D1212680

AMERICAN HORTICULTURAL SOCIETY

PESTS &
DISEASES

AMERICAN HORTICULTURAL SOCIETY

PESTS & DISEASES

PIPPA GREENWOOD

ANDREW HALSTEAD

A. R. CHASE

DANIEL GILREIN

DORLING KINDERSLEY PUBLISHING, INC.

DORLING KINDERSLEY PUBLISHING, INC.
www.dk.com

PROJECT EDITORS *Laura Langley, Martha Swift*
DESIGNER *Rachael Parfitt*

....

MANAGING EDITOR *Louise Abbott*
MANAGING ART EDITOR *Lee Griffiths*

....

DTP DESIGNERS *Chris Clark, Matthew Greenfield*
PRODUCTION CONTROLLER *Martin Croshaw*

....

ILLUSTRATIONS *Sandra Pond and Will Giles*

First American Edition, 2000
2 4 6 8 10 9 7 5 3 1

Published in the United States by Dorling Kindersley Publishing, Inc., 95 Madison Avenue, New York, NY 10016

Copyright © 2000 Dorling Kindersley Publishing, Inc.

All rights reserved under International and Pan-American Copyright Conventions. No part of this publication may be
reproduced, stored in a retrieval system, or transmitted in any form or by any means, electronic, mechanical,
photocopying, recording or otherwise, without the prior written permission of the copyright owner.
First published in Great Britain in 1997 by Dorling Kindersley Limited, London.

Dorling Kindersley Publishing offers special discounts for bulk purchases for sales promotions or premiums. Specific
large-quantity needs can be met with special editions, including personalized covers, excerpts of existing guides, and
corporate imprints. For more information, contact Special Markets Department, Dorling Kindersley Publishing, Inc.,
95 Madison Avenue, New York, NY 10016 Fax: 800-600-9098.

Library of Congress Cataloging-in-Publication Data
Greenwood, Pippa.
  Pests and diseases / Pippa Greenwoood.– 1st American ed.
    p. cm.
At head of title: American Horticultural Society.
ISBN 0-7894-5074-7 (alk.paper)
  1. Garden pests. 2. Plant diseases. 3. Garden pests–Control. I. American Horticultural Society. II. Title.

SB603.5.G742000
635'.049–dc21   99-048249

Reproduced in Italy by Scanner Services SRL
Printed and bound by Star Standard, Singapore

CONTENTS

INTRODUCTION

MAKING THE IDENTIFICATION AND DIAGNOSIS OF A PROBLEM GOES
HALFWAY TO SOLVING IT. THIS BOOK HELPS THE GARDENER CONSIDER
ALL THE FACTORS IN THE GARDEN THAT AFFECT GROWING PLANTS, SO
THAT PROMPT ACTION CAN BE TAKEN IF NEEDED.

IT IS IMPOSSIBLE to garden without encountering pests, diseases, and
disorders on your plants. They are unwelcome in any garden, large or
small. At the very least they spoil a plant's appearance, but if left to spread
and develop unchecked, the more serious ones may dramatically reduce a
plant's vigor, impairing growth, flowering ability, or yield. Some may create
wounds, which are of little significance in their own right but which allow
the entry to secondary organisms, which then might wreak havoc.

The key to a flourishing garden lies not only in quick identification and
treatment of pests and diseases but also in understanding how to keep
plants healthy, thereby preventing problems from occurring in the first
place. Many common problems originate in cultural disorders (the
conditions in which a plant is growing) or are capable of serious damage
only on a plant that is stressed by growing in an unsuitable site or by poor
cultivation. Once a cultural problem has been identified and understood,
it is often quite simple to overcome it and so avoid
a whole host of possible additional problems.

It is vital to identify correctly the pests, diseases, and disorders
themselves. If you are uncertain about what is attacking a plant, it is
impossible to tell whether or not it is something you need worry about and
what, if anything, you should do about it. *AHS Pests and Diseases* makes a
wealth of information on all aspects of the problem side of gardening
available to gardeners and professional horticulturists alike.
By looking at the garden as a whole and then identifying the specific
problem, it allows you to stay one step ahead of pests, diseases,
and disorders in the garden.

HOW TO USE THIS BOOK

THE EASY-TO-USE format provides three ways to help you identify a plant pest, disease, or disorder: by symptom, by plant, and by problem. Symptoms of pests and diseases are shown in color photographs in the *Gallery of Symptoms*, which is cross-referenced to the *A–Z Directory*. Information on beneficial organisms is found in both sections. *Individual Plant Problems* is a plant-by-plant listing, enabling you to look up the problems your particular plant could be suffering from and find their reference in the A–Z and Gallery. A section on *Garden Health and Problems* looks at the garden and plant cultivation as a whole, discussing the background to problems that might occur, while at the back of the book, the comprehensive *Reference Section* contains a glossary and index.

IDENTIFYING AND CONTROLLING PROBLEMS:

BY SYMPTOM

See Gallery of Symptoms, *pp.10–63*

The Gallery section contains hundreds of photographs, enabling you to identify the cause of the symptoms on your plant, then referring you to the A–Z Directory. It is divided into six parts: Leaves; Stems and Buds; Flowers; Fruits, Berries, Nuts and Vegetables; Soil, Roots, Tubers, and Bulbs; and Lawns. At the end are four pages enabling the identification of Beneficial Garden Dwellers.

Whether problem
is a pest, a disease,
or a disorder

Name of problem,
corresponding with
detailed A–Z entry

Page
reference
in A–Z

PLUM CURCULIO   PEST • *See p.161*
Tiny fruit are damaged and may drop. Surviving fruit show crescent-shaped scars and sometimes swelling. Fruit may also be gouged, wormy, brown, and rotten.

PLANTS AFFECTED Many tree fruits
SEASON Spring through autumn

Plants affected
by that particular
problem

Brief description of
visible and other
symptoms

Season when problem
is most likely to occur

Color photograph of affected
plant part with symptoms
clearly visible

Section heading,
color-coded for
easy reference

FRUIT, BERRY, NUT AND VEGETABLE PROBLEMS

GALLERY OF SYMPTOMS

FRUITS, BERRIES, VEGETABLES AND NUTS

IF THE EDIBLE PARTS of a plant are attacked by a pest or pathogen, the whole reason for growing the plant may well be lost. Fruits and berries are particularly prone to attack, since they usually have a high sugar and moisture content. Nuts, peas, and beans are also valuable food sources for many creatures.

In addition, some ornamental trees and shrubs are very commonly grown mainly for their attractive show of berries, and when these are eaten, removed, or spoiled by disease, the plant's appearance is ruined.

In many cases, prolonged protection of the plant may be needed, perhaps by using barriers or traps to keep pests away from the flowers or the developing and ripening fruits. Pesticides can be used with some success, but again these may sometimes need to be applied before the first signs of damage are noticed.

FRUIT PROBLEMS

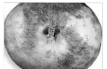

EUROPEAN APPLE SAWFLY   PEST • *See p.126*
Most infested fruits drop off in early summer. Some do develop as ripe fruit but have distinctive ribbon scars where the young larvae fed under the skin.
PLANTS AFFECTED Apples
SEASON Midspring to early autumn

FRUIT SCALD   DISORDER • *See p.130*
Reddish brown patches of discoloration develop on the skin of the fruit. The flesh beneath is usually undamaged, but it may be discolored. Exposed surfaces are most badly affected.
PLANTS AFFECTED Many kinds of fruit
SEASON Mainly summer

BIRDS   PEST • *See p.106*
Many kinds of fruit-eating birds will peck holes in ripening fruits. Wasps may enlarge this damage, and brown rot or other diseases frequently develop once the skin has been broken.
PLANTS AFFECTED Apples, pears, plums, peaches
SEASON Midsummer to autumn

PLUM CURCULIO   PEST • *See p.161*
Tiny fruit are damaged and may drop. Surviving fruit show crescent-shaped scars and sometimes swelling. Fruit may also be gouged, wormy, brown, and rotten.
PLANTS AFFECTED Many tree fruits
SEASON Spring through autumn

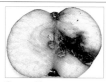

CODLING MOTH   PEST • *See p.116*
This is the cause of wormy apples in late summer. The caterpillar feeds at the core and tunnels out through the side or the eye end of the ripening fruit when it is fully developed.
PLANTS AFFECTED Apples, pears, walnuts, others
SEASON Midsummer to early autumn

WASPS AND YELLOWJACKETS   PEST • *See p.187*
These insects enlarge damage started by birds, but they can also initiate feeding on softer-skinned fruits (*see p.49*). They can make fruit picking hazardous.
PLANTS AFFECTED Tree fruits, grapes, blueberries
SEASON Midsummer to early autumn

BROWN ROT   DISEASE • *See p.110*
Soft, brown rot develops on fruit (here on an apple) and soon becomes studded with raised, creamy white pustules (*see also p.49*). These are often arranged in concentric rings.
PLANTS AFFECTED Cherries, peaches, others
SEASON Late summer and autumn

47

BY PLANT

SEE INDIVIDUAL PLANT PROBLEMS, *PP.193–205*

A comprehensive listing of garden plants by type, with listings of the general and specific ailments that might attack them. The problem can then be identified by referring to the *Gallery of Symptoms* or to the A–Z Directory.

Pests, diseases, or disorders that the plant might suffer from, listed alphabetically

PEARLEAF BLISTER MITE, 157
PLUM CURCULIO, 47, 161
PROLIFERATION, 44
QUINCE RUST, 165
REPLANT DISORDERS, 96
ROOT APHIDS, 168
ROSE LEAFHOPPER, 170

Page reference for color photograph in Gallery of Symptoms

Page reference for entry in A–Z Directory

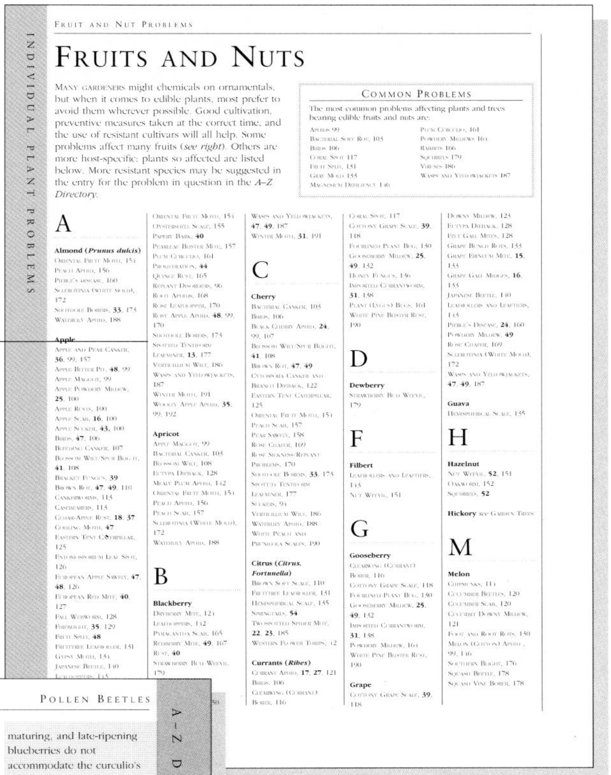

The sample page (Fruits and Nuts) shows:

INDIVIDUAL PLANT PROBLEMS

FRUIT AND NUT PROBLEMS

FRUITS AND NUTS

MANY GARDENERS might chemicals on ornamentals, but when it comes to edible plants, most prefer to avoid them wherever possible. Good cultivation, preventive measures taken at the correct time, and the use of resistant cultivars will all help. Some problems affect many fruits (*see right*). Others are more host-specific; plants so affected are listed below. More resistant species may be suggested in the entry for the problem in question in the *A–Z Directory*.

COMMON PROBLEMS

The most common problems affecting plants and trees bearing edible fruits and nuts are:

A–Z DIRECTORY

POLLEN BEETLES

Redheaded pine sawfly (*Neodiprion lecontei*) is one common species that feeds on a wide variety of pines and even other conifers. Caterpillars are white with black spots and a reddish head. They overwinter as cocoons in duff (decaying organic matter) beneath the host tree. European pine sawfly caterpillars are a grayish green and often feed on mugo, Scots, Japanese black, and other pines. Sawfly adults do not bother the trees, except for causing minor injury when inserting eggs in twigs or needles. There may be 1 or several generations a year, depending on species.
CONTROL Pine sawflies have many natural enemies, but they do not always provide adequate control. If plants or infestations are small, handpick larvae and destroy or prune off infested branches. For species that overwinter as cocoons, rake up ground debris and the cocoons in it under pines. Conifers do not tolerate extensive defoliation, and sawflies often seem to defoliate trees "overnight," so watch susceptible plants carefully for early signs of damage and/or infestation. Species such as European pine sawfly are cryptically colored, and the small larvae of all species are easily overlooked. Insecticidal soap can control larvae when they are small; spot treat infested branches. Other labeled insecticides may be needed for extensive infestations.

PLANT (LYGUS) BUGS
SYMPTOMS Leaves at the shoot tips of many plants, such as fuchsias, roses, hydrangeas, currants, forsythias, mints, dahlias, and

chrysanthemums, are misshapen, with many small holes (*see p.29*). Foliage may be flaked with white spots. Flowers of dahlia and chrysanthemum open unevenly or are killed, and those of fuchsia (*see p.46*) abort at an early stage. Raspberry and strawberry fruits fail to develop normally and are distorted or "buttoned."
CAUSE Plant bugs, such as the fourlined plant bug (*Poecilocapsus lineatus*) and tarnished plant bug (*Lygus lineolaris*), both of which are about ¼–¼in (5–6mm) long when adult. They feed on developing seeds or suck sap from the shoot tips, and some secrete a toxic saliva that kills some of the plant cells. Later, as leaves expand from the damaged shoots, these dead areas may tear into many small holes. At times, honey locust plant bug (*Diaphnocoris chlorionis*) and ash plant bug (*Tropidosteptes amoenus*), among others, are important pests of shade trees.

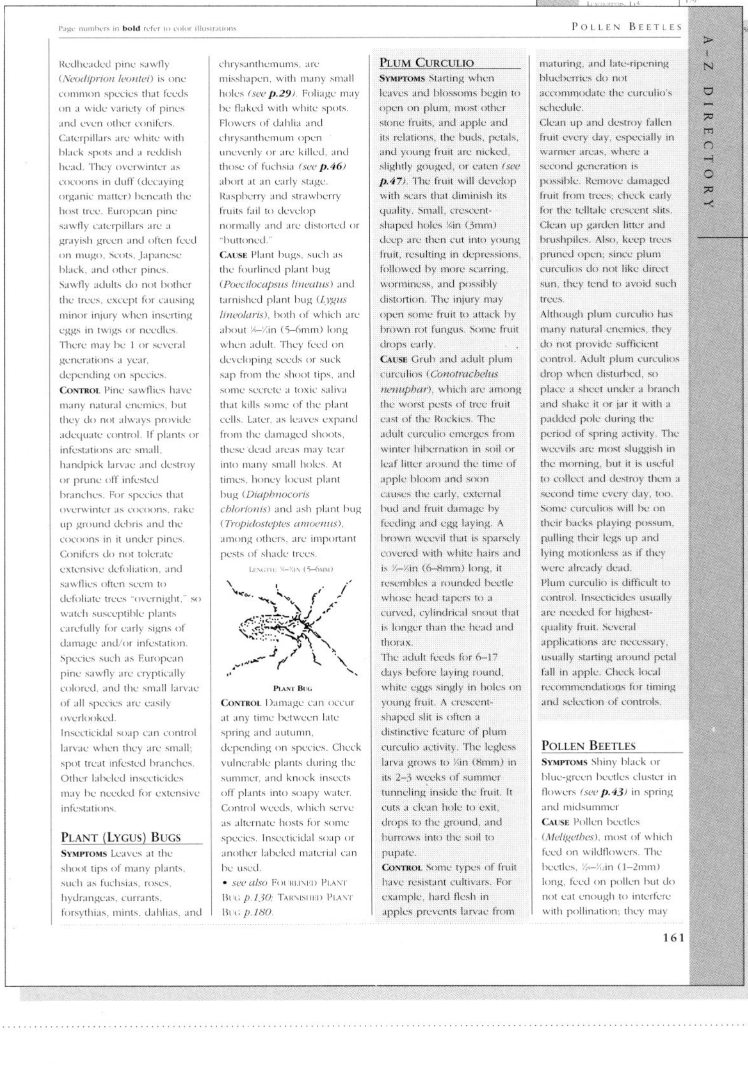

LENGTH: ¾–¼IN (5–6MM)

PLANT BUG

CONTROL Damage can occur at any time between late spring and autumn, depending on species. Check vulnerable plants during the summer, and knock insects off plants into soapy water. Control weeds, which serve as alternate hosts for some species. Insecticidal soap or another labeled material can be used.
• *see also* FOURLINED PLANT BUG *p.130;* TARNISHED PLANT BUG *p.180.*

PLUM CURCULIO
SYMPTOMS Starting when leaves and blossoms begin to open on plum, most other stone fruits, and apple and its relations, the buds, petals, and young fruit are nicked, slightly gouged, or eaten (*see p.47*). The fruit will develop with scars that diminish its quality. Small, crescent-shaped holes ⅛in (3mm) deep are then cut into young fruit, resulting in depressions, followed by more scarring, worminess, and possibly distortion. The injury may open some fruit to attack by brown rot fungus. Some fruit drops early.
CAUSE Grub and adult plum curculios (*Conotrachelus nenuphar*), which are among the worst pests of tree fruit east of the Rockies. The adult curculio emerges from winter hibernation in soil or leaf litter around the time of apple bloom and soon causes the early, external bud and fruit damage by feeding and egg laying. A brown weevil that is sparsely covered with white hairs and is ½–¼in (6–8mm) long, it resembles a rounded beetle whose head tapers to a curved, cylindrical snout that is longer than the head and thorax.
The adult feeds for 6–17 days before laying round, white eggs singly in holes on young fruit. A crescent-shaped slit is often a distinctive feature of plum curculio activity. The legless larva grows to ⅜in (8mm) in its 2–3 weeks of summer tunneling inside the fruit. It cuts a clean hole to exit, drops to the ground, and burrows into the soil to pupate.
CONTROL Some types of fruit have resistant cultivars. For example, hard flesh in apples prevents larvae from

maturing, and late-ripening blueberries do not accommodate the curculio's schedule.
Clean up and destroy fallen fruit every day, especially in warmer areas, where a second generation is possible. Remove damaged fruit from trees; check early for the telltale crescent slits. Clean up garden litter and brushpiles. Also, keep trees pruned open, since plum curculios do not like direct sun; they tend to avoid such trees.
Although plum curculio has many natural enemies, they do not provide sufficient control. Adult plum curculios drop when disturbed, so place a sheet under a branch and shake it or jar it with a padded pole during the period of spring activity. The weevils are most sluggish in the morning, but it is useful to collect and destroy them a second time every day, too. Some curculios lie on their backs playing possum, pulling their legs up and lying motionless as if they were already dead. Plum curculio is difficult to control. Insecticides usually are needed for highest-quality fruit. Several applications are necessary, usually starting around petal fall in apple. Check local recommendations for timing and selection of controls.

POLLEN BEETLES
SYMPTOMS Shiny black or blue-green beetles cluster in flowers (*see p.43*) in spring and midsummer.
CAUSE Pollen beetles (*Meligethes*), most of which feed on wildflowers. The beetles, ½–⅛in (1–2mm) long, feed on pollen but do not eat enough to interfere with pollination; they may

161

BY PROBLEM

See A–Z Directory, *pp.97–192*

Comprehensive entries for the pests, diseases, and disorders that may be found on garden plants clearly describe the symptom(s), cause, and control of each problem. Preventive and control measures include organic, biological, and chemical methods as appropriate. In addition, suggestions are given for techniques for avoiding and minimizing further damage. This section also contains information on beneficial organisms. The A–Z section is cross-referenced to the Gallery section and to other associated entries. Some entries are accompanied by black and white illustrations.

Page reference in **bold** type indicates that symptoms are illustrated in the Gallery section

GALLERY OF
SYMPTOMS

EVEN FOR EXPERIENCED gardeners, the correct
identification of the exact cause of a plant
problem – be it a pest, disease, or disorder –
can be difficult. For ease of comparison with
affected plants, the detailed photographs in this
section are grouped by the parts of plants
attacked and show similar types of symptom
together so that differences can be seen.

LEAVES

DAMAGE TO THE FOLIAGE can spoil a plant's appearance and, if any part of the plant is edible, the potential crop may be reduced. Leaf markings may take the form of spots, either flat (*pp.12–14*) or raised (*pp.14–17*) to the touch, often with the fruiting bodies of fungi visible; blotches (*pp.17–20*); mottling (*pp.20–22*); or discoloration (*pp.22–25*). Leaves may also be distorted (*pp.25–27*), dying (*pp.28–29*); or damaged (*pp.29–31*). Many pests are visible to the naked eye (*p.32*).

The majority of leaf markings are caused by diseases. Weaker fungal diseases are likely to cause extensive damage only to a plant already lacking in vigor. Plants are particularly vulnerable if they are growing in unsuitable conditions, have not been well cared for, or have suffered some other serious attack. Cultural and other remedies may be necessary to both improve the general health of the plant and to control the specific problem.

Leaf marking can occur at any stage but is most serious when young foliage is attacked. Leaves with extensive variegation are especially prone to damage.

MARKINGS ON LEAVES

VIRUS DISEASE • *See p.186*

On orchids, dark brown or black (or occasionally yellow) streaks or spots appear on the leaf. Flowering is often affected, and the plant's overall vigor will usually decline.

PLANTS AFFECTED Orchids; many other plants
SEASON All year

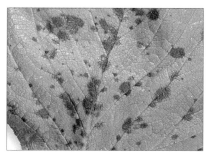

STRAWBERRY LEAF SPOT DISEASE • *See p.179*

Reddish purple spots are found on the leaves, which may later enlarge (*see p.17*). Off-white fungal growth may develop over the surface. Flowers can be affected.

PLANTS AFFECTED Strawberries
SEASON Mainly midsummer to autumn

IVY ANTHRACNOSE DISEASE • *See p.139*

Light to darker brown, circular spots develop on English ivy. The spots turn black and dry or stay moist. Stems can develop similar symptoms but usually do not die.

PLANTS AFFECTED English ivy (*Hedera helix*)
SEASON All season

DELPHINIUM BLACK BLOTCH DISEASE • *See p.122*

Black blotches appear on the leaves, which enlarge and often spread to the leaf stalks and stems. The leaves may eventually die off.

PLANTS AFFECTED Delphiniums, larkspur
SEASON Late spring to autumn

LEAF SPOT (FUNGAL) DISEASE • *See p.143*

Rounded, gray or brown spots develop on the leaves (here of a castor bean) and may join together. Fruiting bodies are often apparent on the spots.

PLANTS AFFECTED Most plants
SEASON Varies with host plant

WATER SPOTS DISEASE • *See p.188*

Sunken white, yellow, or brown circles of variable size appear on the upper sides of leaves. Areas of raised green tissue may remain within the spots. The spots may turn brown and die.

PLANTS AFFECTED African violets, gloxinias
SEASON Any time (usually in winter)

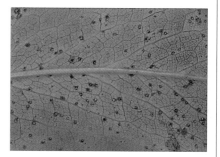

RUST DISEASE • *See p.171*

On *Mahonia*, dark brown, spore-filled pustules occur on the lower leaf surface, with bright orange spots on the upper surface (*see p.24*). Leaves may fall early, but overall plant health is rarely affected.

PLANTS AFFECTED Mahonias; many other plants
SEASON Late spring to early autumn

MARKINGS ON LEAVES *CONTINUED*

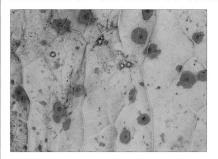

ALTERNARIA LEAF SPOT
DISEASE • See p. 98

Gray-brown, round spots are seen on the leaf surface, often with concentric rings on them. Affected areas may drop away, leaving a ragged leaf.

PLANTS AFFECTED Brussels sprouts, cauliflowers
SEASON Mainly midsummer to late autumn

FOURLINED PLANT BUG
PEST • See p. 130

Groups of small brown spots occur on new foliage, and leaves may become distorted and eventually drop off. Colorful insects may be visible.

PLANTS AFFECTED Shrubs and herbaceous plants
SEASON Spring into summer

LEAF SPOT (FUNGAL)
DISEASE • See p. 143

Purple-brown or buff-colored spots appear on pansy leaves and may join together. The affected areas may fall away, leaving holes.

PLANTS AFFECTED Pansies, many other plants
SEASON Varies with host plant

ROSE BLACKSPOT
DISEASE • See p. 169

Purple-black spots, often with yellow haloes, are seen on leaves. The spots may join together or remain separate. Leaf yellowing and premature leaf drop are common symptoms.

PLANTS AFFECTED Roses
SEASON Mainly early summer to autumn

Blotches appear shiny and may be up to 1/2 in (1.5cm) in diameter

Main part of leaf tissue remains healthy green color

Surface of spot is rough and slightly raised

SPOTTED TENTI-FORM LEAFMINER
PEST • See p. 177

Apple and crabapple leaves show small, oval, blotchy mines. Heavily damaged leaves may turn brown and drop. Fruit may also drop or ripen early.

PLANTS AFFECTED Apples and crabapples
SEASON Late spring through summer

TAR SPOT OF MAPLE
DISEASE • See p. 181

Large, black blotches with bright yellow haloes develop on upper leaf surfaces. Leaves may fall early and the tree can look disfigured, but overall vigor is not usually affected.

PLANTS AFFECTED Maples
SEASON Late spring to autumn

MARKINGS ON LEAVES CONTINUED

MYROTHECIUM SPOTS AND ROTS
DISEASE • See p. 149

A wide variety of symptoms occur, such as water-soaked spots that turn black, stem girdling and cankers, holes in leaves, and root and crown rot.

PLANTS AFFECTED Many plants

SEASON Between 60-85° F (15-30° C)

PEA LEAF AND POD SPOT
DISEASE • See p. 156

Yellow or brown, often sunken, spots are found on the leaves and pods. There is general yellowing of adjacent tissues. Fruiting bodies are usually apparent.

PLANTS AFFECTED Peas

SEASON All season, but mainly summer

RHODODENDRON LEAF SPOT
DISEASE • See p. 168

Brownish purple spots on leaves often have a pink or purple ring around the edge of each one. Concentric ringing is also seen, with central fruiting bodies.

PLANTS AFFECTED Rhododendrons and azaleas

SEASON All year (mainly late summer onward)

RAISED MARKINGS ON LEAVES

OAK LEAF BLISTER/CURL
DISEASE • See p. 152

Upper leaf surfaces have raised areas; depressed areas are on the undersides. Blisters start yellow-green then turn white and brown. Leaves may curl.

PLANTS AFFECTED Many plants

SEASON Between late spring and late summer

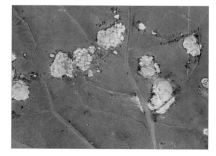

WHITE BLISTER
DISEASE • See p. 189

Shiny, white, raised spots are seen on the lower leaf surface of brassicas (here on a cabbage), often arranged in concentric rings. The upper leaf surface is yellowed and usually distorted.

PLANTS AFFECTED Edible brassicas

SEASON Mainly early summer to late autumn

LINDEN GALL MITE
PEST • See p. 145

Red or yellowish green, tubular structures containing microscopic mites grow on the upper leaf surfaces. Heavily infested leaves may be distorted.

PLANTS AFFECTED Lindens (*Tilia*)

SEASON Late spring to autumn

RAISED MARKINGS ON LEAVES CONTINUED

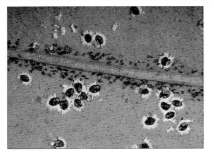

MULBERRY WHITEFLY
PEST • *See p. 148*

Leaves are sticky and shiny or may be covered with patches of black sooty mold. Numerous tiny black, white-fringed insects appear on the undersides.

PLANTS AFFECTED Mulberry, mountain laurel
SEASON Between 60-85° F (15-30° C)

COTTONY CAMELLIA (OR TAXUS) SCALE
PEST • *See p. 118*

Honeydew and sooty mold develop on the upper leaf surfaces. Oval, yellow or brown scales live on the underside, and egg bands are deposited in summer.

PLANTS AFFECTED Mainly camellias and hollies
SEASON All year

RUST
DISEASE • *See p. 171*

On periwinkles, numerous small, dark brown, spore-filled pustules are found on the leaf undersides. Leaves become pitted and distorted. The whole plant may become distorted and die back.

PLANTS AFFECTED Periwinkles (*Vinca*) and others
SEASON All season (mainly summer and autumn)

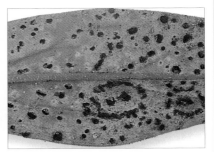

RUST
DISEASE • *See p. 171*

On geraniums, dark brown, fungal pustules are seen on the lower leaf surfaces, usually arranged in concentric rings within larger spots. There is yellow discoloration on the upper surfaces.

PLANTS AFFECTED Geraniums (*Pelargonium*), others
SEASON All season

RUST
DISEASE • *See p. 171*

On irises, numerous raised, dark brown pustules are found on leaves. Leaves yellow and may die back prematurely. Older leaves are usually the worst affected. Vigor is rarely affected.

PLANTS AFFECTED Irises, many other plants
SEASON Mainly late summer to autumn

RUST
DISEASE • *See p. 171*

On snapdragons, concentric rings of tiny, dark brown, spore-filled pustules are seen on lower leaf surfaces. A yellow halo appears around the edge of each spot.

PLANTS AFFECTED Snapdragons; many others
SEASON All season (mainly spring and summer)

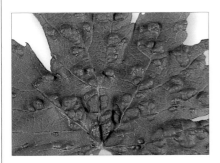

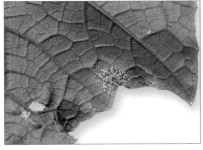

GRAPE ERINEUM MITE
PEST • *See p. 133*

Parts of the leaf bulge upward. The underside of affected areas is covered in creamy white hairs that turn brown. Microscopic mites live among the hairs.

PLANTS AFFECTED Grapevines
SEASON Late spring to autumn

CUCUMBER POWDERY MILDEW
DISEASE • *See p. 120*

Powdery white or gray patches occur in scattered round spots on the tops of the leaves. The spots enlarge, merge, and spread to the undersurface.

PLANTS AFFECTED Squash family, daisy family
SEASON All season

COTTONY HYDRANGEA SCALE
PEST • *See p. 118*

Oval, white, waxy egg masses appear on the leaves and stems. Flat, oval, yellowish brown scales occur on the leaf undersides, next to the veins.

PLANTS AFFECTED Mainly hydrangeas
SEASON All year (eggs late spring to midsummer)

RAISED MARKINGS ON LEAVES CONTINUED

Leaf tissue between pustules usually remains green

Affected leaves may fall rapidly, thereby weakening the plant

Bright orange or yellow spots are seen on lower leaf surface

ROSE RUST
DISEASE • *See p. 176*

Bright orange clusters of spores appear on the lower leaf surfaces, with dark brown, overwintering spores developing from midsummer. Leaves fall prematurely.

PLANTS AFFECTED Roses

SEASON Mainly summer and autumn

GRAPE GALL MIDGES
PEST • *See p. 133*

Grape leaves develop spinelike, red, pointed galls that project from the surface. Leaves may be lightly to very heavily affected.

PLANTS AFFECTED Grapevines

SEASON Late spring

APPLE SCAB
DISEASE • *See p. 100*

Grayish green or khaki, scabby spots develop on the leaf surface. Slight blistering or puckering may also occur. Leaves yellow and fall prematurely, and the tree is weakened.

PLANTS AFFECTED Edible and ornamental *Malus*

SEASON Mainly late spring and summer

PEARLEAF BLISTER MITE
PEST • *See p. 157*

The foliage develops yellowish green or pink, slightly raised patches, which later turn black. These patches form spots or a band on each side of the midrib.

PLANTS AFFECTED Pear trees

SEASON Midspring to autumn

HEMISPHERICAL SCALE
PEST • *See p. 135*

Convex, dark brown, hemispherical scale insects infest leaves (here of a fern) and stems. They are often accompanied by sticky honeydew and sooty mold.

PLANTS AFFECTED Many greenhouse plants

SEASON All year

ELM LEAF GALL APHIDS
PEST • *See p. 126*

Elm leaves develop raised areas in several shapes. If cut open, small aphidlike insects may be seen.

PLANTS AFFECTED Elms

SEASON Spring through summer

RAISED MARKINGS ON LEAVES CONTINUED

RUST
DISEASE • *See p.171*

On *Moraea*, leaves develop patches and soemtimes rows of yellow to orange to brown dotlike pustules. Severe cases will kill individual leaves and reduce overall plant vigor.

PLANTS AFFECTED *Moraea*, many others
SEASON Late spring through autumn

RUST
DISEASE • *See p.171*

Orange, raised pustules appear on the lower leaf surface (here of a mallow), later turning buff-brown. The upper leaf surface has corresponding yellow or orange spots. Leaves may die back.

PLANTS AFFECTED Hollyhocks, mallows, others
SEASON Late spring through autumn

CURRANT APHID
PEST • *See p.121*

Leaves develop individual blistered or puckered areas that may coalesce and discolor (see p. 27). Yellowish aphids may be found singly or in large groups on the leaf undersurfaces.

PLANTS AFFECTED Currants
SEASON Midspring to early summer

OAK GALL WASPS
PEST • *See p.152*

Flat, circular disks or galls containing tiny grubs form on the leaf surfaces. They are reddish at first, then yellowish brown when mature. Twigs, buds, and other parts may develop galls.

PLANTS AFFECTED Oaks (*Quercus*)
SEASON Spring and summer

OAK LEAF GALLS

Variable growths caused by a number of insects, mites, and fungi occur on leaves and twigs, differing in color, shape, and surface texture. Most are harmless and require no control. Also see left.

PLANTS AFFECTED Oaks
SEASON Spring and summer

WILLOW LEAF-GALL SAWFLIES
PEST • *See p.190*

Coffee-bean-sized swellings, which are red or yellowish green, form on willow leaves. Each gall contains a small, caterpillar-like larva.

PLANTS AFFECTED Willows (*Salix*)
SEASON Early summer to early autumn

BLOTCHY MARKINGS ON LEAVES

SPINACH LEAFMINER
PEST • *See p.177*

Pale green blotches later dry up and become brown. White maggots live within the mined areas and later turn into brown pupae, from which adult flies will emerge.

PLANTS AFFECTED Spinach and beets
SEASON Late spring to late summer

STRAWBERRY LEAF SPOT
DISEASE • *See p.179*

Early spotting (*see p.12*) develops into large blotches, each with a gray center. These may appear slightly raised. Off-white fungal growth may develop.

PLANTS AFFECTED Strawberries
SEASON Mainly midsummer to autumn

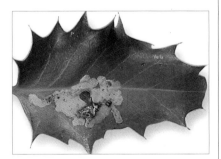

HOLLY LEAFMINERS
PEST • *See p.136*

Irregular, yellowish purple blotches occur on the upper leaf surfaces. There may also be linear tunnels in the leaf coming from the central blotch.

PLANTS AFFECTED Hollies (*Ilex*)
SEASON All year

BLOTCHY MARKINGS ON LEAVES CONTINUED

DOGWOOD ANTHRACNOSE
DISEASE • *See p.123*

Leaves and flower bracts develop yellow spotting, usually beginning at the base of the plant and progressing upward. Spots may drop out to leave shotholes.

PLANTS AFFECTED Dogwoods
SEASON Spring into summer

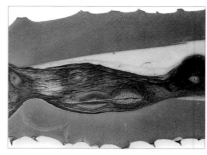

YUCCA LEAF SPOT
DISEASE • *See p.192*

Circular, brown or gray-brown spots appear on leaf surfaces with concentric rings and central fruiting bodies. The spots may join together.

PLANTS AFFECTED Yuccas
SEASON All year (mainly midsummer onward)

SHOTHOLE
DISEASE • *See p.173*

Spots or blotches of discolored tissue develop. The damaged areas then fall out, leaving holes (*see p.30*) looking as if shot out. No insects are present, and fungal growth is rarely visible.

PLANTS AFFECTED Ornamental and fruiting *Prunus*
SEASON Mainly mid- to late summer

RUST
DISEASE • *See p.171*

On fuchsias, numerous tiny, pale orange pustules are found on the lower leaf surface, with the upper surface showing yellow-orange or purple discoloration. Leaves may wither and fall prematurely.

PLANTS AFFECTED Fuchsias, willowherbs, others
SEASON Mainly early summer to autumn

LARKSPUR LEAFMINERS
PEST • *See p.142*

Brown, dried-up areas extend from the leaf tips to the leaf stalk. Small white grubs live within the mined areas. Adult flies cause pale spots on the leaves.

PLANTS AFFECTED Delphiniums and monkshoods
SEASON Early to late summer

APPLE RUST
DISEASE • *See p.100*

Off-color spots appear on apple and crabapple leaves, and sometimes fruits, petioles, and young twigs. Spots release rusty orange powder when mature and disturbed by motion or rain. See p. 37.

PLANTS AFFECTED Apples, crabapples, junipers
SEASON Spring and autumn

ROSESLUGS
PEST • *See p.170*

Pale green caterpillars with brown heads graze the leaves, causing white or brown dried-up areas. They usually feed on the lower leaf surface but may occur on the upper surface in shaded areas.

PLANTS AFFECTED Roses
SEASON Early summer to early autumn

VIRUS
DISEASE • *See p.186*

On raspberry, yellow-green flecks, mottles, or ring spots are seen on the leaves. The leaves may become small and distorted, and the plant will have a reduced crop. Growth is very poor.

PLANTS AFFECTED Cane fruits; many others
SEASON Spring to autumn

DRYBERRY MITE
PEST • *See p.124*

Pale yellow blotches form on the upper leaf surface, with reduced hairiness of the lower leaf surfaces. Leaves at the shoot tips are often distorted.

PLANTS AFFECTED Bramble fruits
SEASON Late spring to early autumn

BLOTCHY MARKINGS ON LEAVES CONTINUED

Galls may form between the leaf veins or along them

Spots are usually creamy white, but on purple-tinged leaves they are often red or pink

Felt galls disfigure but cause little real damage to plants

PEAR SAWFLY

PEST • *See p.158*

Small caterpillars covered in black slime graze the leaf surface, causing it to dry up and turn brown. The larvae often feed on the upper leaf surface.

PLANTS AFFECTED Woody rose family members
SEASON Early summer to midautumn

BIRCH LEAFMINER

PEST • *See p.106*

Small grubs tunnel within the leaves and make blotchy patches that begin pale and blisterlike and then turn brown and dry.

PLANTS AFFECTED Birches
SEASON Late spring into summer

FELT GALL MITES

PEST • *See p.128*

Microscopic mites cause the abnormal growth of dense patches of hairs (here on beech), usually on the underside of the foliage. In late summer the hairs dry up and become brown.

PLANTS AFFECTED Some deciduous trees
SEASON Late spring to autumn

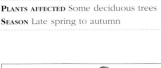

COLUMBINE LEAFMINERS

PEST • *See p.117*

Increasingly wider white lines, or a slowly enlarging blotch, show up on leaves. Tiny maggots live with the damage and can be seen when backlit.

PLANTS AFFECTED Columbines
SEASON Spring through autumn

LILAC LEAFMINER

PEST • *See p.145*

Irregular, blotchy, brown mines develop where whitish green caterpillars have fed inside the foliage. The caterpillars then roll up the leaf tips with silk threads and complete their feeding there.

PLANTS AFFECTED Lilac, privet, and ash
SEASON Early summer to early autumn

EDEMA

DISORDER • *See p.125*

Raised, pale green and (later) brown spots are found on the lower leaf surface (here of an ivy geranium). The upper leaf surface may show corresponding yellow spotting.

PLANTS AFFECTED Many plants
SEASON Winter to spring

BLOTCHY MARKINGS ON LEAVES CONTINUED

Fruiting bodies can develop on lesions

Large areas of leaf may be killed as blotches join together

Affected areas become dry

HELLEBORE LEAF BLOTCH
DISEASE • See p. 135

Slate-gray or gray-brown blotches are seen on the leaves. The lesions may eventually join together. Leaf and flower stems and flowers may also be affected.

PLANTS AFFECTED Hellebores
SEASON Mainly early summer to autumn

ROSE POWDERY MILDEW
DISEASE • See p. 170

White, powdery fungal growth is found on the leaves. They may become distorted, generally yellowed, and fall early. Stems can also be affected.

PLANTS AFFECTED Roses
SEASON All season (mainly summer to autumn)

HORSE CHESTNUT LEAF BLOTCH
DISEASE • See p. 137

Tan-brown, irregular blotches appear, each with a bright yellow margin, on the leaves. The leaf margins and tips are most severely affected.

PLANTS AFFECTED Horse chestnuts (*Aesculus*)
SEASON Midsummer to autumn

MOTTLED MARKINGS ON LEAVES

AZALEA LACEBUG
PEST • See p. 102

Tops of leaves show pale speckling, and the undersides are marked orangish red and dotted with relatively large, sticky brown or black spots. Undersides may have little pointed projections on them.

PLANTS AFFECTED Azaleas and mountain laurel
SEASON Midspring through summer

POTATO LEAFHOPPER
PEST • See p. 163

Leaves are stunted, developing yellow to brown margins, and may be generally off-color and distorted. Twigs may be stunted and have swollen areas.

PLANTS AFFECTED Potatoes, maples; others
SEASON Mostly summer

SOUTHERN RED MITE
PEST • See p. 176

Very fine pale yellow mottling occurs on leaves; a severe infestation makes them look off-color and sickly. Leaves may drop. Tiny red mites may be visible.

PLANTS AFFECTED Many broadleaved evergreens
SEASON Mainly spring and autumn

MOTTLED MARKINGS ON LEAVES CONTINUED

VIRUS
DISEASE • *See p. 186*

Yellow flecks, spots, mottles, or sometimes ring spots are seen on the leaves. Leaves may be small and distorted, and overall growth poor. Here on geranium (*Pelargonium*).

PLANTS AFFECTED Many plants
SEASON All season

EUONYMUS SCALE
PEST • *See p. 126*

Pale yellow mottling and elongate white scale insects are found on the foliage. Stems become encrusted with the dark brown, pear-shaped female scales. Heavy infestations may cause dieback.

PLANTS AFFECTED Evergreen *Euonymus*
SEASON All year

ROSE LEAFHOPPER
PEST • *See p. 170*

A coarse, pale mottling develops on the upper leaf surface. Pale yellow insects live on the underside of the leaves. Roses growing in warm, sheltered places can become heavily infested by summer.

PLANTS AFFECTED Many woody plants
SEASON Midspring to midautumn

RHODODENDRON LACEBUG
PEST • *See p. 168*

A coarse, pale yellow mottling develops on the upper leaf surface. A rusty brown deposit and insects are found on the lower leaf surface.

PLANTS AFFECTED Rhododendrons, *Kalmia*
SEASON Early spring to late summer

ROSE VIRUS
DISEASE • *See p. 171*

Yellow flecks, spots, mottles, vein-banding, or ring spots are found on the leaves. Flowers may show slight color-breaking symptoms and growth may be affected, but these are both rare.

PLANTS AFFECTED Roses
SEASON All season

CUCUMBER MOSAIC VIRUS
DISEASE • *See p. 120*

Yellow mottles and blotches are seen on leaves (here of a squash), which are distorted (*see p. 25*). The whole plant is stunted and may die prematurely.

PLANTS AFFECTED Wide host range
SEASON All season

MOTTLED MARKINGS ON LEAVES CONTINUED

DRACAENA THRIPS
PEST • *See p.123*

Black, white-banded, narrow-bodied, elongate insects cause a silvery brown discoloration of the upper leaf surfaces of the younger foliage.

PLANTS AFFECTED Some houseplants
SEASON All year

TWOSPOTTED SPIDER MITE
PEST • *See p.185*

Early stages of spider mite attack show as a fine, pale mottling of the upper leaf surface. Tiny, yellow-green mites are found on the underside of the leaves.

PLANTS AFFECTED Greenhouse and garden plants
SEASON Midspring to late autumn

RUST
DISEASE • *See p.171*

Numerous dark brown, spore-filled pustules are found on the underside of the leaf (here on a plum). Bright yellow or orange spots are seen on the upper surface. Leaves fall prematurely.

PLANTS AFFECTED Plums and many other plants
SEASON All season

CAMELLIA YELLOW MOTTLE
DISEASE • *See p.113*

Yellow or white mottled markings and patches of discoloration form on leaves. General growth is not affected. Usually only isolated branches are affected.

PLANTS AFFECTED Camellias
SEASON All year

TULIP FIRE
DISEASE • *See p.183*

Buff-colored or bleached flecks develop on the leaves. Early infection causes extensive leaf distortion and the development of fuzzy, gray fungal growth. Flowers may also be affected.

PLANTS AFFECTED Tulips
SEASON Mid- to late spring

PRIVET THRIPS
PEST • *See p.165*

Elongate, narrow-bodied insects cause green leaves (*above right*) to develop a silvery brown discoloration (*above left*), especially during late summer. The thrips are found on the upper leaf surfaces.

PLANTS AFFECTED Privet and lilac
SEASON Early summer to early autumn

DISCOLORED LEAVES

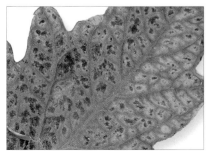

MAGNESIUM DEFICIENCY
DISORDER • *See p.146*

Yellow, brown, or otherwise discolored areas form between the leaf veins and around the leaf edge (here on a tomato). Older leaves are the worst affected.

PLANTS AFFECTED Many plants
SEASON Mainly late spring to autumn

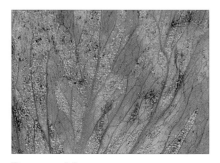

DOWNY MILDEW
DISEASE • *See p.123*

Angular, yellow-discolored areas on the leaves (here on lettuce) rapidly turn pale brown and papery or soft. Off-white fungal growth often develops beneath the leaf.

PLANTS AFFECTED Lettuce; many other plants
SEASON All season

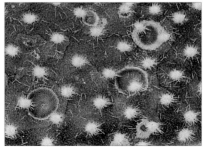

CACTUS CORKY SCAB
DISORDER • *See p.112*

Pale, roughened areas appear on the surface and may become brown and sunken. In extreme cases, holes develop as the affected tissue dies.

PLANTS AFFECTED Cacti, other succulents
SEASON All year

DISCOLORED LEAVES CONTINUED

VIRUS
DISEASE • *See p. 186*

Virus symptoms include yellow vein-clearing (here on a sweet pea), mottling, mosaicing, spotting or ring spotting seen on the leaves. Leaves may be distorted (*see p.25*) and general growth is stunted.

PLANTS AFFECTED Sweet peas; many others
SEASON Mainly late spring to late summer

VIRUS
DISEASE • *See p. 186*

Yellow streaking or flecking is seen on leaves (here on *Narcissus*); symptoms may occur on flower stems or petals. Plants can become stunted. Growth and performance may be unaffected.

PLANTS AFFECTED Many plants
SEASON All season

BEGONIA POWDERY MILDEW
DISEASE • *See p. 106*

White or pale gray, powdery fungal growth is found mainly on upper leaf surfaces. Affected leaves turn papery and soft. May affect stems and buds.

PLANTS AFFECTED Begonias
SEASON Mainly spring to autumn

TWOSPOTTED SPIDER MITE
PEST • *See p. 185*

If heavily infested, leaves lose much of their green color and dry up. Fine silk webbing may appear between the leaves and the mites swarm over the plant.

PLANTS AFFECTED Greenhouse and garden plants
SEASON Midspring to late autumn

HERBICIDES
DISORDER • *See p. 135*

Among other symptoms, yellow spots and blotches appear (here on a rose), which may turn brown as the leaf tissue dies off. Plant growth can be stunted and the plant may die.

PLANTS AFFECTED Any plant
SEASON Mainly spring to summer

ONION THRIPS
PEST • *See p. 154*

Leaves become covered with fine white or off-white mottling. Tiny, elongated insects may be found on the leaves. Damage is especially severe during heat and drought.

PLANTS AFFECTED Onions, leeks, cabbage
SEASON Summer

DISCOLORED LEAVES CONTINUED

IRON DEFICIENCY
DISORDER • *See p. 139*

Yellowing between the veins on leaves (here of a rhododendron) is seen. The youngest leaves are affected worst. Overall growth may be reduced.

PLANTS AFFECTED Many acid-loving plants
SEASON Varies with host plant

POWDERY MILDEW
DISEASE • *See p. 164*

Powdery, white or tan fungal growth appears on the leaf surface (here on oak). Leaves, particularly young ones, may be distorted and die off early.

PLANTS AFFECTED Oaks; many other plants
SEASON Late spring to autumn

BLACK CHERRY APHID
PEST • *See p. 107*

Leaves at the shoot tips become curled, with black aphids on the underside. Affected leaves often turn brown in midsummer.

PLANTS AFFECTED Cherry trees
SEASON Late spring to late summer

POTASSIUM DEFICIENCY
DISORDER • *See p. 162*

Leaf tips and edges are scorched and may show brownish purple spotting on the underside (here on a geranium). Flowering and fruiting will be poor.

PLANTS AFFECTED Many plants
SEASON Mainly midsummer to autumn

PIERCE'S DISEASE
DISEASE • *See p. 160*

Lower leaves are yellow-mottled then turn brown and dry on the edges. The discoloration expands, although veins usually remain green. Leaves are often distorted. Stems wilt and plants may die.

PLANTS AFFECTED Grapes
SEASON Late spring into summer

RUST
DISEASE • *See p. 171*

Bright spots appear on the upper leaf surface, with pustules on the underside (here on a mahonia; *also see p.12*). Leaves may fall prematurely, but overall health of the plant is rarely affected.

PLANTS AFFECTED Mahonias; many other plants
SEASON All season

DISCOLORED LEAVES CONTINUED

DOWNY MILDEW
DISEASE • See p.123

Pale green or light brown, angular patches of discoloration are seen on the leaves (here of a *Geranium*). Off-white, slightly fuzzy fungal patches develop beneath.

PLANTS AFFECTED Many plants
SEASON All season (during high humidity)

CUCUMBER MOSAIC VIRUS
DISEASE • See p.120

Leaves may be distorted and reduced in size and also discolored, with blotches and mosaic patterns (*see p.21*). On some hosts, flowers show color breaking.

PLANTS AFFECTED Wide host range
SEASON All season

CHRYSANTHEMUM LEAFMINER
PEST • See p.115

White or brown sinuous lines develop where the leaf-mining grubs have been feeding. In heavy attacks most of the leaf area becomes discolored.

PLANTS AFFECTED Chrysanthemums
SEASON Midspring to late autumn

POWDERY MILDEW
DISEASE • See p.164

White, powdery fungal growth develops on the upper leaf surface (here of a *Geranium*). The leaf can become distorted, and the leaf stalk may also be affected.

PLANTS AFFECTED *Geranium*, many other plants
SEASON Varies with host plant

FOLIAR NEMATODES
PEST • See p.129

Brown areas enclosed by the larger leaf veins form islands or wedges in the leaves. Eventually the whole leaf will become discolored.

PLANTS AFFECTED Many plants
SEASON Mainly late summer to late autumn

CUCURBIT DOWNY MILDEW
DISEASE • See p.121

Leaf undersurfaces are marked with purple-white, fuzzy spots; the upper surfaces show yellow spots. The spots spread. New shoots shrivel and die.

PLANTS AFFECTED Squash family
SEASON After midsummer or all season

DISTORTED LEAVES

GOOSEBERRY MILDEW
DISEASE • See p.132

Powdery fungal growth is seen on puckered leaves, usually on the upper surfaces. Young leaves wither and die off. Stems and fruits may be infected.

PLANTS AFFECTED Gooseberries and blackcurrants
SEASON All season

APPLE POWDERY MILDEW
DISEASE • See p.100

Powdery white fungal growth develops on leaves. On young leaves the upper and lower surfaces may be attacked, and the foliage withers and dies.

PLANTS AFFECTED Apples and crabapples
SEASON Spring to autumn

VIRUS
DISEASE • See p.186

Growth may be distorted and stunted (as on this tobacco plant) and the plant usually dies off early. Other symptoms include yellow mottling, spotting, or mosaicing on the leaves.

PLANTS AFFECTED Wide range of plants
SEASON Mainly summer and autumn

DISTORTED LEAVES CONTINUED

Withered remains of leaf still attached to gall

Texture is firm but compressible and becomes softer with age

Gall is rounded but may also be forked with fingerlike protrusions

CAMELLIA GALL
DISEASE • *See p.112*

Large galls, up to 1/3in (18cm) long, develop in place of leaves. The surface becomes covered in spores and may appear white in places. The plant's overall vigor is rarely affected.

PLANTS AFFECTED Camellias

SEASON Late summer to autumn

PEACH LEAF CURL
DISEASE • *See p.156*

Leaves become puckered; they are pale green at first but soon turn red and purple. A powdery, white spore layer develops on the surface.

PLANTS AFFECTED Peaches, nectarines

SEASON Spring and early summer

LAUREL PSYLLID
PEST • *See p.142*

Leaves at the shoot tips become yellow or red, with thickened, downcurled margins. Later, the damaged areas dry up and turn brown. Fluffy white nymphs may be seen on the lower leaf surface.

PLANTS AFFECTED Bay (*Laurus nobilis*)

SEASON Late spring to midautumn

CYCLAMEN MITE
PEST • *See p.121*

Nonwoody plant parts become distorted or undersized. Leaves become mottled or streaky and drop early, and the entire plant may be stunted.

PLANTS AFFECTED Many plants

SEASON Spring through autumn

BOXWOOD PSYLLID
PEST • *See p.109*

Shoot extension is severely restricted, and the cupped leaves form cabbage-like structures. Flattened, pale green, aphidlike insects may be present and excrete a white, runny liquid.

PLANTS AFFECTED Boxwood (*Buxus*)

SEASON Midspring to midsummer

IRREGULAR WATERING
DISORDER • *See p.139*

Leaves (here of a rhododendron) become puckered and distorted but retain their normal color. Not all leaves will be affected.

PLANTS AFFECTED All plants

SEASON All season (mainly summer)

DISTORTED LEAVES CONTINUED

VIRUS
DISEASE • *See p. 186*

The plant (here a *Passiflora*) may be distorted and stunted and will usually die off early. Leaves often also display yellow mottling, spotting, mosaicing, or veining.

PLANTS AFFECTED Many plants
SEASON Mainly summer and autumn

HERBICIDES
DISORDER • *See p. 135*

Among other symptoms, leaves (here of a geranium) become cup-shaped, often with the veins close together. Stems and petioles may be curled or distorted (*see below right*).

PLANTS AFFECTED Any plant
SEASON Mainly spring and summer

TAXUS BUD MITE
PEST • *See p. 181*

Buds and growing tips enlarge abnormally and develop russeting. Twisting and distortion, and sometimes death of the new growth, follows.

PLANTS AFFECTED Yew (*Taxus*)
SEASON Spring and summer

RHODODENDRON GALL MIDGE
PEST • *See p. 168*

New foliage appears distorted or twisted and sometimes has yellow spots. Edges may be curled under and brown. Later growth may be similarly affected.

PLANTS AFFECTED Large-leaved rhododendrons
SEASON Spring

LEAF-CURLING PLUM APHID
PEST • *See p. 142*

In the spring leaves become tightly curled and crinkled, due to aphids feeding on the underside of the leaves. Leaves remain distorted all summer.

PLANTS AFFECTED Plums, prunes
SEASON Early to late spring

CURRANT APHID
PEST • *See p. 121*

Leaves at the shoot tips develop raised, red or yellowish green, puckered areas. Pale yellow aphids may be found on the underside of affected leaves.

PLANTS AFFECTED Ccurrants
SEASON Midspring to early summer

TARSONEMID MITES
PEST • *See p. 180*

Microscopic mites live and feed at shoot tips and in flower buds. Their feeding causes scarring on the stems and progressive distortion and stunting of the foliage. Growing tip may be killed.

PLANTS AFFECTED Many plants
SEASON All year

HONEYLOCUST POD GALL MIDGE
PEST • *See p. 136*

Leaves at the shoot tip fail to expand and resemble small seedpods. Each galled leaflet contains several whitish orange maggots.

PLANTS AFFECTED Honeylocust (*Gleditsia*)
SEASON Early to late summer

HERBICIDES
DISORDER • *See p. 135*

Among other symptoms, stems and petioles (here of a tomato plant) may become curled and distorted. Leaves narrow or curl up (*see top, center*), and stems may be roughened.

PLANTS AFFECTED Any plant
SEASON Mainly spring and summer

LEAVES DYING OFF

FROST
DISORDER • *See p.130*

The foliage (here of a hydrangea) becomes withered and hangs limply. It may become blackened or turn pale green or brown. The exposed parts of the plant are most severely affected.

PLANTS AFFECTED Many plants
SEASON Late autumn through early spring

POTATO LATE BLIGHT
DISEASE • *See p.163*

Brown patches develop mainly around tips and edges, and leaves eventually wither and die. White fungal growth may appear and topgrowth collapse.

PLANTS AFFECTED Potatoes, tomatoes, petunias
SEASON Mid- to late summer

KEITHIA THUJINA NEEDLE BLIGHT
DISEASE • *See p.141*

Tiny, black, slightly raised spots are embedded in the foliage, leaving pits or holes as the spores are released. Foliage turns brown and dies back.

PLANTS AFFECTED *Thuja plicata*
SEASON Mainly late summer and early autumn

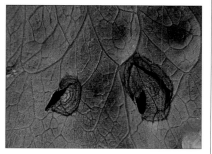

DROUGHT
DISORDER • *See p.124*

Leaves (here of a hosta) wilt and later dry out or shrivel, often turning brown and papery. In the early stages lowered temperatures and watering may revive the plant; later, dieback or death occurs.

PLANTS AFFECTED All plants
SEASON Mainly summer

PEA WILT
DISEASE • *See p.156*

Leaves turn yellow and die back. Internally the stem's vascular system is stained brown, but this is visible only if the outer stem is stripped away. The entire plant wilts and is killed rapidly.

PLANTS AFFECTED Peas and sweet peas
SEASON Mainly summer

GRAY MOLD
DISEASE • *See p.133*

Fluffy gray fungal growth (here on lettuce) appears on leaves, often with brown or orange slimy rotting of the stem and base of the plant.

PLANTS AFFECTED Lettuce; many other plants
SEASON All season, depending on weather

LEAVES DYING OFF CONTINUED

NARCISSUS LEAF SCORCH
DISEASE • See p. 150

Leaves are red-brown and scorched as they emerge. Brown spots with fungal bodies are found on the leaves. Bulbs do not rot or show discoloration.

PLANTS AFFECTED *Narcissus*, amaryllis, crinums
SEASON Spring

VERTICILLIUM WILTS
DISEASE • See p. 185

Foliage wilts and dies, and soft stems wilt. Usually only part of the plant is affected initially. The leaf veins and vascular tissue are discolored.

PLANTS AFFECTED Many plants
SEASON All year

FERTILIZER BURN
DISORDER • See p. 128

Leaves wilt and develop dry, brown tips or edges. Dry areas may also occur between veins. Damage may be confined to one side of the plant.

PLANTS AFFECTED Many plants
SEASON Mostly spring and summer

HOLES IN LEAVES

MEXICAN BEAN BEETLE
PEST • See p. 146

Lacy holes develop between leaf veins; the holes enlarge and become ragged, while the rest of the leaf turns brown. Pods and stems may show damage.

PLANTS AFFECTED Beans
SEASON Spring through summer

SLUGS
PEST • See p. 174

Slugs feed mainly at night and eat irregular holes in foliage or graze away the surface tissues. A silvery slime trail is sometimes left on plants. Snails (*see right*) cause similar damage.

PLANTS AFFECTED Many plants
SEASON Spring through autumn

SNAILS
PEST • See p. 175

Irregular holes are eaten in the foliage, and a silvery slime trail may be found nearby. Slugs (*see left*) cause similar damage. A flashlight inspection may be required to identify the culprits.

PLANTS AFFECTED Many plants
SEASON Early spring to late autumn

PLANT (LYGUS) BUGS
PEST • See p. 161

Leaves at the shoot tips develop many small, brown-edged holes. The leaves are often distorted, and flower buds may be killed or damaged.

PLANTS AFFECTED Many plants
SEASON Late spring to late summer

FLEA BEETLES
PEST • See p. 129

Small, rounded holes are scalloped out of the upper leaf surface (here of a wallflower). Small, blue-black or black, yellow-striped beetles, which jump off the foliage, may be seen.

PLANTS AFFECTED Brassicas; eggplant
SEASON Midspring to late summer

BLACK VINE WEEVIL (DAMAGE BY ADULT)
PEST • See p. 107

Adult black vine weevils eat irregular notches from the leaf margins (here of a rhododendron). On shrubs the leaves closest to the ground are attacked.

PLANTS AFFECTED Many plants
SEASON Midspring to midautumn

HOLES IN LEAVES CONTINUED

FROST
DISORDER • *See p. 130*

Leaves (here on oak) emerge with smooth-edged holes mostly in the interior of the leaves, and they may be deformed and smaller than normal. No evidence of insect occurrence is present.

PLANTS AFFECTED Mainly trees and shrubs
SEASON Spring; sometimes late autumn

LEAF-CUTTING BEES
PEST • *See p. 142*

Semicircular or elliptical pieces are removed from the leaf margins (here of a rose). The smooth outline of the missing pieces distinguishes leaf-cutting bee damage from other leaf-eating pests.

PLANTS AFFECTED Many plants, especially roses
SEASON Early to late summer

CABBAGE LOOPER
PEST • *See p. 112*

Large, normally irregular holes occur in leaves; flower buds, flowers, and fruit may be damaged as well. On cabbages, the caterpillars make holes in the heads. Excrement pellets occur throughout.

PLANTS AFFECTED Brassicas, vegetables, flowers
SEASON Entire growing season

WATERLILY LEAF BEETLE
PEST • *See p. 188*

Both the adults and larvae feed on the upper leaf surface, making elongate strips that rot away to form holes. Leaves turn yellow and decay prematurely.

PLANTS AFFECTED Waterlilies
SEASON Late spring to late summer

CANKERWORMS
PEST • *See p. 113*

Leaves are eaten except for the midrib and major veins. Plants with severe infestations look burned. Variously colored caterpillars walk in "inchworm" fashion and may hang from threads.

PLANTS AFFECTED Many trees and shrubs
SEASON Midspring to early summer

SHOTHOLE
DISEASE • *See p. 173*

Leaves develop spots (*see p.18*) where the tissue dies and falls away, leaving holes, usually with a slight browning at the edges of the holes (shown here on a *Prunus*).

PLANTS AFFECTED *Prunus*, many other plants
SEASON Mainly summer and autumn

JAPANESE BEETLE
PEST • *See p. 140*

Leaves have a few to many small holes chewed between the veins; leaves eventually turn lacy and brown. Large areas of foliage, even on large trees, may be affected.

PLANTS AFFECTED Many plants
SEASON Late spring through summer

BIRDS
PEST • *See p. 106*

Birds rip pieces off leaves with their beaks, causing ragged tears on the foliage (here of a cabbage). In heavy attacks most of the soft parts of the leaves will be removed.

PLANTS AFFECTED Various plants
SEASON All year

BLISTER BEETLE
PEST • *See p. 108*

Leaves are chewed between the major veins; damage usually occurs quickly and may disfigure or kill the affected plants. Adults swarm over plants and release an irritant chemical if disturbed.

PLANTS AFFECTED Many flowers and vegetables
SEASON Midsummer

HOLES IN LEAVES CONTINUED

RUSTY TUSSOCK MOTH
PEST • *See p.171*

Holes are eaten in the leaf margins by hairy caterpillars. Plumes of black hairs project from the head and rear, with four tufts of buff hairs in the middle.

PLANTS AFFECTED Mainly trees and shrubs
SEASON Late spring to early summer

HORNWORM
PEST • *See p.137*

The foliage of tomato and its relatives develops large ragged holes, or the leaves are eaten down to the main veins. Large excrement pellets accumulate on the ground beneath.

PLANTS AFFECTED Tomato family
SEASON Summer into autumn

SQUASH BEETLE
PEST • *See p.178*

Squash leaves show damage ranging from a few holes to complete skeletonization. The plant may die. Larvae can be found feeding on leaf tops while adults feed underneath.

PLANTS AFFECTED Squash family
SEASON Spring through summer

IMPORTED CURRANTWORM
PEST • *See p.138*

Soft parts of foliage are rapidly devoured, leaving just the stalks and larger veins. The larvae are pale green with black spots or uniformly green.

PLANTS AFFECTED Gooseberries, red/white currants
SEASON Midspring to late summer

WINTER MOTH
PEST • *See p.191*

Small holes are eaten in newly emerged spring foliage; these holes increase in size as the leaves expand. The pale green caterpillars loosely bind leaves together with silk threads.

PLANTS AFFECTED Tree fruits, blueberries
SEASON Early to late spring

PEA LEAF WEEVIL
PEST • *See p.156*

Uniform, U-shaped notches are eaten from the leaf margins (here of a broad bean leaf). The grayish brown beetles do not usually cause extensive damage.

PLANTS AFFECTED Broad beans and peas
SEASON Late spring to late summer

INSECTS ON LEAVES

BEECH APHIDS
PEST • *See p.105*

Pale yellow aphids covered with a fluffy, white wax form dense colonies on the underside of beech leaves. Foliage at the shoot tips may be distorted.

PLANTS AFFECTED Beeches (*Fagus*)
SEASON Late spring to late summer

OAKWORMS
PEST • *See p.152*

Damage starts with individual oak leaves becoming lacy and brown; later, only the midribs remain. Entire branches lose their leaves. Variously colored two-horned caterpillars are visible.

PLANTS AFFECTED Oaks
SEASON Early spring into summer

COLORADO POTATO BEETLE
PEST • *See p.116*

Large, ragged holes occur on leaves; flowers are chewed; green fruit show gashes that turn brown. Excrement deposits occur along with damage.

PLANTS AFFECTED Potato family
SEASON Midspring onward

PINE SAWFLIES
PEST • *See p.160*

Needles are partially or completely eaten on individual branches or entire plants. Partially eaten needles turn red-brown and dry. Older foliage is generally eaten, but new growth may also be attacked.

PLANTS AFFECTED Pines, spruces, hemlocks, firs
SEASON Early spring to early autumn

MEALYBUGS
PEST • *See p.146*

Flattened, oval insects covered in a white, mealy or fluffy wax live on the underside of leaves and in the leaf axils. These sap-feeding insects excrete honey-dew, which makes the foliage sticky.

PLANTS AFFECTED Many greenhouse plants
SEASON All year

CABBAGE APHID
PEST • *See p.111*

Dense colonies of gray-white aphids live on the underside of brassica leaves and on the shoot tips of young plants. Mottled yellow patches develop on leaves.

PLANTS AFFECTED Brassicas
SEASON Late spring to early autumn

HEMLOCK WOOLLY ADELGID
PEST • *See p.135*

Anywhere from a few to many masses of small, dirty white specks occur at the base of needles. Severe infestations are unattractive and usually kill the tree.

PLANTS AFFECTED Hemlocks
SEASON Spring to early summer

JUNIPER WEBWORM
PEST • *See p.141*

Dead patches develop in juniper bushes as the foliage turns brown and dries up. The patches are bound together by silk webbing produced by the caterpillars.

PLANTS AFFECTED Junipers (*Juniperus*)
SEASON Late spring to early summer

LARCH ADELGID
PEST • *See p.142*

Small, black, aphidlike insects concealed under fluffy white wax feed by sucking sap from the foliage. Heavy attacks can distort the needles and make the foliage sticky with the pests' sugary excrement.

PLANTS AFFECTED Larches (*Larix*)
SEASON Midspring to late summer

STEMS AND BUDS

THE STEMS OF A PLANT can be compared to the skeleton of animals, their support giving the plant its characteristic shape and holding the leaves, flowers, and buds in the position in which they function best. Since the stems contain the plant's vascular, or transport, system they are also fundamental to its function, so when stems are damaged by a pest or by disease, the buds, flowers, and leaves carried on them may deteriorate, too.

Stems may be attacked in a variety of ways, by pests that gnaw the outer tissues (sometimes ringing the whole stem), feed from them by sucking sap, or even tunnel through them. Pest damage may then allow pathogens to enter and so cause further infections, which in turn may spread down the stem and into the crown of the plant; if this occurs, the whole plant may be killed. The tissues of the stem may also be prevented from working by the presence of fungal pathogens that literally clog up the vascular system, so preventing it from functioning.

STEM PROBLEMS

RHODODENDRON BORER
PEST • *See p.166*

Leaves wilt and turn yellow. Branches have small holes in the crotches, and sawdustlike material appears outside and holes and on the ground.

PLANTS AFFECTED Rhododendrons and azaleas
SEASON Autumn and spring into summer

VERTICILLIUM WILTS
DISEASE • *See p.185*

Soft stems and leaves wilt (*see p.29*). Conducting tissue is stained brown, causing longitudinal streaking, which is visible only if the bark is removed.

PLANTS AFFECTED Many trees and shrubs
SEASON Symptoms most apparent in summer

SHOTHOLE BORERS
PEST • *See p.173*

Small holes in the bark, resembling damage by shotgun pellets, are the emergence holes of small, brownish black beetles. Attacks occur mainly on trees growing under stressful conditions.

PLANTS AFFECTED Plums, cherries, almonds
SEASON Late spring to midsummer

PHLOX NEMATODE
PEST • *See p.159*

Stems are stunted and abnormally swollen, and there may be splitting at the base. Leaves at shoot tips are narrow and may consist of little more than the midribs (as on the top stem, above).

PLANTS AFFECTED Perennial and annual phlox
SEASON Midspring to midsummer

TWO-LINED CHESTNUT BORER
PEST • *See p.185*

Zigzag tunnels appear under bark. Branches may wilt and die back. Small D-shaped holes appear in bark. Foliage may be thin, small, and off-color.

PLANTS AFFECTED Oaks
SEASON All year

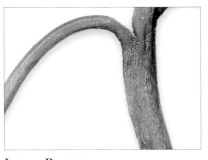

LILAC BLIGHT
DISEASE • *See p.145*

Young shoots wilt and die, with the older stems developing cankers. Angular brown spots appear on leaves which then die off. Gray mold growth is often present, masking the symptoms.

PLANTS AFFECTED Lilacs (*Syringa*)
SEASON Late spring and early summer

BARK BEETLES
PEST • *See p.104*

The larvae of several species of beetle feed underneath the bark of recently dead or dying trees and shrubs. This network of tunnels was made by elm bark beetle grubs.

PLANTS AFFECTED Many trees and shrubs
SEASON All year

STEM PROBLEMS CONTINUED

Soil mix is waterlogged

Flowers, leaves, and stems have collapsed

DAMPING OFF
DISEASE • *See p. 122*

Seedlings collapse. The stem base is discolored and may shrink inward, often appearing water-soaked initially. Fluffy white fungal growth may be present. Seeds may rot completely and not emerge.

PLANTS AFFECTED All seeds and seedlings
SEASON Mainly late winter and spring

WATERLOGGING
DISORDER • *See p. 188*

Foliage wilts and yellows, as if suffering from drought, but the condition does not improve if more water is applied. The entire top growth may flop over (as with the cyclamen above).

PLANTS AFFECTED Any plant (especially if in pots)
SEASON All year

HERBICIDES
DISORDER • *See p. 135*

Among other symptoms, leaves are narrowed and may be cupped, and leaf veins appear parallel. Here, conifer foliage is distorted. Petioles and stems may show spiral twisting.

PLANTS AFFECTED Many plants
SEASON Mainly early to midsummer

GRAY MOLD
DISEASE • *See p. 133*

Discolored patches develop on stems (here of a rose) and may girdle them, causing dieback. Fluffy gray fungal growth and black fungal resting bodies can develop on affected areas.

PLANTS AFFECTED Soft and woody-stemmed plants
SEASON All year

HONEY FUNGUS
DISEASE • *See p. 136*

A white fungal mat, smelling strongly of mushrooms, develops beneath the bark on stem bases, trunks, and roots. The woody tissue beneath discolors. This is also called mushroom rot.

PLANTS AFFECTED Trees, shrubs, some other plants
SEASON All year

RASPBERRY CANE SPOT
DISEASE • *See p. 166*

Purple spots with silvery white centers develop on the canes. The spots enlarge rapidly, and the canes may split and die. Leaves and flowers may be affected.

PLANTS AFFECTED Raspberries, other cane fruits
SEASON Early summer to autumn

STEM PROBLEMS CONTINUED

BACTERIAL CANKER DISEASE • See p.103
Patches of bark flatten and sink inward. Amber-colored, resinlike ooze may appear close by. Foliage withers and dies off or buds fail to open. Branches may be killed by girdling cankers.

PLANTS AFFECTED Ornamental and fruiting *Prunus*
SEASON Mainly spring and autumn

ENDOTHIA CANKER DISEASE • See p.126
A grayish green area slowly expands on trunks, branches, or exposed roots. Small orange to brown spots develop as the disease progresses.

PLANTS AFFECTED Oaks, beeches, other trees
SEASON All year, mainly in summer

SEIRIDIUM CANKER DISEASE • See p.173
Foliage (here on a cypress) yellows and dies. Bark becomes roughened as cankers develop. Resin oozes from the infected areas and tiny, black fruiting bodies appear. Cankers may ring stems.

PLANTS AFFECTED Several conifers
SEASON All year, mainly autumn and winter

SMUT DISEASE • See p.174
Raised, blisterlike areas develop on stems (here on *Trollius*). These erupt to produce black, powdery spore masses. Affected stems may be killed if the pustules are sufficiently large.

PLANTS AFFECTED Many plants
SEASON Mainly summer

POOR PRUNING See p.94–95
This pruning cut – here on birch – has removed a branch too close to the trunk, so the wound has failed to heal successfully. Infection has entered the wound, causing the wood to deteriorate.

PLANTS AFFECTED Any tree or shrub
SEASON All year

OLEANDER APHID PEST • See p.153
Leaves become distorted and discolored, with similar damage often occurring on buds and young stems. Specks, honey-dew, and black mold cover the leaves. Pests are plainly visible.

PLANTS AFFECTED Oleander (*Nerium*), milkweeds
SEASON Spring to autumn

FIREBLIGHT DISEASE • See p.129
Flattened areas develop on the bark (here of a pear tree) and may exude bacterial ooze. The wood beneath is stained red-brown. Flowers wither and die, followed by adjacent leaves.

PLANTS AFFECTED Apples, pears, and relatives
SEASON Late spring to summer

WOOLLY APPLE APHID PEST • See p.192
Fluffy white patches develop on branches, especially on pruning wounds and in cracks in the bark. Infestations on young shoots cause knobby swellings.

PLANTS AFFECTED Apple and related plants
SEASON Midspring to midautumn

BEECH SCALE PEST • See p.106
An off-white, powdery wax accumulates in crevices in the bark of beech trees. It is secreted from tiny, sap-feeding scale insects. Heavy infestations may be linked with the development of canker.

PLANTS AFFECTED Beeches (*Fagus*)
SEASON All year

STEM PROBLEMS CONTINUED

GIANT WILLOW APHID
PEST • See p. 132

Dense colonies of relatively large, grayish black aphids develop on willow stems. The bark and ground under the tree becomes sticky with honeydew excreted by the aphids.

PLANTS AFFECTED Willows (*Salix*)
SEASON Midsummer to midautumn

EUROPEAN FRUIT LECANIUM
PEST • See p. 127

Little brown mound- or shell-like objects occur on the stems. Black powdery mold (sooty mold) often occurs in the same area.

PLANTS AFFECTED Many trees and shrubs
SEASON Spring into late summer

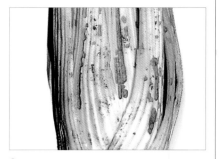

SLUGS
PEST • See p. 174

The softer parts of leaves and leaf stalks are eaten (here of celery, causing elongate grooves between the veins). Damaged parts turn brown and may be infected by secondary rots.

PLANTS AFFECTED Soft tissue of many plants
SEASON Spring to midautumn

SCLEROTINIA
DISEASE • See p. 172

Stems (here of a Jerusalem artichoke) become discolored and covered in dense, white, fluffy fungal growth. Large black sclerotia (fungal resting bodies) are embedded in the fungal growth.

PLANTS AFFECTED Wide range of plants
SEASON Mainly early autumn, but all year

APPLE AND PEAR CANKER
DISEASE • See p. 99

Flattened areas of discolored bark crack and split, forming concentric rings of flaky bark. White or red fungal bodies may develop on the cankered areas.

PLANTS AFFECTED Mainly apple and pear
SEASON All year

SYCAMORE MAPLE SOOTY BARK DISEASE
DISEASE • See p. 180

Green or yellow staining develops under bark. Later, black spore masses or blister-like outgrowths develop on the stems. Large areas of bark die and break off.

PLANTS AFFECTED Sycamore maple (*Acer*)
SEASON All year

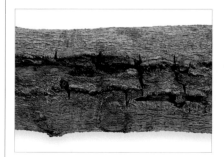

IRREGULAR WATERING
DISORDER • See p. 139

Longitudinal cracks or splits in bark may penetrate into the woody tissue. Older splits have swollen edges due to the formation of scar tissue.

PLANTS AFFECTED All woody plants
SEASON All year

MOWER INJURY
DISORDER • See p. 148

Patches of bark at the base of a shrub or tree trunk are missing; similar damage may occur on surface roots. Older scars show signs of healing or may be sites of attack by insects and disease.

PLANTS AFFECTED Trees and shrubs
SEASON Visible all year

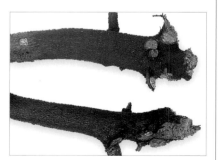

VOLES
PEST • See p. 186

Branches or whole plants die as a result of these small rodents gnawing away the bark on the stems or roots. Damage often occurs in winter, but the results may not be apparent until summer.

PLANTS AFFECTED Many trees and shrubs
SEASON All year

STEM PROBLEMS CONTINUED

APPLE RUST
DISEASE • *See p. 100*

Bizarre-looking, slimy orange horns emerge from hard, irregularly rounded structures on stems (especially red cedars) during moist weather. Also see page 18 for effects on apple leaves.

PLANTS AFFECTED Junipers; apples and crabapples
SEASON Spring and autumn

JUNIPER SCALE
PEST • *See p. 141*

Flat, yellow-white, rounded scales encrust the stems, often causing yellowing of the green parts. Heavy infestations of this sap-feeding insect can cause stems to die back.

PLANTS AFFECTED Juniper, cypress, arborvitae
SEASON All year

MEALYBUGS
PEST • *See p. 146*

Pinkish gray or white insects infest the stems and leaf axils. They are often covered with a fluffy, white, waxy substance. Honeydew excreted by the mealybugs allows sooty mold to grow.

PLANTS AFFECTED Many plants
SEASON All year

BRACKET FUNGUS
DISEASE • *See p. 109*

Bracket- or shelf-shaped, fungal fruiting bodies of variable size grow out from the tree, most commonly at the base of the trunk, but sometimes high in the crown. Also see below and pages 38-39.

PLANTS AFFECTED Most trees and some shrubs
SEASON All year (mainly autumn)

BRACKET FUNGUS
DISEASE • *See p. 109*

Here, dark red-brown, woody-textured bracket fungus grows on the trunk or base of trees. The lower surface is creamy white and covered in pores.

PLANTS AFFECTED Most trees and some shrubs
SEASON All year (mainly autumn)

BRACKET FUNGUS
DISEASE • *See p. 109*

Here, a semi-circular, rubbery, annual bracket fungus develops on trunks or branches, reddish brown and smooth or slightly ridged with a paler undersurface.

PLANTS AFFECTED Most trees and some shrubs
SEASON All year (mainly autumn)

STEM PROBLEMS CONTINUED

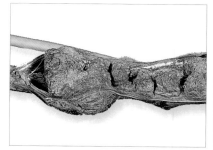

CROWN GALL – AERIAL FORM
DISEASE • See p.119

Roughened, rounded growths break out from within the stem (here of a logan-berry), rupturing it. Galls become woody and (if extensive) stems may die back.

PLANTS AFFECTED Many woody plants

SEASON All year, mainly summer

COOLEY SPRUCE GALL ADELGID
PEST • See p.117

On Douglas fir, cottony strands appear on needles, which bend and twist. On spruces, conelike galls form at base of shoots. Galls dry and remain on tree.

PLANTS AFFECTED Douglas fir, spruces

SEASON Spring through summer

BRACKET FUNGUS
DISEASE • See p.109

Overlapping, variably colored fungal structures are found on the trunk or large limbs of trees. The brackets often have wavy edges. See page 37 and right.

PLANTS AFFECTED Most trees and some shrubs

SEASON All year (mainly autumn)

BRACKET FUNGUS
DISEASE • See p.109

Single or overlapping, small bracket fungi grow on stems or trunks (here on dead wood). The upper surface may be concentrically zoned in shades of tan, brown, cream, and gray.

PLANTS AFFECTED Most trees and some shrubs

SEASON All year (mainly autumn)

NANTUCKET PINE TIP MOTH
PEST • See p.149

Pine needles at branch tips turn yellow and then brown and dead. Holes occur at the bases of needles, buds, and shoots. Plants may be stunted.

PLANTS AFFECTED Two-and three-needled pines

SEASON Midspring into summer

CANKER
DISEASE • See p.113

These are small cankers (here on mulberry) that may girdle and then kill stems. Tiny red-brown pustules appear around the cankered area. Leaves and shoots may die back.

PLANTS AFFECTED Many woody plants

SEASON All year

STEM PROBLEMS CONTINUED

BRACKET FUNGUS
DISEASE • See p.109

Hoof-shaped or rounded, fungal fruiting bodies appear on the bark of dead or living stems (here of an apple tree). Also see below and pages 37-38.

PLANTS AFFECTED Most trees and some shrubs
SEASON All year (mainly autumn)

BACTERIAL FASCIATION
DISEASE • See p.103

Numerous small, bunched, distorted, thickened, or fasciated leaves grow, usually around the stem base (here of a geranium, *Pelargonium*).

PLANTS AFFECTED Annual or herbaceous plants
SEASON Mainly spring and summer

COTTONY GRAPE SCALE
PEST • See p.118

In early summer this scale insect deposits its eggs under pads of white wax (here on a pyracantha), which can be drawn out in long threads. Heavily infested plants lack vigor.

PLANTS AFFECTED Grapes, currants, peaches, others
SEASON All year (eggs in spring/summer)

BRACKET FUNGUS
DISEASE • See p.109

Variably colored and shaped fungal structures are found around the base of trees or in the near vicinity of the roots. Also see above and pages 37-38.

PLANTS AFFECTED Most trees and some shrubs
SEASON All year (mainly autumn)

QUINCE RUST
DISEASE • See p.165

Yellow specks on leaves and other green parts develop into enlarged, misshapen areas, then they curl and drop. Green twigs develop swollen areas and then die back.

PLANTS AFFECTED Rose family
SEASON Spring into autumn

PINE ADELGIDS
PEST • See p.160

Small, black, aphidlike insects suck sap from the young shoots. The adelgids are hidden under a fluffy, white wax that is secreted from their bodies. This often resembles mold or snow.

PLANTS AFFECTED Pines (*Pinus*)
SEASON Midspring to late summer

HERBICIDES
DISORDER • See p.135

Among other symptoms, abnormal roots and other outgrowths form on stems (here of a brassica), causing them to become distorted. The foliage may not be affected.

PLANTS AFFECTED All plants
SEASON Mainly late spring and summer

MOSSYROSE GALL WASP
PEST • See p.148

Roughly spherical swellings covered in reddish or yellowish green, mossy leaves develop around the stems of certain roses and occasionally on foliage.

PLANTS AFFECTED Roses
SEASON Midsummer to early autumn

SPITTLEBUG
PEST • See p.177

Globules of frothy white liquid appear on stems and sometimes on foliage. Inside the froth is a yellowish green, sap-feeding insect, which is the nymphal stage of the adult spittlebug.

PLANTS AFFECTED Many plants
SEASON Late spring to early summer

39

STEM PROBLEMS CONTINUED

PHYSICAL INJURY
See pp. 70–71

Winds, heavy snow, browsing animals, poor pruning practices, or vandals may cause tearing of bark and injury to the wood beneath. Jagged wounds are slow to heal, and pathogens may enter them.

PLANTS AFFECTED Woody plants

SEASON All year

RUST
DISEASE • *See p.171*

Bright orange spore masses develop on the stems (here of a blackberry), often appearing from ruptures in stems. Large fissures remain on the stems after spores disperse.

PLANTS AFFECTED Bramble fruits; many others

SEASON All season

RASPBERRY CANE BORER
PEST • *See p.166*

Two distinctive rows of punctures occur below the tip of a raspberry cane, which usually wilts and dies back above the dots. Entire canes may die.

PLANTS AFFECTED Cane fruits, roses

SEASON

ASPARAGUS BEETLE
PEST • *See p.101*

Both larvae (*above left*) and adults (*above right*) eat the foliage and also chew bark from the stems, causing them to dry up and turn a yellowish brown color.

PLANTS AFFECTED Asparagus

SEASON Late spring to early autumn

EUROPEAN RED MITE
PEST • *See p.127*

The spherical winter eggs are very tiny, but there may be so many that they give the bark a reddish color, especially on branch undersides.

PLANTS AFFECTED Apples, plums

SEASON Eggs early autumn to late spring

FORSYTHIA GALL
DISEASE • *See p.130*

Rough-surfaced, nearly spherical, finely knobby, woody galls develop on stems. Several galls may be fused together. Old galls are black. The growth and development of the stem is not affected.

PLANTS AFFECTED Forsythia

SEASON All year

ROSE CANKER AND DIEBACK
DISEASE • *See p.169*

Stems die back and discoloration occurs, either in patches or all over the affected stem. Tissues may dry out. Growth above the affected areas dies off.

PLANTS AFFECTED Roses

SEASON Mainly late spring into summer

BLIND SHOOTS
DISORDER • *See p.107*

Shoots that should bear flower buds form, but no flower buds develop (here on a rose). Leaf and stem growth otherwise appear perfectly healthy, with no sign of dieback.

PLANTS AFFECTED Flowering shrubs

SEASON Mainly in summer

PAPERY BARK
DISORDER • *See p.155*

Bark peels off as a thin, papery brown sheet. Small- to medium-sized shoots are most commonly affected, but any may show symptoms. Shoots can die back. Apple trees are particularly affected.

PLANTS AFFECTED Woody plants

SEASON All year, mainly spring and winter

STEM PROBLEMS CONTINUED

WITCHES' BROOMS
DISEASE • *See p.192*

Closely packed, densely branched clusters of twigs grow from normal stems. The stems do not die back but bear numerous small leaves. Adjacent growth is perfectly normal.

PLANTS AFFECTED Trees
SEASON All year

PEAR SCAB
DISEASE • *See p.158*

Irregular, dark spots develop on the young stems and may cause girdling. Olive-brown pustules are found on the undersurface of leaves and on affected stems. Stems may die back.

PLANTS AFFECTED Pears (*Pyrus*)
SEASON All year, particularly spring

CORAL SPOT
DISEASE • *See p.117*

Raised red, orange or coral-colored, hard pustules develop on dead or dying stems. Affected stems die back farther; if the infection spreads to the crown, the whole plant may be killed.

PLANTS AFFECTED Woody plants
SEASON All year

LUPINE APHID
PEST • *See p.145*

Large, whitish gray aphids cluster on the flower stems and underside of leaves. Heavy infestations cause the plant to wilt. Honeydew and sooty mold soil the foliage.

PLANTS AFFECTED Lupines
SEASON Late spring to late summer

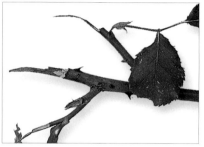

DEER
PEST • *See p.122*

Various species of deer come into gardens and eat foliage, flowers, and stems. Browsed stems invariably have ragged cuts caused by a deer's lack of incisor teeth in its upper jaw.

PLANTS AFFECTED Most plants
SEASON All year

BLOSSOM WILT
DISEASE • *See p.108*

Raised, rounded, buff-colored fungal pustules appear on twigs and stems (here of an apple tree), often associated with adjacent flowers withering and dying soon after opening.

PLANTS AFFECTED Apple, pear, plum, cherry
SEASON Mainly late spring and summer

BUD PROBLEMS

BLINDNESS OF BULBS
DISEASE/DISORDER • *See p.107*

Flower buds fail to form or do not develop fully (here on a daffodil) and open partially or not at all. Leaves are unaffected and appear healthy.

PLANTS AFFECTED *Narcissus*, many other bulbs
SEASON Spring

TAXUS BUD MITE
PEST • *See p.181*

Buds swell, dry up, and die on isolated branches or on the entire plant. New shoots are not produced. Severe infestation leads to misshapen, stunted growth. See also p. 27.

PLANTS AFFECTED Yews
SEASON

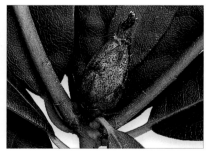

RHODODENDRON BUD BLAST
DISEASE • *See p.167*

Buds form but turn dry and brown. Numerous tiny, black, bristlelike fungal growths develop on the surface. Affected buds remain on the plant.

PLANTS AFFECTED Rhododendrons
SEASON All year, evident late spring and summer

41

FLOWERS

MOST GARDENS ARE packed full of plants grown largely because of their flowers, be they annuals, biennials, perennials, shrubs, climbers, or trees. In fruit and vegetable gardens, flowers are often equally important, because without them the edible fruits would never develop. Keeping flowers free from pests and diseases is therefore vital.

Flowers are usually short-lived, yet during their brief lifespan there may well be several pests or pathogens that could attack and therefore spoil them. They may be discolored (p.42) or disfigured by infestations of pests (p.43), deformed (pp.44–45) or damaged by pests (p.46). In many cases, however, even if a few blooms are spoiled, later flowers may be unscathed, having missed the attentions of the pest or the infection period of the pathogen.

Flowering in general is also greatly influenced by cultural and weather conditions, in particular soil moisture and fertility and the level of sunshine. Growing a plant in a suitable spot is the best way to ensure a good display of flowers.

DISCOLORED FLOWERS

GRAY MOLD   DISEASE • See p.133
Spots of discoloration appear on the petals (here of a rose). Spots may be edged with a dark ring. No fungal growth is apparent. In extreme cases the whole flower deteriorates.

PLANTS AFFECTED Many flowers
SEASON Mainly spring and summer

RHODODENDRON   DISEASE • See p.168
PETAL BLIGHT
Spots of discoloration develop on the petals. These enlarge and appear water-soaked. The flower collapses and rapidly discolors all over.

PLANTS AFFECTED Rhododendrons and azaleas
SEASON Spring

VIRUS   DISEASE • See p.186
Petals show "color breaking," with streaks of discoloration (here on a tulip). The petals do not deteriorate. Flowers may be reduced in number and size and show distortion.

PLANTS AFFECTED Tulips, many other plants
SEASON Bloom season

WESTERN   PEST • See p.189
FLOWER THRIPS
Pale flecking develops on petals (here of a gloxinia), and yellowish brown insects are seen on flowers and foliage. Infested blooms have a shortened life.

PLANTS AFFECTED Many greenhouse plants
SEASON All year

PESTS VISIBLE ON FLOWERS

ROSE APHIDS
PEST • *See p. 169*

Green, yellowish green, or pink aphids cluster on flower buds and stems. Heavy infestations reduce the quality of the blooms. White cast aphid skins litter the buds and foliage.

PLANTS AFFECTED Roses

SEASON Midspring to late summer

POLLEN BEETLES
PEST • *See p. 162*

Tiny black, metallic blue, or bronzy green beetles crawl around the center of blooms, where they feed on pollen. No direct damage is caused, but they can be a nuisance on cut flowers.

PLANTS AFFECTED Many flowers

SEASON Midspring to late summer

MELON (COTTON) APHID
PEST • *See p. 146*

Small black or dark green aphids infest the flowers (here chrysanthemum) and the undersides of leaves. Sooty mold grows on the aphids' excrement.

PLANTS AFFECTED Chrysanthemums and others

SEASON Mainly summer to autumn

SLUGS AND SNAILS
PESTS • *See pp. 174-75*

Damage caused by slugs and snails is usually indistinguishable. On daffodils, above, foliage is ignored but petals can be reduced to brown-edged fragments. A silvery slime trail is usually left behind.

PLANTS AFFECTED Wide range of plants

SEASON Spring to autumn

APPLE SUCKER
PEST • *See p. 100*

Flattened, tiny, pale green insects suck sap from blossom clusters. Heavy attacks make the petals turn brown and can be confused with frost damage. Fruit set can be greatly reduced.

PLANTS AFFECTED Apple trees

SEASON Mid- to late spring

SPITTLEBUG
PEST • *See p. 177*

A frothy, white liquid covers yellowish green insects (here on *Potentilla*), which are the immature nymphs of the adult spittlebugs. They also suck sap from foliage and stems (*see p. 39*).

PLANTS AFFECTED Many plants

SEASON Late spring to early summer

SQUASH BUG
PEST • *See p. 178*

Pale green to yellow dots on flowers and leaves coalesce into larger brown spots. Growth wilts, leaf edges become dry, and the plant dies. Gray young and brown adults swarm over the plant.

PLANTS AFFECTED Squash family

SEASON Spring through summer

JAPANESE BEETLE
PEST • *See p. 140*

Flowers have holes chewed in them or are completely eaten away. Adult beetles are often found in pairs or large groups and, when disturbed, drop down toward the ground before flying away.

PLANTS AFFECTED Many plants

SEASON Late spring through summer

BLISTER BEETLE
PEST • *See p. 108*

Flowers are completely eaten or heavily damaged. Adults often attack one plant en masse and then migrate to another. Blister beetles come in a wide range of colors.

PLANTS AFFECTED Many flowers and vegetables

SEASON Midsummer

DEFORMED AND DISTORTED FLOWERS

ASTER YELLOWS   DISEASE • *See p.102*

A wide variety of symptoms occurs. In general, plants develop abnormalities such as twisted, curled, and extra leaves, bunchy or elongated growth, and off-color or freakish flowers (as here).

PLANTS AFFECTED Many nonwoody plants
SEASON Summer

SMUT   DISEASE • *See p.174*

Anthers become swollen and distorted and packed full of masses of dark brown or black spores. Anthers burst to release spore masses. Flower stems may be distorted.

PLANTS AFFECTED Several plants
SEASON Mainly summer

FROST ON BUDS AND FLOWERS   DISORDER • *See p.130*

Petals become discolored (here of a camellia), usually brown and either soft or, less frequently, dry. Exposed flowers are most badly affected.

PLANTS AFFECTED Many flowers
SEASON Mainly spring and late autumn

ROSE BALLING   DISORDER • *See p.169*

Outer petals on an unopened or only partially opened bud are pale brown and dry. Initially, inner petals are unaffected, but they may die off when secondary organisms invade.

PLANTS AFFECTED Roses
SEASON Mainly summer

BOLTING   DISORDER • *See p.108*

Plants grown for their leaf crop become elongated and produce flowers prematurely (here on a brassica). This limits the cropping period. Early cultivars are particularly susceptible.

PLANTS AFFECTED Many leafy vegetables; onions
SEASON Mainly summer

PROLIFERATION   DISORDER • *See p.165*

Flower buds form within the center of the flower (here a rose). These remain as buds or develop into stems bearing flowers and occasionally leaves. Only the flowers or buds are affected.

PLANTS AFFECTED Roses, also pears and apples
SEASON Late spring and summer

DEFORMED AND DISTORTED FLOWERS *CONTINUED*

FASCIATION
DISORDER • *See p.128*

Stems become fused together, producing broad, ribbonlike stems (here on delphinium). The stems usually bear leaves and flowers but become curled and distorted.

PLANTS AFFECTED Many plants
SEASON All year on perennial stems

SCLEROTINIA
DISEASE • *See p.172*

Brown spots become wet and covered in fuzzy white growths. The spots contain rather large black spore bodies. Symptoms occur on flowers and most other aboveground plant parts.

PLANTS AFFECTED Many plants
SEASON Spring to autumn

WIND
DISORDER • *See p.191*

Petals (here of a camellia) become scorched and discolored, usually brown. Damaged areas are usually dry, not soggy. Flowers on exposed areas of the plant are most susceptible.

PLANTS AFFECTED Many plants
SEASON Mainly spring

WESTERN FLOWER THRIPS
PEST • *See p.189*

Petals and sometimes foliage show scarring, white or silvery streaking, and sometimes distortion. Flowers often fade rapidly, and buds may not open.

PLANTS AFFECTED Many annuals and perennials
SEASON Midspring through summer

Fuzzy fungal growth begins to cover whole flowerhead

Flowerhead loses shape and dies off

GLADIOLUS THRIPS
PEST • *See p.132*

Tiny creamy yellow or black, narrow-bodied insects feed in the flower buds and on the foliage. Infested blooms have pale mottled petals, and buds may turn brown and fail to open.

PLANTS AFFECTED Gladioli
SEASON Mid- to late summer

GRAY MOLD
DISEASE • *See p.133*

At this advanced stage of gray mold, the flowers rapidly become covered in dense, gray fungal growth (here on a geranium). Dieback may spread. For earlier symptoms *see p.42.*

PLANTS AFFECTED Many flowering plants
SEASON All year

DAMAGED FLOWERS

NECTAR ROBBING
PEST • *See p. 150*

Some short-tongued bees cannot reach the nectar from the front of some flowers, so they bite a hole at the base of the flower. Bees taking nectar in this way do not assist with pollination.

PLANTS AFFECTED Large-flowered plants

SEASON Summer

BIRDS
PEST • *See p. 106*

Birds may peck the petals of some flowers (here a crocus) to shreds, leaving fragments scattered nearby on the soil. They sometimes select certain colors but are not consistent.

PLANTS AFFECTED Crocus, primroses, and others

SEASON Early spring to summer

PEONY WILT
DISEASE • *See p. 158*

Stem tissue is discolored and shrinks inward, commonly at the base or, as above, below flower buds. Fuzzy gray fungal growth develops, and black fungal bodies are found on or in stems.

PLANTS AFFECTED Peonies

SEASON Spring to summer

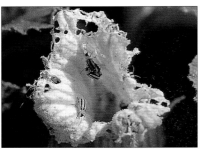

Male earwigs (top) have curved pincers, while females (bottom) have straight ones

Ragged holes are eaten in petals

STRIPED CUCUMBER BEETLE
PEST • *See p. 120*

Seedlings are completely eaten. Young plants have holes on all parts. Older leaves are lacy, and the entire plant may die. Beetles are obvious on plants.

PLANTS AFFECTED Squash family

SEASON Spring into autumn

PLANT (LYGUS) BUGS
PEST • *See p. 161*

Flower buds abort; infested plants are largely flowerless. Foliage is distorted and has many small holes, due to plant bugs damaging leaves at the shoot tips.

PLANTS AFFECTED Many plants

SEASON Late spring to late summer

EARWIGS
PEST • *See p. 125*

Earwigs emerge after dark, usually in mild weather, to feed on petals (here of a cosmos) and on foliage at shoot tips. This results in holes developing in the blooms and the expanded leaves.

PLANTS AFFECTED Clematis, dahlias, and others

SEASON Late spring to early autumn

FRUITS, BERRIES, VEGETABLES AND NUTS

IF THE EDIBLE PARTS of a plant are attacked by a pest or pathogen, the whole reason for growing the plant may well be lost. Fruits and berries are particularly prone to attack, since they usually have a high sugar and moisture content. Nuts, peas, and beans are also valuable food sources for many creatures.

In addition, some ornamental trees and shrubs are very commonly grown mainly for their attractive show of berries, and when these are eaten, removed, or spoiled by disease, the plant's appearance is ruined.

In many cases, prolonged protection of the plant may be needed, perhaps by using barriers or traps to keep pests away from the flowers or the developing and ripening fruits. Pesticides can be used with some success, but again these may sometimes need to be applied before the first signs of damage are noticed.

FRUIT PROBLEMS

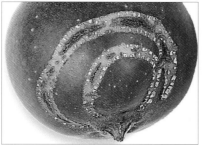

EUROPEAN APPLE SAWFLY
PEST • *See p.126*

Most infested fruits drop off in early summer. Some do develop as ripe fruit but have distinctive ribbon scars where the young larvae fed under the skin.

PLANTS AFFECTED Apples
SEASON Midspring to early autumn

FRUIT SCALD
DISORDER • *See p.130*

Reddish brown patches of discoloration develop on the skin of the fruit. The flesh beneath is usually undamaged, but it may be discolored. Exposed surfaces are most badly affected.

PLANTS AFFECTED Many kinds of fruit
SEASON Mainly summer

BIRDS
PEST • *See p.106*

Many kinds of fruit-eating birds will peck holes in ripening fruits. Wasps may enlarge this damage, and brown rot or other diseases frequently develop once the skin has been broken.

PLANTS AFFECTED Apples, pears, plums, peaches
SEASON Midsummer to autumn

PLUM CURCULIO
PEST • *See p.161*

Tiny fruit are damaged and may drop. Surviving fruit show crescent-shaped scars and sometimes swelling. Fruit may also be gouged, wormy, brown, and rotten.

PLANTS AFFECTED Many tree fruits
SEASON Spring through autumn

CODLING MOTH
PEST • *See p.116*

This is the cause of wormy apples in late summer. The caterpillar feeds at the core and tunnels out through the side or the eye end of the ripening fruit when it is fully developed.

PLANTS AFFECTED Apples, pears, walnuts, others
SEASON Midsummer to early autumn

WASPS AND YELLOWJACKETS
PEST • *See p.187*

These insects enlarge damage started by birds, but they can also initiate feeding on softer-skinned fruits (*see p.49*). They can make fruit picking hazardous.

PLANTS AFFECTED Tree fruits, grapes, blueberries
SEASON Midsummer to early autumn

BROWN ROT
DISEASE • *See p.110*

Soft, brown rot develops on fruit (here on an apple) and soon becomes studded with raised, creamy white pustules (*see also p.49*). These are often arranged in concentric rings.

PLANTS AFFECTED Cherries, peaches, others
SEASON Late summer and autumn

FRUIT PROBLEMS *CONTINUED*

ROSY APPLE APHID
PEST • *See p.171*

Small, grayish pink aphids infest the foliage and fruitlets in spring. They cause leaf curling and yellowing, and affected fruits remain small and distorted with a pinched appearance at the eye end.

PLANTS AFFECTED Apples

SEASON Early spring to late summer

PEAR MIDGE
PEST • *See p.157*

Pear fruitlets become abnormally swollen, turn black, and drop off the tree in early summer. These fruitlets contain many small, whitish orange maggots. The whole crop may be lost.

PLANTS AFFECTED Pears

SEASON Late spring to early summer

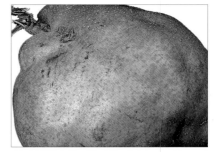

PEAR STONY PIT VIRUS
DISEASE • *See p.158*

Fruits become knobby and pitted, with hard patches throughout the flesh. Affected fruits usually appear only on isolated branches.

PLANTS AFFECTED Pears

SEASON Late summer to early autumn

PEAR SCAB
DISEASE • *See p.158*

Blackish brown, scabby patches appear on the skin of the fruits. The fruits are often small and misshapen and may be spoiled by splits, since secondary organisms rapidly cause rot.

PLANTS AFFECTED Pears

SEASON Late summer to early autumn

CORN EARWORM
PEST • *See p.117*

The top parts of corn ears are chewed away, and holes appear in tomatoes and peppers. The larvae may be found along with its excrement. Young foliage may be eaten, as well as cornsilks.

PLANTS AFFECTED Corn, tomatoes, peppers

SEASON Late spring through summer

APPLE BITTER PIT
DISEASE • *See p.99*

Pale brown spots of discoloration appear within the flesh, or sometimes on the fruit's skin. Those on the skin are usually slightly sunken. The fruit is otherwise perfectly normal in shape and size.

PLANTS AFFECTED Apples

SEASON Mainly autumn and in storage

EUROPEAN APPLE SAWFLY
PEST • *See p.126*

After initially tunneling under the skin, larvae bore into the core of fruitlets. Wet, blackish brown excrement comes out of the entry hole. Also see p.47.

PLANTS AFFECTED Apples

SEASON Midspring to midsummer

FRUIT SPLIT
DISORDER • *See p.131*

Straight or branched splits develop in the skin. The splits are usually single, but several may occasionally appear on one fruit. Secondary organisms such as brown rot may invade and cause rot.

PLANTS AFFECTED Most fruits, especially apples

SEASON Mid- to late summer

EUROPEAN CORN BORER
PEST • *See p.127*

Leaves have tiny holes in them, and fruits and seeds are bored and chewed. Stems have small holes and sawdustlike material nearby. Stems bend and break.

PLANTS AFFECTED Corn; vegetables and flowers

SEASON Late spring into summer

FRUIT AND BERRY PROBLEMS

WASPS AND YELLOWJACKETS
PEST • *See p.187*

These familiar stinging insects are attracted to ripe fruits. They can make extensive cavities in some softer-skinned fruits. Also see p.47.

PLANTS AFFECTED Tree fruits, grapes, blueberries
SEASON Midsummer to midautumn

BROWN ROT
DISEASE • *See p. 110*

Fruits (here a cherry) turn brown and rot and rapidly develop numerous raised, creamy white pustules (*see also p.47*). The fruits then dry out but remain hanging on the tree.

PLANTS AFFECTED Stone fruits; sometimes apples
SEASON Late summer to autumn

REDBERRY MITE
PEST • *See p. 167*

Blackberries fail to ripen completely, with parts or all of the fruit remaining red. Ripening becomes progressively unsatisfactory as the season develops. The cause is microscopic mites.

PLANTS AFFECTED Blackberries
SEASON Late summer to midautumn

POWDERY MILDEW
DISEASE • *See p.164*

Fruits (here grapes) develop a white, off-white, or grayish beige fungal coating in patches or all over. They fail to swell fully, may be small or distorted, and may crack or split.

PLANTS AFFECTED Some fruits
SEASON Summer

GOOSEBERRY MILDEW
DISEASE • *See p. 132*

Powdery or felty white fungal growth develops on the skin, soon turning buff or pale brown. The fungus may be rubbed off. Fruits may be undersized.

PLANTS AFFECTED Gooseberries, blackcurrants
SEASON Summer

PYRACANTHA SCAB
DISEASE • *See p.165*

Greenish black, scabby fungal growth develops on the berries, which may cause them to split and die off. In extreme cases the whole surface of the berry may be obscured.

PLANTS AFFECTED Pyracanthas
SEASON Autumn

FRUIT AND VEGETABLE PROBLEMS

RASPBERRY FRUITWORM
PEST • *See p. 166*

The stalk end dries up and becomes grayish brown. An elongate, whitish brown grub may be found feeding in the core or plug of the fruit. Fruit may drop.

PLANTS AFFECTED Raspberries
SEASON Midsummer to early autumn

TOMATO GREENBACK
DISEASE • *See p. 182*

A partial or complete ring of unripened tissue appears around the stem end of a ripening fruit. The flesh and skin remains either green or yellow.

PLANTS AFFECTED Tomatoes
SEASON Summer

GRAY MOLD
DISEASE • *See p. 133*

Soft, pale brown areas develop on the fruit (here strawberries) and rapidly increase in size. Fuzzy gray fungal growth develops on the surface, and the fruit rapidly rots.

PLANTS AFFECTED Strawberries, other fruit
SEASON Late spring to early autumn

BLOSSOM END ROT
DISEASE • *See p. 108*

A sunken, leathery, dark brown to black patch develops at the bottom end of the developing fruit (here tomatoes). The remainder of the fruit ripens normally but remains distorted.

PLANTS AFFECTED Tomatoes, peppers
SEASON Summer

TOMATO FRUIT SPLITTING
DISORDER • *See p. 182*

Fruits develop normally and then split shortly before they are ready to pick. The split may dry out or may become infected with secondary fungi.

PLANTS AFFECTED Tomatoes
SEASON Any time fruit occur

STINKBUG
PEST • *See p. 179*

Fruit develop off-color, yellowish spots or dimples. Some fruits become bent or distorted. Green or brown bugs may be visible. The adults release a distinctive odor when disturbed.

PLANTS AFFECTED Tomatoes, many others
SEASON Late spring through summer

VEGETABLE PROBLEMS

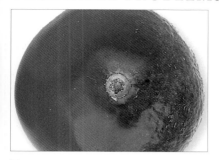

TOMATO BLOTCHY RIPENING
DISORDER • *See p. 181*

Randomly distributed, hard, yellow or green patches of flesh remain unripened. The rest of the fruit develops and ripens normally.

PLANTS AFFECTED Tomatoes

SEASON Summer and early autumn

TOMATO LATE BLIGHT
DISEASE • *See p. 182*

Brown, discolored areas develop within ripe and unripe fruits and are visible on the surface. Discolored areas may shrink inward and suffer secondary rotting.

PLANTS AFFECTED Tomatoes and potatoes

SEASON Summer and early autumn

BEAN AND PEA WEEVIL
PEST • *See p. 105*

Beans kept for seed may have circular holes where adults have emerged. The grubs feed on the cotyledons, but damaged seeds will usually germinate.

PLANTS AFFECTED Beans and peas

SEASON Midsummer to midautumn

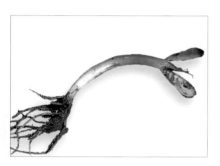

SEEDCORN MAGGOT
PEST • *See p. 173*

White fly maggots feed on germinating seeds, making holes in the cotyledons and stems. Seedlings may die or emerge with the growing point killed or crooked.

PLANTS AFFECTED Corn, peas, beets, others

SEASON Mid-spring to early summer

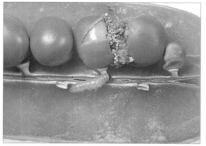

PEA MOTH
PEST • *See p. 156*

Small cream-colored caterpillars with dark spots feed inside pea pods on the developing seeds. Piles of excrement pellets indicate where the caterpillars have been feeding.

PLANTS AFFECTED Peas

SEASON Early to late summer

PEA LEAF AND POD SPOT
DISEASE • *See p. 156*

Yellow or brown, often sunken, patches develop on the pods. Dark brown or black pycnidia (fungal fruiting bodies) may be visible on affected areas.

PLANTS AFFECTED Peas

SEASON Spring to summer

CORN SMUT
DISEASE • *See p. 118*

Individual kernels on ears become enlarged and distorted. Initially pale gray in color, they rupture to release masses of powdery black spores. The rest of the plant develops normally.

PLANTS AFFECTED Corn

SEASON Mid- to late summer

MICE
PEST • *See p. 147*

Rows of germinating peas, beans, and other seeds, bulbs, and corms are disturbed by burrowing mice. Only below-ground parts are eaten; the shoots are left lying on the soil surface.

PLANTS AFFECTED Peas, beans, corn, many others

SEASON Early spring to midsummer

CARROT RUST FLY
PEST • *See p. 113*

Elongate, yellow-white fly maggots tunnel in certain taproots, causing orange-brown discolored lines on the outside of the roots. Secondary rots may extend the damage.

PLANTS AFFECTED Carrots, parsnips, parsley

SEASON Early summer to late autumn

VEGETABLE PROBLEMS CONTINUED

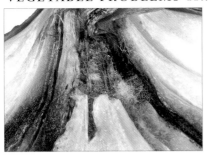

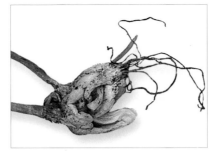

ONION NECK ROT DISEASE • See p.153
The neck area of the onion turns pale brown and soft and appears semi-transparent. Fuzzy gray fungal growth and black sclerotia may develop. The onion can become mummified.

PLANTS AFFECTED Onions, shallots
SEASON Late summer and after harvest

ONION NEMATODE PEST • See p.153
Microscopic, wormlike animals live within the bulb and leaves. Infested plants are swollen and distorted, with softened tissues that are susceptible to secondary rots.

PLANTS AFFECTED Onions, leeks
SEASON Late spring to early autumn

ONION WHITE ROT DISEASE • See p.154
Dense, fluffy white fungal growth appears around the basal plate. Small black sclerotia may be visible, and the bulb starts to rot.

PLANTS AFFECTED Onions, leeks, shallots, garlic
SEASON Summer and in storage

NUT PROBLEMS

NUT WEEVILS PEST • See p.151
The kernel is eaten by a white grub with a brown head. The fully fed grub bores a circular hole in the ripe nut shell (here of a hazelnut) when it leaves to pupate.

PLANTS AFFECTED Hazelnuts, others
SEASON Mid-summer to early autumn

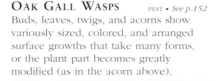

SQUIRRELS PEST • See p.179
Squirrels often strip trees before the nuts are fully ripe, and the ground becomes littered with broken nut shells. Nuts are buried, sometimes in lawns, for consumption during the winter.

PLANTS AFFECTED Hazelnuts, walnuts, others
SEASON Late summer to midautumn

OAK GALL WASPS PEST • See p.152
Buds, leaves, twigs, and acorns show variously sized, colored, and arranged surface growths that take many forms, or the plant part becomes greatly modified (as in the acorn above).

PLANTS AFFECTED Oaks (*Quercus*)
SEASON Late summer to midautumn

SOIL, ROOTS, TUBERS, AND BULBS

PESTS AND PATHOGENS that attack below ground level are common, but because the symptoms they cause are usually first seen above ground, they may well be misidentified. Often the only way to identify a soil-borne problem conclusively is to dig up part or all of the plant, a process which in itself may obviously cause considerable and long-term damage.

Most soil-borne problems, caused by pests or pathogens that attack roots, tubers, bulbs, or corms directly, are potentially very damaging, simply because the root system or the base of the plant is so fundamental to the survival of the plant as a whole. Early investigation, identification, and, where possible, control is therefore essential. Generally, control is difficult, however, since locating and targeting an underground pest or pathogen with a pesticide is not easy.

SOIL PROBLEMS

BLACK VINE WEEVIL (DAMAGE BY LARVAE) PEST • *See p. 107*
Plump, white, legless larvae with pale brown heads feed on roots, corms, and tubers, particularly on plants grown in containers. Plants lack vigor.

PLANTS AFFECTED Many plants
SEASON Late summer to midspring

LEATHERJACKETS PEST • *See p. 144*
Leatherjackets are the larvae of crane flies. They are grayish brown, legless maggots with no obvious head. They eat roots and seedling plants and also cause problems in lawns (*see p. 58*).

PLANTS AFFECTED Many garden plants
SEASON Midspring to late summer

SOWBUGS AND PILLBUGS PEST • *See p. 176*
Sowbugs may be gray or pinkish brown; pillbugs curl up when disturbed. They feed on decaying vegetation in soil and occasionally eat seedlings.

PLANTS AFFECTED Seedlings
SEASON All year

FUNGUS GNAT (LARVAE) PEST • *See p. 131*
The larvae of fungus gnats, or sciarid flies, are white, legless maggots with black heads. They feed on decaying vegetation and seedlings.

PLANTS AFFECTED Greenhouse and houseplants
SEASON All year

WHITE GRUBS PEST • *See p. 189*
White grubs have plump, white bodies, curved like the letter C, with brown heads and three pairs of legs. They eat roots and make cavities in root vegetables and potato tubers.

PLANTS AFFECTED Many garden plants
SEASON Mostly midspring and late summer

CUTWORMS PEST • *See p. 121*
Cutworms are the soil-colored caterpillars of several species of moths. They kill small plants by severing the stems or by gnawing away the outer part of the stems at soil level.

PLANTS AFFECTED Mostly annuals and vegetables
SEASON Mainly midspring to midautumn

SLIME MOLD FUNGAL PEST • *See p. 174*
Small to fairly large patches of vomitlike material appear on mulch, soil high in organic matter, wood, or low down on tree trunks. Older patches emit clouds of dustlike spores if disturbed.

PLANTS AFFECTED Soil, mulch (also turf)
SEASON Spring to autumn

SOIL PROBLEMS CONTINUED

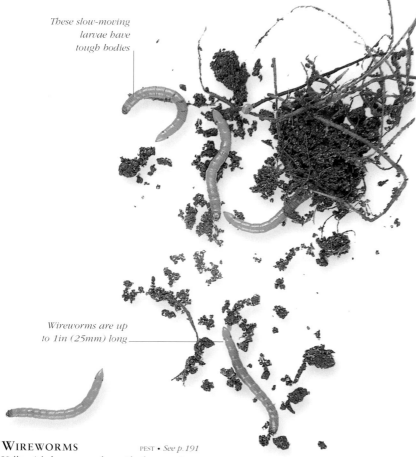

These slow-moving larvae have tough bodies

Wireworms are up to 1in (25mm) long

WIREWORMS
PEST • *See p.191*

Yellowish brown grubs with three pairs of short legs at their front eat roots and bore into root vegetables. They cause the most damage where grass has been dug to create flower or vegetable gardens.

PLANTS AFFECTED Seedlings, potatoes, others
SEASON Early summer to midautumn

MILLIPEDES
PEST • *See p.147*

Millipedes are common scavengers in the garden, feeding on rotting vegetation and occasionally damaging seedlings or fruit touching the soil. They may enlarge damage caused by other organisms.

PLANTS AFFECTED Seedlings, potatoes, tomatoes
SEASON Spring to autumn

SPRINGTAILS
PEST • *See p.177*

Small, white insects come to the surface of potted plants or are washed out of the pot when the plant is watered. Most cause no harm to the plant, since most feed on dead plant material.

PLANTS AFFECTED Potted plants
SEASON All year

BULB PROBLEMS

BULB BLUE MOLD
DISEASE • *See p.111*

Reddish brown lesions develop on the flesh of the bulb and may be sunken. Fluffy, white or blue-green fungal growth may appear on top of lesions.

PLANTS AFFECTED Most bulbs in storage
SEASON Mainly late summer to autumn

NARCISSUS NEMATODE
PEST • *See p.150*

Plants are stunted and distorted. If the bulb is cut in half transversely, brown concentric rings can be seen where the microscopic nematodes are feeding. Infested bulbs rot and die.

PLANTS AFFECTED Daffodils
SEASON All year; mostly noticed in spring

NARCISSUS BULB FLY
PEST • *See p.149*

Infested bulbs rot in the soil or produce a few distorted leaves in the spring. One large maggot feeds in the center of the bulb and fills it with its muddy brown excrement.

PLANTS AFFECTED Daffodils, amaryllis, and others
SEASON Late summer to early spring

BULB PROBLEMS CONTINUED

TULIP FIRE
DISEASE • See p.183

Tiny, irregularly shaped, black sclerotia (fungal resting bodies) develop on the bulb, clustered around the neck. The bulb may rot or appear firm. Foliage that appears above ground may be withered.

PLANTS AFFECTED Tulips
SEASON Late summer

GLADIOLUS CORM ROT
DISEASE • See p.132

Brown, ridged areas of discoloration appear on the corm. The corm dries out and becomes mummified. No fungal growths or sclerotia are visible.

PLANTS AFFECTED Gladioli, crocus, bulbous iris
SEASON In storage

GLADIOLUS CORM ROT – FOLIAGE SYMPTOMS
DISEASE • See p.132

Yellow flecking and (later) striping develops toward the tips of the outer-most leaves. The discoloration spreads and the leaves turn brown and die.

PLANTS AFFECTED Gladioli, crocus, bulbous iris
SEASON Late spring and summer

ROOT AND TUBER PROBLEMS

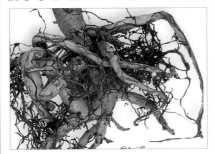

FOOT AND ROOT ROTS
DISEASE • See p.130

Roots discolor (here on daphne), often turning black or brown and shrinking inwards. Deterioration usually starts at the root tips, and roots may disintegrate.

PLANTS AFFECTED Most plants
SEASON All year

IRIS SOFT ROT
DISEASE • See p.139

Roots and rhizomes deteriorate rapidly, turning soft and slimy. The infection usually starts on the leaves but spreads quickly. Foliage may fail to develop, or it yellows and dies back.

PLANTS AFFECTED Rhizomatous irises
SEASON Mainly spring and summer

CLUBROOT
DISEASE • See p.116

Numerous irregularly shaped swellings develop on roots of cabbage and related plants. Swellings do not contain any insect larvae or grubs. The entire root system may be distorted and swollen.

PLANTS AFFECTED Cabbage family
SEASON All year

ROOT APHIDS
PEST • See p.168

Infested plants grow slowly and tend to wilt in sunny weather. Aphids, usually globular and creamy brown, feed on the roots. They often secrete a white, waxy powder from their bodies.

PLANTS AFFECTED Lettuce, beans, and others
SEASON Mid- to late summer

POTATO CYST NEMATODES
PEST • See p.162

Pinhead-sized, spherical cysts, which may be white, pale yellow, or brown, form on the roots. These are the swollen bodies of the female nematodes.

PLANTS AFFECTED Potatoes, tomatoes
SEASON Mid- to late summer

ROOT MEALYBUGS
PEST • See p.169

These tiny, sap-feeding insects have white, elongate bodies and can be found in large numbers. They secrete a white, waxy powder from their bodies, which coats roots and soil particles.

PLANTS AFFECTED Potted plants
SEASON All year

ROOT AND TUBER PROBLEMS CONTINUED

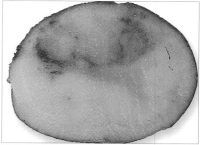

POTATO SPRAING
DISEASE • *See p. 164*

Tan-colored arcs of discoloration appear in the flesh. Corky tissue may be present around the discolored areas. The tubers are occasionally distorted. Foliage and stems may be mottled yellow.

PLANTS AFFECTED Potatoes

SEASON Late spring onward

POTATO SCAB
DISEASE • *See p. 163*

Raised, roughened, scabby patches develop on the skin of the tuber. Scabs have ragged edges. The damage is usually superficial.

PLANTS AFFECTED Potatoes

SEASON Late spring onward

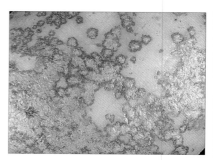

POTATO SILVER SCURF
DISEASE • *See p. 164*

Pale and inconspicuous silvery gray markings develop on the tuber skin. The size, shape, flesh, and eating quality of the potato are not affected.

PLANTS AFFECTED Potatoes

SEASON Mainly in storage

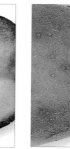

POTATO LATE BLIGHT
DISEASE • *See p. 163*

Sunken, darkened areas develop on the skin. The flesh is discolored by a dry, reddish brown rot. Secondary organisms cause soft rot and an unpleasant smell.

PLANTS AFFECTED Potatoes and tomatoes

SEASON Late summer onward

POTATO POWDERY SCAB
DISEASE • *See p. 163*

Small, nearly circular scabby areas appear on the tuber skin. The scabs have raised margins and burst to release masses of brown spores.

PLANTS AFFECTED Potatoes

SEASON Summer onward

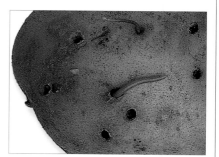

WIREWORMS
PEST • *See p. 191*

Elongate, yellowish brown grubs with three pairs of legs at the head end bore into the tubers. They are mainly a problem where grass has recently been dug over to make a vegetable garden.

PLANTS AFFECTED Root vegetables, potatoes

SEASON Early summer to midautumn

ROOT AND TUBER PROBLEMS CONTINUED

SLUGS
PEST • *See p. 174*

Slugs make small, round holes in the skin of potato tubers but hollow out extensive cavities once they are inside. Some potato cultivars are particularly susceptible to slug damage.

PLANTS AFFECTED Potatoes, root vegetables
SEASON Midsummer to midautumn

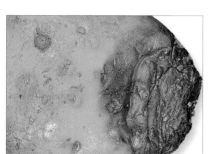

POTATO DRY ROT
DISEASE • *See p. 162*

One end of the tuber shows wrinkled skin and then shrinks inward rapidly, forming concentric rings of wrinkles and discoloration. Pink, white, or blue-green fungal pustules may develop.

PLANTS AFFECTED Potatoes in storage
SEASON Any time of year

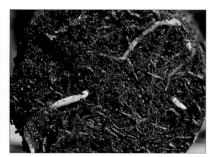

PYTHIUM ROOT ROT
DISEASE • *See p. 165*

The entire plant wilts, and parts may die. Inspection of the rootball finds dead and rotted roots among healthy-appearing ones. Seedlings die quickly.

PLANTS AFFECTED Many plants
SEASON All year

POTATO GANGRENE
DISEASE • *See p. 163*

Slightly sunken, round-edged areas develop on the tuber shortly after lifting. Lesions may remain defined or enlarge. The tuber rots, turning pale pink.

PLANTS AFFECTED Potatoes
SEASON Summer and autumn

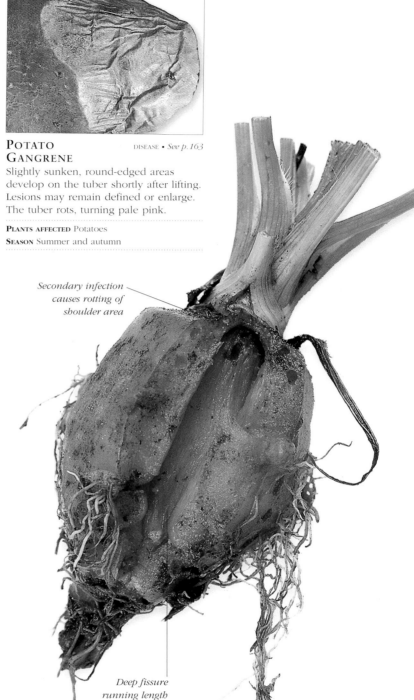

Secondary infection causes rotting of shoulder area

Deep fissure running length of root

IRREGULAR WATERING
DISORDER • *See p. 139*

Longitudinal cracks appear in roots (here of a carrot). Top growth appears perfectly normal. Secondary organisms may cause deterioration of root.

PLANTS AFFECTED Many root crops
SEASON Mainly summer and autumn

GALLERY OF SYMPTOMS

LAWNS

LAWNS ARE VERY POPULAR and one of the most widely used areas of a yard. Even if you do not want a perfect lawn (but instead expect an area that is practical, usable, and a good shade of green, there will still be times when problems need to be addressed.

There are several common fungal infections and pests. The majority of problems, whether caused by a pest, a pathogen, or poor cultivation, result in areas of grass turning yellow or brown. At first sight, differentiating between the various causes may not be easy. Most fungal problems do involve the development of visible (if small) fungal growths; a few, such as fairy rings or other toadstools, are very distinct. Lawn pest problems are generally easier to identify, and the culprits are more readily visible.

In all cases, prompt action is advisable, since once turf grasses weaken or their growth becomes thinner, coarse grasses, mosses, and weeds colonize rapidly. Among these, dog lichens (*see facing page*) are commonly mistaken for a disease, but in fact are part fungus and part algae.

LAWN PROBLEMS

LEATHERJACKETS   PEST • *See p.144*
These cranefly larvae generally cause damage when they are becoming fully grown. Patches of turf turn yellow-brown, and holes may be seen where birds have been searching for the grubs.
PLANTS AFFECTED Turf, roots of many plants
SEASON Midsummer

SLIME MOLD   DISEASE • *See p.174*
Numerous gray, yellow, or off-white spheres are clustered together on individual blades of grass. These may appear to "dissolve" when wet. Turf growth and health are not affected.
PLANTS AFFECTED Many plants, including turf
SEASON Mainly summer and autumn

BURROWING BEES AND WASPS   PEST • *See p.111*
Small, conical heaps of powdery soil form on the lawn. Each has an entrance hole where a solitary bee leaves and enters. No significant damage is caused.
PLANTS AFFECTED Turf
SEASON Midspring to midsummer

WHITE GRUBS   PEST • *See p.189*
Plump, creamy white grubs with brown heads sever roots, making it easy for skunks and birds to rip up turf to feed on them. The grubs are curved, with three pairs of legs (*see p.53*).
PLANTS AFFECTED Turf, other plant roots
SEASON Early autumn to early spring

TURF THATCH FUNGAL MYCELIUM   DISEASE • *See p.185*
Bleached yellow or reddish patches of grass develop. Dense white or off-white fungal growth appears around the grass roots.
PLANTS AFFECTED Turf
SEASON All year

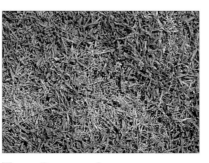

TURF DOLLAR SPOT   DISEASE • *See p.183*
Patches of grass die off and turn straw yellow. The individual patches are usually 4in (10cm) or less in diameter. The fungus causing this disease is most prevalent during warm, damp weather.
PLANTS AFFECTED Turf
SEASON Summer to autumn

EARTHWORMS   PEST • *See p.124*
Some earthworms deposit heaps of muddy excrement on the surface of lawns. These worm casts become smeared by foot traffic or mowers and may spoil the lawn's appearance.
PLANTS AFFECTED Turf
SEASON Mainly autumn to spring

LAWN PROBLEMS *CONTINUED*

ANTS
PEST • *See p. 98*

Heaps of fine soil appear on the lawn's surface above ant nests; if they are disturbed, variously colored ants will be seen. Ant heaps get in the way of mowers and make the lawn uneven.

PLANTS AFFECTED Turf

SEASON Late spring to early autumn

TURF RED THREAD
DISEASE • *See p. 184*

Patches of grass begin to deteriorate. Numerous pale red or pink, gelatinous, hornlike fungal growths are attached to individual grass blades. Later, fluffy, pale pink fungal growth develops.

PLANTS AFFECTED Turf

SEASON Mainly late spring to early autumn

DOG LICHENS
See facing page

Small, unevenly shaped, gray, leaflike growths, off-white beneath, develop in grass, particularly when turf is sparse and weak. Lichen is not a pest or disease; it should be treated as a weed.

PLANTS AFFECTED Turf

SEASON All year

TURF SNOW MOLD
DISEASE • *See p. 184*

Patches of dying grass develop and then enlarge and turn brown. Deteriorating grass may be covered in pale pink, fluffy fungal growth.

PLANTS AFFECTED Turf

SEASON Mainly autumn and winter

MOLES
PEST • *See p. 148*

Moles create a network of tunnels in the soil in which they live and leave the excavated soil in heaps on the surface. Collapsed mole tunnels give the lawn an uneven surface.

PLANTS AFFECTED Turf

SEASON All year

TURF FAIRY RINGS
DISEASE • *See p. 184*

Rings of dead or dying grass, or sometimes other patterns of discoloration, develop on a lawn. One or more rings of lush grass grow adjacent to these. Brown toadstools grow out of the ring.

PLANTS AFFECTED Turf

SEASON Mainly late summer and autumn

BENEFICIAL GARDEN DWELLERS

GARDENS ARE INHABITED BY a wide range of insects and other organisms, but only a small proportion are plant pests. Most are neither particularly helpful nor harmful to the gardener. There are, however, some that are very beneficial, feeding on pests, pollinating flowers, or improving the soil.

Predatory and parasitic insects may not occur in large enough numbers to totally prevent pests from causing damage, but they may keep pest populations under control. Pollinating insects are essential for good crops of most fruits and some vegetables. Any insects that move from one flower to another can effect the transfer of pollen.

Most insecticides do not discriminate between pests and beneficial insects. It is therefore important to avoid unnecessary chemical usage, saving them for plants that would be seriously damaged by pests or diseases if control measures were not taken.

LADYBUGS (LADY BEETLES)
Most ladybugs (*see p.141*) prey on aphids, but some feed on scale insects, spider mites, or mealybugs, and others on powdery mildew fungal spores. Not all are red with black spots; some are yellow or orange with black spots, while others are black with red spots.

FLOWER BUG
Flower bugs, also known as minute pirate bugs, are quite small and are general predators of aphids, thrips, other small insects, mites, and their eggs. They have needlelike mouthparts with which they pierce their prey and suck out the contents.

PARASITIZED APHIDS
Several species of tiny parasitic wasp (*see p.182*) lay eggs in nymphs. The grub develops as an internal parasite that kills the aphid, causing it to become very swollen and straw brown in color. The adult wasp emerges through a hole it makes in the mummy (dead aphid).

LADYBUG LARVA
Although less familiar than the adult beetles, ladybug larvae are equally voracious predators of aphids and other pests. The active larvae are black with orange or white markings. A larva will eat 200–400 aphids before it is fully fed and ready to pupate. See page 141.

HOVER FLY (FLOWER FLY) LARVA
Both the larval and adult stages (*see p.137*) feed on aphids. The larvae have flattened, semitransparent bodies. The adult flies have yellow and black striped abdomens, giving them a wasplike appearance, although their bodies usually look smoother. Also called syrphid flies.

TACHINID FLIES
There are many species of tachinid flies, many quite tiny. Most have larvae that are parasites of insects, especially caterpillars. The maggots feed inside the body cavity of their host insect, causing its death by the time the tachinid larvae are ready to pupate. See page 180.

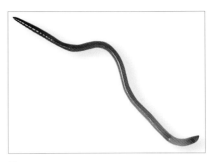

EARTHWORMS
Earthworms (*see p.124*) burrow extensive tunnels in the soil through which water can drain and air can reach plant roots. Worms feed on dead plant material, and their presence in slow-acting compost piles speeds up the conversion of debris to compost.

CENTIPEDES
Most centipedes live in the surface layers of the soil and shelter under stones, logs, and pots. They are active at night, preying on a wide range of small soil animals and their eggs. The front pair of legs curve forward and are modified to act as jaws. See page 114.

Distinctive yellow and black markings

Wasp grasps victim and uses sting to paralyze victim

PRAYING MANTIDS
These rather large and unique-looking insects eat a wide variety of other insects, including both pest species and beneficial ones. In spite of their indiscriminate menu, they are well worth attracting to and retaining in the garden. See page 164.

SOLITARY WASPS
Unlike social wasps, these tunnel out individual nests in rotten wood and sandy soil, or they make use of beetle tunnels in dead wood. Some make small mud nests. All provision their nests with insects for their larvae. There are many species of various sizes. See page 187.

BUMBLEBEES

Bumblebees make their nests in the ground, often in abandoned mouse holes. They are valuable pollinating insects: they will visit flowers in poor weather when honeybees stay in their hives. At full strength in midsummer a nest can house 200–500 bees.

HONEYBEES

Many plants, especially most fruits, require insects to carry pollen from one flower to another to fertilize the flowers and allow seeds and fruits to set. The hairy bodies of honeybees become heavily dusted with pollen when they visit flowers to collect nectar.

WOLF SPIDERS

Most spiders spin sticky webs to capture flying or crawling insects, but wolf spiders run rapidly over the soil or vegetation to hunt down their prey. The females are frequently seen in early summer carrying their silken egg sacs under their abdomens. See page 176.

SHREW

These small, mouselike predators, which have elongate snouts, are rarely seen but may be numerous in wild areas and rough grass. They are active during the day and at night, when they feed on a wide range of insects, slugs, sowbugs, and earthworms.

PARASITIC WASPS

Many species of parasitic wasps lay their eggs in the larvae, pupae, or eggs of other insects. The larvae develop inside the host insect, which is killed when the parasite is ready to pupate. Some wasps have long egg-laying organs to enable them to reach concealed insects.

The ricelike objects on the back of the hornworm above are the pupae of a braconid wasp. They emerge to parasitize other insects and should not be disturbed if found in the garden. Also see Braconid Wasps p. 109, Trichogramma Wasps p. 182, and Wasps p. 187 for more information.

SONG THRUSH
The song thrush specializes in feeding on snails. It breaks the snail's shell by smashing it against a stone. It often makes regular use of certain stones, and these "anvils" become littered with pieces of snail shell. Its diet also includes worms, insects, and berries.

GREEN LACEWING
Lacewings derive their name from the many veins that give the wings a lace-like appearance. Other types of adult lacewings (*see p.141*) have black or brown bodies. The larval stages are voracious predators of aphids and sometimes other small insects.

GROUND BEETLES
Also known as carabid beetles, these insects live mainly on the soil surface, but some climb up plants in search of insects to eat. They are mostly black, brown, or metallic green. The larvae prey on a range of insects, slugs, and pest eggs. See page 134.

TOADS
Toads, like frogs, need ponds in which to breed in the spring, but for the rest of the summer they may be found well away from water. They are mainly active after dark, when they feed on a variety of insects, sowbugs, worms, and spiders.

Beetle's jaws are strong for killing and eating insects

Long legs to help chase prey

GYPSY MOTH DISEASES
Several fungi and viruses attack gypsy moth larvae and can cause tremendous population decreases. Larvae cease feeding and then turn black and die; they are often found hanging from branches or bark, sometimes in a "V" shape. See page 134.

TIGER BEETLES
These colorful predators feed on a variety of insects and occur mainly in sandy areas. Their larvae live in pits in the soil from which they emerge to seize passing insects. The adults run over the soil surface and readily fly up in sunny weather or when approached.

GARDEN HEALTH AND PROBLEMS

GARDEN PLANTS COEXIST with many other living things – some beneficial, many benign, but some harmful. Favorable growing conditions and good gardening practices make plants strong and more able to tolerate potentially harmful organisms, but when serious attack by pests or diseases occurs, the gardener must choose an appropriate method with which to bring the problem under control.

THE BALANCE OF LIFE

EVERY GARDEN FORMS a miniature ecological system that is unique, with its own combination of plants, soil conditions, topography, and climate. These factors, together with the interaction of the various creatures that live within the garden (including predators, parasites, pathogens, saprophytes, and herbivores), determine what thrives, what survives, and what deteriorates or dies. The aim of the gardener is to encourage desirable growth – usually, that of ornamental and edible plants – but this must be achieved within a healthy ecological balance that involves other life forms. A garden purged of insects or fungi, for example, would soon become unproductive. The activities and life processes of other forms of plant and animal life, together with their death and decay, are crucial to the growth and health of garden plants. Since all the organisms in a garden will influence the overall working and functioning of the plants and the garden as a whole, any action taken by the gardener may have an effect on plants or animals other than that being treated. When considering pest or disease control it is critical to be aware of such effects.

THE ENERGY FOR GROWTH

Plants manufacture energy by the process of photosynthesis, in which the action of sunlight on green leaf pigments enables plants to combine

INTERACTION IN THE GARDEN

Even in the smallest corner of the garden, plants, creatures, and environmental factors interact to form a rich and complex ecological system. Any action taken by the gardener may affect numerous links in the varied and interlocking cycles and webs of life.

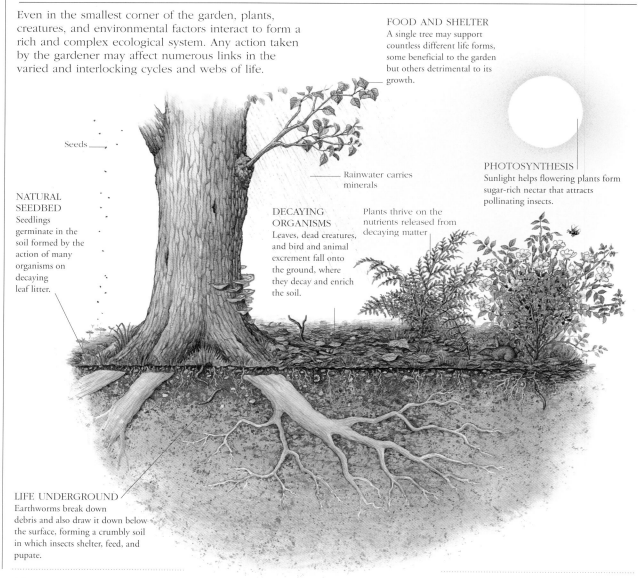

Seeds

FOOD AND SHELTER
A single tree may support countless different life forms, some beneficial to the garden but others detrimental to its growth.

Rainwater carries minerals

PHOTOSYNTHESIS
Sunlight helps flowering plants form sugar-rich nectar that attracts pollinating insects.

NATURAL SEEDBED
Seedlings germinate in the soil formed by the action of many organisms on decaying leaf litter.

DECAYING ORGANISMS
Leaves, dead creatures, and bird and animal excrement fall onto the ground, where they decay and enrich the soil.

Plants thrive on the nutrients released from decaying matter

LIFE UNDERGROUND
Earthworms break down debris and also draw it down below the surface, forming a crumbly soil in which insects shelter, feed, and pupate.

carbon dioxide from the air with water to make sugars and starch. Sugars may be used for other purposes, such as aiding pollination and seed dispersal. Many plants are insect-pollinated, and the secretion of sugar-rich nectar by flowers is an effective means of encouraging bees and other insects to visit blooms. While doing so insects pick up pollen when they come into contact with the anthers, and this is transferred to the pistils of other flowers, effecting pollination.

Sugars also make fruits and berries sweet and attractive to birds and mammals. The seeds are dispersed away from the parent plant when they are spat out or have passed through the animal's gut.

ESSENTIAL NUTRIENTS

The starches and sugars used by plants for growth must be augmented by essential nutrients (*see pp.68–69*), drawn from the soil or, in the case of parasitic plants, from their hosts. For the cycle of life to continue, these nutrients must be returned to the soil. Dead or waste organic material, whether decomposing plant or animal matter, is broken down by the actions of fungi, bacteria, earthworms, and others that feed on decaying plant material. Certain larger fungi and many microfungi, described as saprophytic, live on dead organic material and, by breaking it down, may release components which are then used by other organisms in the vicinity. Their primary role, however, is one of clearing up debris that would otherwise accumulate. In a similar way, numerous garden creatures live on debris and are to be encouraged because of their recycling function.

RECYCLING ACTIVITY
Sowbugs occasionally cause plant problems, but they have a valuable role in processing garden debris.

As any organic matter deteriorates it releases and uses certain nutrients and so alters the range and quantity of materials available to plants and other organisms in the garden. Although deteriorating plant material may harbor plant pathogens, it may also provide a useful overwintering or breeding site for beneficial insects, so it is important to reach a compromise between extremes of garden neatness.

FOOD AND FEEDERS

Plants form the basis of all food webs. There is a huge range of invertebrate animals, including nematodes, millipedes, insects, mites, sowbugs, slugs, and snails, that feed directly on plants. Many

PLANT ASSOCIATIONS
Gardeners' time frames often differ from those of nature. While mistletoe on tree branches (usually, of apple) will weaken the host over many years, most gardeners prefer the short-term attraction and novelty value of its presence.

of them specialize in feeding on particular parts of a plant; some may feed on a variety of plants while others may be specific in their choice of food plant.

Most pests and disease-causing organisms have a relatively restricted host range, attacking only one type of plant or perhaps a few closely related ones. An outbreak of one pest or disease could therefore remove the main food source of another potential pest or pathogen, thereby indirectly minimizing the damage it causes. Plant pests in turn are under attack from predators and parasites that help prevent pests from becoming so abundant that their plant hosts are killed.

PREDATOR
The praying mantid feeds on a wide variety of both harmful and beneficial insects.

SOIL AND NUTRIENTS

THE STRUCTURE AND texture of soil, and the range of nutrients it contains, have a great impact on plant growth and development. Texture – basically whether a soil is light and sandy, heavy and clayey, or something in between – influences plants' ability to develop strong root systems that enable uptake of water and nourishment, and it affects the soil's ability to retain moisture and, to a certain extent, nutrients. These nutrients consist of a range of elements and minerals. Although some are present in only small ("trace") quantities, deficiencies, either due to natural factors or caused by unreplenished or heavy demands by plants, will cause symptoms in plants that are often mistakenly perceived as the results of attack by pests and diseases (*see table, facing page*). Sometimes, pest and disease problems develop following a deficiency (or excess), because the plant is weakened and more vulnerable.

Soil pH influences the range of nutrients that are in a form available to plants. For example, soils of a high pH (alkaline or chalky, pH above 7.0) may "lock up" iron and manganese so that plants become chlorotic. In fact, in an alkaline soil most trace elements are less readily available than in an acidic (pH below 7.0) or neutral (pH 7.0) soil. Similarly, an acidic soil is more likely to produce plants that suffer a deficiency of magnesium. An unusually high level of one nutrient may also

CROSS-SECTION OF GARDEN SOIL
Garden soil has a distinct structure, with three layers – the top-soil, the subsoil, and the bedrock (not shown here). The topsoil is the uppermost layer and is usually a dark color. It contains a high level of organic matter and soil organisms and is the layer in which you dig and plant. The subsoil has a much lower level of organic matter, nutrients, and organisms.

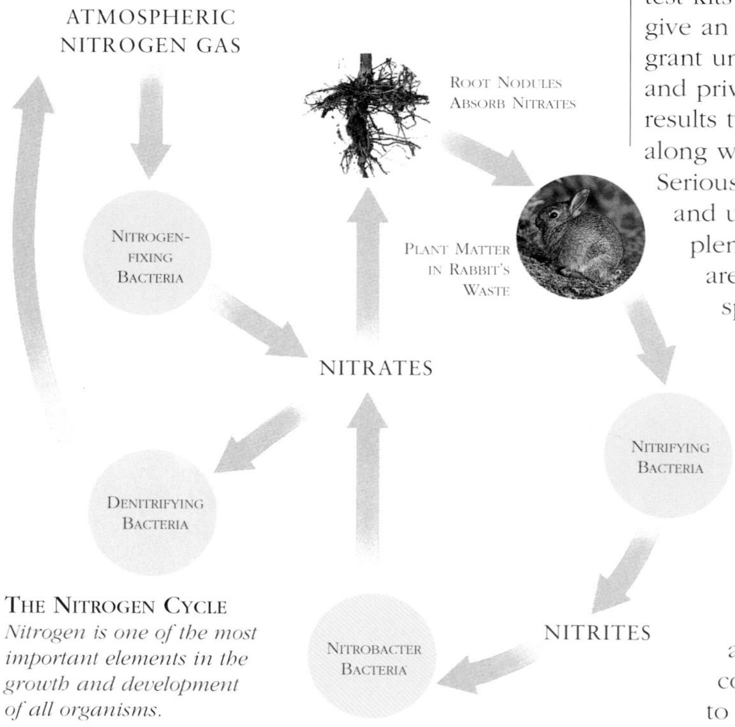

influence the availability of another. For example, tomatoes fed with a high-potassium fertilizer to encourage a heavy crop of fruits may also show yellowing between the veins and around the edges of older leaves due to magnesium deficiency.

BALANCING NUTRIENT LEVELS
Checking the nutrient status and soil pH is worth-while, especially when working a new garden. Soil-test kits enable you to determine the soil pH and give an idea of the levels of major nutrients. Land-grant universities, Cooperative Extension offices, and private labs also do soil tests for a fee. Test results typically include pH and nutrient analysis along with corrective recommendations.

Serious deficiencies are quite rare in most gardens, and using a general fertilizer or regular use of plenty of organic material and good husbandry are usually adequate. Occasional use of specific materials may also be beneficial. It is important to realize, however, that overfeeding can be damaging both to plants and many other soil organisms.

OTHER SOIL LIFE
Many garden creatures, including a number of pests, spend their lives, or a stage in their lives, within the soil. Generally, however, gardeners are far better occupied in improving soil texture and composition than in attempting to control its inhabitants. Although it is easy to become preoccupied with potentially

THE NITROGEN CYCLE
Nitrogen is one of the most important elements in the growth and development of all organisms.

ATMOSPHERIC NITROGEN GAS

ROOT NODULES ABSORB NITRATES

NITROGEN-FIXING BACTERIA

PLANT MATTER IN RABBIT'S WASTE

NITRATES

DENITRIFYING BACTERIA

NITRIFYING BACTERIA

NITROBACTER BACTERIA

NITRITES

USING A KIT TO TEST SOIL NUTRIENTS

1 Preparing. This test for phosphorus is part of a kit to test the pH and major nutrient levels of soil. Mix 1 part soil and 5 parts water and allow to stand until the liquid is fairly clear. Use the pipette to transfer liquid to the testing chambers.

2 Testing. Make sure the water extract reaches the level marks on the color chart. Open the correct capsule (blue in this test) and pour the powder into the chamber. Fit the cap onto the tester and shake until the powder has dissolved.

3 Results. Allow the color to develop in the test chamber for a few minutes. Then compare this with the color chart against a white background and in natural daylight. Read off the results and take further action if required.

damaging garden organisms, the vast majority of creatures in soil are harmless, and some are very beneficial (*see pp.60–63*). The activity of each type of organism affects the population levels of others living in the vicinity, and so any action taken by the gardener will usually exert an effect on something else.

Some animals and fungi can enhance the productivity or the performance of plants; examples include pest predators, parasites, and mycorrhizae, which are fungal associations formed on the root of a plant that allow the plant to become more efficient at nutrient uptake. Mycorrhizae may sometimes be visible in the soil as tiny fungal strands attached to the roots – these are often mistakenly presumed to be harmful. Some also produce fungal fruiting bodies or toadstools around the base of the plant; again it may be presumed, incorrectly, that all toadstools are harmful.

NITROGEN FIXERS

Certain bacteria that "fix" nitrogen, making it available to the plant, inhabit nodules on plant roots. If these roots are left in the soil once the crop has been harvested, they will also improve the nutrient status of the soil for any plants grown there subsequently. The nitrogen-fixing bacteria are invisible to the naked eye, but the nodules are seen as distinct swellings on the roots (*see facing page*). The presence of these root nodules on legumes can be used to great benefit when following a rotation system for growing vegetables (*see p.96*).

NUTRIENT REQUIREMENTS AND ASSOCIATED PROBLEMS

Element	Specifically aids	Symptoms of deficiency	Possible causes of deficiency	Remedies
NITROGEN (N)	Leaf and shoot growth.	Pale foliage, poor growth, and may develop reddish or yellow discoloration. Older leaves affected first, since the nitrogen is moved from these into the newer growth when in short supply.	Most common on soils with low organic matter or where un-decomposed organic matter is added to soil in large quantities.	See p.151
PHOSPHORUS (P)	Root growth, seed formation.	Red or purplish coloring, short and slender stems, and lower leaves may be yellow. The plant's overall growth is affected.	Most common on acidic soils or following heavy watering or rain.	See p.159
POTASSIUM (K)	Flowering and fruiting; wood maturation; tissue strengthening.	Leaves may show scorching of the tips. Fruiting and flowering may be reduced, and on tomatoes it causes blotchy ripening.	Most common on sandy and alkaline or chalky soils.	See p.162
MAGNESIUM (MG)	Chlorophyll formation (the green pigment in plants).	Leaves, particularly the older ones, show yellowing between the veins and around the edges. When it is in short supply, magnesium is moved from the older tissues into the new ones, so young foliage rarely shows any symptoms.	Most common on sandy soils and following heavy watering or rain or heavy applications of potassium.	See p.146
CALCIUM (CA)	Formation of plant cell walls.	The most commonly seen symptoms are bitter pit on apples and blossom end rot of tomatoes. Foliage may also be reduced in size and distorted.	Most common on acidic soils and on plants growing in any soil that is not adequately watered to allow the plant to take up calcium.	See p.112
IRON (FE)	Chlorophyll formation.	Leaf yellowing, mainly between the veins and most apparent on the young leaf growth.	Most common on alkaline soils.	See p.139
MANGANESE (MN)	Chlorophyll formation.	Yellowing between the veins on young leaves, sometimes with small, dead spots.	Most common on alkaline soils and waterlogged or poorly draining soils.	See p.146

NATURAL UPSETS

IN ANY NATURAL environment, there are factors that are not ideal for plant growth. These naturally occurring problems are often the result of adverse weather conditions that either cause physical wounds through which infections may enter or, more commonly, simply weaken the entire plant so that it is more likely to succumb to pests and diseases.

Often the gardener can compound problems, either through "contributory negligence" – leaving drought-stricken plants unwatered, for example – or by unintentionally inflicting damage such as that caused by poor pruning or by overly tight tree ties. By far the most common contributory factor, however, is the poor choice of plants for a given site. If a plant is not suited to the prevailing conditions and climate (or microclimate), it will rarely thrive and will be more prone to problems.

A less than fully hardy plant may be so set back in a cold, exposed site each year that it never makes a good specimen. A moisture-loving plant will fare badly on dry soil; a desert plant may rot in waterlogged ground. Always check before buying that the plant is suited for survival in the conditions your garden offers.

WATER AND DROUGHT

Water is a fundamental plant requirement, used in photosynthesis (*see pp.66–67*), to maintain turgidity (the ability of stems to stand upright), and to transport nutrients into and around the plant tissues.

Plants vary in their requirement for water, and some are better than others at surviving dry conditions. Wilting is the most common symptom of drought; if soil moisture levels are restored fairly

DAMAGE CAUSED BY ENVIRONMENTAL FACTORS

FROST DAMAGE
A scorched appearance is the most common symptom of frost damage. Soft new growth is most vulnerable to damage, with blackening and withering of shoot tips. Pruning should not be left so late in the season that regrowth cannot mature.

Frost-damaged
Pieris japonica
leaves

LIGHTNING DAMAGE
The larger and more ragged wounds are, the more slowly they will heal. Until a wound has completely callused over with scar tissue, it is vulnerable to invasion by pathogens.

Withered maple leaves

DROUGHT
Wilting can be reversed if caught early. Soft, floppy leaves may expand again if water is added, but leaves that have dried and become crispy will not recover. There are also several wilt diseases with similar symptoms (see p.191).

Poor
growth

ANIMAL DAMAGE
Few plants can withstand repeated injury caused by browsing deer and rabbits, which may cause considerable problems in gardens in rural areas or close to parkland.

rapidly it can be reversed. Prolonged drought can, however, cause parts or all of the plant to die. If water levels are consistently low, the plant may survive but be small and fail to perform well. Poor flowering, buds that fail to develop or drop off prematurely, and small fruits with tough skins are common symptoms. Dry soil is most obviously associated with dry weather, but light soil texture and drying winds may also be factors.

WATERLOGGING AND IRREGULAR WATERING

Excess water can be just as harmful as drought. If soil is waterlogged, plant roots may deteriorate rapidly, largely due to the lack of oxygen. Water-logged soil favors the development of pathogens, such as damping-off or foot- and root-rotting fungi. In the early stages, however, chlorosis or yellowing, often associated with the veins of leaves, is a common symptom.

POOR PRUNING
Stubs left after pruning are readily colonized, as here, by rotting fungi that may spread.

Many plants cannot adapt to an erratic water supply. Plants that are growing in containers are very susceptible, because they tend to dry out readily and may then be overwatered by an over-enthusiastic gardener. Symptoms include poor or slow growth, bud drop, and cracked or split fruits.

EXTREMES OF TEMPERATURE

In addition to drought symptoms, high temperatures often cause scorching of leaves, particularly on plants growing under glass or under plastic. Low temperature injury is most commonly seen as frost damage (*see facing page*), causing withering of shoots, foliage, or flowers or even death of the whole plant. Plants growing in very cold areas or in containers may also suffer root injury resulting from freezing of the root ball. This may then be followed by poor growth, dieback, or even death. Fruit set is frequently affected by low temperatures because the activity of pollinating insects may be restricted and flowers themselves damaged.

Snow and hail can injure leaves or, in the case of snow, weigh down and break branches. This problem is particularly common when a heavy fall of snow has partially melted and refrozen. However, snow provides an insulating "blanket" (especially to the soil) and prevents or lessens wind or cold injury to the plants that it covers.

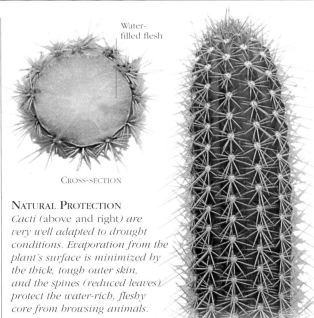

Water-filled flesh

CROSS-SECTION

NATURAL PROTECTION
Cacti (above and right) are very well adapted to drought conditions. Evaporation from the plant's surface is minimized by the thick, tough outer skin, and the spines (reduced leaves) protect the water-rich, fleshy core from browsing animals.

STRONG WINDS

Wind may cause physical injury and scorching of foliage, and a prevailing strong wind may also prevent a from plant growing to its full potential size or even alter its shape. Wind blows away the moisture around a transpiring plant leaf and so will, in turn, increase the plant's water requirements and make it more likely to suffer from drought if a plentiful supply of water is not available. In very windy seasons or sites, pollination may also be poor resulting from pollinating insects being restricted in their activities.

Healthy *Primula malacoides* flowers

Flowers dying off

Leaves turn yellow and flop over

WATERLOGGING
The water in saturated soil displaces air between soil particles, creating an anaerobic environment in which plants cannot function normally. The symptoms therefore resemble those of drought, and plants may mistakenly be given yet more water.

TYPES OF PLANT DISEASE

T HE DISEASE-CAUSING organisms (pathogens) most prevalent in gardens are fungi and viruses. In addition, several bacterial infections and a few diseases caused by mycoplasmas occur.

FUNGAL INFECTIONS

This major group of infections is caused by microfungi that are extremely small and rarely visible to the naked eye. Examples include downy mildews, powdery mildews, fungal leaf spots, and rusts. A few fungal infections are systemic (found throughout the plant), but the majority are restricted to certain plant parts. The larger fungi – those that produce easily visible fungal structures such as fungal brackets or toadstools – are less common but may prove extremely damaging.

VIRUS INFECTIONS

Virus particles are submicroscopic, being invisible with the aid of a normal microscope, but they can be detected with an electron microscope or immunological assay tests. However, the symptoms they cause are generally easily visible, most commonly as yellow or white leaf markings and distortions. Virus particles are found throughout an infected plant, but their symptoms may be apparent on only one area, or their appearance may vary from one part of the plant to another. Virus infections may occur alone or in combination with other virus infections. It is impossible to identify precisely which are involved from the symptoms alone. Mycoplasmas are submicroscopic and similar to bacteria but cause viruslike symptoms.

BACTERIAL INFECTIONS

Problems caused by bacterial infections are usually localized, but since many cause rapid deterioration of plant tissues, their effect may be quite dramatic. Sometimes the bacteria are apparent as bacterial ooze, for example on a tree infected with bacterial canker or fireblight. Many bacterial infections are accompanied by a distinct fishy odor.

HOW DISEASES ARE SPREAD

Most fungal infections are spread from plant to plant or within a plant by spores. These are occasionally large enough to be visible with the naked eye. Their type, size, and quantity depends largely on the specific fungus. Most spores are spread either on air currents or by rain splash. Bacteria are spread by similar means. Some pathogens may also be carried by animals, especially insects as they move from plant to plant. Soil-borne infections are usually spread either in association

MICROSCOPIC AND SUBMICROSCOPIC ORGANISMS

FUNGUS
The majority of fungi produce visible symptoms, and in most cases the fungal mycelium and sometimes the spores are apparent, too. The spores of the majority of rust fungi (here hollyhock rust) are released from within raised pustules. Their detailed structure (inset) is visible only with the aid of a microscope.

VIRUS
Infection by virus particles (inset) usually results in visible symptoms, such as leaf distortion (here from cucumber mosaic virus) and yellow patterning, often accompanied by overall poor growth and stunting. Virus-infected plants may also be symptomless, or the extent of the symptoms may vary greatly.

SPREADING DISEASE
Using cutting tools such as pruners on an infected plant and then on a healthy one without disinfecting them can spread disease.

COLOR BREAKING
A characteristic symptom of virus attack is slashing or striping of flower color. Usually unwanted, it has in some cases, particularly in tulips, been developed through breeding to produce novel color patterns in otherwise healthy plants.

with soil particles or in soil moisture. Some, such as *Phytophthora*, have spores called zoospores that can propel themselves in water. Weather conditions greatly affect disease spread and development, and in most cases moisture on the plant surface encourages infection and spread. Humidity and the resultant film of moisture on the plants may also cause a marked increase in disease spread and development.

Viruses are most commonly spread when sap from an infected plant is transferred to another potential host. Pruning tools, physical injury, grafting, and taking cuttings are all common routes. Even handling – for example, dividing – an infected plant may be sufficient to transfer virus particles to a healthy host. Many viruses are also transmitted by garden creatures that, because of this role, are known as vectors. The most common are sap-feeding pests such as aphids, leafhoppers, and nematodes. Some viruses are seed-borne.

INCREASING VULNERABILITY

A plant that has suffered a severe attack of, say, powdery mildew, with consequent loss of leaves, may be severely stressed, particularly if infection occurs in several consecutive years. The plant may well then be more prone to attack by another pathogen or insects or be especially sensitive to drought due to leaf loss and root damage. In a similar way, a peach tree that has been damaged by peachtree borers is very prone to attack by the fungus causing Cytospora canker (*see p. 122*), which gains entry via the wounded bark.

It cannot be reiterated too often that stresses brought about by unsuitable growing conditions or extremes of weather (*see pp. 70–71*) and problems associated with nutrient deficiencies and phytotoxicity (plant damage caused by excessive nutrient levels or use of unsuitable chemicals) are often responsible for symptoms of illness as well as lowering a plant's ability to resist infection and disease development.

MOST COMMON PLANT DISEASES

Disease	Type	Method of spread	Conditions making plant more susceptible	Season
POWDERY MILDEWS	Fungi	Water/rain splash; air currents.	Dry soil/root conditions; moist or humid environment around leaves.	Spring, if dry, and summer to autumn.
DOWNY MILDEWS	Fungi	Water/rain splash; air currents.	Humid air around foliage; damp spring and autumn weather; stagnant conditions. Plant debris in vicinity; dead/damaged plant parts.	All year.
RUSTS	Fungi	Water/rain splash; animals; wind.	Damp, warm, stagnant conditions; moisture film on leaves.	Mainly damp periods spring through autumn.
FUNGAL CANKERS	Fungi	Water/rain splash; air currents.	Damage to bark from pruning wounds; pest attack; frost crack.	All year.
FUNGAL WILTS	Fungi	Pruning tools; infected root material; infested soil.	Damage creating open wounds when spores in vicinity.	All year.
BACTERIAL SOFT ROTS	Bacteria	Water splash, water films; pruning tools; insects.	Damage to the plant's surface allowing entry of bacteria; poor storage conditions.	All year.
FUNGAL LEAF SPOTS	Fungi	Mainly water/rain splash; some air currents.	Poor growing conditions; weather extremes; other diseases.	Mainly spring and summer.
BACTERIAL BLIGHTS	Bacteria	Rain splash, insects	Warm, wet weather; stem injuries from natural causes or pruning; lush vegetative growth resulting from excessive nitrogen fertilizer.	Spring.
CUCUMBER MOSAIC VIRUS	Virus	Sap-feeding pests; handling; pruning and taking cuttings; occasionally seed-borne.	Presence of any factors that encourage spread (*see left*).	Mainly late spring and summer.
PHYTOPHTHORA/ PYTHIUM	Fungus	Soil- and water-borne.	Injury to plant; overly wet soil conditions.	All year.

TYPES OF GARDEN PEST

ANIMALS BECOME PESTS when their activities begin to have an adverse effect on plants. They may do this by reducing plant vigor so that yields of fruits and vegetables, or the decorative qualities of ornamentals, are impaired. In addition to the direct damage caused by their feeding activities, pests can have indirect effects on plants. Those feeding on the edible parts of fruits and vegetables may not be numerous enough to reduce yields, but nevertheless they make them unpalatable due to the presence of insects and their excrement. Many sap-feeding insects soil their host plants with a sugary excrement called honeydew that encourages the growth of sooty molds.

Pests can also transmit some virus and fungal diseases of plants on their mouthparts or bodies. Some plant diseases are dependent on the presence of pest-damaged tissues and cannot become established without this initial help.

While some garden pest problems are local, others are the result of migrations from elsewhere. Pests may be imported in purchased plants or gifts. Potato leafhoppers can fly in from agricultural crops, such as freshly cut alfalfa, while corn earworm moths, which are capable of longer flights, may come to the northern US and Canada from southern overwintering areas.

Snail uses its rough "tongue" or radula to break up plant tissues

SOLITARY FEEDER
While snails can occur in great numbers in gardens, they are essentially lone operators when browsing on plants. Each individual is, however, capable of causing extensive damage.

Pests affect plants in a variety of ways. Some attack specific plant parts, while others feed on or damage several different types of plant tissue.

SAP-FEEDING PESTS
Sap-feeding pests such as aphids, adelgids, and scale insects have needlelike mouthparts that are inserted into plants in order to suck sap. No visible holes are made in the leaves, but many sap-feeders have a toxic saliva that results in often dramatic leaf and stem distortion and/or discoloration. Some sap-feeding pests – including aphids, leafhoppers, and thrips – can transmit virus diseases. Most sap-feeders infest the foliage, stems, and flowers, but there are some species of aphids and mealybugs that also attack roots.

FLOWER PESTS
Relatively few pests specialize in feeding on flowers or flower buds, but these are attacked by many general plant pests such as earwigs, caterpillars, and Japanese beetles. Pests often associated with flowers are pollen beetles, strawberry bud weevil, and gladiolus thrips. Chipmunks and some birds may destroy flowers and flower buds.

GALL-FORMING PESTS
Some pests secrete chemicals into their host plants when they deposit eggs or as they feed. This induces a variety of abnormal growths, known as galls, that enclose the causal organisms. The gall-forming habit is found among many types of insects, mites, and nematodes. Plant galls can also be caused by fungi and bacteria.

ROOT-FEEDING PESTS
The larvae of a wide range of insects bore into or destroy roots, corms, bulbs, and tubers. Their activities are often slow to be discovered and can be difficult to eliminate. Some controls involve

PESTS EN MASSE
A single aphid or even a small colony presents no threat to a healthy plant. The speed at which they multiply, however, quickly results in heavy infestations that soon sap plants' vigor.

FEEDING DAMAGE
The depredation caused by feeding is a major factor in pest damage. However, they also create open wounds on plants that may act as entry points for secondary infections.

disposing not only of the affected plant but of the soil in the vicinity of the root ball. Many root pests arrive as eggs laid by winged insects; others may be imported into gardens via container-grown plants. Plants purchased or received as gifts should always be tipped out of their pots and the root ball examined for signs of pest activity before planting.

FRUIT PESTS
Fruits and seeds are attacked by the larvae of many insects, including a variety of moths, sawflies, and beetles. Wasps, birds, raccoons, woodchucks, squirrels, and many other animals can also be a problem. Some pests, such as plant bugs, reduce the quality of fruits by causing skin blemishes; others render them inedible. Damage to ripening fruits increases the chances of infection by fungal rots, which greatly reduces their storage life.

STEM PESTS
Most pests attacking plant stems feed from the outside and include most of the sap-feeding pests. Bark beetles feed as larvae under the bark of woody plants, while the larvae of clearwing moths bore into the center of stems. Mammals, such as rabbits and deer, can damage bark, especially during winter.

LEAF PESTS
Plant foliage can bear a greater variety of pests than any other part of a plant. In addition to the sap-feeding pests listed above, there are pests that feed on the leaf tissue itself, such as slugs, snails, earwigs, caterpillars, beetles, and adult black vine weevils. Some insects, such as the larvae of certain flies, moths, sawflies, and weevils, feed within the leaves as leaf miners.

HOW PESTS ATTACK

WHITEFLIES

SAP-FEEDERS
Adelgids, aphids, leafhoppers, mealybugs, plant bugs, psyllids, scale insects, spider mites, spittlebugs, thrips, whiteflies.

EARWIG

FLOWER PESTS
Aphids, birds, caterpillars, earwigs, Japanese beetles, pollen beetles, slugs, snails, strawberry bud weevil, thrips.

BLACK VINE WEEVIL

ROOT-FEEDERS
Black vine weevil grubs, cabbage maggots, carrot rust fly larvae, cutworms, nematodes, onion maggots, root aphids, root mealybugs, slugs, white grubs, wireworms.

GALL WASP LARVAE

GALL-FORMERS
Adelgids, aphids, gall midges, gall mites, gall wasp larvae, nematodes, psyllids, sawflies.

WASPS

FRUIT PESTS
Birds, codling moth larvae, European apple sawfly, Japanese beetle, nut weevil, Oriental fruit moth, pea moth larvae, plum curculio, raspberry fruitworm, squirrels, wasps.

SCALE INSECTS

STEM PESTS
Many sap-feeding pests (see above), plus bark beetles, clearwing moth larvae, deer, rabbits, squirrels, voles.

CATERPILLAR

LEAF PESTS
All sap-feeding pests (see above), plus adult black vine weevils, beetles, caterpillars, earwigs, leaf-cutter bees, nematodes, sawfly larvae, slugs, snails.

PEST LIFE CYCLES

T HE LIFE CYCLES of pests are as diverse as the
pests themselves, but they can be divided into
two broad categories: complete and incomplete
metamorphosis. The latter involves little more than
a gradual increase in size as the pest reaches
maturity, with the immature stages usually
resembling the adult animal. This form of growth
is shown by nematodes, slugs, snails, millipedes,
sowbugs, mites, and some insects, including
earwigs, aphids, leafhoppers, froghoppers,
grasshoppers, whiteflies, mealybugs, scale insects,
plant bugs, and thrips. The feeding habits of the
immature stages are often the same as the adult,
and so all active stages in the life cycle are capable
of causing damage.

COMPLETE METAMORPHOSIS

More advanced insects, such as butterflies, moths,
beetles, flies, ants, bees, sawflies, and wasps,
undergo complete metamorphosis. Here, the larval
stages are very different in appearance from the
adult, and there is a pupal stage in which the larva,
usually enclosed within a protective casing, changes
into the adult insect. With these insects the feeding
habits of the larvae are often different to those of
the adult, and it is usually the larvae that cause

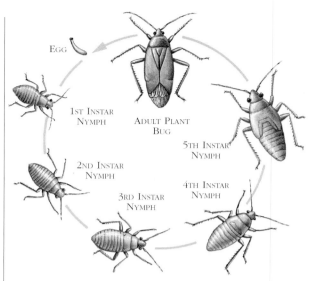

INCOMPLETE METAMORPHOSIS: PLANT BUG
*Pests that undergo incomplete metamorphosis look broadly
similar at each stage of their lives and gradually acquire
the adult features.*

damage to plants. For example, caterpillars of
butterflies and moths feed on leaves, while the
adults feed on nectar. Some beetles, however, cause
damage during both the larval and adult stages.

HOW PESTS DEVELOP

Pests generally start life as eggs, although aphids
give birth to live young for most of the year,
producing eggs only in the autumn to overwinter.
Invertebrates, such as insects, mites, sowbugs, and
millipedes, do not have any bones or internal
skeletons. Instead, they have a hard outer covering
to their bodies. Like a suit of armor, this restricts
growth, so it must be shed from time to time to
allow the animal to increase in size. This process is
known as ecdysis. After the old outer skin has been
cast off, the soft new skin underneath is stretched
by the animal before it hardens, thus creating more
space for growth. The number of stages, or instars,
between the newly hatched nymph or larva and the
adult animal is usually between four and twelve,
depending on the species.

HOW PESTS REPRODUCE

Most adult pests are either male or female and mate
in a conventional manner. There are, however,
exceptions. Slugs and snails are hermaphrodites
with both male and female genitalia. They mate
with others of their species, and both partners will
subsequently lay eggs. Some insects are capable of

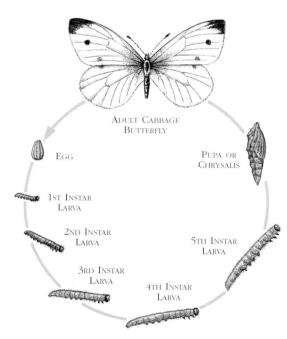

COMPLETE METAMORPHOSIS: CABBAGE BUTTERFLY
*The more advanced types of insect undergo a complete
transformation in appearance and often in feeding habits
during their lives.*

APHID GIVING BIRTH
Aphids give birth to live young in spring and summer, but as daylength shortens and temperatures fall in autumn they lay eggs instead, which will overwinter.

breeding without mating (parthenogenesis). In some, such as black vine weevil, only females are known to exist. Aphids occur as females only during spring and summer; males are produced in late summer when mating is necessary to produce overwintering eggs. Some gall wasps have alternating asexual all-female generations and sexual generations with males and females.

PEST LIFESPANS

The length of time required to complete the life cycle depends on factors such as temperature, the availability of food, and the nature of the pest. Most pests are able to complete their development within a year, but some require much less, while others take longer. Wireworms, for example, feed on roots in the soil for up to five years before they pupate and become adult click beetles. Aphids, by cutting out the egg stage, are able to go from young nymph to adult insect in as little as seven days.

Pests that have more than one generation in a year complete their development more rapidly in warmer weather. Twospotted spider mite takes 55 days to complete its life cycle at 55°F (10°C) but only 12 days at 70°F (21°C). Most outdoor pests have one to three generations a year. Greenhouse pests such as whitefly and spider mite can go through as many as 12 generations a year due to the warm, sheltered conditions in which they live.

SEASONAL CHANGES

Pests have evolved alongside the plants they feed on, and so they begin to attack their hosts at the time of year when the appropriate plant tissues will be available. This is strongly related to temperature and daylength, which not only control plant growth processes such as bud burst, flowering, fruiting, and aging, but also bring pests out of winter dormancy and allow egg hatching. Similarly, the life cycles of predatory insects, such as ladybugs, are related to that of their prey, aphids.

SURVIVING THE WINTER

The means by which pests overwinter varies, although each species will usually have one particular stage in its life cycle in which it survives the colder months of the year. This may be the egg, one of the nymphal or larval stages, the pupa, or adult. The overwintering stage generally occurs in some sheltered place, such as in the soil, in the crevices of bark, or inside dense shrubs and conifers. Many insects and mites go into a form of hibernation called diapause from which they will not emerge until they have experienced a sufficient period of cold. This prevents them from emerging prematurely whenever the winter weather turns mild. Some greenhouse pests, such as whitefly, continue feeding and breeding throughout the year, albeit more slowly in winter than in summer.

ANNUAL POPULATIONS

While some pests are a problem every year, others are only occasional problems. Serious outbreaks may be due to a combination of favorable weather conditions and a relative absence of predators, parasites, and diseases of the pest. Minor pests often need a run of several good reproductive cycles before they are numerous enough to become a significant problem. Hot, dry summers favor certain pests such as spider mites and thrips, while slugs and snails thrive under damp conditions. Cold winters do not kill all pests, since those native to a given area have a cold-tolerant overwintering stage. Mild winters can allow some pests that would normally go dormant (such as aphids) to continue feeding and breeding, resulting in higher populations in spring.

LADYBUG LARVA EATING APHID

ADULT LADYBUG EATING APHID

THE BENEFICIAL LADYBUG
Both the larval and adult stages of ladybugs feed avidly on aphids, making them doubly valuable to gardeners. Some are also predators of scale insects, thrips, mealybugs, or mites.

GARDEN HEALTH AND PROBLEMS

APPROACHES TO CONTROL

WHEN SOMETHING goes wrong in a garden, and pests or diseases are to blame, the first consideration is whether control measures are necessary, and if so what action should best be taken. Not all infections or infestations merit control. A powdery mildew infection at the end of the season on a herbaceous plant may look unsightly, but if the leaves are going to die back shortly anyway, the infection has little if any detrimental effect on the plant and may not be worth treating. Similarly, it may be easier and more sensible to pick off one or two caterpillars on a cabbage than to attempt to control them with an insecticide.

Some problems cause rapid and severe damage, while others may cause some damage but are probably more worrying to the gardener than they are injurious to the plant. It is therefore important to balance the need to spray with the damage the pest or disease actually causes. Farmers have an "economic threshold" – the point at which a pest or disease is causing or is likely to cause sufficient loss to merit the time and money spent on control measures. This is something the gardener should consider, modifying the equation to include the extent to which a problem reduces a plant's yield or esthetic value, before reaching for the sprayer.

USING PESTICIDES

There is no doubt that chemical controls (*see pp.86–91*) offer rapid, safe, and usually complete solutions to pest or disease problems. If correctly used, garden products today have been so carefully formulated and tested (*see pp.86–87*) that possible adverse side effects are minimal. Most gardeners

INTEGRATED PEST MANAGEMENT IN THE GARDEN

The integrated approach to controlling problems combines appropriate plant choice and good gardening practice, preventive measures to avoid problems, and sensible use of pesticides only when warranted by serious pest or disease attack.

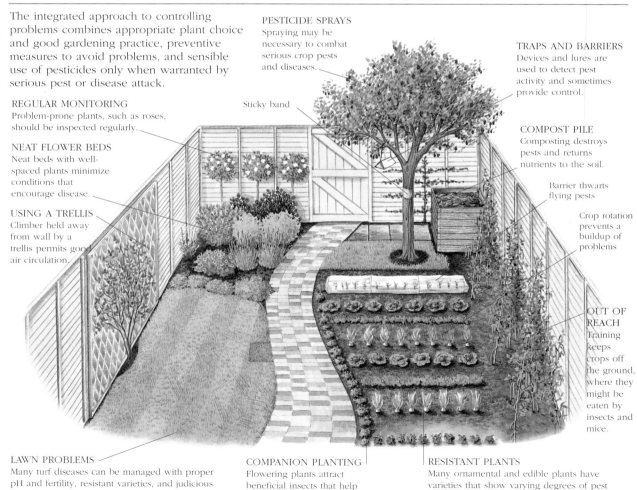

PESTICIDE SPRAYS
Spraying may be necessary to combat serious crop pests and diseases.

TRAPS AND BARRIERS
Devices and lures are used to detect pest activity and sometimes provide control.

REGULAR MONITORING
Problem-prone plants, such as roses, should be inspected regularly.

Sticky band

COMPOST PILE
Composting destroys pests and returns nutrients to the soil.

NEAT FLOWER BEDS
Neat beds with well-spaced plants minimize conditions that encourage disease.

Barrier thwarts flying pests

USING A TRELLIS
Climber held away from wall by a trellis permits good air circulation.

Crop rotation prevents a buildup of problems

OUT OF REACH
Training keeps crops off the ground, where they might be eaten by insects and mice.

LAWN PROBLEMS
Many turf diseases can be managed with proper pH and fertility, resistant varieties, and judicious watering practices.

COMPANION PLANTING
Flowering plants attract beneficial insects that help control vegetable pests.

RESISTANT PLANTS
Many ornamental and edible plants have varieties that show varying degrees of pest and disease resistance.

who do not follow organic gardening methods are also happy to use inorganic or chemical fertilizers. The inorganic approach to gardening may still be more widespread than the organic, but increasing numbers of people who would not call themselves organic gardeners use many organic methods.

"GREEN" GARDENING

In recent years, organic or so-called "green" gardening has become increasingly popular. Many gardeners have started to question the use of too many garden chemicals, and some use purely organic methods. Organic gardening avoids the use of manufactured chemicals, but some organic gardeners use Bordeaux mixture or products containing pyrethrum, since these are both made from "natural" ingredients.

The organic approach also advocates the use of only naturally occurring materials such as manure for improving soil fertility, and materials such as leaf mold for mulching or improving soil texture.

It embraces other environmental concerns, too, such as the use of coir or bark-based growing media in preference to peat-based products, and of recycled materials wherever possible.

Organic gardening also makes full use of what are, essentially, good gardening techniques, such as the pruning out of infected material and good garden hygiene (*see pp.92–96*). Resistant or tolerant plant cultivars and trap and barrier methods (*see pp.80–83*) are also important to the organic gardener.

To succeed at organic gardening it is also important to take all possible steps to encourage populations of beneficial creatures such as naturally occurring pest predators and parasites (*see pp.84–85*). The avoidance of many chemicals will make this easier, but it should be remembered that some of the products accepted by many organic gardeners (for example, rotenone) are not selective in their activity and so may affect the beneficial organisms that the organic gardener is trying so hard to encourage.

INTEGRATED PEST MANAGEMENT IN THE GREENHOUSE

The enclosed environment of a greenhouse can favor some problems but may also assist control. While pests flourish in the warm, sheltered atmosphere, they may also be excluded or targeted more successfully by traps, sprays, and the release of beneficial predators or parasites.

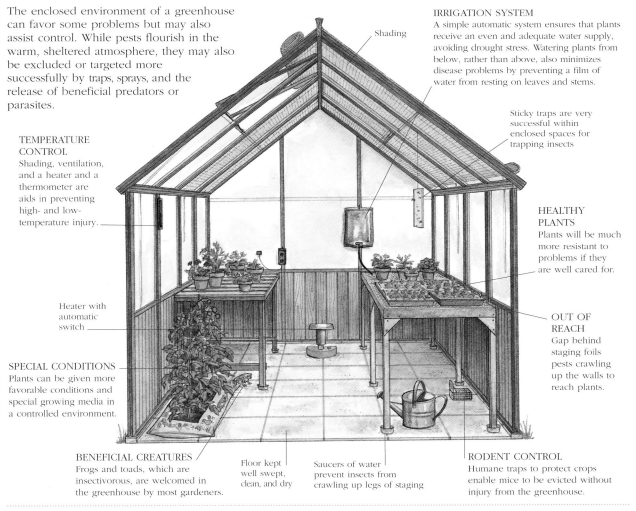

IRRIGATION SYSTEM
A simple automatic system ensures that plants receive an even and adequate water supply, avoiding drought stress. Watering plants from below, rather than above, also minimizes disease problems by preventing a film of water from resting on leaves and stems.

Shading

Sticky traps are very successful within enclosed spaces for trapping insects

TEMPERATURE CONTROL
Shading, ventilation, and a heater and a thermometer are aids in preventing high- and low-temperature injury.

HEALTHY PLANTS
Plants will be much more resistant to problems if they are well cared for.

Heater with automatic switch

OUT OF REACH
Gap behind staging foils pests crawling up the walls to reach plants.

SPECIAL CONDITIONS
Plants can be given more favorable conditions and special growing media in a controlled environment.

BENEFICIAL CREATURES
Frogs and toads, which are insectivorous, are welcomed in the greenhouse by most gardeners.

Floor kept well swept, clean, and dry

Saucers of water prevent insects from crawling up legs of staging

RODENT CONTROL
Humane traps to protect crops enable mice to be evicted without injury from the greenhouse.

CHEMICAL-FREE CONTROLS

Relying solely on chemicals to control pests and diseases can bring long-term problems in the form of pesticide resistance, harm to harmless animals, and consequent damage to the environment. Integrated pest management (IPM) is a more environmentally friendly approach to tackling pests and diseases. It includes recognizing the role that natural enemies play in reducing pest numbers and devising complementary control measures that enable pest predators and parasites to survive. This may involve more careful monitoring of pest and disease infestations to determine whether pesticide treatments are needed and, if so, when they should be applied to achieve the best effect. Biorational (environmentally conservative) tactics should also be considered. This approach can significantly reduce the number of spray applications made.

Good garden practices (*see pp.92–96*), such as removing badly infested or diseased plants, ensuring plants have adequate water and nutrients, growing plants and cultivars suitable for the local soil and climate conditions, and selecting cultivars with pest or disease resistance, are all part of an integrated control approach to limiting pest and disease problems, as is the use of biological controls (*see pp.84–85*). Picking off pests by hand

A Beer Trap for Wasps
Half-fill a jar with beer and seal it with some paper and a rubber band. Make a small hole in the paper. In their attempts to reach the attractive beer, the wasps should fall through.

at an early stage can prevent many problems from escalating. Some pests can be washed off with a strong stream of water from a garden hose. Pests that are most active at night, such as slugs and snails, can be gathered up with the aid of a flashlight on damp evenings. Always pick off any pests in or near ponds by hand, since many pesticides are dangerous to fish and other pond life.

There are also a number of traps and barriers that either prevent pests from reaching their intended goal or draw them to a more tempting destination. Some, such as beer traps for slugs and wasps, eliminate the pests; others are monitors, indicating when controls will be most effective.

PHEROMONE TRAPS
Pheromones are volatile chemicals produced by some insects as a means of communicating with others of the same species. They play an important role in maintaining the organization of social insects such as ants, bees, and wasps. Pheromones are also used by some insects, usually females, as a means of attracting males for mating purposes.

The pheromones of some pest species, such as codling moth, clearwing borers, and corn earworms, have been identified and the chemicals synthesized for use in pheromone traps, which are sold in kit form (*see facing page*). Once the trap is in position male

COMPANION PLANTING
Companion plants were once thought to deter pests from crops. It is more likely, however, that their bright flowers attract pest predators, initiating a form of biological control (see p.84).

HOW TO ASSEMBLE A PHEROMONE TRAP

1 Kit contents. A self-assembly pheromone trap kit should include a fold-together, open-sided box with hanging wire, some sticky sheets, and some synthetic pheromone lures.

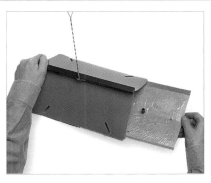

2 Assembling. Make up the box and place a sticky sheet on the bottom. Put a pheromone lure on top of this sheet. The sheet and pheromone should be replaced after six weeks.

3 Hanging. Hang the trap by its wire on the tree, at about head height and within the central canopy. It should be put in position at the expected beginning of the insects' flight period.

moths fly into it, expecting to find a virgin female, but instead get caught on a sticky sheet or in a contaner. The main function of these traps is to record the moths' main flight and egg-laying period accurately so that, if necessary, insecticides can be applied at the right time to control the newly hatched larvae. On isolated apple trees pheromone traps may catch sufficient male moths to reduce the mating success of females, therefore limiting the number of fertile eggs that are laid.

A STICKY TRAP
This trap is used to catch winged insects that are attracted by the yellow color of the strips. The strips are covered in non-drying glue and so trap the insects when they fly onto them.

STICKY BANDS AND TRAPS

Some insects cannot fly, so it is possible to prevent them from gaining access to their host plants by placing a sticky barrier in their path. Sticky bands are wrapped around tree trunks to trap gypsy moth caterpillars as they move up and down the tree in late spring. Buy the bands or make them with duct tape and sticky insect barrier. Do not apply the sticky material directly to tree trunks. The bands can also trap wingless fall cankerworm moths as they emerge and move up the trunk to lay eggs.

Other crawling insects that can be deterred by sticky or greasy barriers are earwigs, ants, and adult black vine weevils. A band around the base or the rim of containers can be very effective. Flea beetles can be made to jump on to a sticky trap: grease a piece of wood or cardboard then draw it, grease side down, along the tops of plants, being careful not to touch them with it, but agitating the foliage with your hand or a stick. Flea beetles jump when disturbed and will be caught on the trap.

Sticky traps are also useful in greenhouses for catching winged insects such as whiteflies, thrips, and fungus gnats. The best traps consist of yellow plastic strips that are covered in nondrying glue. These can be purchased or made by coating yellow plastic plates with sticky insect barrier or oil. They are suspended above the plants; when insects land on them, they are unable to escape. Such traps may not give adequate control on their own, but they can give an early indication of the presence of pests. It is often easier to see whiteflies on a yellow trap than to find them by searching on the underside of leaves. Early detection of an infestation allows the pest to be controlled by introducing biological controls or by using appropriate insecticides before the plants are damaged.

GARDEN HEALTH AND PROBLEMS

OTHER TRAPS

Other traps can be used to protect flowers from earwigs, and roots from wireworms. Grapefruit, beer, and shingle traps can be used against slugs and snails. The earwig trap uses an inverted flower pot filled with dry grass and placed over a stake among susceptible plants. Earwigs feed at night and will crawl into the trap to shelter from the daylight. You can then remove the pot and pick out the earwigs. To limit wireworm damage, put a potato on a stick and bury it: the wireworms will move in, preferring it to plant roots. The potato with its pest inhabitants can be regularly removed and renewed.

Hollowed-out grapefruit halves can be propped up on stones on the ground in flower beds; slugs and snails are attracted to the smell, crawl in, and remain there. The grapefruit skin can be picked up in the morning, complete with the slugs, which can be disposed of by destroying them in a strong salt solution. A jar half-full of beer can be almost buried in the ground, where the smell will attract slugs and snails, which fall in and drown. (For a beer trap for wasps, *see p.80*.)

BARRIERS

There are various barriers that can be constructed in the garden to deter pests and provide a non-chemical alternative to control. They range in size from fruit cages (*see below*) and large glass cloches to individual plastic cloches (*see facing page*).

To protect smaller fruit-bearing plants such as strawberries or currants against bird and animal damage, use mesh netting to construct a low frame, making sure that the base is secured with bricks to prevent the pests from getting in underneath. Apple and pear clusters can be individually enclosed in bags made from muslin or pantyhose. Although

EARWIG TRAP
Earwigs are a particular nuisance on chrysanthemums, because they crawl to the top of stems and eat the buds and petals. This earwig trap is an easy and effective control.

time-consuming, this can be effective and should be done when the fruit is almost ripe – the time it is most likely to be attacked by wasps or birds.

In a greenhouse, there are a variety of traps that can be used (*see p.79*); these include putting legs of tables in saucers or pots of water. This will prevent insects from climbing up onto the plants. Slugs may be deterred with copper-foil barriers.

Some animals, such as toads, are highly beneficial in the garden (*see pp.60–63*) and should be encouraged. Others, such as deer, rabbits, gophers, and moles, can cause extensive damage. Fences can be used for rabbits and deer; wire netting buried at least 6in (15cm) below ground with

FRUIT CAGE

PROTECTIVE ROWCOVER

PROTECTIVE COVERS
The fruit cage (far left) is made from wire or plastic netting supported by metal posts. This type of cage can help protect small fruit trees or bushes from bird and animal attack. The rowcover (left) protects and insulates plants and seedlings while allowing light and air to reach them. This tunnel is constructed by using strong wire hoops to support a sheet of the spun polypropylene material.

30in (75cm) above should deter rabbits. Deer will need a much taller barrier or electric fence. Mice (*see p.147*) and moles (*see p.148*) need traps.

HORTICULTURAL ROWCOVERS

In recent years, several types of horticultural rowcover have become available. These are finely spun light-weight materials, usually white and made of polypropylene or other plastics, that can be laid over developing vegetable crops. The rowcover gives the young plants valuable protection against wind and cold and also exclude pests such as birds, cabbage worms, cabbage maggots, cucumber beetles, and flea beetles.

When using rowcover to give protection against pests it is essential to adopt a crop rotation system (*see pp.92–96*). If, for example, radishes are sown where radishes or cabbages were grown the previous year and then covered with rowcover, adult cabbage maggots may emerge from pupae buried in the soil and will then be trapped under the covering with the crop.

COLLARS

Seedlings of cabbage and other related vegetables, such as rutabaga, are prone to attack by cabbage maggots. A ready-made collar, or one made using a piece of carpet, tarpaper, or cardboard, is placed on the ground around the stem of each seedling. This prevents the female flies from laying their eggs in the soil; instead, they will lay them on the collar, where they will dry up before hatching.

HOT WATER TREATMENT

This form of pest control is carried out mostly by commercial growers but can be attempted by gardeners. It is used against certain bulb pests, such

AN INDIVIDUAL CLOCHE
A cut-off plastic bottle placed over young plants in early spring makes an ideal slug deterrent and also acts as a mini-cloche, enabling soil around the roots to warm up more quickly.

as narcissus nematode and bulb fly, and also against nematodes on some herbaceous plants such as chrysanthemum, as well as cyclamen mite. The technique involves immersing dormant bulbs or plants in water held at a temperature that is high enough to kill the pest without harming the plant. For details of these treatments, see chrysanthemum nematode (*p.115*) and narcissus nematode (*p.150*).

Care must be taken to ensure that the temperature is kept constant throughout the period of treatment, since too much heat damages the plants while insufficient heat allows the pest to survive. After treatment, bulbs are planted out in fresh soil, while herbaceous plants are potted up to produce cuttings.

REPELLENTS

Repellents are used principally against birds and mammals, where the aim is to deter feeding or encourage them to move elsewhere, rather than to cause them any harm.

Humming tapes are used to protect plants against birds, while devices that produce ultrasonic sounds are available for frightening away moles and cats. Other means of keeping pets and pest animals away from plants rely on using irritant substances, such as pepper dust, or compounds that give plants unpleasant tastes or smells, such as soap or rotten egg solids. Repellents may need frequent renewal. It is also advisable to change the type of repellent in use to avoid the target animals becoming familiar with the sound, smell, or taste and losing their aversion toward it.

Collar about 4in (10cm) in diameter

Cabbage transplant

COLLAR
Prevent adult cabbage maggots from laying their eggs in the soil around the stems of vulnerable young plants by placing a disk or collar around the stem base.

BIOLOGICAL CONTROLS

THIS APPROACH to control involves enlisting the help of pests' naturally occurring enemies – predators, parasites, and fungal, bacterial, or viral pathogens. These natural enemies limit pest populations but are not always successful in stopping them from causing unacceptable damage. This is often because environmental conditions favor the pests, plants may be very susceptible, or tolerance for injury or infestation is low.

Biological control occurs naturally in gardens; ladybugs eat aphids, for example, and thrushes attack snails. Today, however, the term "biological control" is more commonly taken to refer to the use of natural enemies that are introduced under suitable conditions to give effective control. This approach has more success in greenhouses, where specific predators and parasites can be purchased for use against many major pests. There are few successful biological controls for plant diseases, but in some parts of the world insects, mites, and fungal diseases are being used to control alien plants that have become weeds.

BENEFITS OF BIOLOGICAL CONTROL

Biological controls may be more suitable to use than pesticides. When used on food plants, such as tomato and cucumber, for example, there is no

Thrush can eat hundreds of snails per season

VALUED BIRDS
While a few birds are a nuisance in the garden, many have a useful role, feeding on snails, slugs, and many pest insects. Also, their esthetic appeal cannot be denied and may be valued for that reason alone.

problem with pesticide residues on the edible parts. Similarly, the risk of chemicals causing spray damage is avoided.

Predators and parasites can seek out pests living in places that are difficult to reach with pesticides. Once released, natural enemies can be left to get on with controlling the pests; chemical controls often require repeat applications, particularly during the summer when high temperatures allow pests to breed rapidly. Some biological controls are selective, controlling particular pests with no harmful effects on nontarget species. Certain pests, such as greenhouse whitefly and twospotted spider mite, may develop resistance to pesticides, making biological control the best option.

ENCOURAGING PEST PREDATORS

The mixture of flowers and other plants found in a typical garden is helpful in providing, directly and indirectly, food and shelter for a wide range of beneficial insects, birds, and pest-eating animals such as bats, skunks, and toads. Installing a pond can also help because it provides a breeding site for frogs and toads. In the autumn many of these pest predators will seek out sheltered places where they can survive the winter. A thorough neatening of the garden at the end of the summer may be pleasing to the eye, but this could result in the loss of many potential allies in the battle against pests.

The choice of chemicals used on garden plants can also have a significant effect on natural populations of pest predators. Some pesticides are more selective than others for pests, and their use limits the disruption caused to nonpest animals. Insecticidal soap, for example, gives good control of aphids but has little residual effect on most beneficial insects and mites.

A COLORFUL GARDEN
Bright flowers, particularly in shades of purple and yellow, and those offering pollen and nectar, will attract beneficial insects such as hoverflies, whose larvae feed on several kinds of aphid.

BUYING AND USING BIOLOGICAL CONTROLS

The predators, parasites, and pathogenic agents that are commercially available are intended for use against specific pests. It is therefore essential that pests are accurately identified. The various biological controls are compatible with each other and can be used in combination; however, they must not be used together with most chemical controls or immediately afterward. Predators and parasites are very susceptible to most insecticides and must be regarded as an alternative to chemical control rather than an additional treatment. The instructions for use should give a safe interval that must elapse between the application of chemicals and of the biological control.

Most biological controls are living animals that should be released onto the infested plants as soon as they have been obtained, although some can be held for brief periods under refrigeration. Directions are normally provided with the organisms. They may sometimes be bought through garden centers but more usually are sold by mail-order firms who often advertise in gardening magazines.

APPLYING BIOLOGICAL CONTROLS

Pest predators, parasites, and pathogens are all organisms with rather specific environmental requirements, thriving within a particular range of temperature, humidity, and even daylength. Pathogenic nematodes, for example, need relatively warm soil around 65-75°F (18-24°C), although some are adapted to cooler conditions. They are applied by drenching into moist soil. *Bacillus thuringiensis*-

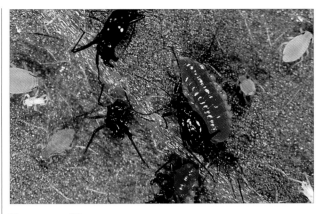

PREDATORY MIDGE
Aphids are among the most damaging and common of pests. The larvae of a tiny midge, Aphidoletes aphidomyza, *will kill and eat up to 80 aphids each.*

based sprays become less effective with increasing exposure to sunlight so should be sprayed late in the day. Since Btk must be ingested to be effective, temperatures must be sufficiently warm to encourage caterpillars to feed. Because of environmental limitations, biological controls are likely to be used outdoors only from midspring to autumn. In greenhouses, most can be used into winter but may require supplemental lighting to increase daylength. Suppliers should supply detailed instructions for each species, and some also offer guidelines tailored to particular pest problems and situations. Remember that predators need time to breed before they become numerous enough to overcome pests.

TYPES OF BIOLOGICAL CONTROL

Pest	Name of biological control	Type of predator or parasite	How it works
APHIDS	Aphidoletes aphidimyza	Predatory midge	Larvae feed on aphids.
	Aphidius species	Parasitic wasps	Larvae develop inside the aphids' bodies.
CATERPILLARS	Bacillus thuringiensis kurstaki	Bacterium	Disrupts the gut wall of caterpillars.
FUNGUS GNATS (SCIARID FLIES)	Hypoaspis miles	Predatory mite	Feeds on the flies' larvae.
TWOSPOTTED SPIDER MITE	Phytoseiulus persimilis	Predatory mite	Eats the eggs, nymphs, and adult spider mites.
GREENHOUSE WHITEFLY	Encarsia formosa	Parasitic wasp	Attacks the pest's scale-like nymphal stages.
MEALYBUGS	Cryptolaemus montrouzieri	Predatory ladybug	Both the adult and larval ladybugs eat the eggs and active stages in the mealybug's life-cycle.
SLUGS	Phasmarhabditis hermaphrodita	Pathogenic nematode	Infects slugs with a fatal disease.
SOFT SCALE	Metaphycus helvolus	Parasitic wasp	Develops in the immature scale nymphs.
BLACK VINE WEEVIL	Heterorhabditis bacteriophora Steinernema carpocapsae	Pathogenic nematodes	Infect grubs with a fatal disease.
WESTERN FLOWER THRIPS	Amblyseius species	Predatory mites	Eat the immature thrips nymphs.

CHEMICAL CONTROLS

PLANT PESTS AND diseases have always been problems for gardeners and farmers alike. It is, however, only fairly recently that an industry has existed to develop and market products for keeping plants in good health. In the nineteenth century these included some dangerous pesticides based on arsenic, cyanide, mercury, and other chemicals. A few pesticides, such as the plant-derived insecticides rotenone and pyrethrum, sulfur, and the copper fungicide Bordeaux mixture, survive from that time and are still in use today.

SAFETY STANDARDS

Most of the chemicals currently in use have, however, been developed since 1945. Some developed at that time, such as the insecticides DDT and aldrin, have subsequently been withdrawn, since it was discovered that they persist in the environment and accumulate in the bodies of birds of prey and other predators. The manufacturers of pesticides and the government departments that regulate them have learned from mistakes such as this, and environmental safety is now a high priority. New products now available and in development include insecticidal soaps, horticultural oils, pheromone (sex attractant) traps, and many derived from microorganisms.

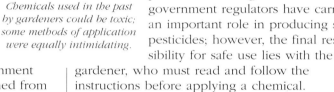

PATENT FUMIGATOR
Chemicals used in the past by gardeners could be toxic; some methods of application were equally intimidating.

Before any new product can be marketed it must be thoroughly researched to test factors such as its effectiveness, its persistence, any effects on nontarget plants and animals, and its long- and short-term effects on humans. These tests start in the laboratory and move on to field trials. This process may take ten to twelve years to complete and can cost millions of dollars. No other chemicals apart from pharmaceuticals are as thoroughly tested before they can be sold.

Insecticides and fungicides are developed for the agricultural market, and only a few of the chemicals available to professional growers are marketed for garden use. These are formulations at the safer end of the toxicity spectrum, and some can be applied without wearing special protective clothing. Manufacturers and government regulators have carried out an important role in producing safe pesticides; however, the final respon-sibility for safe use lies with the gardener, who must read and follow the instructions before applying a chemical.

PESTICIDE RESISTANCE

It is possible for some pests and pathogens to build up an immunity or tolerance to chemicals, so that a pesticide that was once an effective treatment

APPLYING CHEMICALS ON FARMLAND
Garden chemicals are largely developed from those used in agriculture and in the professional horticultural trades. However, the formulations in which they are supplied for use in the garden are much safer, eliminating the need for protective clothing and other special precautions, although sensible safety rules should be observed and the manufacturer's instructions strictly followed.

no longer works. Continual use of the same chemical can exert a powerful selection pressure by killing the more susceptible individuals while leaving those with some tolerance to pass this characteristic on to the next generation. Pests can develop significant resistance in about 40 generations and, since some pests have several generations a year, a chemical can fail within a comparatively short time.

Resistance problems are less frequent in gardens than in agriculture or commercial horticulture. This is because most gardeners use chemicals over small areas, and susceptible strains of pests and pathogens continually come in from other areas where different or no chemicals are used. Resistant pests are often found in greenhouses, where the enclosed environment and a rapid reproduction rate can speed up the evolution of resistant whiteflies, spider mites, and aphids. Outdoors, some diseases, such as gray mold, rose blackspot, rusts, powdery mildews, and apple scab, can become tolerant to fungicides, especially the systemic types.

REDUCING RESISTANCE PROBLEMS

Gardeners can reduce the likelihood of resistance occurring by using chemicals sensibly. Where possible, nonchemical alternatives, such as biological controls (*see pp.84–85*) or the removal of badly diseased plants, should be considered. It should be noted that some different active ingredients are chemically related, and it is likely that a pest or pathogen resistant to one will also be "cross-resistant" to similar chemicals. The continual use of the same pesticide or closely related ones should be avoided.

PHYTOTOXICITY

Plants are sometimes damaged by insecticides or fungicides; this is known as phytotoxicity. The manufacturer's instructions should be read and

GREENHOUSE TRIALS
Before potential pesticides are used outdoors, extensive greenhouse trials are conducted. These are designed to test the chemical's efficacy and any harmful effects on plants.

followed carefully to ensure that the correct dilution is being applied. Plants known to be harmed by a chemical will be listed by the manufacturer, but this information is not known for all potential plant and chemical interactions.

The risk of such damage occurring can be minimized by not treating plants already under stress as a result of exposure to bright sunlight, extremes of temperature, or dryness at the roots. Seedlings are more susceptible than mature plants, and petals are more likely to be scorched than leaves. Where there is doubt and there are a number of plants to be sprayed, it is sensible to treat just a part of one plant and watch for adverse reactions over the next few days. Plants that have been damaged may suffer a significant check in growth but will usually make a recovery.

WITHIN A CONTROL DOME

SYSTEM OF CONTROL DOMES

USING CONTROL DOMES TO TEST CHEMICALS
Small-scale tests in enclosed environments, such as the control domes illustrated here, are used to detect possible environmental problems before field trials are held.

CHEMICALS AND THEIR ACTIONS

Insecticides, miticides, and fungicides act in a variety of ways to control pests. Many work on contact: the pest must be hit or walk over a treated surface for the material to be effective. Insecticidal soap, for example, works only when it covers the pest. Others must be ingested, working after the pest consumes the pesticide. *Bacillus thuringiensis kurstaki*-based insecticides disrupt the gut lining, so only caterpillars that consume treated plants parts will die. Some materials act in both ways.

Most fungicides and bactericides are protectants and to prevent disease must be on the plant before infections occur. Protectant fungicides act by preventing spores from germinating or killing spores at germination. Bacteria may be inhibited or killed by protectant bactericides.

Pesticides are sold in a variety of formulations. For the home garden and landscape, most are designed to be sprayed on foliage or drenched into the soil. Ready-to-use preparations can be applied

THE WAYS CHEMICALS WORK

Different problems require chemicals to be applied in different ways. Sometimes, a combination of methods of application is needed to achieve satisfactory control.

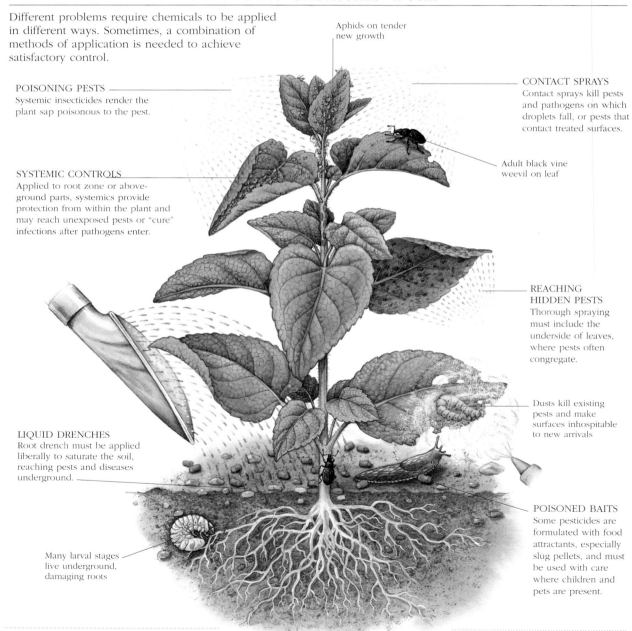

Aphids on tender new growth

POISONING PESTS
Systemic insecticides render the plant sap poisonous to the pest.

CONTACT SPRAYS
Contact sprays kill pests and pathogens on which droplets fall, or pests that contact treated surfaces.

Adult black vine weevil on leaf

SYSTEMIC CONTROLS
Applied to root zone or above-ground parts, systemics provide protection from within the plant and may reach unexposed pests or "cure" infections after pathogens enter.

REACHING HIDDEN PESTS
Thorough spraying must include the underside of leaves, where pests often congregate.

Dusts kill existing pests and make surfaces inhospitable to new arrivals

LIQUID DRENCHES
Root drench must be applied liberally to saturate the soil, reaching pests and diseases underground.

POISONED BAITS
Some pesticides are formulated with food attractants, especially slug pellets, and must be used with care where children and pets are present.

Many larval stages live underground, damaging roots

APPLICATION METHODS

Type	Advantages	Disadvantages
LIQUID SPRAY	Contact and systemic types available. Most have a wide range of applications. Inexpensive.	Handling and accurate measuring of concentrate needed. Requires special equipment for application.
LIQUID DRENCH	Contact and systemic types available. Most have a wide range of uses. Inexpensive.	Handling and accurate measuring of concentrate needed. Difficult to work out precise amounts.
DUST	Used direct from pack, so little is wasted. It is easy to apply direct to the target organism.	Only contact types available. May leave unsightly deposit on plant.
READY-TO-USE SPRAYS	No need to handle concentrate; contents are already correctly diluted. Quick and simple to use.	Expensive and suitable for treatment of relatively small areas of infection/infestation.
PELLETS	In measured doses: easy to apply correct quantity. Repellents in them to deter animals.	May be eaten by pets, children, or wildlife. Can become less active after rain.
AEROSOL	Quick, simple, and easy to use. Required dose applied, so no waste. No equipment needed.	May not control pests hidden or under foliage. Expensive.
GRANULARS	Convenient and simple to apply, especially for turf.	Expensive compared with sprays and may be eaten by wildlife.

directly and concentrates sprayed after dilution. Others are availble in aerosol cans, especially for household and nonplant pests. Granular formulations are common for lawn applications. A few pests, such as slugs, can be controlled with chemicals that are mixed with something attractive to form a poisoned bait. These include rat poisons, slug pellets, and ant baits.

Some pesticides control a wide range of insects, including beneficial insects if they are on the plant when sprayed. This broad spectrum of activity is an advantage where several infestations are to be controlled at one time but a disadvantage where disrupting beneficials creates secondary problems.

PROTECTING PONDS
Fish are extremely susceptible to harm from many garden chemicals, which should not be used on aquatic plants. Avoid chemical fertilizers where they may leach into pond water.

PROTECTING PETS AND WILDLIFE
Be especially careful when using insecticides around pets and wildlife. Birds can be poisoned after ingesting granular insecticides, and pets can become sick after eating slug baits. Keep potential nontarget effects in mind when using any pesticide.

Pesticide selectivity can be enhanced in a number of ways. Timing application only when pests are at intolerable levels and directing sprays for the particular target (rather than broadcast over a large area) are ways of minimizing nontarget effects. Some materials are inherently more selective than others. For example, insecticidal soap works primarily on soft-bodied insects such as aphids and has a very short persistence, losing effectiveness after drying.

PERSISTENCE OF PESTICIDES
The rate at which insecticides and fungicides lose their effectiveness and break down into other compounds varies. This is largely dependent on the degree of stability of the chemical's molecular structure, but it is also affected by factors such as weather and exposure to sunlight. Some organochlorine insecticides, such as DDT and aldrin, are extremely persistent and accumulate in the environment and so have been withdrawn.

Persistence may be a double-edged sword, providing long-term control while reducing labor for repeat applications, but possibly increasing the risk of effects on nontarget organisms and pesticide resistance problems. However, relatively few pesticides remain active for more than a week or two, and some are effective for only a day or a few hours. The less persistent materials are particularly useful when only a quick intervention is needed or where disrupting beneficials poses a problem.

SELECTION OF CONTROLS
With a wide array of options available, making the best choices can seem bewildering. Most counties or regions have a Cooperative Extension office (or its equivalent), part of county or state government and affiliated with an agricultural college, which can help diagnose problems and provide a plan tailored to a site and to personal preference.

GARDEN HEALTH AND PROBLEMS

APPLYING PESTICIDES

PESTICIDES are a great help in controlling pest and disease problems when few or no satisfactory alternatives are available. If used with care and only when needed, they pose minimal threat to people and the environment. Changes in legislation and the increasing concerns about safety to the environment and the user mean that the list of chemicals available is constantly changing. Also, all chemicals are rigorously tested before being marketed.

When considering chemical control, always decide whether the situation really necessitates their use. Slight pest infestations, or those which occur toward the end of the season, may not pose a sufficient threat to the plant.

Selecting the most suitable chemical is also important; whenever possible, use one that controls only the pest organism. Formulations that contain both a fungicide and an insecticide are appropriate only when both the specified pest and disease are present at a level that warrants control.

READING THE LABEL

Always consult the product label to determine precisely what the chemical can be used for and whether it is formulated for use against the problem and on the plant you have in mind. Using a pesticide inconsistently with the label is a violation of federal law for which the user can be held liable.

Products that carry a label recommendation for use on edible crops may also specify a minimum interval that must elapse between the application of the chemical and the harvest of the fruit or vegetable.

The timing, application rate, and frequency of application are also important; information about all of these factors is available on the label. Applying a

HEALTHY VEGETABLES
To make sure that vegetables and fruits are safe to eat after chemical treatment, adhere to the directions and restrictions on the product label.

pesticide at the incorrect rate, frequency, or time may prove ineffective, damaging, or simply wasteful, and so it is essential to follow the instructions.

RULES FOR SAFETY

When applying chemicals, there are a number of general rules that should be followed.

Chemicals must always be applied according to the instructions. Avoid contact with your eyes and skin, and avoid inhaling the chemical. Labels should include a section of Precautionary Statements, giving warnings about protective clothing. Chemical-resistant clothing and perhaps a respirator are suggested for handling and applying pesticides. Different products should not be mixed together unless this is indicated on the label or leaflet.

Keep children and animals away, and never eat, drink, or smoke while applying chemicals. Do not apply in windy, hot, sunny, or completely calm weather to minimize the threat of chemical drift affecting adjacent plants. Spray in the late afternoon, early evening, or early morning.

EQUIPMENT FOR APPLICATION

You may need to invest in some special equipment to apply chemicals. This should all be labeled clearly and kept separately, so that it is used for

---

PESTICIDE TOXICITY TERMS

The label on almost every pesticide container displays a signal word that indicates the pesticide's level of toxicity to humans.

DANGER appears on pesticides that are highly toxic; it is accompanied by **POISON** and the skull and crossbones symbol if oral, dermal, or inhalation risks are very high.

WARNING indicates moderate toxicity.

CAUTION ratings are given on pesticides that are slightly toxic to relatively nontoxic.

Pesticide labels also carry additional information on how to safely use the product.

MIXING AND APPLYING CHEMICAL SPRAYS

1 Measuring. Measure out the required amount of concentrate accurately. Avoid making up more than necessary, and always read the instructions carefully. Wear rubber gloves, and take care not to spill any of the chemical.

2 Mixing. Part-fill the sprayer with water, and then carefully pour the concentrate in. Rinse out the measurer with water, then add this to the sprayer. Fill up to the required level with water, then close all containers.

3 Applying. If possible, spray both surfaces of the leaves. This is particularly important if contact action sprays are used. Spray at dusk to minimize risk to pollinating insects and to lessen phytotoxic reactions.

no other purpose (*see below*). Use completely different equipment for the application of weedkillers, because even trace amounts of these can cause serious damage to garden plants. A small sprayer is suitable for most chemicals unless you have a very large area to treat. One that produces a fine spray is needed for controlling most pests and diseases. Insecticide or fungicide drenches or weedkillers can be applied using a watering can fitted with a dribble bar.

Clean all equipment regularly. When rinsing it out after use, spray all washings onto suitable plants. Never dispose of any dilute or concentrated chemicals by pouring them down a toilet or drain, into watercourses, or onto land where they may contaminate underground water.

APPLYING CHEMICALS IN ENCLOSED SPACES

When chemicals such as sprays or aerosols are used in enclosed spaces such as greenhouses or conservatories, particular care is needed to avoid contact or inhalation. Temperatures are often higher and ventilation much lower than outside. Greenhouses or conservatories that open directly into the house pose further difficulties, so wherever possible, doors or windows into the house should be tightly closed.

The risk of damaging the plants being treated is also greater, due both to the raised temperatures and to the magnifying effect that glass may have on the sun's rays. To minimize problems, do not apply during the hotter, brighter parts of the day, and make sure plants are watered and foliage is dry.

STORING CHEMICALS

It is very important to store garden chemicals safely, since even small amounts can be harmful to people, animals, and garden plants. Below are tips to help you store chemicals correctly. Rules for safe storage should also be applied to the equipment you use to apply chemicals. It is worth marking items such as watering cans clearly so that they are not confused with equipment for general garden use.

STORAGE TIPS

• Store chemicals in a safe place, preferably a locked cabinet inaccessible to children or animals.
• Keep chemicals in their original containers, with their tops tightly closed.
• Make sure all containers are clearly labeled and kept separately.
• Clear out cabinets annually so that you do not accumulate old and obsolete products. To dispose of them, wrap them well and contact your local pesticide authority. Watch out for and dispose of leaking products similarly.

SAFETY HAZARDS

• Do not transfer any chemical out of its original container into another one, especially soft-drink and other beverage bottles.
• Buy sufficient chemicals for only one to two years' use, and do not store them for a long period of time. Chemicals become less effective once they have been opened and may go out of date.
• Do not keep surplus quantities of made-up solutions and sprays. Dispose of them and rinse out equipment immediately after you have finished treating plants.
• If you need to get rid of old chemicals, do not simply add them to household rubbish or pour them down household drains. Dispose of them safely (*see left*) without removing them from their original containers.

PREVENTIVE MEASURES

WELL-GROWN, vigorous plants are not immune to pests and diseases, but they are less likely to be badly damaged. Attention should be paid to selecting plants and cultivars that are likely to do well under the local soil and climatic conditions. It is worthwhile paying more for good-quality seeds, bulbs, and plants from reputable suppliers. Cheap offers from dubious sources may be in poor condition or may carry pests and diseases that may be difficult to eliminate once introduced into a garden or greenhouse.

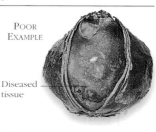

RESISTANT CULTIVAR
Some cultivars of broccoli have been bred for resistance to clubroot, a devastating soil-borne disease.

RESISTANT CULTIVARS

Many cultivars of plants have been developed in recent years to withstand common strains of fungal or bacterial disease or to lessen susceptibility to pest attack. These include some fruits and vegetables that virtually eliminate the risk of several serious problems in the vegetable garden. Resistant cultivars suggested by local experts as well as knowledgable gardeners are highly recommended for general garden use.

CARE OF YOUNG PLANTS

Take care to ensure that planting or sowing is done properly; sowing too early or late (when soil may be cold and wet), or planting pot-grown plants too deeply or with a potbound root system, will result in plants that will always struggle and fail to make good growth. Growing media should be well-drained and not allowed to become waterlogged. Practice good technique: for example, thin, prick out, and pot on seedlings (*see facing page*) as soon as necessary, rather than neglecting them until the task is well overdue. Crowded seedlings, competing for limited resources of nutrients, water, and light, will be weak and undersized and may never make vigorous plants. Also, the younger a plant is, the more swiftly it is able to recover from being transplanted.

MAINTAINING HEALTHY PLANTS

Plant problems can arise at any time of the year but are more prevalent during the spring to autumn season, during their peak growing period. It is a good idea to make regular tours of inspection in order to detect problems before they become serious. It is important to look for plants that are under-performing; this may show as slow growth, often with symptoms of discoloration, distortion, or damage that should be investigated as soon as possible.

Plants showing signs of attack by pests or diseases should not be ignored, since it is very likely that other plants may also become affected. Control measures are most effective when problems are detected early, diagnosed accurately, and dealt with early on. In a group of plants, removal of the affected one(s) is a sensible precaution to help stop the problem from spreading.

CHOOSING HEALTHY PLANTS AND BULBS

Vigorous growth

SELECTING HEALTHY BEDDING PLANTS
Choose plants that are free of any sign of pests or disease. Look for compact growth with a good leaf color and a well-developed root system. Avoid those with yellowing leaves, leaf spots, weak growth, or wilted parts.

BUYING BULBS
Since there is a good deal of variety in the quality and size of bulbs available to the gardener, they should be closely examined before buying. Bulbs should be as fresh and firm as possible (see bottom right) and without signs of mold or discolored patches. The bulb shown top right has both diseased tissue and damaged outer scales, so it would not be a good choice. Undersized bulbs may not flower in their first year, so always try to choose the largest bulbs available of the chosen cultivar.

POOR EXAMPLE

Diseased tissue

GOOD EXAMPLE

GOOD PLANTING

1 Sowing. Sowing into a seed tray is a good way of raising large numbers of seedlings, but they will soon need more space to allow them to develop. Overcrowding will restrict their growth.

2 Pricking out. Select the stronger seedlings, then carefully remove them from the tray. Handle them by gently holding the seed leaves rather than the stem, which is easily bruised.

3 Transplanting. Space the seedlings out and plant out or put into pots once they are well established. Avoid damping off by using sterile soil mix, rather than garden soil, and clean water.

As plants grow and develop, thin out any that have become overcrowded. This improves their vigor and allows air to circulate around stems and leaves, thus reducing damp air conditions that favor germination and infection by fungal spores.

FERTILIZING PLANTS

Most plants will benefit from supplementary fertilizing to increase yields of fruits and vegetables and to increase the quality and quantity of flowers. Organic fertilizers include garden compost, various manures, bone meal, dried blood, and seaweed extracts. These all provide a variety of nutrients, although not necessarily in the right balance required for optimum plant growth.

Manmade fertilizers can be essentially single-nutrient compounds, such as ammonium sulfate (supplying nitrogen) or superphosphate (phosphorus), but more widely used by gardeners are general fertilizers (such as 5-10-5), which provide all the major nutrients. These are available as granules for adding to the soil, or in soluble form for watering in or spraying on the leaves (foliar feeding). The slow-release fertilizer pellets now available will give container-grown plants the nutrients they need throughout the growing season.

Fertilizing is generally done during the spring and early summer, when plants are making rapid growth. Fertilizers applied in autumn or winter may be largely wasted: dormant plants do not need fertilizer, and nutrients added then may be washed away by rain before spring.

WATERING

Watering is always crucial in a garden, particularly at critical stages in a plant's development such as the seedling stage and when flowers and fruits are being produced. In dry periods, it is important to water before plants show signs of drought stress and to water at regular intervals.

Watering is best done in early to midmorning to minimize loss to evaporation and to allow foliage to dry. Water that remains on foliage for long periods increases the chance for foliar diseases to occur. Covering the soil surface with a mulch will help retain moisture in the soil. Rain barrels can be used to gather water from the roof. This source of water is suitable for most plants but is best avoided for seedlings and cuttings, since it might spread fungi that cause damping off and stem rots.

SUPPORTING CLIMBING PLANTS
Plants that cannot support their stems need tying up to keep them off the ground, where growth will be vulnerable to insects and slugs. Even self-clinging climbers need help when young.

DRAINAGE

Waterlogged soil can be just as damaging as dry
soil to plants. A heavy soil, such as clay, has only
small spaces between the soil particles, making it
moisture-retentive and difficult for water to drain
through. Improve heavy soil texture by digging in
coarse organic matter, such as compost, leaf mold,
or manure, to enhance drainage and aeration.

Sandy soils are easy to work and warm up
quickly in spring, but they do not retain moisture
well. These soils also benefit from liberal addition
of organic matter, which improves their capacity to
hold moisture and nutrients. Chalky, alkaline soils
are usually very well drained, allowing moisture
and fertility to leach away easily, and they likewise
benefit from the addition of organic matter.

WEEDING

Good weed control is important. If weeds gain
dominance, other plants may become more
vulnerable to problems. Weeds can be removed by
hand or by hoeing, suppressed with mulches and
landscape fabrics, or controlled with many other
nonchemical techniques. Also, like cultivated plants,
weeds may attract pests and pathogens and are a
source of reinfestation after problems have been
controlled on cultivated plants. They also help pests
and diseases survive in the absence of cultivated
hosts, diminishing the value of crop rotation.

REMOVING DEAD PLANT MATERIAL
*Unless features such as winter seedheads are desired, dead or
dying flowers and foliage, together with their stalks or stems,
should be removed, because they can become sites for rots and
fungal growth that may spread to living plant material.*

REMOVING SUCKERS TO KEEP PLANTS STRONG
*Most roses are grafted onto a rootstock, and suckers will emerge
from below the graft union. Gently clear away soil from where
the sucker arises, then cut it or pull it off.*

REMOVING OTHER UNWANTED GROWTH

To keep plants strong, suckering growth from the
roots needs to be removed, particularly on grafted
plants such as roses and most fruit trees. These are
usually grafted onto rootstocks that will produce
sucker growth of inferior quality to, but usually of
greater vigor than, the named cultivar. If possible,
the suckers should be traced back to the roots from
which they arise and cut off at the source. Cutting
them off at soil level simply encourages more
suckers. Avoid damaging roots when digging the
soil around roses, cherries, and other plants prone
to suckering, since this can stimulate sucker growth.

DEAD, DISEASED, AND DAMAGED GROWTH

Although the routine pruning of plants that require
it is usually best carried out at a particular time of
year, it is, with very few exceptions, safer to
remove any dead, diseased, or damaged growth
from a plant as soon as it is noticed, rather than
waiting for the usual pruning time. Removal of
branches that have been broken by storms or other
causes should be finished with a clean cut to speed
callusing. Branches infected with fungal diseases,
such as fireblight, canker, or tip dieback, should be
cut out well below the signs of infection to prevent
the further spread of these diseases.

ROUTINE PRUNING

Not all plants require pruning, but many woody
plants do benefit from some form of thinning or
reduction in size. This may be done on an annual
basis, such as with apple trees, in order to promote
the development of spurs that will produce flower
buds and fruits. Other plants may need infrequent
pruning, with the intention of doing no more than

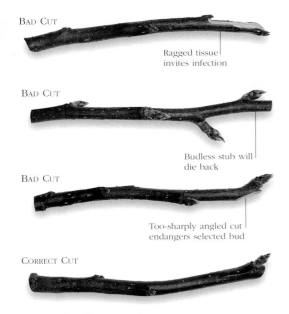

BAD CUT

Ragged tissue invites infection

BAD CUT

Budless stub will die back

BAD CUT

Too-sharply angled cut endangers selected bud

CORRECT CUT

GOOD AND BAD PRUNING CUTS

Make sharp pruning cuts close to a strong bud, with the cut sloping away from the bud. Avoid making ragged cuts or leaving stubs above the bud. Use a sharp knife or pruners.

removing the occasional branch or shoot that is growing too far in the wrong direction. Always prune to correct situations where branches cross each other, since in rubbing together they may create wounds that are open to infection.

Pruning also provides an opportunity to thin shrubs and trees with a dense system of branches to provide a more open center. This improves growth and the development of flowers and fruits by allowing sunshine in. There is also a better flow of air among the foliage and branches, which will

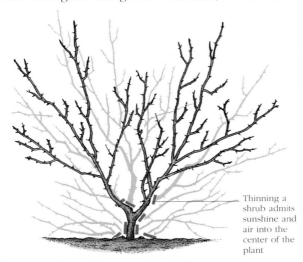

Thinning a shrub admits sunshine and air into the center of the plant

PRUNING TO AVOID CROWDED GROWTH

Cut out some of the older stems in order to encourage new growth. Thin the stems if overcrowded to create a more open center. This will help reduce the incidence of diseases.

help foliage dry and deter the germination of fungal spores. With flowering shrubs, removing one third of the older stems yearly will revitalize the plants by stimulating the development of young shoots.

MAKING CORRECT CUTS

Bad pruning can cause problems, rather than curing or preventing them, so it is important to make cuts correctly with clean, sharp tools (and to disinfect tools between cuts). Invest in good- quality pruners to remove stems up to the thickness of a pencil; anything larger is better tackled with loppers or a pruning saw. Shoots should be cut cleanly back to a strong bud with a slanting cut (*see left*). Never leave a stump of stem above the bud, since this will result in dieback.

Do not cut a branch off absolutely flush with the trunk or branch from which it arises. There will be a slight thickening, or collar, at the base of the branch; the cut should be made just outside this point. If the collar is also removed, the growth of scar tissue over the pruning wound is impaired and can result in a large exposed area of inner wood.

It is sometimes necessary to remove large branches from trees. Before doing so, it is generally wise to seek the advice of a professional arborist; major work such as this can result in an unstable or unbalanced tree.

Large branches are heavy, and it is often advisable for safety reasons to remove them in smaller pieces instead of making a single cut. This also reduces the danger of the branch dropping as it is being

CROSSING BRANCHES

Crossing branches rub against each other, wearing away the bark and creating entry points for disease.

cut and tearing a strip of bark from the trunk. This risk can be further reduced by initially making a cut on the underside of the branch before completing the task by sawing down from the top.

WOUND PAINTS

The use of commercial wound paints on large pruning cuts is much less often recommended today than in the past. There is some evidence to show that they can restrict the natural healing process that occurs around correctly made pruning cuts. However, where trees and shrubs are known to be susceptible to fresh wound-infecting diseases, it may be helpful to use a wound paint.

COMPOST PILE
Some types of infested or diseased material must never be composted, but many pathogens may be destroyed by the heat generated in the center of the pile. Never leave rotten apples on top of compost like this; instead, bury them deep within the pile.

RAKING UP OLD LEAVES
*Dead leaves harbor slugs and encourage gray mold (*Botrytis*) and other diseases. Keep the garden neat by gathering plant debris and putting it on the compost pile.*

DISPOSAL OF DEBRIS AND PRUNINGS

At the end of the growing season, rake up fallen leaves to remove overwintering fungal spores and places for pests. Composting garden debris is an excellent way of returning nutrients and organic matter to the soil, but there are some basic rules that must be followed when composting unhealthy plant material. Most pests and diseases cannot survive in the heat generated by compost piles, but it is advisable to cover infested plants with compost or with a layer of grass clippings or weeds. Plants with root pests or diseases should never be put onto compost pile. Instead, dispose of them with the rest of your household trash, as should prunings from plants with canker or dieback.

REPLANTING AND CROP ROTATION

Growing the same or closely related plants in the same piece of ground in successive years can lead to a buildup of problems. Vegetables, bedding plants, and bulbs are, however, particularly prone to some pests and diseases, and changing the growing site is not guaranteed to protect them. Many insects have winged adults which will have little difficulty in locating their host plant's new position. Similarly, many diseases are spread by windblown spores. There are, however, some less mobile problems, such as nematodes and root rots, that can be avoided by adopting a diligently practiced crop rotation system.

There are other good reasons for changing the growing sites of plants. Roses and apples suffer from replant disorders. If replacement plants are put in the same place from which an apple or rose has recently been removed, it is possible that the new plant will fail to thrive. Microorganisms associated with the roots of the old plant seem to have an antagonistic effect on the new plant. Crop rotation in the vegetable garden also helps make

better use of the available nutrients, since plants differ in their nutritional requirements. When devising a crop rotation system, it is advisable to group related plants together in order to get maximum advantage when next year the planting sites are changed around. A simple rotation for the vegetable garden involves a three-year cycle; at the end of this time each of the three groups will have been grown for one year in a different area.

SIMPLE CROP ROTATION

GROUP 1	GROUP 2	GROUP 3
Cabbage	Potato	Beans
Brussels sprouts	Tomato	Peas
Cauliflower	Carrot	Onions/Shallots
Kale	Parsnip	Leeks
Broccoli	Celery	Lettuce
Turnip	Parsley	Corn
Rutabaga	Beet	Squash
Radish	Swiss chard	Cucumber

FIRST YEAR	SECOND YEAR	THIRD YEAR
GROUP 1	GROUP 2	GROUP 3
GROUP 2	GROUP 3	GROUP 1
GROUP 3	GROUP 1	GROUP 2

A BED OF GROUP 3 CROPS, INCLUDING PEAS AND BEANS

A–Z
DIRECTORY

THIS DICTIONARY SECTION contains entries for pests, diseases, disorders, and beneficial organisms likely to be found in the garden. Some occur in varying forms on many plants and have a general entry with cross-references. Many others are largely host-specific and so have a plant name as part of the entry name.

Suggested controls and preventive measures present nonchemical and chemical methods wherever appropriate.

ADELGIDS

Conifers, particularly pines (*Pinus*), spruce (*Picea*), larch (*Larix*), Douglas fir (*Pseudotsuga menziesii*), hemlock (*Tsuga*), and fir (*Abies*), are attacked by adelgids. These black aphidlike insects suck sap from foliage, stems, and bark. Some adelgids, particularly on spruce, cause conelike galls. On other conifers, they may feed on needles, branches, trunks, or cones, and are often covered by a fluffy, white wax. Some alternate between spruce and another conifer. Infestation on nonspruce hosts may cause distorted needles or yellowing. Heavy infestations by some adelgids give trunks, branches, or foliage a snowy appearance. Galls on spruce rarely pose a threat to the tree, but high numbers on twigs or trunks can cause dieback. See individual entries for controls.

• *see also* BALSAM WOOLLY ADELGID *p.104;* COOLEY SPRUCE GALL ADELGID *p.117;* EASTERN SPRUCE GALL ADELGID *p.125;* HEMLOCK WOOLLY ADELGID *p.135;* LARCH ADELGIDS *p.142;* PINE ADELGIDS *p.160.*

AIR POLLUTION

SYMPTOMS Because air pollutants are taken in by a plant's respiratory system, foliar symptoms generally appear first. The first clue may be markings that range from silvery to bleached to yellow to purple and black and from small flecks to large patches, streaks, or wavy bands. Leaves can appear scorched or slimy, papery and brittle and can collapse, wither, or develop shotholes. They may bulge, curl, tear, or roll up or down. Foliage can be stunted and grow slowly, or it can age early, show premature autumn coloration, and drop. The rest of the plant also is affected, from overall stunting and other growth disorders to specific failures. Branches die back without healthy leaves. Buds fail to form or open properly. Flowers show color breaking, petal curling, or premature dropping. Fruit quality and yield are reduced. Unless a nearby pollution source or recent pollution event can be identified, it is hard to distinguish air pollution damage from that of many pathogens, pests, and other environmental and nutritional problems. Often, only laboratory analysis provides a definitive diagnosis.
CAUSE Pollutants, including ozone, sulfur dioxide, fluorides, metal compounds, and ethylene. Even at a very low concentration, a pollutant can accumulate in plant tissue to harmful levels. Such chronic exposure can have a more adverse effect than a high atmospheric concentration lasting 1–2 days. Species and cultivars have greatly differing levels of tolerance, and an individual plant's reaction changes with age; usually, young plants and nearly mature foliage suffer worst.
CONTROL Maintain vigor.

ALGAE

SYMPTOMS Powdery deposits develop on the plant's surface; they are commonly green or gray-green and can be rubbed off, usually leaving no discoloration on the plant tissue. The plant's growth and development are rarely affected.
CAUSE Generally nonparasitic, microscopic, plantlike organisms that develop in films of moisture on plant surfaces. They are particularly common on plants growing in moist situations. Leaves and trunks or stems are most frequently affected, especially those on the north-facing side.
CONTROL Algal deposits can usually be washed off. Improve air circulation around the plant, and reduce dampness to prevent regrowth.

ALTERNARIA LEAF SPOT

SYMPTOMS Gray or brown spots appear on affected foliage *(see p.13)*. They frequently show concentric rings of tissue dieback with central, raised fruiting bodies of the fungus. In extreme conditions, spots may join together, causing extensive areas of leaf to wither and die and sometimes drop. The damage usually remains as distinct, nearly circular spots. Areas of pale or variegated foliage are most readily affected. Plants commonly affected include potatoes, carrots, and brassicas.
CAUSE Various species of the fungus *Alternaria*. The spores are airborne when carried by rain or water splash. They thrive in wet weather and poor air circulation and on plants growing lushly.
CONTROL Remove and dispose of affected leaves. Discard crop debris at the end of the season. Improve air circulation by spacing plants well and weeding between the rows. Avoid overhead watering and excessive use of high-nitrogen fertilizers. Spray with a fungicide containing mancozeb or copper.
• *see also* POTATO EARLY BLIGHT *p.163.*

ANDROMEDA LACEBUG

SYMPTOMS The leaves of *Pieris* are speckled or mottled gray or yellow. On the undersides are shiny, black, hard drops of excrement, among which may be seen dissimilar nymph and adult lacebugs. Damage may be only unsightly, or it may cause leaves to drop, which, in turn, can cause significant dieback, diminished plant vigor, and stunting. Most severe injury occurs on plants in full sun.
CAUSE Nymph and adult andromeda lacebugs (*Stephanitis takeyai*), which suck the foliage juices from the underside. The loss of chlorophyll causes the mottling and, possibly, serious damage. The darker, spiny nymph does not resemble the ⅛in (3mm) adult, whose lacy venation of the boxy wings continues over the head and thorax. Plant damage occurs all year.
CONTROL Maintain healthy plants. Avoid planting in sites with full sun. Some cultivars are purported to have moderate resistance to lacebugs. When symptoms first appear from either nymphs or adults, spray lower leaf surfaces with insecticidal soap or another insecticide.

ANTHRACNOSE

Various fungi cause patches or spots of discoloration to appear on infected plant tissue. Leaf, stem, or (in beans) pod tissue may be killed, and in severe cases the entire plant may die.
• *see also* BEAN ANTHRACNOSE *p.105;* DOGWOOD ANTHRACNOSE *p.123;* IVY ANTHRACNOSE *p.139;* SYCAMORE ANTHRACNOSE (BLIGHT) *p.180.*

ANTS

Some ant species are beneficial predators of insects, including pests such as aphids and scales. Many are harmless to plants. A few indirectly cause injury by protecting aphids and scales, while several damage plants outright. Carpenter ants

(*Camponotus*) tunnel into soft wood and may nest in live trees as well as buildings. Although they do not eat wood, feeding on insects, honeydew, and other liquids, their activity can weaken trees structurally. Allegheny mound ants (*Formica exsectoides*) build large mounds and kill small trees in their way. They feed on other insects. Both carpenter and Allegheny mound ants, as well as the notorious fire ants of the southern US, bite and emit irritating formic acid.

LENGTH: ⅛–⅜IN (3–10MM)

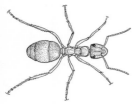

BLACK ANT

CONTROL Ants can be reduced in numbers, but they cannot be completely eliminated. Most kinds of ants are at most a nuisance rather than a significant pest. Control measures, such as pouring boiling water over mounds, should be confined to nests that cause the worst problems. Granular insecticides can be mixed with the upper soil of mounds, or liquid formulations can be used for drenching. Baits with insect growth regulators do not provide immediate control. For large infestations, the services of a professional may be needed.

APHIDS

Many species of aphid, sometimes called plant lice, occur in gardens, and some species feed on only certain kinds of plants. Generally, affected plants show reduced vigor with varying degrees of leaf distortion or galls. The upper leaf surface becomes sticky with the sugary

honeydew excreted by aphids, sometimes combined with their cast skins; a black sooty mold often grows on the honeydew. A few species of aphid feed on roots, twigs, or stems. Aphids may be red, green, yellow, pink, black, grayish white, or brown and are very small but often occur in large numbers. Winged forms may also be present. Most kinds overwinter as eggs on alternate hosts. Some viral diseases are spread by aphids.

CONTROL Natural enemies often provide adequate control. Yellow sticky cards or boards can be used to monitor aphids on greenhouse plants. Aphids can be dislodged with a blast of water from the hose. Insecticidal soaps, horticultural oil, and other materials are available as sprays.

• *see also* BALSAM TWIG APHID *p.104;* BEAN APHID *p.105;* BEECH APHIDS *p.105;* BLACK CHERRY APHID *p.107;* CABBAGE APHID *p.111;* CURRANT APHID *p.121;* ELM LEAF GALL APHID *p.126;* GIANT WILLOW APHID *p.132;* HONEYSUCKLE APHID *p.137;* LEAF-CURLING PLUM APHID *p.142;* LUPINE APHID *p.145;* MELON (COTTON) APHID *p.146;* MILKWEED APHID *see* OLEANDER APHID *p.153;* PEA APHID *p.155;* PEACH APHIDS *p.156;* ROOT APHIDS *p.168;* ROSE APHIDS *p.169;* ROSY APPLE APHID *p.171;* WATERLILY APHID *p.188;* WOOLLY APPLE APHID *p.192.*

APPLE AND PEAR CANKER

SYMPTOMS Areas of bark sink inward (*see* **p.36**), usually starting near a wound or bud. The bark becomes discolored and then shrinks and cracks, forming concentric rings of flaky bark. The branch may become swollen around the cankered area. As the canker enlarges, the shoot may be girdled, so foliage and

growth above it start to die back. Stems and trunks may be attacked, and very occasionally immature fruits are infected and rot. In summer, raised, white fungal pustules develop on the canker; in winter, raised, red fruiting bodies grow. Apples and pears are frequently affected; poplars (*Populus*), beeches (*Fagus*), willows (*Salix*), hawthorn (*Crataegus*), and mountain ash (*Sorbus*) also succumb.

CAUSE The fungus *Nectria galligena*, which is spread mainly in spring as windborne spores that enter through wounds.

CONTROL Prune out entire spurs or branches where possible. On larger branch or trunk infections, carefully pare away all infected and damaged bark and wood, cutting back to completely clean tissue. Improve general growing conditions, particularly soil drainage, since poor drainage may aggravate the disease. Do not grow susceptible cultivars. Sprays used for apple scab and apple powdery mildew should also help suppress canker.

APPLE BITTER PIT

SYMPTOMS Tiny sunken brown spots may develop on apple skin (*see* **p.48**). The flesh is spoiled by numerous pale brown spots or freckles. Affected apples may have an unpleasant, slightly bitter taste. The symptoms may appear while the fruits are on the tree but often develop only during storage. Large fruits and heavily yielding trees are more prone to this disorder.

CAUSE Calcium deficiency in the fruit. Calcium levels in the soil may be perfectly adequate, but in dry conditions the tree cannot take up the amount it needs. Too high a level of

magnesium or calcium in fruits may also be a cause.

CONTROL Keep apple trees well watered and mulched. Maintain even growth by feeding with a balanced fertilizer; avoid excessive use of high-nitrogen fertilizers. Spray developing fruits with calcium nitrate solution.

APPLE MAGGOT

SYMPTOMS Apple or crabapple skins have brown streaks and slight dimples, and brown tunnels meander through the pulp, perhaps with a maggot at the end each one. The surfaces of harder winter apple varieties are pitted, while softer varieties may decay around the injured sites. Infested fruit becomes soft and rots, often dropping from the tree. Other susceptible fruits include pears, apricots, plums, hawthorn, and juneberry.

CAUSE The apple maggot, or railroad worm, which is the larva of a fruit fly, *Rhagoletis pomonella*. The black adult fly resembles a small (¼in/6mm) housefly. The female lays eggs in late spring and summer, puncturing the skin of the fruit. The pale maggots, ⅜in (1cm) long, tunnel deeper into the fruit, and then tunnel out while the damaged fruit is still hanging on the branch or (usually) after it has dropped prematurely.

CONTROL Frequently gather and destroy dropped fruit. Hang sticky red sphere traps about 6ft (1.8m) high around the tree canopy, starting in late spring to early summer. Maintain the traps until late summer. Also hang the traps in nearby host trees, such as crabapple and hawthorn. A multipurpose fruit spray can be applied every 10 days until late August. Begin spraying shortly after the flies are first detected.

APPLE POWDERY MILDEW

SYMPTOMS Leaves are covered in a white, powdery fungal growth (*see p.25*). Young leaves breaking from infected buds often show symptoms. If attacked early, the foliage rarely reaches full size and is distorted and dies prematurely.
CAUSE The fungus *Podosphaera leucotricha*, which overwinters in the apple buds or on the young stem growth (as silvery white patches). This fungus may also occasionally attack pears and quinces but does not cause serious damage. Disease spread and development is most rapid in hot summers and if there are heavy dews at night.
CONTROL Keep apple trees well watered, since dry soil seems to encourage powdery mildew development. Mulch well. Prune out severely infected growth and mildewed stems. Prune established trees to improve air circulation. Spray with a suitable fungicide, and grow resistant cultivars.

APPLE RUSTS

SYMPTOMS In spring and autumn, discolored spots appear on apple and crabapple trees. Leaves (*see p.18*) are the most common infection sites, and the spots on the undersurface enlarge, swell, turn from yellow to rusty, and release clouds of rusty powder when disturbed. Often fruit and sometimes petioles and green twigs are affected. Diseased parts may become dwarfed, distorted, or killed and fall early. Surviving fruit is of poor quality. The first season of infection may kill a seedling, but a mature tree usually survives. Later infections may kill branches and eventually the tree.
CAUSE Species of the rust fungus *Gymnosporangium*.

The most common and destructive is cedar-apple rust (*G. juniperi-virginianae*). These rusts require 2 hosts to complete their life cycle: apple and, usually, a red cedar or another juniper. The spores require at least 4 hours in water, such as rain or dew droplets, on the plant surface to germinate.
CONTROL Many older apple cultivars are more resistant than newer ones. Asian crabapple species tend to be resistant. If possible, destroy nearby evergreen host species, particularly individuals with obvious symptoms. Plant on the leeward side of a windbreak planting or a building. Increase air circulation. Remove galls (*see p.37*) from nearby red cedars and other junipers. Destroy infected leaves and fruit. Systemic fungicides may kill pathogens, but most fungicides only prevent infection and must be sprayed on leaf undersides thoroughly and repeatedly in spring and autumn.

APPLE SCAB

SYMPTOMS Blackish brown, scabby patches develop on the fruits, with similar but more greenish gray spots on the leaves (*see p.16*), of ornamental and edible *Malus* species. In severe cases, the fruit may be almost entirely covered with scabby patches and be small and misshapen. Infected fruits may crack or split and develop brown rot. Affected leaves fall early and may show extensive infection on the stalk. A very similar disease affects poplars.
CAUSE The fungus *Venturia inaequalis*, which overwinters on scabby patches on the young stems and on fallen infected leaves. Scabs usually are most prevalent in wet seasons

and on trees with overly crowded branches.
CONTROL Rake up and dispose of affected leaves as they fall. Prune out cracked or scabby shoots. Spray with an appropriate fungicide, and grow resistant cultivars.

APPLE SUCKER

SYMPTOMS Flattened, tiny, pale green insects occur on blossom clusters in spring (*see p.43*). Heavy infestations kill the flowers and prevent fruit set.
CAUSE Sap-feeding, aphidlike insects, *Psylla mali*, which hatch from overwintering eggs as apples leaf out. Most of the damage is caused by nymphs during the blossom period. The adult stage resembles a winged aphid and is present after petal fall.

ACTUAL SIZE 🐛

APPLE SUCKER

CONTROL Using horticultural oil during the late dormant period can help control the egg stage. Applying insecticide at the greenbud stage, before flowering, will provide some control.

ASH (LILAC) BORER

SYMPTOMS In late summer, especially after a very dry and warm spell, green ash foliage and branch tips wilt. Branches show boring damage, sometimes are girdled, and break off easily. Castings and sawdust are on the bark or the ground under small bore holes. White caterpillars are sometimes seen. Tunneling is visible under the bark and in the wood. Extensive sapwood injury and girdling can weaken stems or trunks, leading to breakage. Plants attacked repeatedly show

rough bark with many gaps and ridges.
Lilac can show similar symptoms, mostly in the crown and first 3ft (90cm) of stem or trunk. At the site of tunneling, the stem is swollen and cracked, the bark may be broken away, and flagging branches or dieback may be present. Privet, fringetree, and mountain ash are sometimes affected as well.
CAUSE The ash borer (*Podosesia syringae*), the larva of a clearwing moth. The larva feeds mostly on sapwood but sometimes also on heartwood. It bores 2 characteristic holes: the lower entrance is rough sided, and the upper exit is round.
CONTROL Carefully inspect any susceptible nursery stock before purchasing or transplanting. Maintain vigor by deep watering (especially during drought), fertilizing, and controlling other damage, especially bark injury. After planting, wrap the trunk and larger limbs to make a barrier and prevent sunscald. Occasionally unwrap and check for eggs and borers, especially in spring. If an unwrapped base is cleared of grass, weeds, and debris, birds may eat eggs and larvae. Probe borer holes with a wire before adult emergence, or dig out the larva or pupa with a sharp knife. Prune infested or weakened branches before moths emerge. Moths can be monitored and partially controlled by pheromone traps. Residual bark sprays can be applied 10 days after the first borer moth is trapped, and repeated if moths are still trapped after 6 weeks. Bark sprays with beneficial nematodes control some clearwing borers.
• *see also* CLEARWING BORERS *p.115*.

ASH SPANGLE GALL MITE

SYMPTOMS Instead of producing the usual ash seeds, the flowers become converted into lumpy, brown, woody galls. They persist on the tree and can be a distinctive feature after leaf drop.

CAUSE Microscopic gall mites (*Eriophyes fraxinivorus*), which suck sap from flowers in spring and secrete chemicals that convert the flowers into galls.

CONTROL Since this mite has no adverse effect on a tree's growth and the condition is only cosmetic, control is not necessary.

ASIAN LONGHORNED BEETLE

SYMPTOMS The trunk, branches, or exposed roots of hardwood trees, notably maples and willows but also birch, ash, rose of Sharon, poplar, and other hardwoods, have holes ⅜in (1cm) or larger in diameter. The bark shows smaller, darkened, oval to round, roughly cut depressions nearby. Coarse sawdust is piled at the tree's base or caught in branch crotches. Bark may be sloughed off damaged areas. High winds break off branches. A branch or small trunk may be girdled just under the bark, or extensive tunneling might be evident.

Repeated attacks and branch breakage can lead to general crown dieback and death.

CAUSE The Asian longhorned beetle (*Anoplophora glabripennis*). The beetles are 1–1¼in (2.5–3.2cm) long and glossy black with white spots, and the long antennae are banded with alternating black and white. They tend to attack the same tree repeatedly, although they can fly hundreds of feet if necessary. They are also active, rapid walkers as they feed on leaves and young twig bark. The white, grublike larvae feed under the bark and in heartwood.

CONTROL Outbreaks of this recently arrived pest have been detected in the New York area and Chicago. Several thousand trees have been destroyed to control the infestations. Beetles may have arrived in wood packing material from Asia. There are no chemical or other controls yet identified and registered for this pest. If you see the beetle or its large bore hole, contact your agriculture authorities. State agriculture authorities, the Cooperative Extension Service, or university specialists to notify them of suspected infestations.

ASIATIC GARDEN BEETLE

SYMPTOMS Starting in early summer, irregular holes and edge damage appear in the leaves and blossoms of many garden flowers, some vegetables, and shrubs and trees. New damage is particularly noticeable after a warm night, with leaves often eaten from the edges inward. In autumn or early and midspring, grass thins or dies in patches. Examination of sod reveals root damage, and C-shaped white grubs.

CAUSE The Asiatic garden beetle (*Maladera castanea*), which causes chewing damage as both larva and adult. Related to the Japanese beetle and rose chafer, the adult is chestnut brown, ⅓–⅜in (8–11mm) long, and round. Beetles emerge in early to midsummer to feed during the late evening and night. They are strongly attracted to light, but remain buried in the soil near their food plants during the day.Grubs, which overwinter in soil, are present in late summer and spring, feeding on roots of grasses and other plants.

CONTROL Clean up weedy areas. Many pupae can be destroyed by thorough spring cultivation. Adults can be handpicked at night. Check around the bases of damaged plants during the day, and destroy the beetles. Attract birds, which feed on adults. Cover plants with netting when adults are active. Insecticides control grubs in turf. Pyrethrum-based sprays may deter adult feeding.

ASPARAGUS BEETLE

SYMPTOMS Asparagus foliage thins and stems turn brown (*see p.40*). Tips and buds may have chewing injury. New shoots are sometimes peppered with small black eggs. Small red-and-black beetles and sluglike dark larvae may be present.

CAUSE Adults and larvae of a leaf beetle, *Crioceris asparagi*. The beetles are ¼–⅓in (6–8mm) long, black with 6 yellow blotches on their back and a reddish thorax. They emerge from the soil or mulch in late spring and begin laying eggs on the spears, stems, and foliage. The sluglike larval stage is grayish black and up to ⅜in (1cm) long.

LENGTH: ¼–⅓IN (6–8MM)

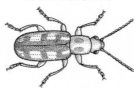

ASPARAGUS BEETLE

CONTROL Hand removal of larvae and adults is feasible for small plantings. Knock larvae off plants; they are usually unable to climb back up. Cut spears close to the ground. Rogue out volunteer asparagus plants. Insecticides can be applied to leaves.

ASPARAGUS RUST

SYMPTOMS During a warm, moist period, asparagus spears develop numerous yellow to orange red spots. These small, powdery pustules darken to reddish brown and finally to black, firmer blisters, which burst when touched to release a fine, dusty cloud of spores. Plant tops may yellow, turn brown, and then die in early to midsummer. The rust may spread rapidly. Damage is severe if the tops are infected over several growing seasons.

This is the most significant disease on *Asparagus officinalis*. Other *Asparagus* species – *A. plumosa* (asparagus fern), *A. asparagoides* (florist's fern), and *A. sprengeri* – may be slightly affected. In all hosts, most aboveground parts are susceptible.

CAUSE The asparagus rust fungus (*Puccinia asparagi*), which completes its entire life cycle on 1 host. Its spores can drift hundreds of miles on the breeze and come down in rainfall. They require moisture for germination on a host; a humid season or a location with heavy dew, fog, or mists favors it.

Repeated rust generations develop until drought occurs or autumn begins. The fungus overwinters on old stems or in the soil.

CONTROL Resistance varies widely. Cut an infected plant at the crown and discard it; do not compost it. Control volunteer and wild asparagus. Deny the fungus a damp foothold: a more open planting allows good air circulation. Do not water from overhead, and do not handle or cut plants that are wet. Also, do not overfertilize with nitrogen. There are a number of effective fungicides. Some treatment regimens call for spraying the intact bed in midspring, while others target the plants immediately after harvest.

ASTER WILT

SYMPTOMS Rapid wilting of the plant, followed by death. The stem base is blackened and shrinks inward. A faint, furry, pale pink or white fungal growth may develop.
CAUSE The fungus *Fusarium oxysporum* f. sp. *callistephi*. It is most common in heavy or wet soils but can attack asters in any soil, and even in seed trays. The fungus is usually introduced on infected seedlings or plants but may also be present in the soil.
CONTROL Promptly remove and dispose of infected plants and the soil in the vicinity of their roots. Use a fresh site for future plantings of asters, and plant only healthy-looking stock. Discard any with dead roots or damaged stem bases. Avoid planting asters on heavy soils, or improve soil texture before planting. Grow resistant cultivars.

ASTER YELLOWS

SYMPTOMS In early summer, nearly 200 species of flowering ornamentals, vegetables, and nonwoody fruit plants show a very wide range of abnormalities, especially in new growth. For example, the veins of immature leaves turn slightly yellow while the rest of the tissue stays green, as on China aster (*Callistephus*). The leaf then pales, without spotting, perhaps losing all color, and its edges may brown. New leaves, perhaps only those in a section or half of a plant, emerge yellow and spindly, the petioles elongated and the blades dwarfed. Adventitious growth of stems erupts with a witches'-broom look. Six or more leaves may unfold from an axil that usually gives rise to only 2. The plants are usually stunted. Flowers do not open at all if the plant is affected early. Those that do

bloom are dwarfed, perhaps distorted, and a sickly yellow-green (virescent), regardless of the normal flower color (*see p.44*). The flower stems are stunted, with short internodes, and the many secondary shoots result in a bunchy look, as with delphinium. Seeds are sterile. Vegetables may develop warty skins and ripen early without flavor. Except for garden chrysanthemums, which may die in a few months, most plants survive.
CAUSE Aster yellows, caused by at least 2 strains of a mycoplasmalike organism (MLO), a microorganism that in size and other qualities is somewhere between a virus and a bacterium. In various regions and on prominent hosts, it may also be known as California aster yellows, western aster yellows, lettuce Rio Grande disease, lettuce white heart, celery yellows, potato purple top, potato late break, and strawberry green petal. The MLO is spread mostly by the aster, or 6-spotted, leafhopper (*Macrosteles quadrilineatus*), which picks it up by feeding on diseased plants. This slender, wedge-shaped relative of the cicada grows to ⅛–⅛in (3–4mm). The pale yellowish green to gray body has 6 pairs of black spots on the front of the head. After multiplying inside the insect for 10 days, the MLO can infect another plant that the leafhopper feeds on. It can be infectious for 3 months or more. Aphids may also spread aster yellows. Plant-to-plant contact can transmit the MLO, but it is not carried in seeds and cannot live long in the soil.
CONTROL Some plants, such as carrot, tomato, and potato, have resistant varieties. Rotate to unsusceptible vegetables – for example, beans, peas, and other

legumes. Destroy an MLO-diseased plant. Before winter, remove the aboveground debris of daisy family members, including *Chrysanthemum*, *Coreopsis*, *Erigeron*, and *Gaillardia*. For similar reasons, control nearby weeds year-round. Keep highly susceptible cultivated plants at least 200ft (60m) away from weed borders. Sterilize garden tools and wash your hands after working with infected plants. Once evident, aster yellow symptoms may be suppressed by antibiotics. Leafhoppers can be caught in large numbers in blacklight traps. To block the frequently windblown insect, grow windbreaks of corn or sunflowers. To completely exclude leafhoppers from plants, use floating rowcover, cheesecloth at 22 threads per inch (2.5cm), or wire at 18 strands per inch. Encourage natural enemies that prey on them. Spray leaf undersides with insecticidal soap or pyrethrin, or apply a systemic insecticide to the soil to kill leafhoppers.
• see also LEAFHOPPERS *p.142*.

AZALEA GALL

SYMPTOMS Pale green, waxy growths develop in place of foliage or occasionally in place of petals. Sometimes they have a pinkish red color. The galls later turn white as a powdery spore layer develops on their surface, and at the end of the summer they wither and turn brown. The infected plant continues to grow and flower normally. Symptoms may occasionally develop on rhododendrons.
CAUSE The fungus *Exobasidium vaccinii*, which is common on outdoor and indoor Indian hybrid azaleas (*Rhododendron indicum*). Spores are carried on air currents and by insects, and months may elapse between

infection and the appearance of symptoms.
CONTROL Remove galls promptly before the spore layer develops.

AZALEA LACEBUG

SYMPTOMS From midspring through summer, tan or white speckling appears on the top foliar surfaces of azaleas, especially evergreen types (*see p. 20*). It resembles leafhopper (*see p. 142*) or mite (*see p.147*) feeding damage. Severely damaged leaves may dry and drop off. Damage also appears under leaves, where large, sticky, brown to black droplets cover the surface. Small, dark spiny or lacy-winged insects can be present from spring through autumn.
CAUSE Nymph and adult azalea lacebugs (*Stephanitis pyrioides*), which suck the sap, and with it the chlorophyll, from azalea leaves. The mature azalea lacebug has many veins in its flat top surfaces, from the transparent, lacy wings to the lacy-veined wings with dark markings, and is less than ⅛in (3mm) long. The dark spiny nymphs feed, leaving black varnishlike droppings. The lacy-winged adult bugs may also be present and cause similar damage. Several generations can occur during the season, sometimes with both nymphs and adults present simultaneously.
CONTROL Some azaleas are resistant. Plants grown in full sun may suffer more than those in partial shade. Crush the insects by drawing a leaf between thumb and forefinger. Insects can be blasted off with a jet of water from a garden hose. Apply horticultural oil, insecticidal soap, or other labeled material to control active stages. Coverage under leaves is important.

AZALEA WHITEFLY

SYMPTOMS Tiny, white-winged insects readily fly up from the undersides of the leaves of evergreen azaleas during the summer. The immature nymphs are flat, oval, whitish green, scalelike creatures (*see p.172*) that live on the undersides of leaves. They are present for most of the year. Both adults and nymphs excrete a sugary substance called honeydew that makes the upper leaf surfaces sticky and on which dark sooty mold grows, spoiling the appearance of the foliage.

CAUSE A whitefly, *Pealius azaleae*, which feeds by sucking sap from the leaves of evergreen azaleas.

CONTROL Hairy-leaved varieties of azalea are most prone to infestation, so grow deciduous or smooth-leaved cultivars. Whiteflies can be blasted off with a directed jet of water from a hose. The adult stage, which is reached in midsummer, is more susceptible to insecticides than the eggs or nymphs. Spray the underside of the foliage thoroughly with insecticidal soap or another labeled insecticide. Horticultural oil can also be used against immature stages.

BACTERIAL CANKER

SYMPTOMS Clearly defined areas of bark flatten and sink inward (*see **p.35***). Amber-colored, resinlike ooze may appear, closely associated with injured bark. Only *Prunus* are commonly affected; symptoms are most obvious on cherry trees and far less so on plums. Buds at the tips of affected branches may fail to open. Leaves may appear but later wither and die back due to the ringing

effect produced by the expanding canker. Leaves on affected limbs are often yellowed and small in size. Foliage may develop shothole symptoms.

CAUSE The bacteria *Pseudomonas morsprunorum* (on plum and sweet cherry) and *P. syringae* (on plum, peach, apricot, and cherry). Most infections occur during wet, windy weather in autumn or in damp conditions in spring, when young stems and leaves are readily infected. Spring infections usually start on the leaves and then spread to the wood. Most wood infections occur through injured bark, such as that caused by pruning, frost crack, or leaf fall. Infection during summer is rare.

CONTROL Consider growing resistant cultivars. Prune out infected areas in summer. Spray infected trees with a copper-based fungicide, such as Bordeaux mixture. Sprays should be applied once at the end of summer, once in early autumn, and once in midautumn.

BACTERIAL FASCIATION

SYMPTOMS Numerous small, bunched, often somewhat distorted, thickened, or flattened, fanlike (fasciated) groups of leaves develop around stem bases. The plant may also produce perfectly normal growth.

CAUSE The bacterium *Corynebacterium fascians*, which is soilborne and enters through wounded plant tissue.

CONTROL Remove and dispose of affected plants, together with the soil or soil mix in which they are growing. Avoid spreading the bacteria by washing hands and tools after handling infected plants. Thoroughly scrub pots, trays, and greenhouse staging.

• *see also* FASCIATION *p.128.*

BACTERIAL LEAF SCORCH OF OAK

SYMPTOMS In late spring and summer, oak leaves turn a dull green and start yellowing at the tips and margins, moving inward between veins. A reddish brown band occurs between green and chlorotic tissue. Especially after a period of water shortage compounded by high temperature or high winds, the damaged areas turn dry and brown, and the leaves may roll inward. Symptoms are worse by late summer. Branchfuls of foliage or the entire tree will be wilted and stunted. The oak loses vigor and produces fewer acorns. There may be some branch wilting, stunting, and dieback the first year, affecting from an upper or outer branch to a larger section of the crown. On an individual branch, the disease progresses from the oldest, basal leaves toward the tip. All the leaves and shoots can die, but they will stay attached to the branch until autumn. More branches will succumb in successive seasons, usually followed by complete loss of the oak. Pin, red, and scarlet oaks are the most frequently affected. The symptoms generally resemble those of oak wilt (*see p.152*) but on a much longer time scale.

CAUSE Bacterial leaf scorch of oak, caused by *Xylella fastidiosa*. Living in, moving through, and multiplying only in the xylem, it interferes with a tree's water circulation and possibly spreads toxins. It is probably spread from tree to tree by leafhoppers and spittlebugs that feed on xylem. Oak leaf scorch primarily occurs in regions with moderate winters, and symptoms are enhanced by hot, dry weather, especially drought. Predisposing factors include potassium deficiency,

shallow soil, girdling roots, and root disease.

CONTROL Use all cultural techniques to help oaks avoid or withstand water stress. Do not plant them near a source of excessive reflected heat, such as pavement or a building. Fertilize, mulch well, and water deeply.

BACTERIAL LEAF SPOT

See LEAF SPOT (BACTERIAL) *p.143.*

BACTERIAL SOFT ROT

SYMPTOMS Roots, tubers, rhizomes, fruits, and the dense heads of brassicas are generally the most susceptible areas of host plants. Discolored areas develop, and, as the tissue beneath deteriorates (usually quickly), the injured area may sink inward. Infection usually spreads rapidly and can prove fatal or seriously damaging. This disease is usually accompanied by a foul smell.

CAUSE Various bacteria, most commonly *Erwinia atroseptica* and *E. carotovora*. They usually enter through wounds and are easily spread on pruning tools, by handling, or by insects and other animals.

CONTROL Control is rarely possible, since the infection spreads so rapidly. It may, however, be possible to limit the damage by promptly removing infected areas together with the adjacent tissue. Disinfect pruning tools. Avoid initial injury, where possible.

BAGWORM

SYMPTOMS Leaves show ragged holes or chewing damage after leafing out in spring; eventually, only the main veins are left. Conifers show increased thinning. Branches or an entire tree may be defoliated, which will kill an evergreen or stunt a deciduous tree. Cases made of bits of twigs and foliage may be observed hanging from leaves, twigs, or branches in late summer. Almost any tree or shrub, evergreen or deciduous, including arborvitae, juniper, elm, boxelder, birch, and willow, can be a host. **CAUSE** The bagworm (*Thyridopteryx ephemeraeformis*), which is the case-building caterpillar of a short-lived moth. The larva begins to feed immediately upon hatching about midspring. The bag is carrot shaped and 1–3in (2.5–7.5cm) long, consisting of plant fragments woven together with silk. The caterpillar lives in the bag and carries it around, only partly emerging when feeding branch by branch. In late summer, it attaches the bag with a band of silk to pupate. **CONTROL** Natural enemies provide some control, and pheromone traps catch male moths. Handpick and destroy the bags by late winter, before the eggs hatch. Be sure to remove the silk band, which might girdle and kill the twig or branch. Young bagworms can be killed by Btk *(see p.110)*, insecticidal soap, or another labeled product.

BALSAM TWIG APHID

SYMPTOMS On balsam, Siberian, Fraser, and alpine fir and on white and Colorado blue spruce, needles bend and twist upward and drop prematurely. Severely affected shoots may die. Bark is roughened. Since succulent new growth is the main object of attack, the worst damage occurs in late spring and early summer. Through summer, though, clusters of aphids and white, powdery material may be seen on shoots, which

become so saturated with shiny honeydew that the needles stick to one another. Black sooty mold may grow on the honeydew. **CAUSE** Nymph and adult balsam twig aphids (*Mindarus abietinus*), which are greenish to bluish gray under a waxy, white covering and ⅛in (3mm) long. **CONTROL** Maintain the health of all firs and spruces. Avoid overfertilizing with nitrogen. Check susceptible trees by tapping branches over a white board or inspecting foliage for the aphids or distortion. Knock aphids off the shoots with hard blasts of water. Natural enemies, such as ladybugs and syrphid fly larvae, may be present. Damaged areas can be trimmed off. Horticultural oil or another insecticide applied immediately before budbreak can provide some control if damage was significant the previous year. Superior oil can be applied before eggs hatch as a dormant oil or during the aphids' season of activity.

BALSAM WOOLLY ADELGID

SYMPTOMS The smaller stems on firs develop swollen, lumpy growths at the ends of twigs where small black insects covered with white, waxy material are feeding. Trunks may be covered with a white, powdery substance in heavy infestations, and trees may stop growing. Tops may grow crookedly or horizontally, and new growth may be stunted or drooping. **CAUSE** A sap-feeding insect, *Adelges piceae*, which is active between late spring and autumn. Two or 3 generations may occur annually. **CONTROL** Noble fir is less prone to injury. Natural enemies help keep this pest in check. Water trees to

minimize drought stress, which can increase injury. Smaller specimens can be treated with insecticidal soap. Good coverage of bark and twigs is essential.

BARK BEETLES

SYMPTOMS Tunnels appear in the bark and sapwood of a wide variety of woody plants, especially those that are diseased or dead, but also some that are healthy or newly transplanted *(see p.33)*. Sawdustlike material, masses of pitch, shotholes, or toothpicklike projections may be evident. Affected trees may have yellowing, flagging branches or show serious dieback in crowns. **CAUSE** Many species of bark beetle, which attack conifers and deciduous or evergreen trees and shrubs. Among the most notorious is the European elm bark beetle (*Scolytus multistriatus, see p.127*), which carries spores of the fungal pathogen that causes Dutch elm disease *(see p.124)*. Beetles are about ⅛–⅛in (3.5–4.5mm) long and dark reddish brown. The tunneling pattern is often characteristic of a particular species of beetle; it consists of a maternal tunnel, in which eggs are laid, and larval channels, which radiate away from the original tunnel. Grubs pupate at the ends of the tunnels, and adults chew their way out, leaving small holes in the bark. The black turpentine beetle (*Dendroctonus terebrans*) is a common pest of landscape pines and spruces, leaving obvious "pitch tubes" at entrances to its galleries.

LENGTH: ⅛–⅛IN (3.5–4.5MM)

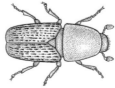

ADULT BARK BEETLE

CONTROL Keep plants as healthy as possible, with minimal drought, compaction, or other stress. Affected branches and dying trees should be promptly pruned, removed, or destroyed. In some cases, removing bark will eliminate breeding sites if felled trees cannot be removed. Bark sprays are sometimes effective if well timed before infestation but may require the services of a professional applicator. Pheromones are available for monitoring certain species. Insecticides are not generally effective once beetles have entered the tree.

BARK SCALDING

SYMPTOMS The bark on a young tree's trunk or larger limbs has bleached, dried-out patches, especially on the side most exposed to the sun. The areas may crack and curl up. Small trees or recently transplanted ones may die. **CAUSE** The sun can scald bark in any season: in summer, the sun is most intense; in winter, the bark sublayers have little moisture to withstand the sun's effects. Bark that is young or otherwise thin is most vulnerable to being killed. **CONTROL** Protect the trunk and vulnerable main branches with trunk wrap throughout the year. This provides the added benefit of a barrier against a host of other possible insults, from insect boring and pathogen infection to damage by rodents, birds, dogs, and lawnmowers. The wrap should be kept on for a few years, perhaps rewrapped as the tree's diameter increases, until the tree is established.

BARK SPLITTING

SYMPTOMS The bark on a tree's or shrub's trunk or any size of branch or twig starts

to split, usually longitudinally but sometimes radially (from a point). Further damage, often caused by secondary insect and disease factors, may include bark peeling and shedding, cankers and branch dieback, damaged sapwood, and tree death.
CAUSE During a spell of large fluctuations in temperature, frost can crack bark that has not completely matured. This typically occurs in late autumn to early winter after rains cause an unseasonal growth spurt. Sometimes spring-acclimated wood is damaged by a very hard late frost. Such cracks usually heal during warm months, but not always completely, and they may reopen the next winter. Bark scalding (see p.104) can kill patches of inner bark, which dry and then crack. Summer drought or winter desiccation can cause cracks deep into the sapwood of a young tree.
CONTROL Plant only trees and shrubs adapted to your climate. Wrap the trunks and major branches of young trees and transplants. Keep all trees adequately watered through dry periods and provide good drainage. Increase vigor and growth by fertilizing, but not late in the season. Always avoid injuring a tree. Injured bark can be neatly trimmed to promote callus formation and healing. A professional arborist may be able to save a badly damaged limb or tree by taking radical steps such as gradually closing the crack with long, bolted rods.

BASAL ROT
See FOOT AND ROOT ROTS p.130.

BEAN AND PEA WEEVILS
SYMPTOMS Holes (from which adult beetles have emerged) are seen in dry beans and peas kept for seed (see

p.51). While the beetle grub is present within the seed, a pale circular patch on the seed coat indicates where it has eaten a cavity in the seed's cotyledon.
CAUSE Several species of seed beetle, up to ⅛in (3mm) long, can attack pea and bean seeds. Pea weevil (*Bruchus pisorum*) attacks young green peas. Adults emerge when seed is later stored. Bean weevil (*Acanthoscelides obtectus*) attacks beans in the garden but may also continue to reproduce in stored seed, unlike other species.

ACTUAL SIZE ●

BEAN AND PEA WEEVIL

CONTROL Feeding damage by the larvae is to the seed's food reserve (the cotyledons) rather than the embryo, so infested seeds can still germinate. Seeds kept for later use can be stored at very low temperature (34°F/1°C) to prevent weevils from developing. Carefully heating seed to 131°F (55°C) for 1 hour will kill weevils inside but still allow germination. Store seed in airtight containers.

BEAN ANTHRACNOSE
SYMPTOMS Sunken, longitudinal brown marks develop on the stems of affected beans. Leaf veins may develop a red coloration and may subsequently turn brown, wither, and die off. A reddish brown spotting develops on infected pods, and a pink, slimy fungal growth may develop during wet weather.
CAUSE The fungus *Colletotrichum lindemuthianum*, which is usually seedborne. The fungal spores are spread by

rain or irrigation splash from young infected seedlings onto adjacent plants.
CONTROL Remove infected plants promptly, and do not save their seed. Grow resistant cultivars. Chemical control is rarely justified.

BEAN APHID
SYMPTOMS Dense colonies of tiny black insects mass on the shoot tips and undersides of leaves (see **p.32**) of lettuce, celery, spinach, pepper, broad and lima bean, English ivy, tulip, nasturtium, carnation, and other plants in summer. Affected plants are weakened, foliage may turn yellow, and bean amd other legume pods fail to develop. The same pest may occur on its overwintering hosts, including euonymus, viburnum, and mock orange (*Philadelphus*).
CAUSE The bean aphid (*Aphis fabae*).
CONTROL Inspect susceptible plants at regular intervals. Infestations on euonymus generally disappear by late spring. Aphids can be dislodged with a directed spray of water. Natural enemies also feed on bean aphids and provide some control. Insecticidal soap or another labeled material can be use for persistent populations.

BEAN HALO BLIGHT
SYMPTOMS Small, angular spots appear on the leaves of green or runner beans, at first appearing water-soaked and then darkening, each one surrounded by a bright yellow halo. Leaves then develop yellowing between the veins; the entire affected leaf may turn yellow and die. Growth is affected and yields are reduced.
If pods or stems become infected, they develop gray, apparently water-soaked patches.

CAUSE The bacterium *Pseudomonas phaseolica*, which attacks green and runner beans. Water splash spreads the bacteria. Initial infection usually starts from infected seed.
CONTROL Pick off affected leaves promptly, and avoid overhead watering. Remove and discard all affected plants at the end of the season, discarding their seed.

BEAUVERIA BASSIANA
This insect-pathogenic fungus naturally occurs on plants and in lawn and garden soil and attacks over 70 insect species. Also known as white muscardine after the white, cottony fungal growth covering the infected insect, *Beauveria bassiana* is commercially available and is used to control whiteflies, aphids, Colorado potato beetles, Mexican bean beetles, and others. Affected caterpillars, such as the European corn borer and sod webworms, may turn noticeably pink before the white growth envelops them. Minimizing the use of fungicides and some herbicides tends to favor this pathogen, especially under the right conditions: warm, humid weather and plentiful hosts.

BEECH APHIDS
SYMPTOMS Pale yellow or bluish insects covered with a fluffy, white waxy material (see **p.32**) form dense colonies on the twigs, shoot tips, and undersides of beech leaves from late spring to midsummer or autumn. The foliage and twigs become sticky with the aphids' sugary honeydew, encouraging the growth of sooty molds.
CAUSE Sap-feeding aphids, woolly beech leaf aphid (*Phyllaphis fagi*), and beech blight aphid

(*Grylloprociphilus imbricator*), which are specific pests of beech trees. Woolly beech leaf aphid lives under leaves and on shoots. Beech blight aphid feeds on small twigs and branches, building to high numbers, and may cause dieback.

CONTROL Although woolly beech leaf aphid may be a locally important pest, infestations are rarely more than cosmetic. Beech blight aphids usually affect only a few branches. Colonies can be pruned off or dislodged with a blast of water. Spray with insecticidal soap, horticultural oil, or another labeled material. For infestations on large trees or high hedges, the services of an arborist may be needed.

BEECH SCALE

SYMPTOMS A white, waxy/powdery substance appears in crevices in the bark of beech trees, especially on the northern side of the trunk and larger branches (*see p.35*). Tiny orange insects live underneath the wax.

CAUSE The beech scale (*Cryptococcus fagisuga*). It has little direct effect on the tree, the greatest damage resulting from canker-causing fungi, which can invade bark attacked by the scale insects. The scale spreads by windblown crawler (nymph) stages in late summer.

CONTROL Horticultural oil, insecticidal soap, or another labeled insecticide control the scale and will likely reduce the risk of disease. Apply at the late dormant stage or in late summer.

BEES

See BURROWING BEES *p.111*; LEAF-CUTTING BEES *p.142*; NECTAR ROBBING *p.150*.

BEETLES

Including more than 250,000 species, over 40 percent of all named insects are beetles. They are characterized by their hard opaque forewings, and they are found almost everywhere insects live. Some beetles, such as ground beetles (*see p.134*), ladybugs (*see p.141*), and rove beetles (*see p.171*) are beneficial as predators of garden pests. A number of beetles attack various parts of plants.

Root damage: *see* BLACK VINE WEEVIL *p.107*; WHITE GRUBS *p.189*; WIREWORMS *p.191*.

Stem damage: *see* ASIAN LONGHORNED BEETLE *p.101*; BARK BEETLES *p.104*; BRONZE BIRCH BORER *p.110*; EUROPEAN ELM BARK BEETLE *p.127*; RASPBERRY CANE BORER *p.166*; SHOTHOLE BORERS *p.173*; TWO-LINED CHESTNUT BORER *p.185*.

Foliage damage: *see* ASIATIC GARDEN BEETLE *p.101*; ASPARAGUS BEETLE *p.101*; BLACK VINE WEEVIL *p.107*; BLISTER BEETLES *p.108*; COLORADO POTATO BEETLE *p.116*; CUCUMBER BEETLES *p.120*; FLEA BEETLES *p.129*; JAPANESE BEETLE *p.140*; LEAF WEEVILS *p.144*; LILY LEAF BEETLE *p.145*; MEXICAN BEAN BEETLE *p.146*; PEA LEAF WEEVIL *p.156*; SQUASH BEETLE *p.178*; VIBURNUM LEAF BEETLE *p.186*; WATERLILY LEAF BEETLE *p.188*.

Flower damage: *see* ASIATIC GARDEN BEETLE *p.101*; BLISTER BEETLES *p.108*; CUCUMBER BEETLES *p.120*; JAPANESE BEETLE *p.140*; POLLEN BEETLES *p.162*; ROSE CHAFER *p.169*.

Seed and fruit damage: *see* BEAN AND PEA WEEVILS *p.105*; NUT WEEVILS *p.151*; RASPBERRY FRUITWORM *p.166*.

Turf damage: *see* BLUEGRASS BILLBUG *p.108*; JAPANESE BEETLE *p.140*; ORIENTAL BEETLE *p.154*; ROSE CHAFER *p.169*.

BEGONIA POWDERY MILDEW

SYMPTOMS Grayish white, powdery fungal growth appears in distinct spots or patches on the upper leaf surface (*see p.23*). Leaves become either dry and brown or, more commonly with fleshy-leaved types, yellowed and soggy. Stems and flowers can be affected. Plants grown in the open are rarely infected.

CAUSE The fungus *Microsphaera begoniae*, which is encouraged by dry soil and high humidity.

CONTROL Unless the disease is noticed early, control is very difficult. Pick off affected leaves promptly. Keep plants adequately moist, and improve air circulation. Spray with a suitable fungicide.

BIRCH LEAFMINER

SYMPTOMS Birch leaves exhibit pale, blisterlike blotches that later turn dry and brown (*see p.19*). The damage is most apparent in late spring, when tender leaves may seem scorched or blighted. Repeated attacks can weaken a tree and make it susceptible to borers and other serious pests. Young transplants may be killed. Many birches are susceptible, especially gray birch (*Betula populifolia*).

CAUSE The birch leafminer (*Fenusa pusilla*), which is the larva of a sawfly. In spring, the larva burrows inside leaves to feed between the surfaces, making a blotchlike mine.

CONTROL Some species, such as river birch (*B. nigra*), are resistant. Maintain vigor and health of trees. On smaller birches, pinch to crush each leafminer in its mine, or prune or pick off and destroy infested leaves.

Adults can be monitored with yellow sticky traps. Later-season foliage makes ideal egg-laying sites, so reduce it. Rake up prematurely fallen leaves. For highly susceptible trees that suffer severe, repeated damage, insecticide application may be necessary. Soil-applied systemics are available.

BIRDS

SYMPTOMS Irregular holes and pits appear on ripening fruit (*see p.47*). Smaller fruits, such as strawberries, cherries, and currants, are eaten whole. Leaves (*see p.30*) and flowers (*see p.46*) may be shredded, and entire buds may be eaten. Seeds, especially of grass, are eaten. Disturbed soil may result from birds attempting to reach food items, including white grubs (*see p.58*).

CAUSE Various birds.

CONTROL Many birds are highly beneficial allies, and many gardeners welcome their presence and encourage them into their gardens by providing food, water, and shelter for nesting sites. If a problem: small trees and shrubs can be netted or grown in a large cage. Netting is the only certain way of deterring birds. Various scaring devices, such as scarecrows, humming tapes, glitter strips, and models of cats or birds of prey, are variably successful. An alternative is to place sticks in the soil and criss-cross the area to be protected with black thread, in which the birds are temporarily entangled. Encourage rapid germination and growth through the vulnerable seedling stage by sowing in warm soil and keeping the young plants watered in dry weather.

BITTER PIT

See APPLE BITTER PIT *p.99*.

BLACK CHERRY APHID

SYMPTOMS Leaves at the tips of shoots of sweet cherry become curled in late spring, and dense colonies of black aphids are visible on the leaf undersides (*see **p.24**). By midsummer, some of the affected leaves turn brown and dry up. Honeydew and sooty mold may be present. Young trees may be killed. Sour cherry is sometimes damaged, but injury is usually less severe. Japanese flowering cherries are rarely affected by black cherry aphid.
CAUSE A sap-feeding aphid, *Myzus cerasi*, which overwinters as eggs on cherry trees
CONTROL Damaged terminals or foliage can be pruned or removed. Spray horticultural oil to kill overwintering eggs. Insecticide sprays just before bloom or after petal fall controls aphids on foliage. Look for aphids on new growth and treat before leaf curling becomes extensive.

BLACK LEG OF CUTTINGS

SYMPTOMS Before or shortly after roots start to form, the base of an infected cutting darkens and atrophies, and the upper parts start to discolor and then die off.
CAUSE Various soil- and waterborne fungi, particularly those that cause damping off (*see p.122*) in seedlings.
CONTROL Use only clean or sterilized rooting media, tools, and water. Take cuttings only from healthy plants, with tools dipped in a 10 percent bleach solution between cuts. As a preventive, treat cuttings with a rooting powder containing a fungicide.

BLACK VINE WEEVIL

SYMPTOMS/CAUSE Both the larval and adult stages of *Otiorhynchus sulcatus* cause damage. The larvae are plump, creamy white, legless grubs with brown heads. They are about ⅜in (1cm) long and have C-shaped bodies. They live in the soil (*see p.53*) and feed on roots and the crown of many perennial herbaceous and weedy plants, which are either severed or have the outer bark removed. Severely damaged plants make slow growth, followed by wilting and death. The grubs also bore into the crowns, tubers, and corms of plants such as begonia, astilbe, and cyclamen. A wide range of garden and indoor plants is attacked; plants grown in pots or other containers are particularly at risk. Larval damage is mostly seen between early autumn and midspring. The adult weevils are ⅓in (9mm) long, pear-shaped and dull black, with pale tan hairs in spots. They are slow-moving, flightless beetles that emerge at night and eat irregular notches from the leaf margins of many plants (*see p.29*), especially rhododendrons, yew, *Euonymus japonica*, and hydrangea. The adults can be found at any time from spring to autumn.

LENGTH: ⅓IN (9MM)

BLACK VINE WEEVIL

CONTROL Remove infested plants from pots and inspect the root and crown areas for larvae. Adult weevils can be searched for by flashlight at night and removed from plants. The larvae difficult to control. Under conditions of adequate temperature and moisture, there has been some success with drenching beneficial nematodes, such as *Heterorhabditis bacteriophora* and *Steinernema carpocapsae*, into the soil of container-grown plants. Nematodes should be watered into the soil or soil mix in late summer, while the soil is warm and moist, but before the grubs have grown large enough to cause serious damage. Nematodes are ineffective in heavy soils or those that are dry or colder than 57°F (14°C). The leaf damage caused by the adults is rarely sufficient to affect plant growth but may be an esthetic concern. Foliage insecticides may be used on this pest. Repeat applications may be needed to control late-emerging adults. Evening applications are best.

BLASTING

See BLINDNESS OF BULBS *below*.

BLEEDING CANKER

SYMPTOMS Yellow or brown ooze bleeds from patches of dead or dying bark on the trunks or large limbs of trees. The ooze may dry on the bark, leaving crusty deposits. Affected bark often cracks, allowing other decay organisms to enter. Stems completely ringed by the lesions will die back. Horse chestnuts, lindens, birches, and apple trees are particularly prone to attack.
CAUSE Various species of the fungus *Phytophthora* (*see p.159*).
CONTROL There is no cure for this disease. An inspection should be made by an experienced arborist to determine the tree's health, and measures taken to maintain it.

BLINDNESS OF BULBS

SYMPTOMS Bulbs produce healthy, normal foliage, but they fail to flower. Either no buds are formed at all, or buds form but are dry and virtually empty (*see p.41*) or contain brown and shriveled flower parts.
CAUSE Occasionally due to bulb fly infestation (*see p.149*) or basal rot (on *Narcissus*), but more often due to cultural problems. An inadequate or irregular supply of moisture and nutrients causes bulbs to decline in size and fail to produce buds or a full complement of floral parts. Excessively crowded clumps, naturalized bulbs that are not fertilized, and bulbs growing in dry conditions are also likely to be affected. Daffodils are frequently affected, especially multiflowered or double-flowered forms.
CONTROL Divide and replant congested clumps into a fresh, well-fertilized site. Ensure an adequate supply of water during dry weather. Feed established clumps in the spring with a complete fertilizer. Do not tie up foliage, and do not cut off foliage for at least 6 weeks after flowering.

BLIND SHOOTS

SYMPTOMS Occasionally, flowering shoots of roses and other flowering shrubs develop normally but fail to produce a terminal flower bud (*see p.40*). The plant is otherwise healthy, and other shoots flower normally.
CAUSE Possibly a disorder, nutrient deficiency, or adverse weather conditions.
CONTROL Prune back the blind shoot to a strong bud or pair of buds. Normal flowering shoots should grow from these buds.

BLISTER BEETLES

SYMPTOMS Flowers *(see p.43)* and/or foliage *(see p.30)* of ornamentals and vegetables show chewing damage. Plants may be completely defoliated. Swarms of slender blackish or grayish, sometimes striped beetles may be present. Prominent among the many host flowers are calendula, China aster, chrysanthemum, dahlia, zinnia, Japanese anemone, and buttercup; many bulbs, such as amaryllis; and clematis. Frequently attacked food plants include beans, beets, chard, spinach, tomato, eggplant, sweet potato, and potato.
CAUSE Adult blister beetles (mostly *Epicauta* species), which are rapid defoliators in the garden, appearing suddenly en masse. The larvae, however, are generally beneficial feeders of grasshopper eggs. When disturbed, adults may drop off plants or exude a material that can blister the skin, so they should not be handled.
CONTROL In midsummer, protect plants with screening or floating rowcover. Knock beetles off plants into soapy water or crush them on the ground – avoid touching them to avoid the irritatingt material, or wear disposable gloves and hand pick .

BLOSSOM END ROT

SYMPTOMS A sunken patch develops at the blossom end of developing fruits. The base of the fruit becomes tough and leathery and darkens to brown or black. Not all clusters or fruits on a cluster will necessarily be spoiled. Tomatoes (especially those growing in containers) and occasionally sweet peppers are attacked.
CAUSE Dry soil, which prevents the plant from taking up sufficient calcium *(see* CALCIUM DEFICIENCY *p.112)*. The low calcium content of the fruits causes cells to collapse and discolor. This is encouraged by a very acidic growing medium.
CONTROL Ensure an adequate, regular supply of moisture at all times, especially on fast-growing and heavily yielding plants. Pick off affected fruits and improve your watering routine. Grow small-fruiting tomatoes.

BLOSSOM WILT

SYMPTOMS Blossoms wither and die shortly after appearing. Dead clusters remain on the tree. Infection may then spread to adjacent leaves, which wilt, turn brown, and die, remaining attached to the branch. Pinprick-size, raised, buff-colored fungal pustules develop on infected areas, and localized dieback may occur *(see p.41)*. *Malus*, *Pyrus*, and *Prunus*, including cherry, plum, apple, apricot, and peach, may be attacked, and sometimes *Amelanchier*.
CAUSE The fungus *Sclerotinia laxa* (on all except apple) and *S. laxa* f. *laxa* (on apple), which may overwinter as cankers on infected stems or as pustules on infected flowers or foliage. The spores are windborne; spread is most rapid during wet weather.
CONTROL Prune out infected flower clusters, preferably before the infection spreads to the foliage or into the spur. Just before flowering, spray with a suitable copper-based fungicide.

BLUEGRASS BILLBUG

SYMPTOMS From late spring to midsummer, bluegrass or perennial rye browns and dies in patches. Dead sections can expand and merge, and dead grass is easy to pull up. Individual bluegrass stems are hollowed out and contain a sawdustlike material, and later in summer the rhizomes and roots may be chewed.
CAUSE The bluegrass billbug (*Sphenophorus parvulus*). The adult is a ⅕–¼in (5–6.5mm) black beetle with a typical weevil-like snout. It is sometimes seen walking on sidewalks and driveways. Soon after emergence in spring, the female deposits eggs in holes it chews in host stems. The ¼–½in (6–13mm), brown-headed, white grub feeds there, hollowing out the plant stem down to the crown and roots. Damage resembles injury from other turf insects and pathogens but is set apart by the stem tunneling.
CONTROL Small patches of dead bluegrass can recover with billbug eradication and cultural care, but larger ones must be reseeded or resodded with a billbug-resistant bluegrass or ryegrass or mixtures. Provide good drainage. To help damaged turf recover and mask symptoms, provide adequate irrigation and moderate fertilization. *Heterorhabditis* nematodes can be drenched on a billbug-infested area to parasitize both adults and larvae. Larvae are generally well protected from pesticides, especially once they get down into plant roots. Several insecticides are available that control adults, timed in spring after they have emerged. Billbug adults are also susceptible to *Beauveria (see p.105)*, which sometimes provides natural control or can be applied like a residual insecticide.

BOLTING

SYMPTOMS Plants produce flowers and seeds prematurely, before the crop has developed fully *(see p.44)*. In onions, this results in smaller than normal bulbs.
CAUSE Various factors may be involved; they may include exposure to low temperatures at a certain growth stage (often induced by a cold, late onset of spring), which then induces flowering, or by excessively dry soil conditions, premature heat, or transplanting too late.
CONTROL Avoid growing early varieties of susceptible crops, since they are usually more prone to the problem. Grow resistant cultivars.

BORON DEFICIENCY

SYMPTOMS Symptoms vary with the crop affected. Beet, turnip, and rutabaga develop cankers and internal brown rot; carrot and radish split. Cauliflower, cabbage, celery, pears, and strawberries occasionally develop symptoms, including leaf distortion, rough stems and leaf stalks, distorted and stunted heads and fruits, and shoot dieback.
CAUSE This disorder may occur if the soil has been limed excessively or if it is allowed to become very dry. Boron is readily leached out of the soil, so heavy rainfall encourage this deficiency on light soils.
CONTROL For vegetables, apply about 1¼oz (35g) of borax per 200 sq ft (20 sq m) before sowing or planting (mix borax with horticultural sand to make even application easier). For pear trees, spray at petal fall with 2½oz (70g) of borax in 6 gallons (22 liters) of water, together with a wetting agent.

BOTRYTIS

See GRAY MOLD *p.133*.

BOTTOM ROT

SYMPTOMS On lettuce or cabbage – or almost any plant whose foliage rests on the ground – the lowest leaves show sunken brown spots, which expand and merge. On lettuce they spread from the midrib, rotting the entire head into a slimy, dripping mass. A grayish brown, fuzzy growth may appear.
CAUSE *Rhizoctonia*, a soil-dwelling fungus that causes diseases from seed decay and damping off to storage rots, as well as bottom rot. *R. solani* generally invades roots and underground parts of stems, but in many vegetables, ornamentals, and other plants, it enters where bottom leaves are in contact with the soil. Wet weather, high humidity, and high temperature promote the fungus, as does a high salt level in the soil. From the leaves and petioles, the rot spreads upward. The grayish fuzzy growth (mycelial mat) represents a later stage in the fungal life cycle.
CONTROL Plant resistant cultivars or those whose leaves are held up from the ground, such as cos lettuce. Rotate with immune crops such as onions and corn. Work in plenty of organic matter to improve soil drainage, and plant in raised beds. Increase air circulation by proper thinning. Remove infected leaves or entire plants. Apply fungicide to the soil.

BOXWOOD LEAFMINER

SYMPTOMS In late spring, boxwood leaves show yellow or brown flecks on the top surface, with corresponding yellow or watersoaked spots beneath. By midsummer, these spots swell into oval blisters or blotches, the leaf becoming yellow-green and puckered. Affected leaves may die and drop prematurely, causing twigs to die back and the shrub to weaken. New growth is stunted.
If symptoms persist longer than a year, the feeding damage creates a rangy, ragged look, and a young shrub may be seriously hurt.
CAUSE The boxwood leafminer (*Monarthropalpus flavus*). It is a midge (fly) larva, a yellowish white to orange maggot reaching only ⅛in (3mm) after its nearly year-long feeding and development within boxwood leaves. The young larvae overwinter in the leaves, resuming feeding between the leaf surfaces in spring. In the early mornings of midspring, newly emerged midges swarm around boxwoods, mating and laying eggs. These yellow-orange flies resemble minuscule, wispy mosquitoes.
CONTROL Some English boxwoods (including 'Pendula' and 'Suffruticosa') are rarely damaged. Larvae can be crushed in the mines, or individual leaves can be removed and destroyed in low-level infestations. Keep new growth cut back in spring to reduce the number of possible egg-laying sites. Contact insecticides can be applied in midspring. Systemic materials can be used later in summer when mines appear.

BOXWOOD PSYLLID

SYMPTOMS Boxwood shoots are stunted, with closely spaced, cupped leaves that resemble cabbages (*see p.26*). Droplets of liquid with a white, waxy coating can be tipped out of the damaged shoots during late spring.
CAUSE The immature nymphs of a sap-feeding insect, *Cacopsylla buxi*, which attack the new growth in spring. The nymphs are flattened, tiny, pale green insects. Winged adults are present in midsummer, but they do not affect the plant's growth.
CONTROL If the boxwood plant has grown to the desired height and is being clipped to keep it in shape, something that restricts shoot extension is not really a problem. Even on untrimmed shrubs, the injury rarely is of aesthetic concern. Dormant applications of horticultural oil have provided good control of the overwintering eggs. Other insecticides can be applied in mid- to late May before leaves cup.

BRACKET FUNGI

SYMPTOMS Variously colored shelflike fungal outgrowths develop on large limbs or the main trunk of affected trees (*see pp.37, 38, 39*). They may appear throughout the tree but are most common on the trunk, particularly toward the base. Some may be found growing from the buttress roots or even attached to roots at some distance from the trunk. Some are annual, but most are perennial and quite woody in texture once mature. Most have a tough leathery or woody upper surface, with spores being produced from pores on the undersurface. Fungal sheets (mycelia) may be visible among the decaying parts. Most bracket fungi cause damage to trees, usually as extensive deterioration of the structural woody tissues. Infected trees often become dangerous because they are weakened structurally, and they may suffer wind snap or wind throw.
CAUSE Various fungi.
CONTROL Precise identification is essential, combined with examination of the tree and consideration of its environment. Because infected trees may be hazardous, employ an arborist to determine the extent of decay and overall health of the tree. Removal of the fungal brackets may limit spread but will not cure the problem, since the deterioration continues within the tree.

BRACONID WASPS

The 2,000 species of braconid wasp are nearly all beneficial, parasitizing pest caterpillars, aphids, and insect eggs, among others. They are harmless to humans, spiders, and plants. Their long ovipositors (egg-laying organs) resemble needlelike stingers, although these wasps do not sting. Most are brown or black. Common hosts include armyworms, codling moths, cutworms, pine shoot moths, tent caterpillars, and beetle larvae, such as that of the elm bark beetle. Some target larvae of flies, such as leafminer or fruit flies. Certain braconids specialize in aphids, such as the economically important green peach aphid; parasitized aphid "mummies" resemble tiny sesame seeds. While certain braconid species can be purchased, native wasps are readily attracted to, and sustained by, a season-long nectar source provided by flowering plants, including dill, parsley, lemon balm, yarrow, and Queen Anne's lace. Like most other beneficial insects, braconids are deterred or eliminated by pesticides. Carefully monitor yellow or red sticky traps to determine the presence of braconids, and then immediately discontinue any spraying program. Never destroy a pest caterpillar bearing cocoons (see *p.62*), whose occupants will do far more overall good than your handpicking the caterpillar.

BRASSICA WIRE STEM

SYMPTOMS Leaves on brassica seedlings, especially those of cauliflower and broccoli, become yellowed and narrowed or may die back.
CAUSE A deficiency of molybdenum, which is most common in acidic soils.
CONTROL Lime the soil to reduce acidity, and water affected plants or seed rows with sodium molybdate.

BROAD MITES

See TARSONEMID MITES *p.180.*

BRONZE BIRCH BORER

SYMPTOMS The foliage of birch trees is sparse and yellow or brown, but not dropping, and dieback may be present. Branch or nearby trunk bark has swollen, twisting ridges. Oval or D-shaped, ⅛in (3mm) holes are present among the ridges. Cutting into the ridges reveals tunnels full of sawdustlike material.
A newly transplanted, young, or weak tree may be girdled and killed. A more robust tree suffers only upper branch loss. Repeated attacks may result in loss of large limbs, and the tree may die. The European white birch (*Betula pendula*) is most susceptible; the paper (or canoe or white) birch (*B. papyrifera*) is less so.
CAUSE The bronze birch

borer (*Agrilus anxius*), which is the whitish grub of a metallic wood-boring beetle. Hatching in early to midsummer, the grub bores through bark and chews flat, irregularly winding feeding tunnels (galleries) in the area between the outer wood and the inner bark. Galleries can damage the tree by girdling the trunk or limbs.
CONTROL Avoid planting susceptible birch species. 'Heritage' and 'Whitespire' birches are resistant clones. Brown-barked species tend to be less susceptible than white-barked ones. Plant species suited to your local climate and maintain vigorous growth; avoid drought and other stresses. For the first few years after transplanting a susceptible tree, wrap the trunk and larger limbs, which may deter borers as well as prevent other damage. Enhance vigor by good fertilization, and water deeply during dry spells. Neatly trim branch stubs. Immediately treat all bark wounds, holes, and surgical incisions with antimicrobial tree-wound dressing.
A flexible wire inserted into bleeding areas may kill a grub in its hole. In winter or before the adults' emergence, prune and discard heavily infested branches. A young tree may need to be completely removed. A residual insecticide sprayed onto the bark applied around early to mid-June can help deter damage. Systemic insecticides are also available but must be applied by professionals.

BROWN ROT

SYMPTOMS A soft, brown area develops on the skin of tree fruits (see *p.47*) and in the flesh beneath when it starts

to deteriorate. The whole fruit is ultimately affected. Raised, creamy white pustules appear on the rotted areas in roughly concentric rings (see *p.49*). Infected fruits either fall off the tree or may become "mummified" and dry and remain attached to the branches. Most tree fruits can be affected, especially apple, pear, plum, peach, and nectarine.
CAUSE The fungi *Sclerotinia fructigena* (on apples) and *S. laxa* (other plants), which gain entry through injured skin. Bird pecks, codling moth exit holes, frost crack, cracking due to irregular growth, and fungal scab infections are all common causes of the initial injury. The spores are readily spread by insects or birds, by rain splash, and by fruits coming into contact with a source of infection.
CONTROL Avoid or minimize possible causes of injury to fruits by taking appropriate control or preventive measures. Remove infected fruits promptly, as well as fallen ones, and dispose of them well away from the garden. Prune out all mummified fruits, together with a short section of the spur to which they are attached.

BROWN SOFT SCALE

SYMPTOMS Yellowish brown, flat, oval scales, up to ⅛–⅛in (3–4mm) long, occur on the underside of leaves and are often clustered along the larger leaf veins. Bay, citrus, ivy, ferns, *Ficus*, and *Schefflera* are often attacked, as well as a wide range of indoor and (in the southern US) outdoor plants. Brown soft scale excretes honey-dew, which fosters the growth of sooty mold.

CAUSE A sap-feeding insect, *Coccus hesperidum*, which breeds continually throughout the year on houseplants, in heated greenhouses, and outdoors in warm climates.
CONTROL In greenhouses in summer, a parasitic wasp, *Metaphycus helvolus*, can be introduced for biological control. *M. luteolus* and other parasitic wasps provide some natural control outdoors, and some ladybugs feed on this species. Heavily infested portions of plants can be pruned off. Horticultural oil can be used before budbreak. Insecticidal soap or another labeled insecticide can be applied when crawlers are present.

BT

A widespread, naturally occurring insecticide, *Bacillus thuringiensis* is a group of more than 35 kinds of bacteria, some of which are commercially produced for controlling butterfly and moth caterpillars (*B. t. kurstaki*, or Btk); fly, gnat, and mosquito larvae (*B. t. israelensis*, or Bti); and beetle larvae (*B. t. tenebrionis*, or Btt). Larvae that ingest Bt are killed by destruction of their digestive systems. This biorational insecticide is saprophytic in soil, living on dead material and sometimes on plants. It is completely harmless to plants, humans, pets, and all other animal life besides the larvae targeted. Be aware, however, that butterfly caterpillars are also susceptible to Bt, but its short residual activity and selective application usually minimize the issue. Although Bt occurs widely in soil, it rarely causes natural insect "epidemics" unless it becomes established in dense or stressed insect populations, mostly because the bacteria are destroyed by sunlight. To extend an application's effectiveness, apply in the evening and make several applications 3 or 4 days apart, starting when the insect eggs hatch or when larvae are very small. Thoroughly and evenly coat leaf and stem surfaces, since the material must be ingested to be effective.

BUD DROP

SYMPTOMS Buds form, usually to full size, but drop while still apparently healthy. The plant is otherwise healthy.
CAUSE A period of dry weather while the flower buds are forming. On very susceptible plants, such as camellia and rhododendron, just a few consecutive days of drought at the end of summer when the buds are forming are enough to do damage. Plants growing in containers are particularly vulnerable because the soil is more prone to drying out. Fertilizing too late in the growing season (after early summer) may also induce bud drop the following spring.
CONTROL Water thoroughly and regularly, and never let the soil or soil mix dry out completely. Apply a deep mulch around the root area. Feed no later than early to midsummer, and avoid excessive fertilizing.

BULB BLUE MOLD

SYMPTOMS Bulbs in storage are most likely to develop symptoms, but they may also occur while bulbs are in the ground. Reddish brown lesions develop on the side of the affected bulb or corm, and pink fungal bodies may subsequently develop

beneath the skin. A pale, bluish green fungal growth appears on top of the lesion as it increases in size (*see* **p.54**). On bulbous irises, this may be accompanied by rapid softening and rotting.
CAUSE Various species of *Penicillium* fungi. These fungi are encouraged by warm, moist storage conditions and poor air circulation. The fungus is believed to enter the bulbs while they are in the ground, but the symptoms develop only if storage conditions are unsuitable.
CONTROL Do not buy any damaged or obviously infected bulbs. Store bulbs only as long as necessary and in a cool but frost-free, well-ventilated spot.

BURROWING BEES

SYMPTOMS Small, conical heaps of fine soil appear in lawns or on bare soil during late spring and summer (*see* **p.58**). They are distinguished from ant nests by the hole at the top of the heap where the bee enters its nest. Each nest consists of a vertical shaft in the soil; this shaft has several side chambers that the bee stocks with nectar and pollen as food for its larvae.
CAUSE Many different species of solitary bees nest in gardens. Many common species belong to the genus *Andrena* and are active in late spring. Although all burrowing bees are solitary, with each female making her own nest, the nests may be clustered together, and the same piece of ground may be used by the bees in successive years. Squash bees (*Xenoglossa* and *Peponapis*) are found in and around gardens and are helpful pollinators of squash and related plants.

CONTROL Control measures are not necessary. Burrowing bees cause no real damage to lawns, and they are of benefit as pollinating insects for fruit trees and other plants. The females have stingers but lack aggressive instincts and do not attack humans.

CABBAGE APHID

SYMPTOMS Between midspring and midautumn, yellow patches appear on the foliage of brassicas, and the underside of these areas have dense colonies of whitish gray aphids (*see* **p.32**). During early summer, the aphids infest leaves developing at the shoot tips of young plants. These leaves become distorted and have a pale, mottled appearance. Heavy attacks can kill shoot tips, causing secondary buds to develop sideshoots, resulting in multiheaded plants.
CAUSE Sap-feeding insects, *Brevicoryne brassicae*, which sometimes also attack rutabaga, collards, kale, Brussels sprouts, and radish. Overwintering eggs or other stages are found on host plant debris.
CONTROL Light infestations can be dislodged with a blast of water. Inspect plants carefully; aphids sometimes are parasitized but superficially appear normal. Till under or compost overwintering debris and avoid planting near infested areas. Insecticidal soap can be applied.

CABBAGE BUTTERFLY

SYMPTOMS Holes are eaten in the leaves of brassicas and some ornamental plants,

such as nasturtium. Green velvety caterpillars with a pale yellow stripe down the back may be seen on damaged leaves. Black-green excrement pellets occur on plant parts and on soil.
CAUSE Cabbage butterfly larvae (*Pieris rapae*), officially called imported cabbageworm, are up to 1⅛in (3cm) long and feed mainly in the hearts of cabbages and many other brassicas. They sometimes are found resting on the upper surface of leaves over the midvein, but usually are detected by examining the undersides, where they often occur along the vein. There usually are 3–5 generations a year, with caterpillars occurring from spring to early autumn. One of the few butterfly pests (others are larvae of moths; *see* CABBAGE LOOPER, *p.112*; CUTWORMS, *p.121*), the white adults are common and easily recognized around their host plants.
CONTROL Wasps are important in regulating populations, and a few cabbage varieties have some resistance. Rowcovers can help protect early plantings. Check brassicas regularly from early summer to early autumn. Destroy host plant residues soon after harvest, and eliminate weeds, which serve as an alternate food source. Take control measures as soon as caterpillars are seen, for they are difficult to control once they have grown larger and have gone into the heart leaves. Handpick larvae on a few plants or in light infestations, or use Btk insecticide (*see* p.110) as needed. Insecticidal soap can provide control of young caterpillars, and several other insecticides are also available.

CABBAGE LOOPER

SYMPTOMS Throughout the growing season, the foliage of low-growing, succulent ornamentals and vegetables – especially brassicas – has large, usually irregular holes (*see p.30*). Older leaves generally show chewing damage first. Flower buds and flowers may be similarly chewed; lettuce and cabbage heads may be bored; tomatoes and other low-growing fruits and vegetables may be eaten. Masses of green or brown excrement pellets may be found between looser leaves or under single leaves. Green "inchworms" may be observed on damaged plants. Vegetables other than brassicas that are attacked include lettuce, celery, beets, peas, lima beans, potatoes, and tomatoes. Among ornamentals, dianthus, chrysanthemum, calendula, and geranium may be eaten.
CAUSE The cabbage looper (*Trichoplusia ni*), which is the ½–1½in (1.3–3.8cm) larva of a brownish moth. This caterpillar is pale green with lighter stripes, especially in younger stages. It has a characteristic "looping" habit, similar to that of inchworms, as it walks. Caterpillars feed for several weeks.
CONTROL Where loopers arrive early, rowcover can offer some protection until temperatures become too warm. Destroy weeds that may serve as alternate hosts. Handpick caterpillars carefully, inspecting under foliage. Destroy crop debris soon after harvest. Attract parasitic wasps and flies with nectar and pollen plants, such as dill, parsley, and sweet clover; do not disturb loopers that are carrying parasite eggs or cocoons. The spined soldier bug, as both nymph and adult, is notable among the general predators that feast on cabbage loopers.
Btk sprays (*see p.110*) work best on the smaller caterpillars. Pheromone traps are sometimes used to detect migration of the moths. Insecticidal soap provides come control. Neem and pyrethrin sprays can be used on small caterpillars.

CABBAGE MAGGOT

SYMPTOMS All brassicas and allied vegetables, such as turnip, rutabaga, and radish, are attacked. Some related ornamentals, including stocks, alyssum, and wallflowers, are sometimes damaged. Affected plants grow slowly and tend to wilt on sunny days. Brassicas seedlings are particularly vulnerable, especially shortly after transplanting.
CAUSE Maggots of a fly, *Delia radicum*, which has 3 or 4 generations from midspring to early autumn, hatching from eggs laid in the soil next to host plant roots. The white, legless maggots, up to ⅓in (9mm) in length, eat the finer roots until just a rotting stump is left. The maggots also tunnel into the swollen roots of radish, rutabaga, and turnip.
CONTROL Established plants usually tolerate cabbage maggot attacks; seedlings, root vegetables, and transplants need protection. Delay planting until after the overwintering adults have ceased flying. (In some areas, peak flight of the spring flies occurs near the full bloom of yellow rocket, a common weed.) Later plantings are sometimes less bothered. Floating rowcover, placed over young plants in early spring, provides protection. Be sure that ends are sealed to keep flies from entering. Destroy host weeds and crop residue. Keep plants well watered. Infestations can be reduced by placing squares or disks made of carpet padding, cardboard, or roofing felt, about 4in (10cm) in diameter, on the soil around the stems of transplants. The female flies deposit their eggs on the disks, instead of in the soil; they then dry up before hatching. A few insecticides are available that provide good control, applied to the soil at planting.

CACTUS CORKY SCAB

SYMPTOMS Buff to tan, corky brown markings develop on the skin and may become sunken (*see p.22*). Central areas often become gray or dark brown. Adjacent areas of the plant usually retain their normal green color. Cacti and many succulents can be affected, especially *Opuntia* and *Epiphyllum*.
CAUSE Unsuitable growing conditions, in particular excessively high humidity or light levels. Sometimes fungi may be involved.
CONTROL Improve growing conditions by improving ventilation to reduce humidity or moving the plant to a shadier position. Take care not to alter conditions too dramatically or rapidly.

CALCIUM DEFICIENCY

SYMPTOMS Symptoms vary according to the plant and plant part affected. The most common are apple bitter pit (*see p.99*) and blossom end rot (*see p.108*). Other symptoms may include browning of the internal tissues of Brussels sprouts and the heads of cabbage, cavity spot of carrots, stunting and blackening of central leaves on celery, tip burn of lettuce, and rolled leaves and spindly shoots on potato. On other plants, the most common symptom is poor growth of young shoots and leaves, often combined with some curling and shoot or leaf deterioration.
CAUSE A deficiency of calcium, either in the soil or soil mix, or because of an inadequate uptake of calcium due to a low moisture content of the soil. This disorder is most common on acidic soils or growing media.
CONTROL Ensure an adequate supply of moisture, and encourage soil moisture retention by mulching, where appropriate. Apply lime to acidic soils.

CAMELLIA GALL

SYMPTOMS Large, pale green swellings, often forked or handlike, develop in place of the leaves (*see p.26*). Each gall may measure up to 8in (20cm) in length. The surface soon becomes covered in a layer of spores, giving the gall a creamy white appearance. Small shriveled pieces of leaf may protrude from the tips of the galls. There are rarely more than 1 or 2 galls on a plant. The overall vigor and flowering of the camellia is not affected.
CAUSE The fungus *Exobasidium camelliae*, which seems to be encouraged by wet weather. The spores are probably spread by insects and by rain splash.
CONTROL Remove galls, preferably before the spore layer develops, and discard them.

CAMELLIA YELLOW MOTTLE

SYMPTOMS Irregular blotching and mottling of camellia leaves, with bright yellow or off-white markings (*see* ***p.22***). Occasionally whole branches may bear white or strongly chlorotic leaves. The overall vigor of the plant appears unaffected.
CAUSE A viruslike organism that occurs within the plant, so propagation should not be carried out using material from any part of a visibly infected plant.
CONTROL Prune out all affected stems.

CANKER

SYMPTOMS The precise symptoms of the various cankers (*see below*) vary with both the host plant and the causal organism. The bark is usually raised and often roughened and may split to reveal the tissues beneath. Ooze may develop around the cankered areas. As cankers enlarge, they often ring the infected stem, so growth above the canker deteriorates and die.
CAUSE Various fungal and bacterial organisms.
CONTROL Improve growing conditions. Remove affected areas and consider treating with an appropriate copper-based chemical.

• *see also* APPLE AND PEAR CANKER *p.99;* BACTERIAL CANKER *p.103;* BLEEDING CANKER *p.107;* CYTOSPORA CANKER AND BRANCH DIEBACK *p.122;* ENDOTHIA CANKER *p.126;* NECTRIA CANKER *p.150;* PHOMOPSIS CANKER *p.159;* POPLAR CANKER *p.162;* ROSE CANKER AND DIEBACK *p.169;* SEIRIDIUM CANKER *p.173.*

CANKERWORMS

SYMPTOMS From spring to early summer, trees and ornamental shrubs suffer chewing damage on young leaves and buds, only the midvein and other large veins being spared. Entire trees may be defoliated by late spring. Oak, linden, beech, apple, and elm are commonly attacked. Greenish, brownish, or black inchworms may be present on damaged foliage.
CAUSE The spring cankerworm (*Paleacrita vernata*) and the fall cankerworm (*Alsophila pometaria, (see **p.30**)* are widespread. The names refer approximately to the seasons when eggs are laid. Several other related species attack ornamentals but are usually of minor importance. Caterpillars of both species vary from pale greenish to brown or black, sometimes with pale lateral stripes, reaching about 1in (2.5cm) long. The caterpillars occasionally drop down a fine thread attached to a twig, waiting to be blown to another leaf or nearby tree.
CONTROL Thorough cultivation to 4in (10cm) under susceptible trees, especially *Malus*, will kill pupae directly or expose them to natural enemies, especially parasites, birds, and several pathogens. Sticky bands around the trunk spread on paper 6–8in (15–20cm) wide can be maintained during the periods of adult activity. Place them in early October for fall cankerworms and in February or March for spring cankerworms. Light or baited traps can catch emerging male moths. Check branches and under loose bark for egg masses. On small trees and shrubs with low-level infestations, caterpillars can be shaken off or removed by hand. Btk (*see p.110*), horticultural oil, neem-based insecticides, and other sprays also provide good control for cankerworms.

CARABID BEETLE

See GROUND BEETLES *p.134.*

CARROT RUST FLY

SYMPTOMS The roots of carrots and related plants, such as parsley, parsnip, and celery, are tunneled. Rusty brown lines appear on the outside of the taproots where tunnels close to the surface have collapsed (*see **p.51***). Damaged roots are susceptible to secondary rots, which can affect their storage during the winter.
CAUSE Larvae of carrot rust fly (*Psila rosae*), which has 2 or 3 generations between late spring and early autumn. The slender, creamy yellow maggots are up to ⅜in (9mm) long.
CONTROL Seedlings of carrots sown after late spring will miss the first generation of larvae; carrots harvested before late summer will miss the second generation. Growing susceptible plants on a fresh site under rowcover prevents female flies from laying eggs. Harvest all carrots in fall in blocks to prevent flies from entering holes left from selective harvesting, and till the soil to kill overwintering stages. Eliminate host weed relatives, such as wild carrot (Queen Anne's lace). Yellow sticky cards, placed above the plants, are used to detect the adult flies. Not planting carrots for a few years may be helpful for severe infestations. Some soil-applied insecticides are available for use at planting.

CASEBEARERS

SYMPTOMS At various times throughout the year, many deciduous and evergreen trees may show feeding damage, mined leaves, and small larvae protected in cases made of twigs, bark, and leaf or needle pieces. The precise set of symptoms depends on the host, the pest, and the time of year. For instance, small rectangular brown mines with projecting cigarlike cases are seen on elm, birch, apple, pecan, and other trees and shrubs. Heavy infestations can cause substantial defoliation, leaving plants appearing scorched and sometimes causing dieback or even death. Damage to fruit or nuts can occur.
CAUSE Most larvae of the casebearer moths (*Coleophora*), which make cases unique to their species. The mining larva, often light yellow-green, enters the leaf directly by hatching from the egg at its point of attachment. It feeds within the leaf for a few days, creating a small, winding mine, a spot, or an angular blotch between veins, then exits from the other side with its case. It continues feeding on new foliage throughout summer.
CONTROL Trees and shrubs can usually tolerate some damage. Hand removal or pruning off of the overwintering larvae in their cases may be practical for smaller shrubs or trees. Rake up leaves and fruits, especially ones that have fallen early. Rake up fallen nuts and destroy them. Casebearers have several natural parasites that help regulate their numbers. Birds are important predators. Btk (*see p.110*) or other insecticides may be needed for heavy infestations, timed when larvae are actively feeding.

CATERPILLARS

Caterpillars are the larval stage of butterflies, moths, and a few other insects such as sawflies. Their color, size, and degree of hairiness vary, but they generally have an elongate tubular body shape with a distinct head. Butterfly and moth larvae have 3 pairs of jointed legs at the head end and 2–5 pairs of clasping legs (prolegs) on the abdomen. Larvae of sawflies look similar but have more than 5 (usually 7) pairs of prolegs. Most pest species are moth and sawfly caterpillars and feed on leaves, sometimes in large groups under webbing. Others live in soil and feed on roots, bore into stems, feed inside leaves, or eat fruits and seeds.

CONTROL Many species and their eggs can be removed by hand, especially on small plants. Many caterpillars feed after dark and are easier to find by flashlight. Other treatments are the use of the biological control Btk (*see p.110*) for many butterfly and moth caterpillars, but it is most effective against sawfly caterpillars and younger larvae. Pyrethrum-based insecticides and other materials can be used.
For a complete listing of moths that damage garden plants, *see p.148*.
• *see also* SAWFLIES *p.172*.

CATS

Despite their value as pets, cats can be a nuisance in gardens. They soil flower borders and vegetable plots and may damage plants. Their urine can scorch foliage, and the bark of trees and shrubs is damaged when cats use them as scratching posts. Domestic as well as feral (untamed) cats present a significant threat to birds,

squirrels, and other wildlife the gardener may consider desirable.

CONTROL Commercial animal repellents often fail to give reliable long-term protection. Devices that emit ultrasonic sounds may encourage cats to go elsewhere, at least temporarily. Cats looking for toilet areas are attracted to loose, dry soil or mulch-covered flower beds. Close planting helps cover up the soil surface with vegetation, making it less accessible. Plastic or other trunk protectors can be wrapped around young tress susceptible to damage from extended clawing.

CAVITY DECAY

SYMPTOMS Once exposed to the elements and open to infection by fungal spores, damaged areas on trees soon (or sometime slowly) deteriorate and form a cavity. The decay may spread farther into the trunk or limb, which may result in dangerous structural damage.
CAUSE Initial injury may result from storm damage, poor pruning practices, or other physical injury.
CONTROL Prevent cavity formation wherever possible by treating storm as soon as possible after it occurs and by always using proper and hygienic pruning techniques. When cavities develop, the rotting wood should not be removed and the healthy wood exposed, in spite of what you may think is proper sanitation: removing the rotten wood and disturbing the healthy wood promotes the breaching of the barriers that trees form in response to injury, and more extensive rot then develops. Trees with cavities should be examined regularly to determine their condition

and safety. Consider consulting a professional arborist for advice.

CEDAR-APPLE RUST
See APPLE RUSTS *p.100*.

CENTIPEDES

Centipedes are animals with many flattened body segments, each of which has 1 pair of legs. This distinguishes them from the superficially similar millipedes, which have 2 pairs of legs per segment. Centipedes also have longer antennae on their heads and run away if disturbed. They are equipped with a pair of poison fangs and are predators of small soil-dwelling animals. They probably serve a beneficial role and are not pests. Their bite is not dangerous, although it may be painful.
LENGTH: 1–2⅓IN (2.5–6CM)

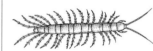

CENTIPEDE

CHINCH BUG

SYMPTOMS In early summer, grass wilts in small, yellow spots, which soon dry and turn brown or light gray and expand into large, irregular patches. Smaller grasses may quickly die, and in several days a whole lawn may be killed. Large-scale lawn damage may resemble that caused by white grubs, disease, and drought. Injury may be most severe in areas of heavy thatch in full sun during hot, dry weather. Inspecting the damaged roots and bases of stems and leaves will reveal the presence of tiny dark bugs, which may also gather on nearby concrete along the grass to bask in the sun. When crushed, they smell

bad, as may be obvious from simply walking across severely infested turf.
CAUSE Nymph and adult chinch bugs (*Blissus*), which have beaks to suck sap from grasses, at the same time injecting a poison. The common chinch bug (*B. leucopterus leucopterus*) and the hairy chinch bug (*B. leucopterus hirtus*) are well distributed. The western and southern chinch bugs (*B. occidus* and *B. insularis*, respectively) are regionally significant.
CONTROL Keep the area free of weeds and debris. Grow resistant cultivars. Remove excess thatch, and keep turf well watered during drought. Strengthen turfgrass with fertilizer. Chinch bugs have many natural enemies, including the fungus *Beauveria bassiana* (*see p.105*), favored by damp conditions; many birds; and other insects, such as parasitic wasps, lacewings, and ladybugs. If infestations are serious, turf can be treated with a commercially available *B. bassiana* preparation or an insecticide.

CHIPMUNKS

SYMPTOMS Corn, cucumber, squash, melon, or other large seeds are dug up, as are flower bulbs. Bulbs, nuts, or tubers may be eaten. Vegetables, flowers, and low-growing fruit, such as strawberries and tomatoes, are eaten. Burrow openings or raised tunnels may be in the vicinity.
CAUSE Chipmunks, which are small, terrestrial rodents that can invade gardens from their wide range of habitats. There are 16 western species of *Eutamias*. The eastern chipmunk (*Tamias striatus*), larger at 8–12in (20–30cm), is especially common in birch

and pine forests. Generally reddish brown, the chipmunk has dark and light stripes (black and yellow in the case of the eastern chipmunk) from its nose to the base of its tail.

CONTROL The chipmunk, like most rodents, is preyed on by a large number of carnivores. Scatter dog or cat hair as a defensive perimeter, or hang the hair in pouches near the ground. Individual plants or bulbs may be protected by cages, buried screen barriers, or hot pepper spray. Various small-animal live traps are available, but check local regulations regarding capture and release. Favored baits include peanut butter, rolled oats, and corn kernels.

CHLOROSIS

SYMPTOMS Plant tissue turns yellow, most commonly in leaves. The loss of the green pigment (chlorophyll) may allow other pigments, which are usually masked by the green, to show, so discoloration may develop.
CAUSE Many unrelated factors. Most common are deficiencies of iron and manganese (so-called lime-induced chlorosis), nitrogen, and magnesium. Water-logging, low temperatures, virus infection, or herbicide contamination may also be responsible. The precise patterning and distribution of the symptoms help determine the cause.
CONTROL Deal with any mineral deficiencies, sources of contamination, or cultural problems. It may take some time to correct the problem.

CHRYSANTHEMUM LEAFMINER

SYMPTOMS Twisting white or brown lines develop in the leaves of chrysanthemums

(*see p.25*), gerberas, marguerites, pyrethrum, and other related composite flowers as well as in those of artichoke, endive, and lettuce. If an infested leaf is held up to the light, a grub or pupa may be seen. Small, pale, raised round scars appear on the upper surface of leaves at shoot tips.
CAUSE Maggots of a leaf-mining fly, *Chromatomyia syngenesiae*, which has 2 generations during the summer on garden plants but can breed continually throughout the year in greenhouses. Several other related leafminers also attack chrysanthemums.
CONTROL Deal with light infestations by picking off mined leaves, or crush the grubs at the ends of their tunnels. Eliminate weedy alternate hosts. Beneficial nematodes, applied as a foliar spray, may provide control. Heavy infestations may need labeled insecticide application 2–3 times at 2-week intervals.

CHRYSANTHEMUM NEMATODE

SYMPTOMS Foliage on chrysanthemums, Japanese anemones, penstemons, and many other herbaceous plants has brown areas separated from green healthy parts by the leaf veins. Eventually, the entire leaf will turn brown or black. Damage progresses from the base of the plant upward
CAUSE Microscopic nematodes, *Aphelenchoides ritzemabosi*. Although present on suitable host plants all year, infestations develop most rapidly during damp weather in late summer and autumn.
CONTROL Destroy badly affected plants. Dormant

chrysanthemum crowns dipped in hot water will produce shoots for cuttings that are free of nematodes: the old stems are cut down and soil washed from the crown before immersing it for 5 minutes in water held at 115°F (46°C). The amount of heat is critical, since too much will damage the plant while too little will allow nematodes to survive.

CICADAS

SYMPTOMS In late spring and summer, fruit and shade trees show wilting of twigs and smaller branches, especially high up in the trees. Branches may die and break off. Severely affected young trees can die. Close examination of the bark near the point of a break shows "stitching" in the form of punctures or slits in lines or of irregular brown scars. A buzzing, slowly throbbing, droning sound may be very noticeable, and stout brown insect skins cling to tree trunks, fences, and other vertical surfaces.
CAUSE Cicadas (*Magicicada*), both the annual species that emerge every year and the legendary periodical cicadas that occur as adults in 13- or 17-year generations. The females lay eggs in twigs by slitting the bark; the nymphs hatch, fall to the ground, and burrow into the soil. There they pierce tree roots and feed on the sap, generally causing little damage. They remain underground until the next spring (annual) or 13 or 17 years later (periodical), emerge from the soil, crawl onto a vertical surface, and shed their nymphal skin to become adults. Adults, which are stocky and 1–2in (2.5–5cm) long, have large eyes and clear wings with

darker veins. Only males "sing," usually 2–3 days after emergence. Although damage is usually light, large broods, especially of the periodical cicadas, can inflict a great deal of damage, especially to young orchards and other trees.
CONTROL Before planting new trees, contact local experts to find out if a large brood is expected soon. If so, delay planting until after it emerges or egg-laying activity is done. Cover young trees during emergence and egg laying. When a large brood is expected, postpone extensive elective pruning. After egg laying, clean up the branch stubs in the tree. Birds eat many cicadas, and a large wasp, the cicada killer, catches them, paralyzes them, and lays its eggs on them.

CLEARWING BORERS

SYMPTOMS Near midsummer, some herbaceous and woody plants drop yellowed, browned, or reddened leaves prematurely. Trunks and lesser stems are tunneled, with fine sawdust expelled from holes, which sometimes ooze sap. Branches or twigs beyond a tunnel may eventually die back, affecting both the appearance and the overall vitality of the plant. Entire plants may die. Bark around bore holes may callus and swell with knotty, gall-like growths, or it may slough off. The tunnels may allow pathogens to establish stem cankers.
CAUSE The wood-tunneling caterpillars of clearwing moths. Most of the major pest species attack 1 or a few host species. Common species in the genus *Synanthedon* include the dogwood borer, which attacks flowering

dogwood and a few other trees; currant borer, which affects gooseberry and currant; and peachtree borer, which attacks peach, plum, and related fruit and ornamental plants. The genus *Melittia* has a few prominent species, including the squash vine borer (*M. cucurbitae*), a major pest of pumpkin and squash.

CONTROL Maintain plant vigor, avoiding drought stress or bark damage while the moths are active to reduce potential egg-laying sites. Trunk wraps or plastic protectors can help eliminate bark injury. Probe a hole with a wire to kill the larva within, or slit the stem to dig it out. If damage is close to the ground, mound soil up until the next spring to allow the wound to heal. Prune off and destroy tunneled growth. Consider removing a badly infested plant. Use screening to protect squash and pumpkin from egg-laying moths. Pheromone traps are sometimes used to monitor activity of clearwing borer moths and may trap enough moths to give good control. Apply superior oil to kill eggs. Residual insecticides may be needed.

• *see also* ASH (LILAC) BORER *p.100;* RHODODENDRON BORER *p.167;* SQUASH VINE BORER *p.178.*

CLEMATIS WILT

SYMPTOMS Leaves and shoots wilt and die back. Wilting usually starts at the shoot tips, leaf stalks blacken where they join the leaf blade, and young foliage wilts. New, healthy shoots may appear from below soil level beneath the wilted area. Discoloration may develop under the lowest pair of wilting leaves. Too much water, graft failure, and insect or slug damage may

also cause wilting, but in these cases clematis do not show the other symptoms.
CAUSE The fungus *Ascochyta clematidina*.
CONTROL Prune out affected stems, cutting back into healthy tissue and below soil level if necessary. Mildly infected plants may resprout.

CLICK BEETLE

See WIREWORMS, *p.191.*

CLUBROOT

SYMPTOMS Roots become swollen, and the entire root system may become distorted (*see p.55*). The foliage is pale, chlorotic, or pinkish and wilts readily, especially during hot weather. Plants fail completely or produce a poor crop. Most edible members of the cabbage family are attacked, and related ornamentals, including wallflowers, stocks, and candytuft.
CAUSE The slime mold *Plasmodiophora brassicae*, which is soilborne and can remain viable in the soil for more than 20 years. The pathogen is easily introduced into a garden on infected plants; on soil adhering to boots, tools, and wheelbarrows; and in soil, manure, or compost. Acidic and waterlogged soils are most prone to clubroot.
CONTROL Improve soil drainage, and lime the soil. Discard all infected plants promptly. Raise your own transplants, or buy plants from only a reputable source and check them carefully before planting. Raise plants in sterilized commercial soil mix in individual pots, and plant out when plenty of roots have formed. Grow resistant cultivars. Practice good weed control.

CODLING MOTH

SYMPTOMS In mid- to late summer, walnuts and pome or stone fruits are tunneled by small white caterpillars with brown heads (*see p.47*). By the time the fruit is ripe, the caterpillars have usually finished feeding. The caterpillar feeds in the core and makes an exit tunnel leading to either the blossom end or elsewhere on the fruit surface.
CAUSE Caterpillars of a small moth, *Cydia pomonella*. Codling moths begin to appear just after apple blossoms fall but may be delayed by cool weather.
CONTROL Folded burlap bands 6in (15cm) wide wrapped around the trunks can be used to trap caterpillars. They should be checked every 10 days and the caterpillars killed. Bands placed in autumn can trap the overwintering pupae. Destroy all fallen fruit promptly, and eliminate nearby host trees or their fruit. Pheromone traps may be useful for trapping the male moths and provide some control. Maintain 1 or 2 traps per tree for the duration of the season. Insecticides, including Btk (*see p.110*) (for larvae, before they enter fruit) and horticultural oil (for eggs), can be used, but timing will be more critical for those than for conventional materials.

COLLAR ROT

See PHYTOPHTHORA *p.159.*

COLORADO POTATO BEETLE

SYMPTOMS From spring, when the soil warms up, and on through the growing season, the leaves of tomato family members and cabbage show large, ragged holes

(*see p.32*), as do those of petunia and flowering tobacco (*Nicotiana*). The plant may rapidly become defoliated, and shoots and stems are also eaten. Stems of tomato transplants may be chewed, causing serious damage. Flowers may have holes chewed in them, or they are completely devoured. Holes may be eaten in green tomatoes or young eggplant; they dry into brown, callused pits. All parts are soiled with black excrement. Small plants suffer extensive damage, and younger ones may be killed. Yields of potatoes and other crops are not affected by moderate foliar destruction, but severe defoliation will drastically reduce yields.
CAUSE The larval and adult stages of the Colorado potato beetle (*Leptinotarsa decemlineata*). The creamy yellow to orangish adult has a hard, hemispherical shell with 5 black stripes. It starts eating young plants in spring, and the female starts laying oval, yellow-orange eggs on leaf undersides as soon as potato foliage opens up. The larva is dark red and matures to orange with a black head. Each side has 2 rows of black spots, and the legs are also black.

LENGTH: ⅜IN (1CM)

COLORADO POTATO BEETLE

CONTROL Alternate rows of potato and bush (green or snap) bean or other nonhost crops. Consider completely rotating out of the host plants for at least 1 year. Protect with floating rowcover until at least midsummer. Kill overwintering beetles by thoroughly tilling the bed in autumn. Starting in early spring, inspect plants and destroy eggs, larvae, and adults. Examine under leaves for egg masses; pick them off or crush them. If the problem is not very severe, handpick adults in the coolness of early morning when they are groggy, or shake each plant over a sheet. Both beetles and larvae can be knocked off into a pail of soapy water. Cut potatoes can be used to attract beetles when they emerge in spring; they then can be easily collected. Toads are excellent predators of Colorado potato beetles. Ladybugs, ground beetles, spined soldier bugs, and wasps are other prominent enemies. *Beauveria bassiana*, a natural insect fungal pathogen *(see p.105)*, kills some adults and larvae. Btt *(see p.110)* works well against the newly hatched larvae. Spray neem or pyrethrins. In some areas, the beetles are resistant to many conventional insecticides, although many still provide some control in most regions.

COLUMBINE LEAFMINERS

SYMPTOMS In spring, columbine leaves develop winding, white trails that start out narrow and become wider *(see **p.19**)*. At other times during the growing season, there may instead be a slowly expanding leaf blotch. Yellowing is possible, and leaves infrequently drop. Plant damage is usually cosmetic.
CAUSE Three closely related leafminers (*Phytomyza aquilegiana*, *P. aquilegivora*, and *P. columbinae*), which are collectively known as the

columbine leafminer complex. All are tiny, pale yellow-green maggots.
CONTROL Despite its appearance, leafminer damage on columbine is not usually severe enough to affect plant health. Floating rowcover protects plants. Yellow sticky cards can be used to detect and possibly trap out the flies; place several around the host plants. Inspect individual plants and remove leaves with larvae. Otherwise, pinch the leaves firmly to crush the maggots in their mines. After frost, destroy plant residues. Autumn cultivation exposes many larvae to the elements and birds. Leafminers are attacked by several parasites, including braconid wasps, that can be attracted with nectar-producing flowers. Sprays of beneficial nematodes have provided control of some leafminers. Several insecticides are available and can be applied when mines are first observed, repeating applications if necessary.

CONIFER WOOLLY APHIDS

See ADELGIDS *p.98*.

COOLEY SPRUCE GALL ADELGID

SYMPTOMS Small, fluffy white balls of waxy threads appear on the undersides of leaves on Douglas fir (*Pseudotsuga menziesii*) in summer *(see **p.38**)*. Heavy infestations may cause distortion and some yellowing of the foliage, which can also be discolored by the growth of sooty molds on the honeydew deposited by the pest.
CAUSE A tiny, blackish brown, aphidlike sap-feeding insect, *Adelges cooleyi*. It can be found on Douglas firs

throughout the year. It may also occur on its alternate host plants – Sitka spruce (*Picea sitchensis*), Colorado blue spruce (*P. pungens*), Engelmann spruce (*P. engelmannii*), and Oriental spruce (*P. orientalis*) – where it causes an elongate, swollen gall at the shoot tips. The gall eventually dries and opens, looking like a small brown "cone."
CONTROL Infestations on Douglas fir are not usually a serious threat to the plant. The spruce generation normally causes little damage, but the brown cones may be of cosmetic concern. Prune off and destroy spruce galls. Avoid planting alternate host spruces nearby and fertilizing infested Douglas fir or spruces. If necessary, insecticidal soap or another labeled insecticide easily controls this insect. Horticultural oil can be used on Douglas fir just before budbreak.

CORAL SPOT

SYMPTOMS Bright, coral to orange raised pustules appear on dead stems *(see **p.41**)*. The pustules appear after the stem has been dead for at least several weeks. Many different plants may be affected, but currants (*Ribes*), *Elaeagnus*, magnolias, and maples (*Acer*) are very susceptible. Dieback occurs, and if the infection spreads down into the crown, the whole plant may be killed.
CAUSE The fungus *Nectria cinnabarina*. Spores are produced all year, and water, either as rain or as irrigation splash, is the main method of dispersal. The fungus enters a plant through a wound or colonizes a dead snag left by physical injury or poor pruning.

CONTROL Prune out all dead or dying stems promptly, cutting well back into sound, healthy wood. Discard wood bearing the pustules. Dispose of garden debris that may be harboring the disease.

CORN EARWORM

SYMPTOMS Tips of ears of corn show feeding damage to kernels, sometimes with a "worm" present and leaving excrement *(see **p.48**)*. Occasionally, ragged holes are chewed in foliage. Extensive mold may follow. Green tomato fruit may show deep holes, especially at the stem end. The leaves, buds, flowers, and pods of beans are eaten. A variety of other food and ornamental plants may be affected. On ornamentals, opening buds can be completely gouged out. Flowers and seeds are devoured, and some stems may be tunneled. The list of attacked annuals and perennials includes calendula, chrysanthemum, dahlia, gladiolus, and rose. Cotton, tobacco, and many wild plants and weeds are also heavily fed on.
CAUSE The corn earworm (*Helicoverpa zea*), the larva of a night-flying moth. It ranges from ¼in to nearly 2in (6–50mm) and varies in color from light green or pinkish brown to almost black. It generally has lengthwise, light and dark stripes, and its underside is lighter.
CONTROL Some varieties of corn are resistant but not immune to attack, particularly those with a tight silk channel. In some areas, plantings can be timed to ripen before earworms are present. With other host plants, such as beans, resistant cultivars and good timing also help. Pheromone traps are available to aid in

predicting severity of infestation and need for control. Deep cultivation in autumn and spring exposes or kills pupae. Screen smaller host plants from egg laying with rowcover. Corn earworm eggs are parasitized by the wasp *Trichogramma minutum*, which can be purchased. Nematodes squirted on ear tips are effective against early larvae. Hand control is feasible with a small crop. After corn is pollinated, pull back the sheath and dig out the earworm; the tip might need to be clipped off.

CORN ROOTWORM
See CUCUMBER BEETLES *p.120*.

CORN SMUT
SYMPTOMS Individual kernels on the ear become hugely swollen and deformed *(see p.51)*. Each is pale gray and ruptures to release large quantities of powdery black spores. The spores may become mixed with rain to produce a black liquid that runs down the plant. Occasionally, other parts of the plant may be affected. The infection is not systemic, and healthy and infected ears may develop on the same plant.
CAUSE The fungus *Ustilago maydis*. The spores are distributed on air currents and by water splash.
CONTROL Remove infected ears before the swellings rupture. Discard all infected plant debris at the end of the season. Do not grow corn on the site for at least 5 years.

COTTONY CAMELLIA (OR TAXUS) SCALE
SYMPTOMS Leaves of camellias, hollies, rhododendrons, evergreen azaleas, and euonymus develop sooty mold on the upper surfaces. Foliage may turn off-color. Flat, oval, yellow-brown objects are attached to the stems or undersides of the leaves, and in early summer the females deposit their eggs under a broad, white, waxy band *(see p.15)*.
CAUSE Sap-feeding scale insects, *Chloropulvinaria floccifera*. They spend most of the year on stems, moving to leaves to lay eggs, when they receive most attention.
CONTROL This scale has natural enemies that often keep it in check. If numbers are too high or sooty mold becomes objectionable, insecticides can be used, including insecticidal soap and horticultural oil when crawlers (nymphs) appear. Oil can also be applied during the dormant season.

COTTONY GRAPE SCALE
SYMPTOMS The foliage of many woody plants, including alder, willow, birch, peach, grapes, currants, gooseberry, and pyracantha, is soiled by sooty mold. Heavily infested plants lack vigor.
CAUSE A sap-feeding scale insect, *Pulvinaria vitis*. Crawlers (nymphs) hatch in early summer and feed initially on the underside of leaves. Before leaf fall, they move back to the bark, where they complete their development and overwinter as adults. When mature in late spring, females deposit eggs in a thick pad of white, waxy fibers *(see p.39)*. The scales are dark brown and up to ¼in (6mm) long.
CONTROL If they are removed by hand, the egg masses can be drawn out in long waxy threads. Several parasites and predators help control this scale. For fruit trees, apply a horticultural oil spray in early spring before budbreak when the plants are fully dormant. Horticultural oil and insecticidal soap can be applied in early to midsummer to kill crawlers.

COTTONY HYDRANGEA SCALE
SYMPTOMS This pest is most visible during late spring and early summer when the females deposit eggs among a mass of white, waxy fibers on the stems and foliage of host plants *(see p.15)*. Hydrangea is the most frequently attacked plant, but this scale also occurs on *Prunus*, linden, maples, and a few other hosts. Heavy infestations reduce the plant's vigor and result in shoot dieback.
CAUSE A sap-feeding insect, *Pulvinaria hydrangeae*. The oval egg masses are up to ¼in (6mm) long. The mature scale is brownish yellow but drops off when the insect dies, leaving the egg mass as the most obvious sign of infestation. Eggs hatch in midsummer, and the flat, oval, pale yellow crawlers (nymphs) live on the underside of leaves next to leaf veins during the rest of summer.
CONTROL Horticultural oil can be applied in late winter or early spring. Insecticidal soap or another labeled material can be used in midsummer against the newly hatched crawlers. Hydrangeas can be damaged by pesticides, so avoid treatment when plants are exposed to bright sunlight or high temperatures. Water the plants first if the soil is dry.

CRANE FLIES
More than 1,600 species of crane flies (erroneously called giant mosquitoes) are found in North America.

A few have soil-dwelling larvae – leatherjackets *(see p.144)* – that feed on roots and the stem bases of small plants. The adults do not bite, and most do not feed.

LENGTH: ⅜–1⅛in (2–3cm)

CRANE FLY

CRAPE MYRTLE POWDERY MILDEW
SYMPTOMS During periods of warm days and cool nights, crape myrtle develops small, dusty, white spots, mostly on shoots and upper leaf surfaces. The circular growths expand into mealy or powdery patches and then may turn yellow while partially or totally engulfing the leaf or shoot. Young leaves may be only one-third normal length and thicker than normal. Curled or otherwise distorted, leaves can be slightly red below. Buds and flowers in the affected area fail to develop normally. The entire plant can be dwarfed.
CAUSE The fungus *Uncinuliella australiana*. Although it prefers high humidity, crape myrtle powdery mildew also flourishes when it is dry, not requiring wet weather to spread, as do most other fungal diseases. The powdery mildew robs its host of nutrients, and deprived plant parts die.
CONTROL Plant in full sun to avoid shade-induced stress and to promote drying. Improve air circulation. Plant resistant cultivars. Various fungicides protect against or suppress powdery mildew, including sulfur, lime-sulfur, Bordeaux mix, compost tea, and baking-soda spray.

CRICKETS

SYMPTOMS At any point in the growing season, feeding damage occurs to roots and stems on a wide variety of plants. Seeds and seedlings are disturbed or completely eaten and larger plants are chewed, with holes and cuts in stems. Turf roots and shoots are also eaten, and the tunneling damages newly seeded grass.
CAUSE Field crickets are rarely a major garden pest, and some are beneficial insectivores, consuming aphids and many dead and dying insects. Active at night, virtually all species have long, heavily muscled legs and stocky bodies ranging from ½–1⅛in (2–30mm) long, and they occur in a wide color range. Many make a familiar chirping sound. Mole crickets, a unique group found in the southern US, have enlarged front legs for digging.
CONTROL Field crickets like the cover provided by dense vegetation and ground litter, so if they are a problem, clean up the garden and thin out plantings. Protect plants with cones or rowcover. Baited traps may be useful. Some birds and predatory wasps favor crickets. Mole crickets are more difficult to control. Individual plants can be protected with metal, screen, or tarpaper cylinders sunk into the ground. Poison baits may be available. Insecticides are available for use on turf.

CROWN GALL

SYMPTOMS Rounded swellings or galls – which are off-white when young and harden and turn brown with age – develop on woody or herbaceous plants. Galls range from less than ⅜in (9mm) to more than 1ft (30cm) in diameter. They usually develop in small groups. Crown gall may appear on the roots or stem base (the crown). Less frequently, symptoms of an aerial form may show at some distance up the stem or trunk (see **p.38**). Galls on woody plants are persistent; those on herbaceous plants are softer and more short-lived. If galls ring the stem or trunk, or cause extensive disruption of water and nutrient flow, the entire plant may decline. If stem or root splitting occurs due to the erupting out of the galls, secondary organisms may gain entry and cause dieback.
CAUSE The bacterium *Agrobacterium tumifaciens*, which is soilborne and capable of living without a living host in the soil. The bacteria enter through wounds and then stimulate rapid proliferation of cells, forming the galls. Gall growth is greatest when the plant is growing rapidly, so infections that occur at the end of the growing season may not produce symptoms until the following year.
CONTROL Improve soil drainage. Check all plants carefully before planting. Keep root and stem injury to a minimum. Remove infected plants and grow root crops (except beets) on the site for at least 1 year to minimize the risk of subsequent infections.

CROWN ROT

SYMPTOMS Deterioration and rotting of the tissues at the crown (the junction of the stems and roots) of the plant. Herbaceous plants are very prone, but woody hosts, such as wisterias, may also succumb. It may then cause deterioration of the stems and foliage, and the entire plant may die.
CAUSE Various soil- and waterborne fungi and bacteria, often several in combination.
CONTROL If dealt with very promptly, it may be possible to save an infected plant. Remove affected areas, cutting well back into healthy tissue.

CRUCIFER BLACK ROT

SYMPTOMS Crucifer seedlings wilt or rot. On young plants, foliage and flower growth is stunted or one-sided. The plant may then turn yellow to brown, wilt, collapse, and die. On an older plant, a leaf edge yellows and turns dark green or brown. Alternately, close to the edge are yellow spots or patches, which may expand into the whole leaf. The veins blacken from the edge toward the middle. The cross-sectioned stem shows a black ring and may weep a yellow ooze. A portion of a plant may develop a hard, odorless rot. The hard rot can be soon followed, perhaps quite quickly, by a wet, smelly decay that will engulf the whole head or most of the plant.
CAUSE The bacterium *Xanthomonas campestris* pathovar *campestris*. Living up to 2 years on debris or seeds in the soil, it can build to a disastrous level in successive years, reaching epidemic proportions in a warm and very wet or humid season. Seeds may start infected, or the plant may be placed in direct contact with contaminated refuse in the soil. Also, the bacterium can live in the soil for a short time. Otherwise, the pathogen is carried to the host by splashing rain or overhead irrigation, water runoff, insects, other animal life, or tools. It enters the plant through a wound or a natural opening. It then spreads through the vascular system; the yellow ooze is the bacteria and broken-down plant cells.
CONTROL Resistance varies. Purchase only seed and plants that are certified disease-free. For untreated seeds, soaking them in 122°F (50°C) water will eliminate *Xanthomonas*. Soaking time varies: broccoli, cauliflower, and collard seeds need just 18 minutes, while cabbage seeds need 25. Let the seeds air dry (to prevent other pathogens from attacking the wet seeds), and then dust them with a fungicide-bactericide preparation. After harvest, completely remove and dispose of debris, including as many of the roots as possible. Use sterile planting media, containers, and tools. Do not plant the same variety in the same place 2 years in a row, and about every 3 years completely rotate out of crucifers in the bed. Remove cruciferous weeds, such as some mustards, shepherd's purse, and pepper grass. Space plants to allow good air circulation. Provide well-drained soil, do not overwater, and do not let drainage water collect. Instead of overhead sprinkling, irrigate in furrows between rows. Keep soil fertility well balanced, with ample nitrogen for strong leaves. Eradicate cutworms and cabbage root maggots, which may spread the bacterium. Infected leaves can be picked off, but if the stem is involved, pull out the entire plant, including the intact root ball, and discard everything. Use a copper-based fungicide according to package directions.

CUCUMBER BEETLES

SYMPTOMS Cucurbit (melons, cucumbers, and squashes) leaves and, sometimes, flowers may be chewed and skeletonized, and stems may be chewed or pitted. Small, yellow beetles with black stripes or greenish beetles with black spots may congregate on stems, in flowers, or under leaves. Seedlings and especially cotyledons can be severely damaged or eaten entirely. Larger plants withstand some damage but may wilt or show mottling from disease. Sweet corn is sometimes affected: in severe cases, silks are clipped, resulting in barren or misshapen ears, or plants fall over from root damage.

CAUSE Several species of cucumber beetle. Striped (*Acalymma vittata*) and western striped (*A. trivitatta*) cucumber beetles are yellow and orange-yellow to cream, respectively, with 3 black lines. They feed especially on cucurbits but sometimes on other plants, including beans, corn, peas, tomatoes, peaches, and various flowers. Larvae feed on cucurbit roots and, occasionally, rinds of fallen fruits. Spotted (*Diabrotica duodecimpunctata*) and western spotted (*D. undecimpunctata*) cucumber beetles are greenish yellow with 11 or 12 black spots. They feed on cucurbits and many other plants, including corn silks, beans, tomatoes, cabbage, potato, and various flowers. The larvae, also called corn rootworms, feed on roots of corn, small grains and other grasses, and legumes. Cucumber beetles are notorious for transmitting the virus that causes mosaic (*see* CUCUMBER MOSAIC VIRUS, *next entry*).

CONTROL Some available cultivars are less attractive to beetles or are resistant to bacterial wilt. In general, most pumpkins, winter squash, and watermelon cultivars are less prone to wilt but still suffer feeding damage. Protect cucurbit seedlings and transplants with floating rowcover or other barriers. Handpick beetles. Promptly rogue out plants that show wilt disease. Eliminate overwintering sites. Plant an early border of attractive host plants as a trap crop, and treat or remove beetles frequently from the trap plants. Especially for western corn rootworm, rotate corn with nonhost plants. Beneficial nematodes can be drenched around crown and roots of cucurbits to help control striped cucumber beetle larvae. Severe infestations may require the use of insecticides. Avoid using them when the flowers are open and pollinators are actively working them.

CUCUMBER MOSAIC VIRUS

SYMPTOMS Plants are stunted and show distinct yellow mosaic patterning (*see p.21*), usually on stunted, deformed foliage (*see p.25*). Flowering is reduced or nonexistent, and plants may die partially or completely. If fruits are produced on cucurbits (squash, pumpkins, or cucumbers), they are small, pitted, and strangely dark green with bright yellow blotches. Their texture is hard, and the fruits are inedible. Changes in petal color may occur.

CAUSE The cucumber mosaic virus, which has an extremely wide host range, including many common ornamental garden plants,

food crops, and weeds. The virus particles are readily spread by handling and by sap-feeding insects, especially aphids.

CONTROL Grow resistant cultivars. Destroy infected plants. Control aphids to minimize the risk of infection spread. Remove weeds. Avoid unnecessary handling of plants, and try to handle healthy plants before touching infected or suspect ones. After handling infected plants, wash hands thoroughly.

CUCUMBER POWDERY MILDEW

SYMPTOMS The top surfaces of leaves of cucumbers or other cucurbits (gourds, melons, pumpkins, and squash) have a powdery white or gray growth in scattered round spots or patches (*see p.15*). The spots merge and spread to the undersurfaces (which may look more silvery at first) and stems, perhaps enveloping entire leaves while becoming tinged brown. The leaves dehydrate, cupping and withering as the actual leaf tissue (under the growth) goes from dark green to yellow-green then brown. The leaves look sunscalded and may die. The entire plant surface, including shoots, flowers, and fruit, may be covered by the growth. The prematurely ripening fruits are small, deformed, and whitened or browned. They have poor taste and texture. The yield is low, and infrequently the plant dies. Ornamental plants, especially in the daisy family, show similar symptoms.

CAUSE Growing more superficially than downy mildew, cucumber powdery

mildew may be 2 fungi (*Erisyphe cichoracearum* or *Sphaerotheca fuliginea*) that produce similar symptoms. Unlike most other fungi, cucumber powdery mildew does not require moist conditions to spread. It is most severe, however, in a cool, humid, shaded garden that is too crowded for adequate air circulation. It thrives during cool nights that follow warm days. Spores are spread by wind and also by hands, shoes, and tools.

CONTROL Disease-resistant and tolerant varieties may be marked "PM" in seed catalogs. Even with such plants, rotate out of cucurbits to avoid fungi that have mutated to overcome the plants' resistance. Keep cucurbits well spaced to promote good air circulation and to allow maximum sunlight. High plant vigor generally reduces the susceptibility of cucurbits, but do not overfertilize. Pick off heavily infected leaves. Otherwise, a strong washing of both sides of the leaves early in the day kills spores and inhibits growth of this superficial fungus. Destroy all debris of potential hosts after harvest. Spray both sides of lightly infected leaves with fungicidal soap. The sulfur-containing products that are typically applied against powdery mildews, such as sulfur dust, lime-sulfur mix, and Bordeaux mixture, can damage many cucurbits, although certain varieties are sulfur tolerant. Test substances on a few leaves before general application.

CUCUMBER SCAB

SYMPTOMS Corky dry spots up to ½in (1.3cm) appear on cucumber and immature muskmelon fruit. A dense, furry, olive-green fungal growth covers the spots in damp conditions. Stem and petiole lesions may also develop; if they girdle the stem or petiole, growth beyond dies.

Cause The fungus *Cladosporium cucumerinum*, which is encouraged by cool, damp conditions.

Control Remove infected areas promptly. Grow resistant cultivars.

Cucurbit Downy Mildew

Symptoms The undersurfaces of cucurbit (cucumber, melon, squash, pumpkin, and gourd) leaves develop downy, purplish white spots (*see p.25*). On the top side of the leaves, and often noticed first, are corresponding small, yellow spots. The downy spots beneath become gray, tan, and then brown or black. As the spots coalesce into large areas, the plant tissue withers and dies. The topside yellowing remains interveinal and angular. Infection generally starts on older, lower leaves. It moves from older to younger leaves along the vine. Fruit is stunted and off flavor. New growth emerges reddish, shrivels, and dies. The leaves and heads of brassicas sometimes also show the growing downy spots, which in this case turn tissue brown and papery.

Cause Cucurbit downy mildew (*Pseudoperonospora cubensis*). Rain, irrigation water, and dew promote spore release; the spores can then carried by cucumber beetles (*see p.119*) and air currents down the vine and around the garden.

Control Some varieties show resistance. Clean up all garden debris after each crop. Rotate cucurbits, particularly where the soil does not freeze deeply. If a planting had downy mildew, avoid putting cucurbits back in that bed for at least 3 years. Space properly to promote good air circulation. Remove infected leaves early to save the plant. Some protection is given by a liquid copper fungicide or Bordeaux mix.

Currant Aphid

Symptoms Leaves at shoot tips become crumpled, with raised, blistered areas that have small, pale yellow insects on the undersides (*see p.17*). The affected leaves are yellowish green or have a reddish coloration (*see p.27*), especially on redcurrants.

Cause Sap-feeding aphids, *Cryptomyzus ribis*, which are active on the foliage between bud burst and midsummer.

Control Damage is often just a cosmetic concern. Natural enemies, such as ladybugs, often provide adequate control. Horticultural oil, applied during the dormant season, late winter to early spring, will kill the egg stage. Insecticidal soap or another labeled material can be applied between bud burst and flowering.

Cutworms

Symptoms Small plants in flower beds and vegetable gardens wilt and die. Examination of the plants shows that the roots at or just below soil level have been severed, or the outer bark has been gnawed away. Root vegetables, such as potatoes and carrots, may have cavities eaten in them. Buds or leaves may be eaten, and there may be holes in tomatoes. Caterpillars, often creamy brown or sometimes greenish brown and up to 1¼in (3.8cm) long, are often found in the soil near recently damaged plants (*see p.53*).

Cause The soil-dwelling caterpillars of several moths.

Control Cutworms tend to work their way along row crops such as sweet corn, carrots, and lettuce, so it is worthwhile sifting the soil near a damaged plant to find them. These caterpillars are more troublesome following fallowing or in weedy plots, so good cultivation will help. Inspect plants at night with a flashlight. Wrap stems of transplants with paper to 1in (2.5cm) above and below ground to deter feeding. A pathogenic nematode, *Steinernema carpocapsae*, can be used in moist, well-drained soil during summer. Spreading ashes around plants may discourage cutworms.

Cyclamen Mite

Symptoms In the cooler parts of the growing season (early to late spring and again in late summer early autumn), any nonwoody part of ornamentals, vegetables, and greenhouse plants become distorted and stunted (*see p.26*). Leaf and flower buds are swollen and blackened. Young foliage is badly crinkled, fails to expand fully, and becomes purple, brownish green, or bronze and maybe brittle. Older foliage is mostly unaffected, as may be blossoms. Other flowers may become mottled, streaked, or green and distorted and drop early. Attacked flowers are neither normal-size nor plentiful. There is dark brown to blackish scarring or streaking on stems and petioles. If fruit develops at all, it is dwarfed and withered. An attacked plant is stunted overall. Delphinium, snapdragon, *Aster novi-belgii*, and gerbera are especially susceptible. Other ornamentals attacked include aconitum, ageratum, azalea, chrysanthemum, crassula, dahlia, lantana, marguerite, and marigold. Food-plant hosts include tomato, pepper, and particularly strawberry. In the greenhouse, African violet, begonia, cyclamen, geranium, and some foliage plants are damaged.

Cause The tiny, sap-sucking cyclamen mite (*Phytonemus pallidus*), which infests buds, unfolding leaves, and crowns.

Control Be sure that the diagnosis is accurate; damage resembles symptoms of virus or other problems. Grow less susceptible plants; for instance, *Aster novae-angliae* resists attack much better than *A. novi-belgii*. Purchase only strawberry plants that are certified mite free. After handling an infested plant at home, wash your hands and sanitize tools before moving to clean plants. Destroy badly infested parts or plants. Keep weeds under control, because they can be mite reservoirs. Any plant diagnosed as infested should be isolated or destroyed; other plants exposed to it then need to be carefully monitored. Predatory mites have been tested with limited success as biological controls for greenhouse plants and strawberries. Usually, miticides labeled for cyclamen mite must be used for complete control. Prune or pinch back plants to improve coverage.

CYTOSPORA CANKER AND BRANCH DIEBACK

SYMPTOMS Conifer needles turn dry and brown, usually first on branches near the ground. Fruit tree and other hardwood foliage is stunted and may be yellow between the veins. Defoliation may follow, although brown leaves may persist among healthy foliage.

Trunks and branches can have multiple dark, oval or elongate cankers that enlarge and become sunken. The bark of a canker dies and separates, whereas bark at the margin may thicken and roll inward. Small black spore-producing bodies may be present. A sticky resin accumulates inside diseased wood before oozing out of cracks, especially on peach and black cherry. The exudate begins as a clear amber and, as it dries, may develop a white crust that blackens from saprophytic fungi. Curly orange threads may grow from the canker. Bases of young twigs develop sunken brown pustules. Twigs may drop immediately or persist for years. It may take decades for large limbs to be girdled and killed by cankers. In the meantime, they are disfigured and show lopsided growth. Buds are killed, and fruit productivity decreases.

CAUSE Cytospora canker and branch dieback, each type of which is caused by a fungus with a limited host range of related trees. The fungi attack dead tissue as well as bark on trees weakened by drought, malnutrition, or environmental extremes. The spores usually enter through wounds created by mechanical injury, twig scars from leaf and fruit fall, and holes made by borers. Wet weather not only promotes spore development but also helps splash spores to new sites on other trees or on the same host. *Cytospora* spores are also spread by running water, breezes, and tools.

CONTROL Plant hardier and generally more vigorous cultivars. Maintain vigor with ample watering, good drainage, and fertilizing. Protect trunks against sunscald and cold by wrapping them or coating them with white latex paint. Do not plant downwind from or near cankered trees. Prune out infected and dead branches, and sterilize tools between cuts. Delay routine spring pruning until after buds swell, when healing is most rapid. Do not injure bark by careless mowing.

DAHLIA SMUT

SYMPTOMS Pale brown, elongate spots with yellow margins develop on leaves in midsummer. The lower, older leaves are affected first. The spots darken, become larger, and may merge, often killing the leaf.

CAUSE The fungus *Entyloma calendulae* f. *dahliae*, which may live in the soil around infected plants and on plant debris. It can persist in the soil in the absence of dahlias for about 5 years.

CONTROL Remove and dispose of severely infected dahlias, and plant replacements on a fresh site. The fungus does not seem to be present in the tubers, so if affected leaves are removed and the tubers appear clear of infected debris, they can be stored and should produce healthy plants and flowers.

DAMPING OFF

SYMPTOMS Seedlings flop over or collapse, often showing discoloration and deterioration around the stem base *(see p.34)*. Initially, these lesions may appear water-soaked. The infection spreads rapidly, causing patches of seedlings to die. An entire tray of seedlings may be killed within a few days. Fluffy white fungal growth may be seen on the surface of the dead and dying seedlings. If infection occurs before germination is complete, many seedlings fail to emerge.

CAUSE Several soil- and waterborne fungi, particularly species of *Pythium*, *Phytophthora*, and *Rhizoctonia*. Infection is encouraged by overly wet compost and prolonged high temperatures. Seedlings without adequate light and grown from seed sown too densely are particularly prone to infection. Damping off is most common when hygiene is poor – if pots, trays, and implements are not properly cleaned, if unsterilized soil mix is used, or if unclean water is used. Sometimes the seeds are contaminated.

CONTROL Observe strict hygiene and use only clean equipment and sterilized soil mix. Use only clean water, especially not water collected in a barrel. Sow seedlings thinly, and make sure that they have adequate light and are not kept too warm for any longer than is needed to encourage germination.

DEER

All species of deer cause problems in gardens. White-tailed deer (*Odocoileus virginianus*) is a common and familiar species. Mule deer (*O. hemionus*) and black-tailed deer (*O. hemionus columbiarius*) are locally important. A wide range of herbaceous and woody plants are eaten, with damage occurring mainly between dusk and dawn. Flowers, foliage, whole shoots, or entire plants can be lost. On woody plants, such as roses, the stems are partly bitten through cleanly, but there remains a ragged edge to the stem *(see p.41)*. Look for the distinctive hoofprints to confirm their presence. The trunks of trees and side branches can be damaged by male deer rubbing their antlers against the bark.

CONTROL It can be difficult to exclude deer from gardens. They can easily jump over obstacles, and a fence about 8–10ft (2.5–3m) high is necessary to keep deer out. Shorter electronic fences are sometimes effective for small areas where pressure from deer is not severe. Deer adapt quickly to visual and sound-producing deterrents. Repellents, depending on offensive taste or odor, may be effective if damage is only light to moderate in small areas and if only a few treatments are needed. They will not work when deer are hungry, and they have to be reapplied after rain. Check with local Cooperative Extension Service or conservation offices about fencing designs and other options.

DELPHINIUM BLACK BLOTCH

SYMPTOMS Black blotches develop on leaves *(see p.12)*, rapidly enlarging and spreading to the stems, petioles, and flower buds. Entire leaves may turn black and die.

CAUSE The bacterium *Pseudomonas delphinii*, which is spread from the soil or by rain or watering splash.
CONTROL Remove and dispose of infected plants, and avoid overhead watering. Plant new delphiniums on a fresh site. Copper-based bactericides can reduce the severity of blotching.

DIDYMELLA STEM ROT

SYMPTOMS Black-brown, sunken blotches develop on the stems of tomatoes *(see **p.33**)* and, occasionally, eggplants at soil or ground level, often combined with the growth of roots above soil level. The older leaves turn yellow. A blackish brown rot, usually at the stem end, develops on the fruit. Numerous black, pinprick-size fungal fruiting bodies appear on the surface of infected areas.
CAUSE The fungus *Didymella lycopersici*, which can be seedborne but is usually spread from plant to plant by rain, watering splash, or handling. The fungus can overwinter on debris from infected plants or in the soil.
CONTROL Remove and dispose of infected plants; do not compost them. Clear up all crop debris at the end of the season, and grow on a fresh site.

DIEBACK

SYMPTOMS The stems of plants start to shrivel and die. Dieback may begin at the tip, the base, or anywhere on the stem; it rarely affects all stems simultaneously. Dark blotches or sunken patches may develop at the point where the deterioration starts. Leaves wilt, yellow, and die. The symptoms may

spread down into the base or the crown, causing the entire plant to die.
CAUSE Various fungi, some that invade healthy stems, and others that enter the plant only through wounds or other points of damage. Dieback, especially from stem tips downward, may also be caused by cultural problems, including poor establishment of young plants, drought, and waterlogging.
CONTROL Prune out affected stems to a point well below any signs of damage. Improve cultural conditions to ensure increased plant vigor.

DOGS

Although not pests in the usual sense of this book, dogs can cause problems in gardens. Their urine can scorch foliage, with females causing circular brown patches in lawns, and males damaging conifers and other plants that they spray.
CONTROL Rinsing the foliage with water to dilute the urine prevents damage, but it must be done soon after the dog has urinated. Commercial animal repellents are available. Fencing may be needed, and some local laws restrict dogs to fenced yards or require the use of leashes.

DOGWOOD ANTHRACNOSE

SYMPTOMS Spots *(see **p.18**)* on the leaves and bracts of species of *Cornus* – especially *C. florida* and *C. nuttallii* and, less severely, *C. sanguinea* and *C. alba* – appear in late spring or early summer, and they may merge into large patches. Tissue can become malformed and wilt, and spots may drop out to leave shotholes. Spots may also

develop on leaf and flower buds, preventing them from opening or producing stunted and deformed growth. Cankers develop on branches, and extensive dieback may occur, killing the tree. These symptoms usually appear first toward the base of the tree and then progress upward.
CAUSE The fungus *Discula destructiva*, which grows and spreads during cool, wet weather and is most prevalent in areas of high rainfall.
CONTROL Prune out infected parts in dry weather, and sterilize tools between cuts. Remove watersprouts, which are highly susceptible. Keep plants healthy through good garden practices, including watering, fertilizing, mulching, and providing adequate light, soil drainage, and air circulation. Grow resistant cultivars or immune species. Copper sprays, sulfur formulations, and Bordeaux mixture and lime-sulfur may help suppress spread.

DOGWOOD BORER

See CLEARWING BORERS *p.115*.

DOWNY MILDEW

SYMPTOMS Yellow, purple-brown, or otherwise discolored areas develop on upper leaf surfaces or, sometimes, fruits or bulbs of a wide range of plants. Each corresponds to a slightly fuzzy, grayish white or, occasionally, purplish fungal growth beneath. The infection may spread, leading to the death of the plant part, large areas of the plant, or the entire plant. Downy mildew is especially common on young plants and those growing in moist, humid environments or during unusually wet seasons. The

symptoms may be confused with those of powdery mildew *(see p.164)*.
CAUSE Several different fungi, particularly species of *Bremia*, *Peronospora*, and *Plasmopara*. These include *Bremia lactucae* (on lettuce), *Peronospora destructor* (on onion), *P. farinosa* f. sp. *spinaceae* (on spinach), *P. parasitica* (downy mildew of brassicas), *P. sparsa* (on rose), *Peronospora* species (on hardy geraniums), *P. viciae* (on pea), *P. violae* (on violet and pansy), and *Plasmopara viticola* (on grape).
CONTROL Remove infected plant parts, and improve air circulation around plants by increased spacing and good weed control. Avoid overhead watering. Dispose of all debris at the end of the season. Grow plants on a fresh site. Spray infected plants (especially the undersides of leaves) with a fungicide that contains mancozeb or copper.
• *see also* CUCURBIT DOWNY MILDEW *p.121*.

DRACAENA THRIPS

SYMPTOMS Indoor plants, especially those with relatively tough leaves, such as *Ficus* and palms, develop a silvery brown discoloration of the upper leaf surface *(see **p.22**)*. Narrow-bodied insects up to ⅟₁₂in (2mm) long may be seen.
CAUSE Sap-feeding thrips, *Parthenothrips dracaenae*. Nymphs are creamy yellow, and adults are darker, with dark bands on pale wings. The wings are folded over the bodies when not in use, which gives the adults their striped appearance.
CONTROL Spray with a pesticide labeled for this use. Damaged leaves will not regain their normal color.

DROUGHT

SYMPTOMS Symptoms vary, depending on the plant affected and whether the drought has been chronic or acute. Common symptoms include poor growth and stunting, wilting of the foliage (see **p.28**), and, in extreme cases, wilting of the stems and flowers (see **p.44**). Prolonged drought may also cause poor flowering, bud drop, and the formation of undersized fruits. Drought followed by sudden watering or rainfall may cause splitting or cracking of fruits and stems.

CAUSE Most commonly, inadequate rainfall or watering; occasionally, an inability of the plant to take up adequate moisture because of a damaged root system. Very free-draining soils, such as those with a high sand content, are particularly prone to drying out. Plants with restricted root runs, such as those growing in containers, are also particularly prone.

CONTROL Make sure that the soil or soil mix never dries out completely. Where feasible, grow plants in open ground or protect containers from direct sunlight. Improve retention of soil moisture by incorporating bulky organic materials (such as compost and well-rotted manure) into light soils and by applying mulch, which reduces water loss by evaporation.

DRYBERRY MITE

SYMPTOMS Pale yellow, rounded blotches develop on the upper leaf surface of raspberry, blackberry, and hybrids (see **p.18**) from late spring onward. On the undersides, corresponding with the yellow blotches, are slightly darker areas. By midsummer, the foliage may

be extensively discolored, and leaves at the shoot tips may be distorted. Loganberry fruit tends to dry out, while red raspberry fruit is often discolored. These symptoms can be confused with those of some viral diseases. Canes affected by the mite normally grow to their usual height and produce an adequate crop, whereas virus-infected plants lack vigor and yield poorly.

CAUSE Microscopic, sausage-shaped mites, *Phyllocoptes gracilis*, which suck sap from the underside of leaves. Young fruit is also damaged. In autumn, they hide in or near buds to overwinter.

CONTROL Plant away from warm, sheltered areas. Chemical controls are not available, but the impact on a plant's health is not as great as the symptoms might suggest.

DRY BUD

SYMPTOMS Buds may be undersize and are usually dry and brown; the plant is otherwise healthy.

CAUSE As with bud drop (see p.111), a period of dry weather while the flower buds are forming. On very susceptible plants, such as rhododendron, just a few consecutive days of drought at the end of summer are enough. Plants growing in containers are particularly vulnerable because they are more prone to dry conditions around the roots.

CONTROL Water thoroughly and regularly, and do not let the soil dry out completely. Apply a deep mulch around the root area.

DRY ROT OF BULBS AND CORMS

SYMPTOMS Foliage turns brown and dies, often with a clear, dark discoloration just

above soil level. Crocus, freesias, gladioli, and montbretias (*Crocosmia*) are particularly affected. Entire plants may die back. The corms develop numerous small sunken lesions, each of which bears many pinprick-size black fungal fruiting bodies.

CAUSE The fungus *Stromatinia gladioli*, which can overwinter on stored corms and may persist in the soil as small, hard, black resting bodies (sclerotia). They can remain viable in the soil for many years, even in the absence of host plants.

CONTROL Check that bulbs are healthy and free from sclerotia before planting. Remove any infected plants. Grow replacement plants, and any others that are susceptible, on a fresh site.

DUTCH ELM DISEASE

SYMPTOMS Areas of the tree's crown show wilting and yellowing. Affected leaves then turn brown and die. Dieback of twigs and branches usually follows, and young shoots may curl over to form "shepherds' crooks." The whole tree may be killed by the end of the first summer. If the bark on affected stems and branches is peeled away, longitudinal, discontinuous brown staining is apparent. If stems or branches are cut across, they may show rings of brown staining in the current year's growth. Feeding damage caused by the elm bark beetle may be seen in the crotches of young stems. The galleries of tunnels caused by the beetle, which spreads the infection, show beneath the bark on larger stems and trunks. Symptoms are much more obvious, and the disease more damaging, during hot, dry weather;

these conditions exacerbate the problems caused by the fungus blocking the tree's vascular system.

CAUSE The fungus *Ceratocystis ulmi*, which causes this disease on elms and on *Zelkova*, spread by elm bark beetles. This disease is responsible for the lost of millions of American elms in the second half of the 20th century. Many areas lost all of their street trees. As a result of this disaster, many municipalities adopted policies for replanting many different tree species and cultivars to avoid another monocultural problem.

CONTROL Remove and dispose of all infected plant parts. Some cultivars and hybrids show some resistance.

EARTHWORMS

Earthworms (see **p.61**) are generally beneficial animals that improve soil conditions. Their tunnels provide aeration and drainage pathways through the soil, and worms help incorporate organic matter by pulling dead leaves into the soil. They can, however, be a nuisance when they excrete small piles of soil-like material onto the surface of lawns (see **p.58**). These worm casts can spoil the appearance of a fine lawn and make the surface muddy and slippery. When lawns are mowed, worm casts become smeared, which creates patches of bare soil that lawn weeds can colonize. Not all earthworms produce worm casts: the culprits are usually species of *Aporrectodea*. They are a problem mainly during spring and autumn when warm, moist soil conditions encourage worm activity in the upper layers of the soil; drought or cold sends worms deeper and reduces casting. **CONTROL** Worm casts can be dispersed by brushing the lawn with a stiff broom or wire rake. This is best done when they are dry and crumbly. During wet periods, walking on the lawn should be kept to a minimum to avoid smearing the casts.

EARWIGS

Earwigs (*Forficula auricularia*), correctly known as European earwigs, are up to ½in (1.3cm) long, dark brown, and easily recognized by the pair of pincers on the rear end of the body. They eat ragged holes in the young foliage, fruit, and flowers of many plants (*see p.46*), especially clematis, dahlias, daylilies, chrysanthemums, and strawberries. During the day, they hide in dark crevices or among the foliage and petals of host plants. They emerge and feed after sunset, so a flashlight inspection is often needed to find them.

LENGTH: ½IN (1.3MM)

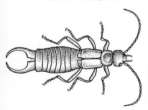

EARWIG

CONTROL Make traps by inverting flower pots on top of bamboo stakes at the height of the plant tops. The pots, loosely stuffed with hay or straw, are used as daytime hiding places by earwigs. Inspect the pots daily, and destroy earwigs found inside. Alternatively, set out low-sided cans filled up to ½in (1.3cm) with vegetable oil.

Newspaper rolled into a tube or hoses placed in the evening can be collected during the day and the earwigs shaken out. Leaves, debris, and other refuges should be eliminated. Several insecticides can be applied around building foundations.

EASTERN SPRUCE GALL ADELGID

SYMPTOMS In early summer, spruce trees (*Picea*), especially the Norway and occasionally the Colorado blue, white, and red, develop swellings at the shoot base that resemble pineapples (*see p.38*). In late summer, the galls begin to dry and turn brown, resembling cones. Galls can persist on trees for many years and spoil their appearance, but do little damage. **CAUSE** Sap-feeding insects, *Adelges abietis*, which produce galls by secreting chemicals as they feed on buds in spring. These chemicals prevent normal shoot development, and, instead, the bases of the leaves become swollen and fused, leaving cavities in which nymphs continue to feed and grow. Slits open in the galls as they dry, allowing the winged adults to emerge. **CONTROL** Spruce gall adelgids must be tolerated on trees that are too tall to be sprayed. On small trees, galls can be pruned out or tolerated, since the adelgids rarely threaten the trees' health. If the aesthetic value is affected, applications of horticultural oil or another labeled insecticide in spring can be effective. This treatment is aimed at overwintering nymphs before they mature and lay eggs on the buds.

EASTERN TENT CATERPILLAR

SYMPTOMS From early to late spring, a wide variety of deciduous shrubs and trees have white, silken webbing around limb crotches. Black caterpillars with white stripes and blue markings may be in the webbing or feeding on leaves. An entire branch or even a whole tree may be defoliated within a matter of days. Despite being weakened, stripped trees are rarely killed. Favorite hosts include wild cherry, apple, and crabapple. Cherry, peach, plum, witch hazel, poplar, ash, birch, and maple are among the many woody ornamental, shade, and forest tree hosts. **CAUSE** The eastern tent caterpillar (*Malacosoma americanum*), which is the larva of a moth. The eggs hatch as leaves begin to open. The gregarious caterpillars spin their multilayered web, enlarging the tent as they grow. Entire branches may be covered. **CONTROL** Tents with caterpillars and cocoons can be removed by hand and destroyed. Avoid torching nests, which can damage the tree. Smaller branches with nests can be pruned out. Inspect trees in autumn or winter for egg masses, and prune or peel them off. Because of diseases, parasites, and predators, eastern tent caterpillar infestations occur in 7- to 10-year cycles. Over 25 species of parasitic flies (such as tachinids) and many wasps (including braconids, chalcids, and ichneumons) are natural enemies, so hesitate before killing caterpillars: check their backs to see whether they are carrying the white eggs or cocoons of their predators.

These beneficials are attracted to pollen and nectar plants, such as small-flowered herbs and wildflowers including catnip and Queen Anne's lace. The spined soldier bug and other predaceous insects also target the caterpillars, and Baltimore orioles can clean up an entire infestation. Btk sprays (see p.110) are most effective against very young larvae. For large larvae, apply labeled insecticides.

EDEMA

SYMPTOMS Raised, wartlike outgrowths develop, most frequently on the lower leaf surfaces (*see p.19*) of African violets, geraniums, and peperomias, for example. Initially, they are the same color as the leaf, but may become corky and brown. Affected leaves may become distorted but do not always die. **CAUSE** The plant takes up more water than it can lose through the leaves through transpiration. As a result, small groups of leaf cells swell as they become filled with water, producing pale green, warty growths. If the growing conditions do not improve, cells rupture and die, turning brown and corky. Edema usually develops when humidity is high and water levels around the roots are excessive. **CONTROL** Do not remove leaves that show symptoms. This disorder is not infectious, and removal of leaves further reduces the rate of moisture loss and so worsens the problem. Reduce watering and/or improve drainage. Increase air circulation around the plants by spacing them farther apart and improving ventilation, as appropriate.

Elm Leaf Gall Aphids

SYMPTOMS Beadlike, knobby, spiral, or bladderlike galls are formed on the upper surface of elm leaves. In severe cases, the entire leaf surface is covered and may be distorted.
CAUSE Several species of aphid. Feeding by the aptly named elm cockscombgall aphid (*Colopha ulmicola*) causes narrow 1in (2.5cm) long serrated galls, which turn from reddish to brown. The elm sackgall aphid (*C. ulmisacculi*) produces small bladderlike growths. The woolly pear aphid (*Eriosoma pyricola*) causes a spiral gall on American elm leaves in spring, and then migrates to pear roots in summer.
CONTROL The galls usually are only a cosmetic concern, rarely affecting the overall health of the tree. Infestations may wax or wane from year to year. Individual infested leaves can be removed where practical. Horticultural oil or other labeled sprays times around budbreak may help.

Endothia Canker

SYMPTOMS A hardwood trunk, limb, stem, or exposed root develops an expanding grayish green lesion with fungal fruiting bodies that are orange-pink changing to cinnamon brown (see **p.35**). Bark and twigs die, and girdled branches are killed. A dozen oak species are highly susceptible, particularly live oak, and beeches are commonly infected. American elm, American holly, silver maple, and fox grape are occasionally damaged.
CAUSE The fungus *Endothia gyrosa*. It is favored by warm weather and trees stressed by water shortage, making its greatest growth in summer. It first gains a foothold on wounded bark. Spores can be carried to the wound by splashing rain, insects, wind, and pruning tools.
CONTROL Maintain a tree's vigor by watering and fertilizing, particularly a transplant or another young tree. Remove dying branches by cutting back well below the canker, and be sure to sterilize the tool between cuts. Excise a small trunk canker with 2in (5cm) of bark outside the obvious margin.

Entomosporium Leaf Spot

SYMPTOMS Pear, quince, and other ornamental and fruiting shrubs and trees have tiny, circular, dead spots on both sides of young leaves. The exact colors vary by host, but their reddish, purplish, or dark brown centers turn gray, maroon, purple, or black, ringed by a thin, deep red, purplish, maroon, or brown margin. The old centers develop black dots, and the unaffected leaf areas may turn yellow.
On leaves, succulent shoots, and seedlings, there are similar spots, which become elongated. In midsummer, the season's new twigs develop lesions. Spots on fruit skins progress as on leaves, darkening, enlarging, and coalescing into roughened, sunken blotches that may crack.
A light infection may be only aesthetically injurious, but a heavy infection can result in severe premature defoliation and fruit drop. Plant growth will be drastically reduced. Some 60 species of the rose family are susceptible. Besides pears and quinces, these include apple, crabapple, mountain ash, hawthorn, serviceberry, pyracantha, and cotoneaster. Evergreens – *Photinia* (red tip, red top, Christmasberry), *Heteromeles* (toyon), and *Raphiolepis* (India hawthorn), for example – can be attacked year-round in an area with mild winters.
CAUSE The fungus *Entomosporium mespili*. Most damage occurs after a rainy period in spring. The spores are splashed (or windblown) to new leaf growth from overwintering twig lesions and old leaves on the ground. An epidemic will take place in a cool, wet summer, with new generations of fruiting bodies in close succession, each creating a new generation of lesions. Temperatures above 86°F (30°C) inhibit the fungus, though, as do dry conditions, and mature leaves are resistant to infection, so in summer the disease typically slows greatly. It builds up again with favorable conditions in autumn.
CONTROL Certain cultivars have some resistance. Clean up fallen leaves and other plant parts to reduce the number of overwintering twig lesions. Avoid overhead irrigation, and keep plants open and well spaced. Do not prune in summer, which might prompt a flush of tender, new growth.

Eriophyid Mite

See GALL MITES *p.132*.

Euonymus Scale

SYMPTOMS The foliage of evergreen euonymus, particularly *Euonymus japonica*, becomes heavily coated with elongate, whitish scales about ½in (2mm) long (see **p.21**), which are the males. The females cluster mainly on the stems and are brownish black, pear-shaped objects, up to ⅛in (3mm) in length, well camouflaged against the bark. Heavy infestations cause yellowish discoloration of the foliage; plants lack vigor and often die back. Other *Euonymus* species, bittersweet, holly, pachysandra, and other plants are also hosts but are much less severely affected.
CAUSE A sap-feeding scale insect, *Unaspis euonymi*.
CONTROL The ladybug *Chilocorus kuwanae leuwonar* has been introduced to help control this pest. Grow resistant or tolerant varieties. The newly hatched crawlers are the most vulnerable stage and are present in mid- to late spring and late summer. Spray at those times with insecticidal soap, horticultural oil, or another labeled insecticide.

European Apple Sawfly

SYMPTOMS Apple fruitlets fall off in early to midsummer with a hole in the side (see **p.48**). This hole is filled with excrement. Mature fruits may be misshapen, with a broad ribbonlike scar on the skin, often running up from the blossom end to the middle of the fruit (see **p.47**).
CAUSE A sawfly, *Hoplocampa testudinea*, which lays eggs in the fruitlets at flowering time. After hatching, the caterpillarlike larva bores into the fruitlet and at first tunnels just beneath the skin before boring into the core. Fruitlets damaged in this way drop off, and when fully fed the larvae leave them (creating the exit hole) and enter the soil to pupate. However, if the larva dies

before it can bore into the core, the fruit will reach maturity.

CONTROL Pick off and destroy fruitlets showing signs of damage. Use sticky white boards to monitor for the adult sawflies. Insecticides applied at petal fall for plum curculio normally also control this pest.

EUROPEAN CORN BORER

SYMPTOMS In early summer, corn or any of nearly 200 other vegetables and ornamentals begin to show signs of insect feeding. Corn leaves are peppered with tiny shotholes, and the midribs and tassels may be broken. Ears and stalks may be tunneled and kernels chewed (*see p.48*). Stalks first suffer from surface scraping, later from burrowing, with frass ("sawdust") seen outside the small entrance holes. These weakened stalks are often bent or broken. Insect larvae may be found at any time. Bean pods and stems, especially of soybeans, are likewise bored, with castings outside the small holes. Pepper fruit may be entered where the stem cap attaches; this and bored branches cause premature leaf and fruit color, fruit decay, or fruit drop. Other food plants notably coming under attack include tomato and eggplant. Stems of ornamentals, especially near cornfields, are tunneled, which may cause dieback or breakage. The small, round holes in dahlia flower stalks and stems presage wilting and death to bud ends, flowers, and foliage above as the borer feeds down through the plant. Other common flowering hosts include aster, chrysanthemum, cosmos,

strawflower, gladiolus, hollyhock, and zinnia.
CAUSE The larva of a small moth, the European corn borer (*Ostrinia nubilalis*). Hatching in early summer, the first-generation larva starts feeding on foliage and then tunnels throughout ears and stalks. The young corn borer is tan or pinkish, later turning grayish and reaching about 1in (2.5cm).
CONTROL Planting late may help avoid this pest but invite damage from corn earworm; consult your Cooperative Extension Service for timed planting advice. Peppers, tomatoes, and other hosts may be more susceptible to borer attack if early corn is growing nearby. Rotate to nonsusceptible crops, especially after a season of infestation. Prune off and destroy infested stems. Dispose of, or shred and plow under, cornstalks immediately after harvest or by early spring. Clean up adjacent grassy or weedy areas. Light or pheromone traps can be used to detect moth activity and plan control measures. Handpick egg clusters and larvae. To reach a tunneling larva, split the stalk open beneath the entry hole. Btk (see p.110) and other labeled insecticides can be used.

EUROPEAN ELM BARK BEETLE

SYMPTOMS In midspring, elms show damage, such as wilting, dieback, or flagging branches, on the shoots, buds, living twigs, and bark around crotches. The branch will have sunburst-patterned galleries beneath bark on the surface of the wood.
CAUSE Not directly a threat, the ⅛in (3mm) European elm bark beetle (*Scolytus*

multistriatus) may carry the spores of the fungus that causes the devastating Dutch elm disease (*see p.124*). Beetles emerge and disperse to healthy elms in midspring. There they feed on young bark. Weakened or unhealthy elms are later chosen for egg laying; the beetles bore into trunks or large branches to make galleries in inner bark. In mid- to late summer, another generation emerges to repeat the cycle.
The adult bores back into elm and starts grooving a gallery oriented parallel to the wood grain where inner bark meets wood, and eggs are laid. Larvae feed through the cambium, boring dozens of slightly wavy galleries radiating outward, basically against the grain, from their mother's, creating a system looking like the silhouette of a long-legged millipede.
CONTROL Keep all elms vigorous by proper cultural care. In an area with both the beetle and Dutch elm disease, remove and discard all dead and dying elm trees. Pheromone traps are available to indicate beetle emergence. Bark sprays with labeled residual insecticide may be needed, timed in early spring and midsummer.

EUROPEAN FRUIT LECANIUM

SYMPTOMS Brown, shell-like, convex objects, up to ⅕in (5mm) in length, encrust the stems of many ornamental and fruit shrubs and trees (*see p.36*), especially those growing against walls or in other sheltered places. Honeydew (*see p.36*) excreted by the insects makes the foliage sticky and promotes sooty molds.
CAUSE A sap-feeding insect, *Parthenolecanium corni*, which usually has 1

generation a year. Its eggs are laid under the scale. Crawlers (nymphs) hatch from the eggs in late spring and feed under leaves, returning to twigs in late summer.
CONTROL The newly hatched crawlers are the most vulnerable stage in the insect's life cycle. Spray in midsummer with insecticidal soap or another labeled insecticide. During late winter or early spring, horticultural oil can be used.

EUROPEAN RED MITE

SYMPTOMS The foliage of apples, plums, and (sometimes) peaches loses its glossy green color and becomes increasingly dull and yellowish green or bronzed (*see p.20*). There is a fine, pale mottling of the upper surface, and large numbers of tiny mites and spherical eggs (*see p.40*) occur on the lower leaf surfaces. Heavy infestations can develop in hot, dry summers and result in early leaf fall. Overwintering eggs laid in crevices on the underside of branches can be so numerous that the bark acquires a reddish hue.
CAUSE A sap-feeding mite, *Panonychus ulmi*, which is blackish red and less than ⅛in (1mm) long. It is generally not a problem on unsprayed trees, where predatory mites and insects keep it at a low level.
CONTROL Inspect leaves carefully after late spring before mite damage is noticeable. Avoid unnecessary spraying for other pests or diseases. Apply horticultural oil during the dormant season against the egg stage. Spray with labeled miticide or fruit tree spray. Several applications are often needed.

EUTYPA DIEBACK

SYMPTOMS Leaves have small, irregular, dark spots. At first rough-textured, the tissue drops out, leaving holes. The leaf yellows, becomes cupped with crinkled edges, and later looks tattered. The trunk or a branch also develops discolored spots, which elongate and deepen into sunken cankers. Some trees, notably apricot, exude a sticky yellowish to orangish gum from the dead area. Its vascular flow interrupted, the branch or whole tree above the canker weakens and almost always dies. Grapevines show similar leaf symptoms. More than 60 species can be affected, notably grape, walnut, apricot, and other *Prunus*. Many ornamental shrubs and shade trees suffer, too, such as honeysuckle, dogwood, tulip tree (*Liriodendron*), oak, ash, and poplar.
CAUSE Eutypa dieback (*Eutypa lata*, syn. *E. armeniacae*), which is also called grape dead arm and Cytosporina dieback of apricot. The pathogen winters in the trunk or branch canker, and then in warm weather produces infective spores, which are splashed by water to leaves, wood wounds, and new shoots. It may also enter through wounds.
CONTROL Prune infected branches or canes at least 6in (15cm) below the canker discoloration. For a tree trunk with a canker, take out the entire plant above the bud union or crown, leaving two to four suckers to take its place. A dry, late-winter day is the best time for such surgery. Sterilize tools between cuts, and treat every wound with a fungicidal protectant.

FAIRY RINGS

See TURF FAIRY RINGS AND TOADSTOOLS *p.184.*

FALL WEBWORM

SYMPTOMS Almost any woody plant, except conifers, has leaves skeletonized by late summer. Large, dirty white, silken webbing covers foliage at branch ends. By late summer, infestations are most severe, and a tree can be completely stripped and even killed. Usually, though, the damage is mostly aesthetic, the webbing always being unattractive. Preferred plants include apple, ash, oak, pecan, sweetgum, black walnut, elm, maple, hickory, willow, and alder. Rose and wisteria are among the smaller ornamental hosts.
CAUSE The caterpillars of the fall webworm moth (*Hyphantria cunea*), which hatch in early summer. They spin large nests on branch terminals and extend them as they feed, which they do entirely within the protective webbing.
CONTROL Clean up debris around trees and other host plants. Pick off and destroy leaves with egg masses. Prune off infested branches, or remove nests by hand. Wind up nests on a stick studded with nails. Last-stage larvae about to pupate can be snagged on sticky bands, which should be checked and maintained as needed. Fall webworms have many natural enemies, including numerous parasites and predators. Spray Btk (*see p.110*) on leaves, on foliage, and into the web, especially when the larvae are small.

FASCIATION

SYMPTOMS Shoots or, less commonly, flower stems become enlarged and flattened, developing a ribbonlike, often slightly curled appearance. Leaves, buds, and flowers develop normally on the distorted stem (*see p.43*). Sometimes many stems are affected simultaneously, but more commonly the majority of the plant remains unaffected.
CAUSE Early injury to the growing point, such as that caused by frost or insect attack, slug damage, or some form of herbicide or mechanical injury. Viral or other infections, such as aster yellows (*see p.102*), may also be involved.
CONTROL Although rather peculiar in appearance, fasciation is harmless and usually does not affect the overall growth and development of the plant. Prune out affected stems.

FELT GALL MITES (ERINEUM MITES)

SYMPTOMS Various trees and shrubs, particularly alder, beech, birch, crabapple, linden, and maple, develop a dense coating of hairs on the underside of the leaves. These hairs are usually creamy white, but on some trees, such as copper beech, some maples, and crabapples, the hairy patches are reddish pink (*see p.19*). Later in summer, the patches dry and become brownish. On some plants, such as walnut and grape, the upper leaf surface opposite the galls appears blistered where felt galls have developed on the undersides.
CAUSE Microscopic mites of various species that are usually host-specific. The galls are produced in response to mite feeding.
CONTROL Light infestations on small trees can be checked by picking off affected leaves. Fortunately, apart from creating the galls and ruining the appearance of the plants, these mites have little impact on the host plant's growth. Most miticides are not effective against gall mites, but several insecticides are labeled for control, including horticultural oil. Applications are usually timed around budbreak as the mites emerge to feed on new foliage or in autumn as they return to buds to overwinter.

FERTILIZER BURN

SYMPTOMS The edges or tips of the leaves of nearly any kind of plant turn dull brown, looking dry and scorched, and then dark brown or black (*see p.29*). Older leaves are usually affected first, sometimes only on one side of the plant. Dry soil and hot weather result in the most drastic damage. A seedling shows signs of root damage or fails to emerge. The stem at any stage of plant maturity may rot at the soil line; plant growth slows and then stops, and the plant dies. Tomatoes, peppers, and cucurbits such as squash and melons suffer from blossom end rot. Fruits have water-soaked spots that become sunken, leathery, and brown or black. Irregular patches or well-defined stripes of lawn yellow and die. The dying area does not expand, and bordering grass stays green.
CAUSE Occurring most frequently in poorly drained soil or in areas with little rainfall, fertilizer burn results from excess fertilizer or a high soil concentration of soluble salts. Fertilizer also burns plants from direct contact. Overlapping runs of

a lawn spreader result in a double fertilizer application. **CONTROL** Always follow fertilizer directions. Immediately clean up any spill, and then repeatedly drench the area with water. Sweep up fertilizer from concrete, from which it could run off to lawn or bed edges. Whenever turning or stopping a drop spreader, close it up. If sprinkling granular fertilizer around individual plants, keep it off leaves and away from stems, spreading it evenly over the entire root zone. Immediately after application, spray down the plants to wash granules and dust off and to start to leach it into the ground. Organic fertilizers generally will not burn. However, fresh poultry and cattle manures are high in salts.

FIREBLIGHT

SYMPTOMS Flowers wilt and wither then die back, followed by adjacent leaves and stems shortly afterward (see **p.35**). The plant may show extensive dieback and be killed within a few seasons. Infections usually occur scattered throughout the crown of the tree or shrub, healthy stems often growing next to infected ones. Infection commonly occurs at flowering time. The bark sinks inward on young stems, and, if pared back, a rusty red discoloration is visible on the wood. Ooze may be produced from affected areas. Symptoms may be confused with those of blossom wilt (see p.108), but the infection occurs only in members of the rose family that produce pomes (applelike fruit), such as apples, pears, hawthorns, *Pyracantha*, and *Cotoneaster*. **CAUSE** The bacterium *Erwinia amylovora*, which is

encouraged by warm, wet weather. The bacteria usually enter the plant through the open flowers, but infection may also take place through stem injuries. Bacteria may be carried by rain splash and be spread on unsanitary pruning tools.
CONTROL Prune out affected stems to a point at least 6in (15cm) into healthy wood. Dispose of all prunings, and sterilize all tools after use on an infected stem. If the infection is widespread, or the plant small, it may be better to remove it entirely.

FLEA BEETLES

SYMPTOMS Small beetles, mostly ⅟₂₅in (2mm) long but sometimes ⅛–⅙in (3–4mm), readily jump off foliage when disturbed. They are shiny black (sometimes with a yellow stripe running down each wing case), metallic blue, or yellowish brown. They chew small, rounded shotholes in the upper leaf surface (see **p.29**) that may not penetrate the leaf. The remaining damaged tissues dry up and turn brownish white. Heavy attacks can kill seedlings and check the growth of older plants.
CAUSE There are many species of flea beetle. On brassicas, including radish and turnip, it is mainly *Phyllotreta*; they also attack wallflowers, alyssum, stocks, aubrieta, and nasturtiums. Potatoes, peppers, eggplant, and ornamental *Solanum* species are sometimes damaged by several species. The damage is caused by the adults; larvae live in the soil and feed on roots, causing only minor injury, except to potatoes, which sustain some surface feeding. Flea beetles are active between midspring and late summer.

ACTUAL SIZE

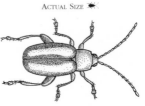

FLEA BEETLE

CONTROL Some damage is usually tolerable but may affect esthetic value. In cases where damage is severe or disease transmission is a concern, such as with corn, grow disease-resistant varieties or cover plants with rowcover when young. Clean up overwintering sites. Beetles are easily disturbed, and many can be trapped with yellow sticky bands placed in or drawn along plant rows. If necessary, several insecticides are available for control.

FLIES

There are a number of fly pests of garden plants, and in all cases damage is caused by the larval stage (maggot) rather than the adults. Other flies – crane flies (see p.118), hover flies (see p.137), and tachinid flies (see p.180) – are not harmful or are even beneficial.
Roots and seeds: see CABBAGE MAGGOT *p.112*; CARROT RUST FLY *p.113*; FUNGUS GNATS *p.131*; LEATHERJACKETS *p.144*; ONION MAGGOT *p.153*; SEEDCORN MAGGOT *p.173*.
Bulbs: see NARCISSUS BULB FLY *p.149*.
Foliage: see BIRCH LEAFMINER *p.106*; BOXWOOD LEAFMINER *p.109*; CHRYSANTHEMUM LEAFMINER *p.115*; COLUMBINE LEAFMINERS *p.117*; GALL MIDGES *p.131*; HOLLY LEAFMINER *p.136*; HONEY-LOCUST POD GALL MIDGE *p.136*; LARKSPUR LEAFMINERS *p.142*; LILAC LEAFMINER *p.145*; PEAR SAWFLY *p.158*; PINE SAWFLIES *p.160*; RASPBERRY

SAWFLY *p.166*; RHODODENDRON GALL MIDGE *p.168*; ROSESLUGS *p.170*; SPINACH LEAFMINER *p.177*; WILLOW LEAFGALL SAWFLIES *p.190*; WILLOW SAWFLIES *p.190*.
Fruit: see APPLE MAGGOT *p.99*; EUROPEAN APPLE SAWFLY *p.126*; IMPORTED CURRANTWORM *p.138*; PEAR MIDGE *p.157*; PEPPER MAGGOT *p.159*; WALNUT HUSK FLIES *p.187*.

FLUORIDE TOXICITY

SYMPTOMS Leaf tips turn brown, often separated from healthy tissue by a yellow band. Leaf edges may turn yellow; green or yellow spots may develop. Spots enlarge, merge, and then turn brown.
CAUSE Accumulation of excess fluorides, which are compounds of the element fluorine. Fluorides are taken up from the soil, which receives them from superphosphate (fertilizer), perlite, and some kinds of peat. Fluoride-treated tap water is a common source. Fluorine is sometimes an airborne pollutant.
CONTROL Grow plants less susceptible to damage. Use fluorine-free water, such as water collected in a rain barrel. Keeping soil pH above 5 will limit uptake.

FOLIAR NEMATODES

SYMPTOMS Brown islands or wedges develop in leaves (see **p.25**), between the larger leaf veins. Eventually, the entire leaf turns brown and dries up. Typically, the youngest leaves at the shoot tips are free of infestation, but the older leaves show progressively severe damage.
CAUSE Two microscopic nematodes, *Aphelenchoides ritzemabosi* and *A. fragariae*, attack a wide range of plants in gardens and greenhouses.

CONTROL Badly infested plants should be removed and discarded. With indoor plants, avoid wetting the foliage: nematodes can emerge from leaves and spread rapidly in a surface film of water.
- *see also* CRYSANTHEMUM NEMATODE *p.115*; NARCISSUS NEMATODE *p.150*; ONION NEMATODE *p.153*; PHLOX NEMATODE *p.159*.

FOOT AND ROOT ROTS

SYMPTOMS Deterioration of basal stem tissues causes the upper parts of the plant to wilt, discolor, and die back. Soft-stemmed plants, especially seedlings and cuttings, are commonly affected, but most annual, biennial, and herbaceous perennial plants may show symptoms. Tomatoes, cucumbers, and melons are frequently affected. The tissues at the stem base may darken, atrophy, become discolored (usually darkening), and occasionally soften. Root rot may occur simultaneously *(see p.55)*. Sometimes called basal rot.
CAUSE Various fungi, often similar to or the same as those responsible for damping off of seedlings *(see p.122)*. Other fungi, including various *Fusarium* and *Verticillium*, may cause foot and root rot symptoms.
CONTROL There is no cure available for infected plants. It may, however, be possible to prevent the spread of the infection by very prompt removal of any infected plants, together with the soil mix or soil around their roots. Unhygienic cultivation techniques, including the use of unsterilized media, dirty trays, pots, and tools, and dirty water, are often responsible for introducing or spreading this infection.

FORSYTHIA GALL

SYMPTOMS Numerous bumpy swellings develop along the length of stems *(see p.40)*. The whole plant or just certain areas of the plant may have them. Individual galls are usually up to ⅜–⅝in (1–1.5cm) in diameter; occasionally, several may be joined or fused together. They are the same color as the forsythia stems. Overall growth and development of the plant is rarely affected, but the plant's appearance can be spoiled.
CAUSE Unknown.
CONTROL If the forsythia becomes disfigured, prune out affected stems to a point several inches beneath the lowest gall.

FOURLINED PLANT BUG

SYMPTOMS Discolored, generally round spots appear in spring on the surfaces of the young foliage of a wide variety of herbaceous and woody plants *(see p.13)*. Accompanying the spots may be depressions in the tissue. Curling or other distortion of a whole leaf is especially likely when the spots coalesce or drop out; the growing leaf may tear, or it may wither and drop. Buds may also suffer deforming irregularities.
Symptoms depend on which of over 250 plant species is host. Most hosts are herbaceous. Chrysanthemum, coreopsis, dahlia, geranium, *Pelargonium*, globe thistle, lavender, lupine, morning glory, Shasta daisy, zinnia, and mint are frequently attacked. Various vegetables, especially legumes, and many weeds are also hosts. Woody plants usually are attacked first on the topmost foliage. All sorts of small fruits suffer, particularly currants and gooseberry.
Among affected ornamental shrubs and trees are azalea, deutzia, dogwood, forsythia, honeysuckle, hydrangea, rose, sumac, viburnum, and weigela.
CAUSE Nymph and adult fourlined plant bugs (*Poecilocapsus lineatus*). The overwintering eggs of this general feeder hatch in mid- to late spring into bright orange-yellow to red nymphs. They are about ½in (2mm) long and have rudimentary black stripes on the wing pads and black dots on the thorax. In about 30 days, the mature fourlined plant bug has developed. The forewings are thickened at their bases and overlap at their membranous ends when folded back and flat. This soft-bodied pest is ¼–⅜₀in (6–7.5mm) and yellow to a bright yellow-green, with 4 lengthwise broad black stripes.
CONTROL The fourlined plant bug has a few enemies among its relatives: damsel bugs, big-eyed bugs, and pirate bugs. Attract these predators to a garden plot with groundcovers and heavy pollen producers. Destroy weeds and plant residues. Protect plants with floating rowcover. Handpick nymphs and adults. Foliar applications of insecticidal soap or another labeled insecticide can help.
- *see also* PLANT (LYGUS) BUGS *p.161*.

FROST

SYMPTOMS Buds discolor, usually turning brown and sometimes becoming soft. Petals of open blooms discolor, usually turning brown, and either retain their shape or wither *(see p.44)*. The buds or flowers on the more exposed areas of the plant are usually the worst affected. Foliage, usually toward the shoot tips and particularly on the more exposed parts of the plant, turns brown or black or appears scorched *(see pp.28, 30)* and may wilt, wither, and die back. Young stem growth adjacent to the frosted leaves may also die back. Russeting of the skin occurs on fruit, usually on the most exposed face of the fruit. Damaged areas may develop a corky, roughened appearance, and the fruit may be deformed. There may be partial or total crop loss.
CAUSE Frost, which is most likely to cause damage on slightly tender plants or those that have budded or leafed out early. Late frosts, occurring once buds have opened, can also be very damaging. Plants that are subjected to the warming of early-morning sun following overnight frost are especially prone to injury.
CONTROL Choose planting positions carefully, especially for early-flowering plants or those known to be readily frost damaged. Provide protection with rowcovers. An autumn dressing of high-potassium fertilizer helps stem growth mature and may help minimize frost damage.

FRUIT SCALD

SYMPTOMS Reddish or brown areas develop on the skin of the fruit *(see p.47)*, on surfaces that are subjected to the full impact of the sun. In extreme cases, the flesh beneath may be damaged, but the discoloration is usually limited to the skin.
CAUSE Strong sunlight on the tender skin of young fruit, which causes scorching or scalding.
CONTROL In temperate zones, scald is generally seen only in unusually hot, bright

summers. Controls usually are not needed but could include artificial shading on specimen trees.

FRUIT SPLIT

SYMPTOMS Shallow cracks occur, usually only just penetrating into the flesh and most commonly running round the stem end of the fruit *(see* ***p.48****)*. These cracks may heal over, but if they occur when the fruit is more mature, the fruit usually succumbs to secondary infections.
CAUSE An erratic supply of water. The splitting occurs when the tree puts on a sudden spurt of growth when moisture becomes available after drought.
CONTROL Keep trees regularly watered, and apply a mulch to moist soil to reduce evaporation of soil moisture.

FRUITTREE LEAFROLLER

SYMPTOMS On any orchard fruit tree, especially apple, or on many ornamental trees and shrubs, the leaves, buds, or blossoms have irregular holes. A few leaves, especially young ones at branch ends, are rolled into tubes held by webbing. Later in the season, immature fruit shows irregular holes. Most deciduous trees, shrubs, and brambles are susceptible to some extent. Leaf damage alone, even when severe, is a minor concern compared with the crop losses suffered by apple and relatives such as pear, quince, and rose and by citrus and walnut. Fruit is likely to decay, and fruit surviving to maturity will be malformed.
CAUSE The fruittree leafroller (*Archips argyrospila*), sometimes called the azalea leaftier, which is the larva of a small moth. Pale green, with a shiny, black head, this caterpillar is ¾–1in (1.9–2.5cm) long. At a branch tip, it ties several leaves together with silk webbing, perhaps enveloping developing fruits. It wriggles to the side when disturbed and may drop down a thread for a short time, and then it returns to its branch.
CONTROL Look for early signs of infestation as the first leaves expand. Scrape off egg masses, handpick caterpillars, or prune off infested terminals. Several species of wasp parasitize leafrollers. Horticultural oil applied before budbreak kills eggs. Btk (see p.110) or another labeled insecticide is most effective if sprayed when 25–50 percent of the eggs have hatched, contacting the larvae before they can roll up leaves to protect themselves.

FUNGUS GNATS

SYMPTOMS Grayish brown flies with slender bodies, ⅛–⅙in (3–4mm) long, run over the soil surface of pot plants or fly slowly and alight on leaves. The larvae are whitish maggots up to ⅕in (5mm) long, with black heads *(see* ***p.53****)*. They live in the soil and feed mainly on decaying organic matter, such as dead roots, but they may damage seedlings or the base of soft cuttings.
CAUSE Several species of fungus gnats (sometimes called sciarid flies), which occur in greenhouses and on house plants. Most are harmless, but some *Bradysia* species damage fine roots and tunnel in soft stems. Young plants or rooting cuttings are usually most sensitive to damage.
CONTROL On established plants, fungus gnats are a nuisance rather than a pest. Maintain good hygiene in the greenhouse, and remove dead leaves and flowers from the soil surface. Use a sterile or an uninfested potting medium or avoid peat-, compost-, and bark-based media, which are attractive to the flies. If seedlings or cuttings are being damaged, Bti (see p.110) or neem-based materials can be drenched into infested soil, according to label directions.

FUSARIUM BULB ROT

See GLADIOLUS CORM ROT *p.132;* NARCISSUS BASAL ROT *p.149.*

FUSARIUM WILT

SYMPTOMS Soft-stemmed plants wilt, either in part or in their entirety. In carnations (*Dianthus*), the flowers fade prematurely and the leaves wilt and discolor. Woodier-stemmed plants may retain their overall shape, but foliage on affected stems wilts and withers. Internal staining of the vascular tissue may occur and is usually brown or black. Death almost always follows, either rapidly or over several seasons, depending on the plant affected. Cool, damp conditions may encourage very pale pink or white, slightly fluffy fungal growth from the infected tissues.
CAUSE Various species of the fungus *Fusarium*, most commonly *F. oxysporum*. The fungi are responsible for the entire or partial blockage (usually by gumlike formations) of the vascular tissues, so the symptoms are very similar to those caused by drought. Dry soil conditions may encourage rapid wilt symptoms, but unlike plants suffering from drought, those affected by fungal wilts do not recover permanently when watered. The fungus may persist in plant debris and may also be capable of remaining viable in the soil for several years.
CONTROL Remove infected plants promptly. Where feasible, remove soil or soil mix from the immediate vicinity of the roots. Do not grow the same or closely related plants on the site again, or at least for a minimum of 5 years.

G

GALLS

See AZALEA GALL *p.102;* CAMELLIA GALL *p.112;* CROWN GALL *p.119*; FORSYTHIA GALL *p.130.*

GALL MIDGES

Gall midges are tiny flies, usually no more than 1/12–⅛in (2–3mm) long, and most of them have larvae that suck on plant juices. The maggots are orange-white and secrete chemicals that affect the development of plant parts and cause them to produce abnormal growths called galls that enclose the larvae. These midges lay their eggs on a particular part of their host plant, such as developing leaves, shoot tips, flower buds, or fruits, and the galls that subsequently develop have a distinctive and characteristic shape that enables identification. Not all members of the gall midge family are pests; *Aphidoletes aphidomyza* larvae feed on aphids and are used as a biological control.

• *see also* GRAPE GALL MIDGES *p.133;* HONEYLOCUST POD GALL MIDGE *p.133;* PEAR MIDGE *p.157;* RHODODENDRON GALL MIDGE *p.168.*

GALL MITES

These microscopic animals can be found on many plants, particularly trees and shrubs. Although tiny, gall mites damage host plants dramatically. They feed mainly on foliage or in buds, and some secrete chemicals that induce the plant to make characteristic abnormal growths. On foliage, many feed on the surface and produce a russetting or bronzing appearance. Gall mites cause raised structures, thickened and curled leaf margins, blisters, excessive growth of hairs, or off-color patches. Bud-feeding mites cause swollen buds, which dry up or proliferate into cauliflowerlike structures, or shoots develop as witches' brooms. With a few exceptions, most gall mites have little harmful effect on their host plants, and the presence of galls can be tolerated.

CONTROL Gall mites are generally not susceptible to conventional miticides for spider mites. For gall-producing species, treatment is usually timed well before galls are apparent.
• see also ASH SPANGLE GALL MITE *p.101*; DRYBERRY MITE *p.124*; FELT GALL MITES (ERINEUM MITES) *p.128*; GRAPE ERINEUM MITE *p.133*; LINDEN GALL MITE *p.145*; MAPLE BLADDERGALL MITE *p.146*; MAPLE ERINEUM GALL MITES *p.146*; PEARLEAF BLISTER MITE *p.157*; REDBERRY MITE *p.167*.

GALL WASPS

Gall wasps, which do not sting humans, are black or brown insects up to ⅛in (5mm) long that are associated mainly with oaks (see **p.52**) and roses. The gall structures are produced by the plant in response to chemicals secreted by the

larval stages, which are white, legless grubs. Although galls are sometimes numerous, they usually have no harmful effect and so control measures are often unnecessary. Occasionally, they cause significant dieback or numerous unsightly galls on their hosts. Pruning and destroying galls in winter or early spring before wasps emerge is generally the best control. Insecticides are rarely effective.
• see also MOSSYROSE GALL WASP *p.148*; OAK GALL WASPS *p.152*.

GIANT WILLOW APHID

SYMPTOMS Dense colonies of unusually large, brownish black aphids occur on the bark of willow trunks, branches, and twigs, mainly in late summer (see **p.36**). The aphids excrete large quantities of sugary honeydew, which makes the stems and ground sticky. Sooty molds often grow on the honeydew, which also attracts wasps and flies.
CAUSE A sap-feeding insect, *Tuberolachnus salignus*.
CONTROL Although very noticeable, this aphid is not generally of significant concern to plant health. Where objectionable, the aphids can be dislodged with a blast of water from a garden hose or controlled with insecticidal soap or another labled insecticide.

GLADIOLUS CORM ROT

SYMPTOMS Concentric brown markings develop on the corm, usually at its base and while in storage (see **p.55**). Crocuses and bulbous irises may also be affected. The corm dries out, becoming mummified but not developing fungal growth. If plants grow from infected

corms, the foliage shows yellow flecking and later striping toward the tips of the outer leaves (see **p.55**). The discoloration spreads downward, and the leaves turn brown and die. Roots of affected corms blacken and may die back.
CAUSE The fungus *Fusarium oxysporum* f. sp. *gladioli*, which persists in the soil and usually enters the plant through the basal plate or roots of the corm.
CONTROL Dispose of plants showing foliage symptoms. Check all corms thoroughly before storing in a cool, dry place and again at the end of storage before replanting. Dry plants off after lifting, and dip corms in a fungicide solution or treat them with sulfur dust. Plant on a fresh site each year.

GLADIOLUS THRIPS

SYMPTOMS In mid- to late summer, the foliage of gladioli develops a fine, pale or silvery mottling with tiny black excrement spots. Flowers also have pale flecking (see **p.45**), and in severe attacks, flower buds fail to open or leaves turn brown. Corms can fail to grow or can show corky damage. Several other plants are reported to be hosts, including *Kniphofia*.
CAUSE Sap-feeding insects, *Thrips simplex*, which tend to be more troublesome in hot, dry summers. Elongate, narrow-bodied insects, up to ¼in (2mm) in length, they live in the flower buds and at the bases of the leaves. Adult thrips are brownish black, while the nymphs are pale yellow.
CONTROL Some damage is tolerable and usually is not significant. At the end of the growing season, remove and discard leaves and stems.

Disinfect corms by treating with hot water (120°F/49°C) for 10 minutes. Store corms below 50°F (10°C).
If severe, infestations can be controlled with foliar sprays of labeled insecticide. Open flowers can be damaged by sprays, particularly if treated in sunny weather.

GOOSEBERRY MILDEW

SYMPTOMS Whitish gray, powdery fungal growth appears on the upper surface of gooseberry foliage (see **p.25**), stems, and fruits (see **p.49**). Severely affected leaves, especially young growth toward the shoot tips, may become distorted and die. Shoot tips may also die back. The mildew on the skin of affected berries turns pale brown or buff as it ages and can be scraped off. Infected fruit is edible but unsightly, turning brown when cooked. Blackcurrants may also be affected.
CAUSE The fungus *Sphaerotheca mors-uvae*, which is encouraged by stagnant air around the branches and by excessive use of high-nitrogen fertilizers. It overwinters on the branches and in buds.
CONTROL Prune out affected branches, prune to thin growth, and improve air circulation within the crown of the bush. Avoid excessive use of nitrogenous fertilizers; a general fertilizer is usually preferable.

GRAPE BUNCH ROTS

SYMPTOMS Clusters of ripe grapes have growths of gray, brown, or black fuzz. Individual grapes to entire bunches may rot.
CAUSE A few unrelated fungi. *Botrytis cinerea*, which also causes gray mold of vegetables, coats grapes with

gray fungal spores. It thrives in stagnant, moist air, ideally at 68–72°F (20–22°C). Spores are blown, splashed, or carried by insects into wounds resulting from sun, hail, windblown sand, pesticides, and even rapid water uptake. The chance of intact tissue being infected through stomata (pores) is increased when moisture makes diseased plant parts, often blossoms, stick to it. Similar infections – Diplodia cane dieback and bunch rot, also known as cane tip blight or summer bunch rot – are caused by *Lasiodiplodia theobromae*. Somewhat different is *Aspergillus niger*, the cause of grape bunch mold and black mold of fruits and vegetables.
CONTROL Purchase only disease-free plants. Some grape varieties are resistant. Handle plants carefully to avoid wounding. Maintain plant vigor. Do not water the foliage. Allow maximum sunshine and air circulation through vines: use training techniques such as 2-wire trellising and midseason cane pruning. Avoid high nitrogen levels in the soil, which enhances foliage growth. At the time of late bloom on the fruit, give a cluster more air by removing nearby leaves, a few individual grapes, or entire clusters. If possible, harvest before cool, rainy periods. Store the fruit as cold (barely above freezing; not just chilled) and dry as feasible. Clean up postharvest residue. Throughout the season, pick decaying fruits so that insects cannot transport the spores. Control flea beetles, grape berry moths, Japanese beetles, leafhoppers, leaf folders, and other grape pests.

Fungicides based on copper, copper sulfate, or lime-sulfur, such as a Bordeaux mix, can provide protection.

GRAPE ERINEUM MITE
SYMPTOMS During mid- to late spring, parts of grape leaves bulge upward (*see p.15*); the underside of these deformed areas is covered in a dense mat of fine, whitish hairs. As summer progresses, the hairs darken and become yellowish or brown. The upper surface of the blistered areas may also become discolored and turn brown. Heavily infested leaves fall.
CAUSE Microscopic gall mites, *Colomerus vitis*, which suck sap from and secrete chemicals into leaves. The chemicals induce the growth of hairs. Apart from the leaf distortion, the mites seem to have little impact on the plant's vigor and ability to produce grapes.
CONTROL Damage generally is insignificant to the health of plants. Individual leaves can be removed if few are affected, but heavy defoliation would be more harmful than tolerating the mites' presence. Where sulfur is used to control mildew, this pest is rarely observed.
• *see also* GALL MITES *p.132*.

GRAPE GALL MIDGES
SYMPTOMS Grape canes, stems, tendrils, flowers, and, especially, leaves develop discolored blisters, swellings, or growths (*see p.16*). Typical abnormalities are ¼in (6mm) reddish or greenish cones or ¼–¾in (6–19mm) round swellings of the same colors. Others might be flat and blisterlike or dramatically protruding and flaring. At first, a small maggot can be found in each one; later exit holes indicate

that the occupant has moved on. Infestations are very rarely heavy enough to affect plant health or yield.
CAUSE Grape gall midges, fly larvae whose feeding causes the growths, which provide both food and shelter for the midges. The shape and color of a gall are characteristic of the midge species. Spinelike or trumpet galls are made by species of *Schizomyia*; round swellings on fruit clusters or on foliage could be produced by the grape tumid gallmaker (*Janetiella breviconda*). Grape phylloxera, an aphidlike insect, creates leaf galls and has stages that feed on roots.
CONTROL Prune out and destroy infested plant parts.
• *see also* GALL MIDGES *p.131*.

GRASSHOPPERS/ LOCUSTS
SYMPTOMS Many types of nonlawn grasses are completely consumed, including grain crops, ornamentals, and, sometimes, sedges. Corn and beans have large, ragged holes in the leaves, and seedlings are eaten. The leaves of other plants are eaten down to the stems. The damage tends to be greatest in summer near grasslands or rangelands after they have dried up. The insects are easily seen resting on plants or flying.
CAUSE Grasshoppers, of which there are hundreds of North American species, ranging from ¼–3in (6–75mm) long, relatively few of which are pests. Colors include many shades of yellow, green, red, and brown, and many are spotted or striped. Their muscular legs enable them to jump powerfully and for distances up to 2½ft (75cm), and most can fly strongly. Populations of certain

species may increase and migrate when environmental conditions are favorable. When swarming, they are often called locusts.
CONTROL Control weedy grasses. Use cones or floating rowcovers to protect plants. After harvest, work the soil well to discourage egg laying. Till the soil occasionally to expose eggs to the elements and predators. Many beneficial organisms prey on grasshoppers, and pathogens provide control, especially when early warm weather is followed by moist conditions. Trap grasshoppers in a jar containing a mixture of 1 part molasses to 10 parts water. The fungus *Beauveria bassiana (see p.105)* and baits with the parasitic protozoan *Nosema locustae* may be sprayed over large areas, but these measures provide only partial control and usually do not act rapidly. Labeled insecticides can be used.

GRAY MOLD (BOTRYTIS)
SYMPTOMS Gray or, occasionally, off-white or gray-brown mold grows on aboveground parts of most plants (*see pp.34, 50*). It sometimes enters through wounds or points of damage. Fruit may be infected by way of the open flowers, the fungus remaining dormant until the fruits start to ripen (*see p.50*). Before the development of the fungal growth, the infected plant tissue usually discolors, often turning brown and soft. Growth above points of infection may deteriorate, with leaves yellowing and wilting, flowers or fruits changing color or dying off (*see p.45*), or the entire plant dying. On flowers,

bleached white or pale brown spots (ghost spots) may form (see **p.42**). The fungus may also produce numerous small black sclerotia (seedlike resting bodies), which are capable of withstanding a wide range of conditions and then infecting plants when conditions are favorable.

CAUSE The fungus *Botrytis cinerea*. Its spores are common in the air and are readily spread by rain or water splash and on air currents. The fungus, which can live on living and dead plant material, may also carry over from year to year in the soil or on infected plant debris.

CONTROL Control is difficult, since the fungus is so widespread. Avoid injury to the plant, and control slugs, snails, and other creatures that eat plants. Remove dead and injured plant parts before they can become infected, and cut back infected areas. Discard plant debris. Under cover, improve ventilation, and water early in the evening to allow plants to dry before nightfall.
• *see also* GRAPE BUNCH ROT *p.133.*

GREENHOUSE WHITEFLY
SYMPTOMS White-winged insects, ½in (2mm) long, readily fly up when plants are disturbed. The adults and the immobile, whitish green, oval, scalelike nymphs live on the undersides of leaves of many houseplants and greenhouse vegetables and ornamentals. The upper leaf surfaces become sticky with honeydew excretion, on which grows a black, sooty mold.
CAUSE A sap-feeding insect, *Trialeurodes vaporariorum*, which breeds continually

throughout the year on indoor plants. Greenhouse whitefly can spread to garden plants during the summer but will not survive a cold winter.
CONTROL Biological control with a tiny parasitic wasp, *Encarsia formosa*, is often the best remedy on indoor plants between midspring and midautumn when temperatures are high enough to suit the parasite. *Encarsia* must be introduced before a heavy infestation has developed, since it needs time to breed before it can start reducing the whitefly population. Sticky yellow traps hung just above plants catch adult whiteflies and indicate when they are starting to appear in a greenhouse. Insecticidal soaps, neem-based materials (for immature stages), and horticultural oil sprays reduce whitefly numbers and have no lasting impact on *Encarsia*. Most other insecticides are dangerous to the parasite and may give poor control of whitefly if a resistant strain is present. Several applications at about 5-day intervals will be required even if the whitefly is susceptible.

GROUND BEETLES
Ground beetles, or carabids, are common, mostly predatory nocturnal beetles that feed on a variety of insects and other invertebrates. They vary in size from ½–1⅜in (2–35mm) and are mostly black, brown, or bronze-green. They have long, slender legs that enable them to run rapidly when disturbed. Adult ground beetles live and feed mainly in or on the soil surface (see **p.63**), but some species climb up plants at night to prey on aphids, small

caterpillars, and other insects. The larvae live in the soil and are also predatory. Some adult ground beetles feed on plant seeds, and while most are harmless, damage can occur on strawberry fruits.

LENGTH: ½–1⅜IN (2–35MM)

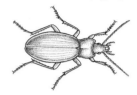

GROUND BEETLE

GROUNDHOG
See WOODCHUCK *p.192.*

GYPSY MOTH
SYMPTOMS Trees and shrubs are severely defoliated in early summer; defoliation often kills conifers, and repeated defoliation can kill deciduous trees. At the height of feeding activity, fecal pellets audibly rain down from trees and accumulate on the ground and other surfaces. Major hosts include alder, willow, basswood, apple, oak (which is especially damaged), hawthorn, and poplar.
CAUSE Caterpillars of a moth, *Lymantria dispar*. The felty brown egg masses are deposited on bark, vehicles, or other solid objects. The gregarious caterpillars, which can blow to nearby uninfested areas, feed on foliage. The hairy, blackish yellow caterpillars are distinctively marked with blue and red warts. The caterpillars can be up to 2¾in (7cm) long.
CONTROL Inspect trees in winter for the egg masses; scrape them off, and destroy them. Look for caterpillars, which hatch from overwintered eggs laid in batches on the bark, from midspring onward. Trunks

can be banded with overhanging burlap strips to trap older caterpillars. They should be monitored frequently and any hiding caterpillars destroyed. Sticky bands placed around the tree also trap moving caterpillars. They have to be maintained every few days if infestations are severe. At the first sign of feeding, small trees and shrubs can be treated with the biological control Btk (see p.110) or sprayed with another labeled insecticide. Small caterpillars are more susceptible than older larvae. see also Gypsy Moth Diseases, *next entry.*

GYPSY MOTH DISEASES
Natural outbreaks of disease among large gypsy moth populations are the most effective control, and some of the organisms most lethal to gypsy moths have been used in eradication measures. The sharp decrease in gypsy moth damage in the eastern US has been largely attributed to the natural spread of *Entomophaga maimaiga*. Lethal viruses are also widespread among gypsy moth populations. The resulting disease blackens and shrivels the larvae (see **p.63**), which hang lifeless from a branch.
The Hamden strain of a nuclear polyhedrosis virus (NPV) has been used as the production standard in Gypchek. Btk (see p110) controls young larvae but not the moth stage.

HALO BLIGHT
See BEAN HALO BLIGHT *p.105.*

HELLEBORE LEAF BLOTCH

SYMPTOMS Slate gray or grayish brown lesions develop on the leaves *(see p.20)*. They may merge, leaving large leaf areas discolored and dead. Flower stems and, occasionally, the flowers themselves may also be attacked, causing flower stems to droop.

CAUSE The fungus *Coniothyrium hellebori*, which spreads especially rapidly in wet weather.

CONTROL Remove and dispose of affected leaves and other plant parts. In certain circumstances, *Helleborus orientalis* appears to show a good degree of resistance to this infection.

HEMISPHERICAL SCALE

SYMPTOMS Scales are evident on the underside of leaves and on stems of a wide range of indoor ornamental plants. Other hosts include gardenia, camellia, citrus, croton, guava, pepper tree, cycads, sumac, myrtle, oleander, and palms. Sugary excrement, called honeydew, falls down and makes upper leaf surfaces sticky. Sooty molds often grow on the honeydew.

CAUSE A sap-feeding insect, *Saissetia coffeae*, which breeds continually throughout the year on houseplants and in greenhouses. It also occurs outdoors in subtropical regions. Mature scales *(see p.16)* have a dark brown, hemispherical shell over their bodies. The shell is up to ⅛in (4mm) across and has an H-shaped ridge on it. Crawlers (nymphs) are flat, oval, and yellowish brown.

CONTROL Heavily infested plants are best disposed of, especially ferns, which generally do not tolerate insecticides. Some scales and honeydew can be removed by wiping the foliage and stems with a damp cloth. Spray with insecticidal soap or another labeled insecticide against the more vulnerable crawlers. Several applications at 7-day intervals may be needed to break the insect's life cycle.

HEMLOCK WOOLLY ADELGID

SYMPTOMS On the twig bark and evergreen foliage of hemlocks (*Tsuga*), especially eastern (Canada) and Carolina hemlocks, are dirty white, woolly tufts, most often attached to twigs at the needle bases *(see p.32)*. Although each globular tuft is only ⅛in (3mm) around, great numbers of them may cover a significant portion of a twig. Foliage appears to be thinning, and dieback may be apparent. The tree loses vigor and needles drop prematurely, eventually to the point of complete defoliation and even death.

CAUSE Hemlock woolly adelgid (*Adelges tsugae*), which feeds on sap during cooler times of the year, the twigs and needle bases being the favored feeding sites. It resembles aphids and often is improperly identified.

CONTROL Susceptible hemlocks are almost always killed within a few years, so infestations must be controlled promptly. Some hemlocks seem somewhat resistant. Examine undersides of twigs from trees, hedges, and specimen plants from several areas. Prune out heavily infested branches, and cut back branches that touch noninfested hemlocks. Look for the woolly masses, which are most obvious in late winter and early spring.

Birds can spread the nymphs from infested to noninfested plants, so avoid placing bird feeders on or around hemlocks. Since fertilizer worsens an infestation, do not fertilize infested plants or surrounding turf. Natural enemies, including *Pseudoscymnus* predatory ladybugs, may help control the pest. Smaller shrubs or trees can be sprayed with horticultural oil in the dormant season or late spring or with insecticidal soap later in the season. Foliar sprays or soil-applied systemics can be used on large plants.

HERBICIDES

SYMPTOMS The leaf blades are distinctly narrowed *(see p.27)*, often to such an extent that the veins are so closely drawn together they appear parallel. Petioles and stems may show spiral twisting, and the foliage may become cupped *(see p.27)*. Brown, scorched spots develop on the foliage *(see pp.23, 34)* and any other part of the plant on which the chemical lands. Stunted rosettes of short shoots and malformed, straplike leaves develop in place of normal side shoots. The symptoms resemble those caused by a witches' broom infection *(see p.192)*. Fruits may not form; if they do, they may be distorted. Tomatoes produce hollow, plum-shaped fruits with few, if any, seeds and little flesh. The stems of brassicas develop roughened gall-like growths at or just above soil level that may appear to be adventitious roots *(see p.39)*. Affected plants may live, but they can fail to bear normally.

CAUSE Herbicides, which can contaminate a plant by inadvertent spraying, drifting spray, using watering cans or spraying equipment that has been insufficiently washed out, and mulching with lawn mowings that contain traces of herbicides.

CONTROL Take great care when spraying, and never do it on hot, windy or gusty days. Protect nearby plants with paper or plastic bags. Where possible, use a watering can and dribble bar rather than a sprayer, since they produce larger droplets that are less likely to cause drift problems. Clearly label equipment used for applying herbicides, and use it for this purpose only. Always wash it out thoroughly after use. Prune out severely damaged areas on trees or shrubs, and feed and water to promote new growth. Severely damaged plants may need to be replaced.

HIGH TEMPERATURES

SYMPTOMS Injury usually results in tissue death and permanent damage. Scorching of leaves, fruits, and flowers is common, often being seen as dry, papery, buff or brown areas. Wilting may occur if the plant is losing more water than it can take up, due to either excessive transpiration or dry soil conditions. Trees or shrubs that have thin bark may show bark death down the exposed side of the stem or trunk. This commonly occurs under cover, especially in greenhouses.

CAUSE Excessively high temperatures or the rapid onset of high temperatures immediately following cool weather.

CONTROL Little can be done once injury has occurred. Prevent further damage by providing shade, improving ventilation, and damping down the greenhouse floor.

HOLLY LEAFMINERS

SYMPTOMS Leaves develop yellowish or purple blotches *(see p.17)* where the internal tissues have been eaten out by a fly maggot. Leaf mines can be seen throughout the year and may be especially abundant on hollies trimmed to form a hedge. This damage has little impact on the health and vigor of hollies. Mined leaves that turn yellow and drop in early summer are likely to be part of the normal loss of old foliage that occurs at that time.
CAUSE The larvae of several small flies, *Phytomyza* species, which lay eggs on young foliage in early summer. There usually are 1 or 2 generations a year, depending on species. Holly leafminer (*P. ilicis*) attacks English holly (*Ilex aquifolium*); native holly leafminer (*P. opacae*) attacks mainly American holly (*I. opaca*) but also English holly. The flies overwinter as late-stage larvae or pupae in the mines, emerging in spring as leaves expand.

HOLLY LEAFMINER DAMAGE

CONTROL Holly leafminer generally must to be tolerated. Yellow sticky cards, hung in or near infested plants, can be used to detect the flies. Look for the flies in spring as leaves first open. Natural controls usually keep the populations in check. Some foliar or soil-applied systemics can be used for severe infestations. Nonsystemic foliar sprays can be used but must be applied before eggs are laid, since insecticides do not penetrate the thick, waxy surface of holly leaves.

HONEYDEW

Honeydew is the sugary excrement produced by some sap-feeding pests, such as aphids, whiteflies, mealybugs, and scale insects. These pests suck sap from the phloem vessels in leaves and stems. The sap they imbibe is very rich in sugars and is only partially digested by the insects, so their excrement is a sticky, sugary liquid that can support the growth of sooty molds, nonparasitic fungi that form black or gray-green deposits on upper leaf surfaces. Light deposits of sooty mold can often be washed from foliage and stems, but it is better to prevent the its buildup by controlling the causal insects before they have a chance to produce honeydew in the first place.

HONEY FUNGUS

SYMPTOMS Affected trees, shrubs, woody climbers, and, occasionally, woody herbaceous perennials start to die back. Resin may exude from around the base of the trunks of infected conifers. The roots and/or stem or trunk bases of infected plants develop a creamy white mycelium (fungal sheet) on them, sandwiched between the bark and the woody tissues beneath *(see p.34)*. The mycelium has a characteristic mushroomlike smell. The fungus also produces tough, brown to black shoelacelike fungal strands called rhizomorphs. They may show branching and are hollow inside, the black outer "rind" being lined with white or faintly pink fungal growth. Rhizomorphs resemble old tree roots and are easily mistaken for them. The rhizomorphs feed on a woody host or the remains of an old tree stump or dead plant. Clumps of toadstools with honey-colored caps and that may be marked with dark brown flecks may appear around the base of infected plants in late summer or autumn. The toadstools may also appear around old tree stumps, following the root line of underground roots or growing from underground rhizomorphs in the vicinity of an infected plant.
CAUSE Various species and races of the fungus *Armillaria*, which cause honey fungus, also called mushroom rot. It is very difficult to differentiate among the species, except on the basis of the damage they cause. Spread occurs either by rhizomorphs, which grow through the soil at the rate of about 3ft (90cm) a year, or by root contact.
CONTROL Remove infected plants promptly, digging out stumps and as much of the root system as possible. Keep plants in good health by regular feeding, mulching, and other relevant care, since this makes them less prone to infection. The spread of disease from the toadstools is minimal, so it is not necessary to clear them away. Certain plants, such as birches (*Betula*), cedars (*Cedrus*), most of the common hedging conifers, cotoneasters, currants (*Ribes*), forsythias, hydrangeas, lilac (*Syringa*), *Malus*, peonies, privet, *Prunus*, rhododendrons, roses, willows (*Salix*), and wisterias, are known to be particularly susceptible and so should not be used as replacement plants in gardens that have honey fungus. Trees, shrubs, and climbers that show a good degree of resistance should be used in preference to others. These include yews (*Taxus*), beeches (*Fagus*), box (*Buxus*), oaks (*Quercus*), celastrus, cercis, catalpas, chaenomeles, clematis, cotinus, elaeagnus, fothergillas, kerrias, passifloras, photinias, pieris, rhus, and tamarix.

HONEYLOCUST POD GALL MIDGE

SYMPTOMS Leaves at the shoot tips of honeylocust (*Gleditsia triacanthos*) fail to expand into the normal form. The leaflets are folded over and make podlike galls *(see p.27)* that contain up to 7 whitish orange maggots. These galls first appear in early summer; by late summer, infestations usually are of no consequence but occasionally are so severe that normal leaf production comes to a complete halt or dieback occurs. The cultivar 'Sunburst' seems to be particularly susceptible and produces pale yellow galls, sometimes with a pink flush.
CAUSE A tiny fly, *Dasineura gleditchiae*. It has 5–10 generations a year, depending on location. Females lay eggs at the shoot tips beginning in late spring.
CONTROL The cultivar 'Shademaster' is reportedly less susceptible to attack. Avoid growing the yellow-foliaged 'Sunburst' where the pest can be troublesome. A few insecticides are available, and use should be timed to when midges are first seen on shoot tips, particularly against the first generation in spring. Tall trees cannot be sprayed properly, and this pest often must be tolerated.

HONEYSUCKLE APHID

SYMPTOMS Grayish green aphids form dense colonies on the shoot tips and flower buds of honeysuckles in late spring and summer. This can result in the formation of witches' brooms and upward folded leaves. The witches' brooms are usually destroyed by cold weather.

CAUSE A sap-feeding insect, *Hyadaphis tataricae*. Eggs are laid on host plants to overwinter. Aphids hatch in spring and feed on shoot tips, injecting a toxin that causes the dormant buds to break and undergo prolific, stunted growth.

ACTUAL SIZE ◆

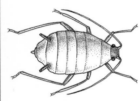

HONEYSUCKLE APHID

CONTROL Check the new growth and flower buds for the presence of aphids from midspring onward. Prune off and destroy witches' brooms and infested growth. Apply insecticidal soap, horticultural oil, or another labeled material before foliage appears to prevent witches' brooms. Resistant cultivars are available.

HORNWORMS

SYMPTOMS The foliage of tomato and its relatives has large, ragged holes, or whole leaves are stripped to the veins or missing. The ground beneath is dotted with dark green droppings. Small stems may also disappear. Green tomatoes sometimes have large chewed holes, which decay or become large, brown calluses on ripe fruit. Small plants can be entirely defoliated and killed.

The season's first damage starts around midsummer. A great deal of a plant's foliage can disappear literally overnight, prompting a closer look and the discovery of green caterpillars bigger than your fingers (*see p.31*). Related plants attacked include potato, eggplant, pepper, tobacco, physalis, petunia, and datura.

CAUSE Hornworms are the larvae of hawk, or sphinx, moths, which resemble hummingbirds. The worst garden pests among them are the tomato hornworm (*Manduca quinquemaculata*, also called tomato worm) and the tobacco hornworm (*M. sexta*). Hornworms are mostly a pale or dark green, infrequently brown or almost black. On the side of each segment is a white, striped marking, a diagonal edged with black (tobacco hornworm) or a sideways V (tomato hornworm); a small, ringed black dot accompanies each stripe. Every caterpillar has a stingless, harmless horn at the rear.

CONTROL Rotate crops out of the host plants. To destroy pupae, cultivate well in late autumn or early spring to kill or expose pupae. Cover crops with rowcover to prevent egg laying. Hornworms are usually well controlled by many natural enemies, including braconid (*see p.109*) and trichogramma (*see p.182*) wasps and other parasites and predators. The wasps are commercially available for release, as are ladybugs (*see p.141*) and lacewings (*see p.141*), which eat the pest eggs. The huge caterpillars are easy to handpick but often well camouflaged. Never kill any caterpillar carrying braconid

cocoons on its back, though, which look like little fuzzy rice grains standing on end (*see p.62*).

Btk sprays (*see p.110*) are very effective against hornworms. Other insecticides are available for use on vegetables but are rarely needed.

HORSE CHESTNUT LEAF BLOTCH

SYMPTOMS Chestnut to tan-brown, irregular leaf blotches (*see p.20*), each with a bright yellow margin, develop from midsummer onward. The damage is often most severe on the leaf margins and leaf tips. Numerous pinprick-size, black fungal fruiting bodies may develop on the upper leaf surface over the spots. Severely infected leaves turn brown, curl, and fall prematurely.

CAUSE The fungus *Guignardia aesculi*, which, although causing early leaf fall, has little effect on the tree's overall health because most of the damage occurs quite late in the season.

CONTROL Gather and dispose of fallen leaves in the autumn to minimize disease carry-over.

HORSE CHESTNUT SCALE

SYMPTOMS Many trees and shrubs, including horse chestnuts (*Aesculus*), lindens (*Tilia*), maples (*Acer*), dogwoods (*Cornus*), magnolias, bay trees (*Laurus nobilis*), elms (*Ulmus*), and *Skimmia japonica*, are attacked. Infestations are most recognizable in early to midsummer when the females deposit their eggs under white, waxy threads; they are secreted from the rear edge of the shell-like covering over the insects' bodies. Mature scales are

brown, up to ⅕in (5mm) long, and found on the trunks and larger branches. After egg laying, the scales die and fall away, leaving circular white egg patches on the bark (*see p.40*). During the summer, young scales – flat, oval, yellowish objects – live on the undersides of leaves. In autumn, they move onto the bark and overwinter as blackish yellow, immature nymphs. Little problem with honeydew and sooty mold occurs with this scale, except on *Skimmia japonica*.

CAUSE A sap-feeding insect, *Pulvinaria regalis*, which has 1 generation a year. The heaviest infestations occur on trees growing in streets and near parking lots, where there is a warm microclimate due to reflected heat.

CONTROL On large trees, horse chestnut scale must be tolerated. Fortunately, it causes little real harm apart from the unsightliness of the egg masses. On small trees and shrubs, scrape off scales and egg masses before eggs start hatching in midsummer.

HOVER FLIES

Many of these flies, also called flower flies and syrphid flies, have black-and-yellow striped abdomens and can be seen sitting on or hovering near flowers. The flies feed on nectar and pollen. Some have larvae that feed on aphids. They may consume as many as 400 before they are ready to pupate and are therefore quite helpful in controlling aphids. Other types of hover fly have larvae that feed on small caterpillars and thrips, in rotting vegetation, in wasp nests, in the mud in pools, or in rot holes in trees.

Although many are beneficial, one hover fly that causes problems in gardens is the narcissus bulb fly *(see p.149).*

LENGTH: ¼–⅝IN (6–15MM)

HOVER FLY

IMPORTED CURRANTWORM

SYMPTOMS Gooseberry bushes become rapidly and severely defoliated *(see p.31)*, often reduced to bare stems by the time the berries are ready for picking. Numerous pale caterpillarlike larvae up to ⅘in (2cm) long and heavily marked with black spots are present. Damage starts in mid- to late spring, and the first generation causes most of the injury, although there may be a partial second and even a third generation. Red- and whitecurrants are also attacked in a similar manner.
CAUSE Larvae of the imported currantworm (*Nematus ribesii*), a sawfly caterpillar. They often feed initially on interior foliage. Adults emerge in spring as foliage expands. Caterpillars develop quickly and drop off the plant to make cocoons in the soil to overwinter.
CONTROL Inspect gooseberry and currant bushes carefully for larvae from midspring. Eggs are often laid on the underside of leaves in the center of bushes, so larvae may go unnoticed until they have eaten upward and outward and there are few

leaves left. Handpick caterpillars or shake them off plants. Natural enemies may not provide adequate control. Insecticidal soap or another labeled material can be used to control the larvae.

INK SPOT

SYMPTOMS Blue-black streaking appears on the outer surface of the bulb. In extreme cases, or if left unchecked, the entire bulb turns black and rots. If infected bulbs produce foliage, it is streaked yellow initially and later develops a red discoloration, particularly toward the tips. Black necrotic spots may develop on the yellowed areas.
CAUSE The fungus *Drechslera iridis*, which produces spores that are spread on air currents. The fungus can overwinter on infected bulbs, in bulb debris, and possibly in soil around infected bulbs.
CONTROL Dispose of any bulbs showing symptoms. Remove any plants that show foliar symptoms, and grow irises on a fresh site. A fungicide containing copper or mancozeb may be helpful.

IRIS BORER

SYMPTOMS Young iris leaves develop dark or water-soaked spots or streaks in midspring to early summer. There may be pinholes, and the leaf edges have ragged, water-soaked chewing damage. Young leaves are slit while still within older leaves. Flower buds, especially at the top of the bloomstalk, may show evidence of boring and feeding, and all affected parts may be slimy. By midsummer, the foliage yellows and wilts and may be loose and rotted at the crown. Brown-headed, large, pinkish grublike caterpillars

may be found in the rhizomes. The rhizome has holes that fill with foul-smelling soft rot, and the decay may spread to attached rhizomes. Rhizomatous irises, particularly bearded irises, are the most frequent hosts. Water-loving Louisiana irises can be another favorite host. Siberian irises are very rarely affected, however, and bulbous irises never are.
CAUSE The iris borer (*Macronoctua onusta*), the larva of a moth, which is by far the most destructive pest of irises. Eggs overwinter in old iris debris and hatch when new leaves are 5–6in (13–15cm) tall. The caterpillar is initially greenish, becoming pink, with a brown or black head. A light stripe runs down its back, and its sides have rows of black dots.
The larva first moves upward while feeding on the leaf surface and edges. Late hatchings may feed up a young flower stalk, damage the buds, and then channel down inside the stalk. The more typical leaf feeder moves down to where a tender inner leaf is covered by an older one. Several younger larvae may feed in each fan.
A few inches above the rhizome, the larva tunnels into the leaf base and eats its way into the rhizome (where only 1 larva will ever be found; the others may have been cannibalized). The iris borer can hollow out this rootstock well into the summer, in the process growing fat and 2in (5cm) long. The malodorous bacterial soft rot (caused by *Erwinia carotovora, see* IRIS SOFT ROT *p.139)* follows, often disintegrating the entire rhizome. The borer may

pupate in the rhizome but usually leaves to pupate several inches deep in nearby soil. The shiny, dark reddish brown pupa is a little smaller than the larva. The short-lived, night-flying moth emerges in late summer or early autumn. It lays eggs, each only ⅟₅₀in (0.5mm) in diameter, in old leaf and flower stalk bases, in other plant debris, and sometimes on the soil near iris plantings.
CONTROL Clean up all leaf, stem, and other debris in late autumn or by early spring to dispose of many of the eggs. To kill the larvae, pinch leaves hard from the base up, especially around obvious damage. You can "X-ray" the borers within the fan of leaves by natural backlighting. Sometimes it is simpler to cut off an infested fan to save the rhizome. When dividing irises in midsummer, carefully inspect all rhizomes. Kill a borer by poking and hooking it with a wire. A partially tunneled rhizome can be saved if it is cleaned up, allowed to dry, and treated. Rhizomes already infected with soft rot can sometimes be saved if the rot is well excised. If a larva has apparently recently vacated a rhizome, search for the pupa by sifting the surrounding soil. (Because the rhizome is at the soil surface, with many shallow roots, transplanting is the only suitable time for this sort of thorough cultivation.) There has been some success drenching beds with insect-pathogenic (beneficial) nematodes in summer. Insecticides are available, including systemics, which should be applied as foliage reaches 6–8in (15–20cm). Repeated applications may be needed.

IRIS LEAF SPOT

SYMPTOMS Water-soaked spots develop on the foliage, later turning brown with gray centers. The spots join together as they enlarge, destroying the foliage. Affected irises are weakened by the loss of foliage and so are less vigorous and may flower poorly.
CAUSE The fungus *Mycospharella macrospora*, which is encouraged by mechanical injury and wet weather. It produces spores that are spread on air currents and by rain and water splash. It overwinters on infected leaves and plant debris.
CONTROL Keep plants well fed, and make sure that they are planted in a suitable, sunny site; they are less susceptible to infection if growing vigorously. If infection occurs after flowering, cut off badly affected areas. If it occurs early in the season, spray affected plants with a fungicide such as mancozeb.

IRIS SCORCH

SYMPTOMS The upper parts of affected leaves wilt and bend over and become reddish brown. The symptoms may initially be confused with those of iris rhizome rot, but the leaf discoloration is different and there is no deterioration of the rhizome. The roots die back; some rot and others disintegrate internally, leaving just a hollow outer "tube" with the threadlike remains of the central cylinder inside.
CAUSE The precise cause is not known, but the problem seems to be caused by root injury in winter or early spring. Winter waterlogging may be responsible.
CONTROL Ensure good drainage. It may be possible

to save slightly affected rhizomes by lifting, removing all deteriorating roots and leaves, washing thoroughly, and replanting on a new, very well-drained site. Foliar feeding, in an attempt to stimulate the production of replacement roots, can help.

IRIS SOFT ROT

SYMPTOMS Foliage yellows and withers, starting at the leaf tips or leaf margins. A soft, often foul-smelling rot develops at the base of the affected leaves and rapidly spreads through the rhizome (*see* **p.55**). As the infection spreads, foliage symptoms become more extreme, and leaves may yellow completely and topple over.
CAUSE The bacterium *Erwinia carotovora* subsp. *carotovora*, which is soilborne and is particularly prevalent in heavy, wet soils and in wet seasons. The bacteria enter the iris through wounds, including those made by iris borers (*see p.138*).
CONTROL Plant irises on well-drained soil. Choose only healthy rhizomes, and plant them shallowly. Avoid injuring the rhizomes, and control pests such as borers and slugs, which may damage them. Remove and dispose of badly infected irises. It may be possible to save rhizomes that are only slightly damaged by cutting off all soft areas back to sound, healthy tissue and treating the cut end with a copper or an antibiotic dust.

IRON DEFICIENCY AND LIME-INDUCED CHLOROSIS

SYMPTOMS Usually seen in combination with manganese deficiency. Leaf yellowing, or chlorosis (*see* **p.24**), often occurs with the development

of brown discolored areas, which start at the leaf margins and then spread between the veins. Immature growth is usually affected earlier and more severely than older growth.
CAUSE Acid-loving plants and lime-hating plants (such as azaleas, ixoras, and gardenias) have roots that are poorly adapted for the absorption of necessary trace elements from an alkaline soil. If conditions are too alkaline, they readily develop deficiency symptoms, particularly of iron and manganese.
CONTROL Avoid growing lime-hating plants on soil that is not sufficiently acidic. Treat affected shrubs with a chelated compound containing iron, manganese, and other trace elements that are available to the plant because they are in a form that does not become "locked up" in the alkaline soil. Use acidic mulches such as chopped, composted oak leaves or conifer bark. Incorporate acidic organic materials into the planting hole at planting. Feed plants with a fertilizer formulated for use on acid-loving (lime-hating) plants. Before planting, consider acidifying soil using sulfur, aluminum sulfate, or ferrous sulfate. Sulfur treatments can also be used around existing plants.

IRREGULAR WATERING

SYMPTOMS Fruits are unusually small and may have a particularly thick skin. The surface may be ruptured, with splits caused when the fruit swells in response to the sudden availability of water (*see* **p.57**). Once the fruit's surface is broken, it is open to infection by secondary organisms, such as gray

mold, which may then cause further, rapid deterioration. Other fruit symptoms may include blossom end rot (*see p.108*). Leaves fail to grow at a regular rate and develop an uneven, almost puckered surface (*see* **p.26**). They may also appear unusually small. Buds may fail to form or form and later drop; bark may split (*see* **p.36**).
CAUSE An irregular or erratic supply of water at the plant roots. Plants growing on a light, sandy soil with a low organic matter content are particularly prone, as are any plants growing in containers.
CONTROL Keep plants adequately watered at all times. Incorporate plenty of bulky organic matter into light soils before planting. Apply a bulky mulch around the root areas to encourage soil moisture retention.
• *see also* BUD DROP *p.111*; DRY BUD *p.124*.

IVY ANTHRACNOSE

SYMPTOMS During a humid summer with frequent heavy rains, English ivy develops large, light to darker brown spots (*see* **p.12**). The spots blacken, and killed tissue may fall away. Similar spots may develop on stems. Irregular circular spots of variable darkness and texture grow there, frequently killing the leaves. If they girdle a main stem, it will collapse and die back.
CAUSE The fungus *Colletotrichum gloeosporioides*, which is also called *C. trichellum*, *Amerosporium trichellum*, and *Glomerella cingulata*. This leaf- and stem-spot fungus requires wet weather or frequent overhead irrigation to spread and invade ivy parts that are injured, stressed by environmental conditions or

nutrient imbalances, or undergoing natural senescence.

Although wounds increase the likelihood of fungal infection, spores can attack undamaged tissue and rest in a latent stage for months, before environmental and plant factors promote further development.

CONTROL Some cultivars are resistant. Provide good air circulation. If groundcover seems too dense, mow annually at a high blade setting; do not mow infected or wet ivy, though, because this will spread the disease. Fertilize, water to prevent drought stress, and be sure that the soil is well drained. Avoid handling English ivy whose leaves are wet, and never walk on it except for maintenance purposes. Cut away and dispose of infected or dead stems and leaves. Clean up all debris. Apply a preventive fungicide, such as Bordeaux mix, copper, sulfur, or lime-sulfur.

JAPANESE BEETLE

SYMPTOMS The growing season sees 2 distinct types of plant damage: in spring and autumn, to roots; in summer through autumn, to foliage *(see **p.30**)*, flowers *(see **p.43**)*, and fruit. In spring, grass dies in large, irregular, brown or bare patches, especially in late spring. The patches can be completely rolled up by hand like a carpet, uncovering C-shaped white grubs. An entire lawn may be killed. Crows, raccoons, and other creatures may do the most significant damage while digging for grubs in

the sod. Primarily grass roots are attacked, although the grubs have reportedly been found on roots of other hosts.

Aboveground damage commences in late spring or early summer, often during the peak rose-blooming period. Leaves and shoots of flowers, vegetables, fruits, and shrubs and trees, especially parts in direct sun, are chewed, and many beetles may be present on a single leaf, flower, or fruit. At first appearing lacy, the foliage skeletonization becomes more irregular until the whole branch or plant is defoliated. Feeding activity ruins scores of herbaceous ornamentals, such as canna, China aster, cosmos, dahlia, hollyhock, and zinnia. In addition to rose (perhaps the most notable host), common woody ornamental plant hosts include flowering quince, rose of Sharon, butterfly bush, heathers, hibiscus, birches, elms, horsechestnut, linden, sassafras, and willows. Corn silks may be eaten. Other vegetables commonly affected include asparagus, beans, okra, and rhubarb. Many fruit crops are also attacked, including grape and apple leaves and peach, nectarine, and raspberry. A fruit may be swarmed over and completely eaten in an afternoon.

CAUSE Larval and adult Japanese beetles (*Popillia japonica*). The brown-headed, grayish white grub, ½–¾in (1.3–1.9cm) and curled, kills or damages grasses and, rarely, other plants by chewing roots. Feeding by the bright, metallic green and brown, ⅜–½in (1–1.3cm) beetle drastically reduces plant vigor, suppressing flowering

and fruiting. Repeat defoliation may kill plants. Infestations tend to be greatest near where both life stages are well provided with preferred hosts: well-maintained sod for the larvae and deciduous plants for the adults. Damage tends to be most severe in sunny, exposed sites. The very mobile beetles become obvious on a sunny day from 70–95°F (21–35°C). They feed only during daylight hours and are minimally active on cool, windy, cloudy days. When approached, they first drop out of sight under leaves, and then strongly fly off.

CONTROL Grubs are naturally controlled in some years by very cold winters with little or no snow cover. Grow flowers and trees the Japanese beetle is not attracted to, such as chrysanthemum, phlox, florist's geranium, and evergreens. Planting corn to produce silk in late summer before or after peak beetle populations can reduce damage.

Remove susceptible wild plants and weeds from the area. These include evening primrose, smartweed, and Indian mallow and such woody plants as elder, poison ivy, sassafras, and wild grape.

In dry summers, turf that is allowed to become dry and dormant is less attractive to egg-laying females. In wetter years, the beetles lay eggs in drier sod. Irrigated lawns generally tolerate more damage than nonirrigated ones. Damaged patches that have just begun to fade can regenerate if kept slightly moist but not sopping wet. Protect plants with floating rowcovers, but regularly check underneath for

emerging adult beetles. On cool, overcast mornings or evenings, when the beetles are most sluggish, shake them off plants and onto sheets or into containers with soapy water. Otherwise, simply handpick them.

Most Japanese beetle traps are baited with both a sex attractant to lure males and a floral lure to draw both males and females. They generally do not help control infestations, although many beetles are trapped. They sometimes are useful indicators of beetle activity. Commercial preparations of spores of *Bacillus popillae*, which causes "milky disease" in grubs *(see p.147)*, can be applied to soil. *B. popillae* does not provide quick results and should not be expected to control a heavy infestation. Soil should be moist and warm (about 70°F/21°C) to be effective. Beneficial nematodes can also be drenched into lawns, which should be well watered after treatment. There have been some successes, but results are inconsistent.

There are general predators and parasites of both adult and grub stages. Many birds relish the beetles, the grubs, or both, including cardinals, catbirds, meadowlarks, grackles, and starlings. Attract parasitic wasps and flies, such as tachinids, to the immediate area with pollen and nectar plants. Controls may be needed when grubs reach about 10 per square foot (100 per sq m): cut and lift up sections of sod to check. Fewer may be tolerated where animals cause damage to turf as they feed on grubs. Generally, treatment is most effective timed when grubs are small, after midsummer, and soil is

moist. Some neem-based materials are labeled as a repellant spray for controlling beetle damage to roses. Other labeled insecticides are available.
• *see also* WHITE GRUBS *p.189*.

JUNIPER SCALE

SYMPTOMS Flat, rounded, or elongate and rectangular white objects with a small yellowish patch develop on the foliage of juniper, cypress (*Cupressus*), false cypress, Leyland cypress, and arborvitae. Heavy infestations cause yellowing and dieback of green shoots (*see p.37*). Entire plants may be killed.
CAUSE A sap-feeding insect, *Carulaspis juniperi*. Eggs and crawlers (nymphs) are present around June in colder areas, to late winter in warmer regions. The rounded scales are protective covers for females and are up to 1⁄16in (1.5mm) long. The smaller rectangular scales cover males.
CONTROL Horticultural oil or another labeled insecticide can be used when crawlers are present.

JUNIPER WEBWORM

SYMPTOMS Patches of brown foliage bound together with silk threads develop. Dark brown caterpillars with paler stripes running along their bodies, up to ⅜in (1.1cm) long, live within the webbing (*see p.32*). Leaves damaged by the caterpillars dry up and die in early summer. Compact, upright junipers, such as 'Skyrocket', can be badly damaged.
CAUSE Caterpillars of a moth, *Dichomeris marginella*, which has 1 generation a year. In southern areas, the moths are active in midspring; in northern regions, they are present

from late spring to early summer. Caterpillars first mine the leaves, later feed externally, and then overwinter. Pupation is in spring. Damage is sometimes overlooked, since it usually occurs first in the plant interior canopy.
CONTROL Several natural enemies attack this pest. Infestations can sometimes be dealt with by cutting out webbed shoots in late spring or early summer. Alternatively, use the biological control Btk (*see p.110*) or spray forcibly with another labeled insecticide.

KABATINA SHOOT BLIGHT

SYMPTOMS Cankers develop on the shoots of Leyland cypress, certain arborvitaes, cypresses, and junipers. The cankers usually develop at the base of small branches and cause dieback and, occasionally, death.
CAUSE Species of the fungus *Kabatina*. The fungal spores are carried on air currents and by rain splash.
CONTROL Remove affected shoots promptly to minimize spread of the disease.

KEITHIA THUJINA NEEDLE BLIGHT

SYMPTOMS Small, black fungal fruiting bodies, each measuring about ⅓in (1mm) across, are embedded in the foliage of *Thuja*. They later split as the spores are released, leaving small, brown sunken pits or holes in the leaves. Foliage, particularly toward the base of the plant, may turn brown (*see p.28*) and die back if the infection is extensive.

CAUSE The fungus *Didymascella thujina*. The spores are airborne, and most infections take place in late summer or early autumn, especially in humid or wet weather. They may overwinter in mucilage attached to the damaged areas.
CONTROL Prune out infected areas promptly, before the spores are released.

LACEBUGS
See ANDROMEDA LACEBUG *p.98;* AZALEA LACEBUG *p.102;* RHODODENDRON LEACEBUG *p.168.*

LACEWINGS
The larvae of lacewings, sometimes called aphidlions, are beneficial insects that feed on aphids and other small insects. Some lacewing larvae carry the sucked-out remains of earlier meals among clumps of bristles on their upper surface. A well-fed larva is up to ⅜in (1cm) long and, apart from a pair of sharp jaws protruding at the front, is hidden under a tangled mass of dead aphids. The harmless adult lacewings have slender, elongate bodies that are pale green, black, or brown. They are aptly named, having 2 pairs of transparent wings, sometimes with darker markings, that have many veins. The adults have long, thin antennae and feed on pollen and nectar or honeydew. Some have unique gold eyes. One species of green lacewing, *Chrysoperla carnea*, overwinters as adults and is often found indoors. Lacewing eggs and larvae

can be purchased for release on greenhouse or garden plants. Look for the tiny eggs on garden plants; they are laid on long stalks, normally on the undersides of leaves. The larvae are cannibalistic, so when releasing eggs, make sure that they are well distributed throughout the garden.

LENGTH: 1⁄12–¾IN (2–20MM)

LACEWING

LADYBUGS
Most of these beneficial insects feed on aphids, as both adult beetles and larvae; some ladybugs also prey on scale insects or spider mites, while others feed on fungal spores. Adult ladybugs are familiar insects, especially those with wing cases that are red with black spots (*see p.60*), but there is great variation, even within some species. The larval stages are generally slate gray to dark blue to nearly black, with orange or white spots on the upper surface. The Australian *Cryptolaemus montrouzieri* is commercially available for controlling mealybugs in greenhouses. Another species, the multicolored Asian ladybug (*Harmonia axyridis*), may be an occasional pest in autumn, when it congregates against buildings and enters houses to overwinter.

LENGTH: UP TO ⅝IN (1.5CM)

LADYBUG LARVA

LARCH ADELGIDS

SYMPTOMS Small patches of fluffy white wax appear on the foliage in early summer. Heavy infestations can cause leaf distortion and yellowing, and sooty molds develop on the pests' sugary excrement (see *p.32*). Trees may appear to be covered with light "snow."
CAUSE Small, black sap-feeding insects, *Adelges laricis*, which resemble aphids and secrete white, waxy fibers. Adelgids of a related species, *A. lariciatus*, feed on and around bud scales and cones. Both have stages on spruce that cause shoot galls.
CONTROL Generally, the damage is of no serious consequence to the trees but mainly a cosmetic concern. Large trees cannot be sprayed effectively but are usually able to tolerate infestations. Small trees can be sprayed with insecticidal soap, horticultural oil, or another labeled insecticide.

LARKSPUR LEAFMINERS

SYMPTOMS The leaves of larkspur, delphinium, and monkshood develop large, brown, dried-up areas extending from the tips toward the leaf stalks (see *p.18*). White maggots up to ⅛in (3mm) in length may be found feeding within the mined areas.
CAUSE Larvae of a leafmining fly, *Phytomyza aconiti*, which has 2 or more generations in summer. Two related species, *P. delphinivora* and *P. delphiniae*, cause similar damage.
CONTROL For light infestations, the damaged parts of leaves can be picked off when damage is first noticed, in late spring to early summer. Collect and

destroy plant debris in autumn and spring. Insecticides are also available and should be applied.

LAUREL PSYLLID

SYMPTOMS During summer, leaves at the shoot tips of sweet bay (*Laurus nobilis*) or cherry laurel (*Prunus laurocerasus*) develop thickened, pale yellow margins, which curl over (see *p.26*). Often just half of the leaf is affected, and later the damaged parts dry up and turn brown. Immature insects (nymphs) feed underneath the curled leaf margins but emerge when ready to molt to the adult stage. These nymphs are gray, flattened, and secrete a fluffy, white waxy material from their bodies. The adults are winged, aphidlike insects, ½in (2mm) in length, which may be seen on the shoot tips during summer.
CAUSE A sap-feeding insect, *Trioza alacris*, which has several generations between late spring and midautumn. Adult psyllids overwinter and then lay eggs in spring on host plants.
CONTROL Natural enemies help provide control. Maintain plant vigor. Deal with light infestations by picking off affected leaves, or spray with insecticidal soap, horticultural oil, or another labeled insecticide when signs of recent damage and nymphs are seen.

LEAF CURL
See PEACH LEAF CURL *p.156*.

LEAF-CURLING PLUM APHID

SYMPTOMS The foliage on plums becomes tightly curled and crinkled during spring (see *p.27*). Green insects, up to ⅛in (2mm) long, and their whitish cast skins can be

found on the underside of the leaves. Damage may also occur on various herbaceous plants, including chrysanthemum, dahlia, cineraria, carrot, aster, and sunflower. Later in the season, the infestation on plums dies out and trees start to produce normal foliage again.
CAUSE A sap-feeding aphid, *Brachycaudus helichrysi*, which migrates back to plums in late summer to lay overwintering eggs near the buds. It sometimes is a greenhouse pest. Mealy plum aphid (*Hyalopterus pruni*), another common species on plums as well as apple, apricot, and peach, also causes leaf curling.
CONTROL Overwintering eggs can be reduced by applying horticultural oil in late winter to early spring. Insecticides labeled for use on plum applied shortly after budbreak help control the newly hatched aphids before they cause extensive leaf distortion. Mealy plum aphid can be controlled similarly. Japanese hybrid plums are not susceptible to this species.

LEAF-CUTTING BEES

SYMPTOMS Circular or elliptical pieces are cut from the leaf margins (see *p.30*) of roses, wisterias, epimediums, and other plants. The smooth circular outline and regular shapes of the missing pieces readily distinguish leaf-cutting bee damage from caterpillar or other damage.
CAUSE Leaf-cutting bees, *Megachile* species, which resemble honeybees but have rusty hairs beneath their abdomens. They are nonaggressive solitary bees, each female constructing her own nest during the summer.

They often visit a plant repeatedly to gather material, and by the time their nest is finished they may have removed several hundred pieces. The female bee uses the leaf pieces to make thimble-shaped cells in her nest. This may be in a hollow plant stem or in a tunnel dug in rotten wood or soil. Quite often, a bee makes use of soil in flower pots, and the cells, resembling old cigar stubs, come to light when the plant is repotted. When a cell has been built, the bee stocks it with nectar and pollen, lays 1 egg, and completes the cell by capping it with circular leaf pieces. A nest may contain up to 20 cells.
CONTROL Damage rarely affects the health of plants. Like other bees, these are useful pollinators and can be tolerated unless small plants are being badly defoliated. Plants can be protected with covers or cones.

LEAFHOPPERS

Leafhoppers are sap-feeding insects, mostly ½–⅛in (2–3mm) long, that live on the undersides of leaves. The adults readily jump off leaves when disturbed, but their wingless nymphs are less active. Their feeding usually causes a coarse, pale mottling of the upper leaf surface. Garden plants frequently attacked are blackberries, plums, salvias, mints, beeches, and many others. Potato leafhoppers are a migratory pest, overwintering only in far southern areas. They inject a toxin as they feed, causing the yellowing and marginal browning called hopperburn. Potatoes, beans, leguminous plants, and young birch, maple, and apple trees are

among the many hosts. Some leafhoppers transmit plant diseases. General control measures for leafhoppers are given in the entry for rose leafhopper (see p.170).
• see also ASTER YELLOWS p.102; POTATO LEAFHOPPER p.163.

LEAFMINERS

Leafmining is a habit adopted by many insects, mainly the larvae of some flies, moths, sawflies, and beetles. The damaged parts of the leaf dry up and become white or brown. The mines may be straight or meandering lines or circular or irregular blotches, and the form of the mine is often distinctive for a particular species. If a mined leaf is held up to the light, the larva or pupa can often be seen at the end or edge of the mined area. Leafminers are usually controlled by removing affected leaves or spraying with labeled insecticide.
• see also BIRCH LEAFMINER p.106; BOXWOOD LEAFMINER p.109; CHRYSANTHEMUM LEAFMINER p.115; COLUMBINE LEAFMINERS p.117; HOLLY LEAFMINERS p.136; LARKSPUR LEAFMINERS p.142; LILAC LEAFMINER p.145; OAK LEAFMINERS p.152; SERPENTINE LEAFMINERS p.173; SOLITARY OAK LEAFMINER p.175; SPINACH LEAFMINER p.177; SPOTTED TENTIFORM LEAFMINER p.177.

LEAFROLLERS AND LEAFTIERS

SYMPTOMS In spring and summer, the leaves of many woody and herbaceous plants are raggedly chewed or skeletonized. Some leaves, often young ones, are twisted, rolled, or folded lengthwise and held with silk strands. Flower buds, blossoms, or developing fruit

have irregular holes. Fruit, vegetable, and ornamental plants are common hosts, including apple and related plants, grape, strawberry, raspberry, filbert, hickory, oak, spruce, hemlock, pachysandra, canna, bean, pepper, rose, geranium, and hydrangea.
CAUSE Leafrollers, leaftiers, and certain webworms, most of which are moth larvae that construct shelters for feeding, resting, or pupation. Some of the more damaging species include oblique-banded leafroller (*Choristoneura rosaceana*), which feeds on apple foliage and fruit as well as on many other plants. Spruce budworms (*C. fumiferana* and *C. occidentalis*) are important forest pests. Fruit tree leafroller (*Archips argyrospila*) is often a problem on deciduous fruit trees, ornamentals, and many herbaceous plants. Oak leafroller (*A. semiferana*) is among several in this group that roll and skeletonize oak foliage. *Archips purpuranus*, sometimes called the pachysandra leaftier (see p.155), is a pest of pachysandra, apple, and other deciduous plants. The typical caterpillar is greenish or pinkish with a dark head and is ½–¾in (1.3–1.9cm) long. It feeds on and lives in the new leaves it rolls or folds up and ties with webbing. It may roll up inside the leaf or otherwise feed on any stage of flower or fruit, from bud to mature fruit or vegetable. The nest provides protection against predators and parasites, the elements, and control sprays. Larvae often wriggle quickly and drop or hang from a silk thread when disturbed.
CONTROL Damage from leafrollers and leaftiers

generally is of minor cosmetic importance. These insects have many natural enemies, including egg and larval parasites and predators such as birds. Destroy leafroller egg masses, often on leaf undersides but sometimes on branches, which often look like clusters of overlapping scales. Handpick or prune off and destroy leaf nests and occupants. Spray Btk (see p.110) on young larvae before they roll their nests. Pheromones are available for some species and are useful for detecting moths and timing sprays. Horticultural oil applied before budbreak helps control egg masses. Other labeled insecticides are also available.

LEAF SCORCH

SYMPTOMS The plant grows well, but its foliage is spoiled by dry, brown areas that are usually first seen around the leaf edges. The entire leaf may ultimately be affected, or the central area may retain its normal color until the end of the season. If the problem is severe, or occurs in for several years, plant growth is affected and dieback may occur. On maples, stems that deteriorate as a result of scorch often develop a white surface discoloration. In extreme cases, extensive dieback, and occasionally even death, may occur.
CAUSE Various factors may be involved. The most common are an overly wet or excessively dry soil, cold winds, or hot, bright sun. Plants lacking in vigor from some other cause, or those that are not yet properly established, are particularly prone to scorch.
CONTROL Attempt to determine which adverse

condition or conditions are involved, and improve growing conditions accordingly. If necessary and feasible, consider moving the plant to a more suitable site.
• see also BACTERIAL LEAF SCORCH OF OAK p.103.

LEAF SPOTS (BACTERIAL)

SYMPTOMS Necrotic patches, usually angular in outline, develop on foliage. Many bacterial leaf spots are surrounded by a bright yellow halo (see **pp.13, 29**). There are no minute, raised fungal fruiting bodies (pycnidia), as seen on fungal leaf spots.
CAUSE Various bacteria may be involved, but especially *Pseudomonas* and *Xanthomonas*. They are usually spread by rain or watering splash from leaf to leaf or, occasionally, from stem lesions to leaves. In most cases, the leaf spotting itself is not very damaging but may indicate that the plant is suffering from another, more serious problem.
CONTROL Remove infected leaves promptly, and avoid overhead irrigation. Use a copper bactericide to protect leaves from infection.
• see also DELPHINIUM BLACK BLOTCH p.122; RHODODENDRON LEAF SPOT p.168.

LEAF SPOTS (FUNGAL)

SYMPTOMS Necrotic spots, usually circular and either gray or brown (see **p.13**), develop on the leaves and may join together, causing large areas of dead leaf tissue to develop (see **p.12**). Occasionally leaves may be killed, but in most cases leaf spots are not very damaging. Sometimes, however, they cause extensive leaf drop.

The spots can show concentric zones of discoloration and may bear numerous, raised, pinprick-size, black or brown fungal fruiting bodies. Many common examples have entries elsewhere under their host name.

CAUSE A wide range of fungi, such as *Alternaria*, *Cercospora*, *Colletotrichum*, and *Helminthosporium*.

CONTROL Remove affected leaves if necessary. Rake up and dispose of fallen leaves at the end of the season to minimize carry-over of spores. Mancozeb can be used for certain leaf spots.

- *see also* ALTERNARIA LEAF SPOT *p.98*; ENTOMOSPORIUM LEAF SPOT *p.126*; IRIS LEAF SPOT *p.139*; IVY ANTHRACNOSE *p.139*; MYROTHECIUM LEAF SPOTS AND ROTS *p.149*; PANSY LEAF SPOT *p.155*; PEA LEAF AND POD SPOT *p.156*; RHODODENDRON LEAF SPOT *p.168*; ROSE BLACKSPOT *p.169*; STRAWBERRY LEAF SPOT *p.179*; WILLOW LEAF SPOT *p.190*; YUCCA LEAF SPOT *p.192*.
- *also see* RUSTS *p.171*.

LEAF WEEVILS

SYMPTOMS Ragged holes are eaten in the foliage of many deciduous trees, especially elm, willow, and poplar. Maple, linden, crabapple, hawthorn, and ornamental cherry are also reported hosts. Tips of arborvitae, chamaecyparis, and juniper are damaged. Small brownish (deciduous plants) or greenish (evergreens) beetles, ⅛–¼in (3.5–6mm) long, may be present in large numbers.

CAUSE The European snout weevil (*Phyllobius oblongus*) and the arborvitae weevil (*P. intrusus*), which feed on young foliage from midspring to early summer.

A variety of other weevil species feed on foliage of ornamental plants. Fuller rose beetle (*Pantomorus cervinus*), black vine weevil (*Otiorhynchus sulcatus*), and two-banded Japanese weevil (*Callirhopalus bifasciatus*) have broad host ranges and are among the more common species.

CONTROL Damage often is tolerable, and even larval stages, which feed on roots of host plants, do not usually cause significant harm. Weevils can be shaken off plants or handpicked and destroyed. Beneficial nematodes are sometimes used for larval stages, drenched into the soil when larvae are present. Labeled insecticides can also be applied for adults if damage becomes intolerable.

LEATHERJACKETS

SYMPTOMS Legless, grayish brown tubular larvae, up to 1–1½in (2.5–3.8cm) long and without obvious heads, occur in the soil (*see **p.53***). They are mainly lawn pests, causing yellowish brown patches in midsummer where the grubs have severed the roots (*see **p.58***). Leatherjackets can also kill vegetable and flower seedlings and young plants.

CAUSE Leatherjackets, which are the larvae of European crane flies (*Tipula paludosa*), or "giant mosquitoes." There are many species of crane fly, but the larvae of the European crane fly sometimes damage lawns, causing patches to die or thin, especially in spring. The flies lay eggs in the soil in late summer or early autumn. Secondary damage from birds probing for larvae to eat may also cause significant damage.

LENGTH: UP TO 1–1½IN(2.5–3.8CM)

LEATHERJACKET

CONTROL By the time leatherjackets have grown large enough to cause noticeable damage, it is generally too late for insecticides to be effective. Check areas of suspected infestations by digging up sod 1ft square (0.09 sq m) and 2in (5cm) deep. If more than 25 leatherjackets are found, then control is suggested. Beneficial nematodes (*see p.151*) can be used against older larvae when the soil is moist and at least 57°F (14°C). Leatherjackets can be removed from lawns by covering small areas with black plastic overnight after heavy rain or irrigation. The larvae will come up onto the lawn surface and can be removed when the plastic is lifted. The adults cause no damage.

LIGHTNING

SYMPTOMS A tree trunk can explode during an electrical storm, with chunks of bark and even wood thrown several yards. Obvious heat-related damage often occurs over much of the remaining plant tissue. Perhaps only the treetop or some limbs are shattered, leaving jagged stubs, or a relatively narrow strip of bark, with a shallow layer of sapwood, is blown off the trunk or bursts into flames. This strip may extend the entire length of the trunk and into the ground, including at least one major root, whose bark and soil cover is also blown off. The resulting rough groove, following the grain, can be continuous or interrupted.

Later, all or part of the tree may brown and die.

In other cases, no gross damage is apparent on the tree, but there may be short ridges several inches long on the trunk. A conifer may exude copious resin. Even in the absence of obvious trunk damage, leaves may yellow and branches die back. On citrus, for example, foliage starts to wilt within 4–6 hours of a strike.

In a large stand of trees with few or no signs of gross trauma, a group of trees to 100ft (30m) across sooner or later turn brown and die. One or more trunks near the center of the dead patch may have stripped bark. Similarly, crops or nursery plants can be killed in a large circle. Lone trees or plants in open fields are the most likely to suffer damage, especially a deep-rooted or decaying tree in moist soil, rather than a healthy tree with shallow roots. Within a group or in a woodland, the most vulnerable tree is the tallest one or a tall one on the windward edge.

CAUSE Direct or nearby lightning strikes. Heavy electric charges in a storm seek to discharge along the most conductive path, which is often between a cloud and the ground. A tree brings the earth's charge closer to the cloud, so it facilitates discharge, often along its entire length, including a major root. If the charge is conducted through the outer sapwood, steam and perhaps other gases are generated instantaneously and explosively, blowing off bark and sapwood. A ground discharge, with the aboveground parts of the tree missed by the lightning bolt, can kill trees and other plants by killing their roots.

Degrees of group fatality and survivable damage is very often centered in a visible "lightning ring" around the point of discharge.

CONTROL Since a healthy tree is more resistant than a declining tree, trees should be watered during dry spells and fertilized to maximize vigor. If a tree looks susceptible because of height or location, or the tree has value to justify the cost, consider having an arborist install a lightning rod, whose copper cable will ground into the soil well away from major roots. Opinions vary, however, on the protective efficacy of instaling lightning rods in trees.

A severely damaged tree may need to be completely removed. Remove damaged branches and bark, which may only be loosened, and neaten all wounds to shut out opportunistic invaders. Water and fertilize to help the plant recover.

LILAC BLIGHT

SYMPTOMS Angular brown spots develop on lilac leaves. Affected leaves die back. Buds blacken and die, and young shoots may be girdled and then wilt and die *(see **p.33**)*. Large, elongated cankers may form on older stems. Secondary gray mold is common and may mask blight symptoms.
CAUSE The bacterium *Pseudomonas syringae*, which is readily spread on air currents and by rain and water splash.
CONTROL Prune out affected areas of the plant promptly, cutting well back into healthy tissue.

LILAC BORER

See ASH (LILAC) BORER *p.100;* CLEARWING BORERS *p.115.*

LILAC LEAFMINER

SYMPTOMS The leaves of lilac, privet, and ash develop brown, shriveled areas *(see **p.19**)* where the internal tissues have been eaten by leaf-mining caterpillars. When half-grown, the whitish green caterpillars emerge from their mine and roll up the leaf tip to form a tube held in place by silk threads. There are several generations a year, with damaged leaves being seen from late spring through summer.
CAUSE Caterpillars of a small moth, *Caloptilia syringella*, which occasionally infest deutzia, mountain ash, and euonymus as well.
CONTROL Pick off affected leaves; clipping privet hedges removes many of the mined or rolled leaves. Btk *(see p.110)* or another labeled insecticide can be applied.

LILY GRAY MOLD

SYMPTOMS Dark green, water-soaked spots develop on the foliage. Affected leaves soon turn brown or bleached and die off. Leaves wither from the base of the stem upward, wilt, and remain hanging on the stem. Flower buds are killed or very distorted. If infection spreads into the stem, the plant topples over. The bulb remains healthy.
CAUSE The fungus *Botrytis elliptica*, which produces numerous spores that are spread on air currents and by rain and water splash. The fungus may persist from year to year as black sclerotia (fungal resting bodies) that develop on infected plant debris. Wet weather encourages disease development and spread.
CONTROL Remove and dispose of infected leaves or all of the top growth, if

necessary. Bulbs from infected plants can be kept, provided that they show no evidence of rot. Remove all debris at the end of the season. *Lilium hansonii* and *L. martagon* show a degree of resistance.

LILY LEAF BEETLE

SYMPTOMS Bright red beetles, ¼in (6–7mm) long with black heads, appear on lilies (*Lilium*), especially Madonna lily (*L. candidum*) and fritillaries (*Fritillaria*), from early spring onward. In midsummer, the larval stage also occurs on the foliage. The grubs have rotund bodies, up to ⅓in (8–9mm) long, and are orange-red with black heads. They cover themselves with their own wet, black excrement. Both grubs and adults eat leaves, flowers, and seedpods. Feeding damage can seriously defoliate plants.
CAUSE A leaf beetle, *Lilioceris lilii*, which is active as an adult from spring until autumn.

LENGTH: ¼IN (6–7MM)

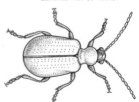

LILY LEAF BEETLE

CONTROL The long period during which the adults and larvae are active makes this a difficult pest to control. With small numbers of lilies and fritillaries, it is possible to protect them by picking the adults and grubs off by hand. The beetles make a rather startling squeaking sound when handled but are nonetheless harmless to humans. Several insecticides are available. The grubs are more vulnerable than the adult beetles.

LIME-INDUCED CHLOROSIS

See IRON DEFICIENCY AND LIME-INDUCED CHLOROSIS *p.139.*

LINDEN GALL MITE

SYMPTOMS From late spring onward, slender, tubular, red or yellowish green projections, up to ⅕in (5mm) long, develop on the upper surface of linden leaves *(see **p.14**)*. The leaves may be badly distorted.
CAUSE Microscopic gall mites, *Eriophyes tiliae*, which induce the galls' growth by secreting chemicals as they feed on the underside of the leaves in early summer. The galls are hollow, and the mites live within them during the summer months.
CONTROL Apart from creating the galls, the mites have no harmful effects on the tree.

LOCUSTS

See GRASSHOPPERS/LOCUSTS *p.133.*

LUPINE APHID

SYMPTOMS Dense colonies of whitish gray aphids, which are up to ⅙in (4.5mm) long, occur on annual and perennial lupines during late spring and summer *(see **p.41**)*. They live on the underside of leaves and on flower spikes, which become sticky with honeydew excreted by the pests. Infestations can be so heavy that plants wilt and die.
CAUSE A sap-feeding insect, *Macrosiphum albifrons*, which overwinters in plant crowns.
CONTROL Look for aphids on leaves and stems from midspring. Dislodge aphids with a blast of water from a garden hose if numbers are high. Alternatively, apply insecticidal soap or another labeled insecticide.

MAGNESIUM DEFICIENCY

SYMPTOMS Yellowing develops between the leaf veins and around the leaf margins, leaving clear green bands immediately adjacent to the veins (*see p.22*). As the green pigment (chlorophyll) deteriorates, other pigments, including yellow and red ones, may become visible. When magnesium is in short supply, it is transported out of the older leaves into the new, developing leaves; older, lower leaves are therefore most readily and visibly affected with these symptoms.

CAUSE A deficiency of magnesium, which often occurs in plants growing in very acidic soils or soil mixes, or after periods of heavy rain or watering. Magnesium is readily leached through the soil when soil water levels are high. The use of high-potassium fertilizers may also increase the occurrence of this deficiency.

CONTROL For a rapid response, apply magnesium as a foliar spray. Use Epsom salts at the rate of 8oz in 2½ gallons (200g in 10 liters) of water, to which is added a wetting agent such as a few drops of mild liquid detergent or soft soap. Several applications are usually needed, at weekly to biweekly intervals. Alternatively, apply Epsom salts to the soil at 1½oz per square foot (40g per sq m).

MANGANESE DEFICIENCY

See IRON DEFICIENCY AND LIME-INDUCED CHLOROSIS *p.139*; PALM FRIZZLE TOP *p.155*.

MAPLE BLADDERGALL MITE

SYMPTOMS Small, wartlike growths appear on the upper surface of maple leaves, especially near the trunk and on large limbs, from early spring to early summer. These bumpy galls are first yellow-green, then pink and blood red, and finally black. A leaf with many galls becomes misshapen, turns yellow, and drops. Although unsightly, this damage is not a threat to the tree's health. Silver maple is the most frequent host.

CAUSE Maple bladdergall mites (*Vasates quadripedes*). The microscopic mites gather on an unopened leaf bud; as soon as the leaf opens, they begin feeding on the undersurface, causing a slight depression. During feeding, the mites inject a substance that promotes abnormal leaf tissue growth around them.

CONTROL The light damage usually does not warrant control measures. Pick off deformed leaves. Horticultural oil applied before budbreak may provide some control.

MAPLE ERINEUM GALL MITES

SYMPTOMS In early summer, a feltlike growth of whitish, green, or red hairs develops on leaf undersides.

CAUSE Microscopic mites that suck sap and secrete chemicals into the foliage, inducing abnormal growth. *Eriophyes elongatus* produces a red erineum on sugar maple; *E. calaceris*, a red erineum on Rocky Mountain maple; *E. modestus*, a green erineum on sugar maple; and *E. negundi*, a white erineum in blister galls on boxelder.

CONTROL Control is usually not needed because, apart from creating the galls, these mites have no harmful effect on their hosts. On small plants, light infestations may be controlled by removing affected leaves.

• *see also* FELT GALL MITES *p.128*.

MEALYBUGS

SYMPTOMS A white, fluffy wax occurs in leaf axils (*see p.32*) and other inaccessible places, such as between twining stems (*see p.37*). Infested plants become sticky with honeydew. Sooty molds may grow on the honeydew. Cacti, foliage plants, and succulents are frequent host plants, but many other houseplants and those grown in greenhouses are attacked.

CAUSE Several sap-feeding mealybugs (*Pseudococcus* and *Planococcus*). They are soft-bodied, grayish white or pink insects up to ⅙in (4mm) long. The wax conceals their eggs.

CONTROL During midsummer, when day length and temperatures are suitable, biological control with a ladybug predator, *Cryptolaemus montrouzieri*, can reduce infestations. Insecticidal soap or another labeled material can be used. Place plants outdoors and make sure that spray coverage is thorough. Several repeat applications may be necessary to provide control. Avoid placing new plants and those that may be infested among clean ones until assured that they are free of mealybugs.

• *see also* ROOT MEALYBUGS *p.169*.

MELON (COTTON) APHID

SYMPTOMS Small, dark green, yellow, and/or black aphids form dense colonies on foliage and flowers. Plants are soiled with cast aphid skins, sticky honeydew, and sooty mold. Heavy infestations cause stunted growth and the early death of blooms. Plants likely to be attacked include chrysanthemums (*see p.43*), cucumbers, melons, okra, begonias, and dahlias.

CAUSE A sap-feeding aphid, *Aphis gossypii*, which can also damage plants by transmitting cucumber mosaic and other plant viruses. While it is mainly a problem in greenhouses, it may also be found outdoors.

CONTROL Outdoors, natural enemies usually provide control. Indoors, biological control with parasitic wasps, *Aphidius colemani*, or predatory midge larvae, *Aphidoletes aphidomyza*, can help during summer. Dislodge aphids with a blast of water, or apply insecticidal soap or another labeled material. Frequent, thorough spraying with insecticidal soap can reduce infestations indoors and outdoors.

MEXICAN BEAN BEETLE

SYMPTOMS Starting in spring, bean leaves become skeletonized and eventually turn brown. This skeletonization progresses to large, ragged holes, the remaining foliage drying up (*see p.29*). Bean pod production is reduced, and the pods and stems themselves are occasionally chewed. Plants may die. Lima bean is very susceptible, but snap beans, soybeans, cowpeas, clover, and alfalfa are also hosts.

CAUSE Larval and adult Mexican bean beetles (*Epilachna varivestis*), which feed from leaf undersides. All stages, including eggs and pupae, often are found simultaneously in summer.

Yellow to reddish, rounded, ¼–⅜in (6–8mm) long, and with 16 dark spots making 3 rows on each wing cover, the adult looks very much like a large ladybug, to which it is related. The larvae are green becoming yellow, and covered with fuzzy spines. There is normally 1 annual generation in colder regions, but 3 or 4 are common in warmer areas Damage is usually greatest in late summer, after populations have built up, and a garden near bean fields may experience a large invasion as the beetles leave the drying field crops.

CONTROL Plant resistant bean cultivars. Grow varieties that bear, or at least become well developed, before local beetle activity. Use floating rowcover. Handpick larvae and adults. Check under leaves daily, and crush the egg masses or simply dispose of the leaves. Remove or till under all plant refuse after harvest to eliminate overwintering sites. Attract beneficial predators and parasites to Queen Anne's lace growing between or near crop rows. The spined soldier bug (*Podisus maculiventris*) is commercially available as an early predator to supplement native populations of assassin bugs and anchor bugs and can be released or lured with commercially available attractants. Ladybugs sometimes prey on the eggs and young larvae. The parasitic wasp *Pediobius foveolatus* can be bought for release in warmer months. Rain or excessive heat may suppress populations. A very cold winter will destroy many overwintering beetles. Pyrethrin sprays or other labeled insecticides can also be used.

MICE

Several types of mice, such as *Mus*, *Microtus*, and *Peromyscus*, cause problems in gardens and buildings. They dig holes in the soil where peas, beans, and corn have been sown, or where crocus corms have been planted. Green shoots are left lying on the soil surface, but the corms and seeds are eaten (*see **p.51***). Mice also cause damage from autumn to spring, when they are indoors and feed on stored fruits, vegetables, seeds, and seedlings.

CONTROL Set mouse traps or bait stations in places where mice are causing damage. Be careful to use bait away from children, pets, or wildlife. In the garden, put traps under the cover of logs or bricks, away from birds and pets. After planting crocuses, press the ground down firmly to make it harder for mice to locate the corms. Get a cat.

MIDGES

See GALL MIDGES *p.131;* GRAPE GALL MIDGES *p.133;* HONEYLOCUST POD GALL MIDGE *p.136;* PEAR MIDGE *p.157;* RHODODENDRON GALL MIDGE *p.168.*

MILKWEED APHID

See OLEANDER APHID *p.153.*

MILKY DISEASE

Caused by the bacterium *Bacillus popilliae*, milky disease infects and kills the grubs of the Japanese beetle (*see p.140*) and other scarab beetles. Naturally occurring but commercially available under several trade names, milky disease is harmless to mammals, birds, plants, and all other insects and ground-dwelling organisms. Formulated as a dust containing infective spores, it is applied directly to a lawn when the soil is not frozen. The spores are viable for several years and infect grubs when they consume spores as they feed. An infected grub will live for 2–3 weeks, spreading the inoculum as it feeds and releasing a large number of spores after it dies. A grub infected with *B. popilliae* becomes increasingly white and opaque as its blood turns from clear to white with spores, hence the name milky spore, and it may show a brown tinge just before death.

Because milky disease requires larval hosts for proliferation and distribution throughout a lawn, avoid using soil insecticides. Since adult Japanese beetles are highly mobile, coordinated neighborhood or community efforts may improve the chance of control with milky disease.

MILLIPEDES

SYMPTOMS Millipedes feed mainly on rotting organic matter but sometimes damage seedlings and other soft plant tissues, such as strawberry fruits. They can also extend damage initiated by other pests, such as slugs on potato tubers.

CAUSE Many species can be found in garden soils (*see **p.54***). The garden millipede (*Oxidus gracilis*) is a common greenhouse pest. Millipedes have long, segmented bodies that may be cylindrical or flat; each body segment has 2 pairs of legs.

LENGTH: ⅝–1⅝IN (1.5–4CM)

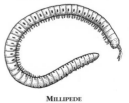

MILLIPEDE

CONTROL Usually not necessary. Protect strawberry fruits by using straw to lift the berries clear of the soil. Damage to potato tubers is generally initiated by slugs, so it is necessary to control them first (*see p.174*). Millipedes are encouraged by organic fertilizers, whose use should be avoided or limited if millipedes are numerous enough to cause problems. Put trap boards out, and collect and destroy millipedes hiding during the day. Several pesticides are labeled for use around foundations, but in very wet years, millipedes may congregate and be hard to control. Sweep them up, and dispose of them away from the house.

MITES

Mites are related to spiders. Those that damage plants fall into several groups: spider mites; eriophyid mites, which include gall and rust mites; and tarsonemid mites, which include broad and cyclamen mites. Most have 4 pairs of legs, although gall mites have only 2 pairs. All are less than ⅛in (1mm) long. They feed by sucking sap from their hosts. Many important pest mites belong to the spider mite group. They cause fine, pale mottling of foliage; this feeding damage can lead to defoliation. Heavily infested plants may become festooned with silk webbing. Eryophyid mites secrete chemicals as they feed that cause the plant to produce abnormal growths that enclose the mites. Rust mites often cause a russetting or bronzing of foliage. Tarsonemid mites infest the shoot tips and flower buds, causing stunted and distorted growth.

Many other mites are harmless and valuable parts of the garden ecosystem, since they feed on fungal growth on rotting plants or on algae (*see* ORIBATID MITES *p.154*). Some mites are predators of pest insects or of other mites and can be used to give biological control in greenhouses. Examples are *Phytoseiulus persimilis* for the control of greenhouse spider mite, and *Amblyseius* for western flower thrips.

• see also

Spider mites: EUROPEAN RED MITE *p.127*; SOUTHERN RED MITE *p.176*; SPRUCE SPIDER MITE *p.178;* TWOSPOTTED SPIDER MITE *p.185*.

Gall (eriophyid) mites: ASH SPANGLE GALL MITE *p.101*; DRYBERRY MITE *p.124*; FELT GALL MITES *p.128*; GALL MITES *p.132*; GRAPE ERINEUM MITE *p.133;* LINDEN GALL MITE *p.133;* MAPLE BLADDERGALL MITE *p.146*; MAPLE ERINEUM GALL MITES *p.146;* PEARLEAF BLISTER MITE *p.157*; REDBERRY MITE *p.167*; TAXUS BUD MITE *p.181*.

Tarsonemid mites: CYCLAMEN MITE *p.121*; TARSONEMID MITES *p.180*.

MOLES

Moles (*Scapanus*) are infrequently seen because they spend most of their lives below soil level. They create a system of underground tunnels and chambers in which they live and feed on earthworms and other soil-dwelling invertebrates. The soil excavated during tunnel construction is deposited in heaps on the surface of lawns and flower beds (*see* **p.59**). Moles also make shallow tunnels, above which the soil is pushed up.

CONTROL A variety of controls and deterrents is available. The cheapest and often most effective method is to use a mole trap. The position of a mole's tunnel is located by probing the soil around a recent molehill with a stick. When found, open up the tunnel with a trowel at least 1ft (30cm) away from the molehill. Insert the trap, taking care to align it with the direction and depth of the tunnel. Cover the trap with sod and an inverted bucket to prevent light from entering the tunnel. If the mole keeps pushing soil into the trap, reset it elsewhere. Alternatives to trapping include flooding the tunnels, which may kill the young or deter the adults, and burying fencing 1½–2ft (45–60cm) belowground and extending it somewhat aboveground, which provides a barrier.

MOSSYROSE GALL WASP

SYMPTOMS Wild roses, sucker growth on grafted roses, and some rose species develop roughly spherical galls, up to 2⅜in (6cm) across, on 1-year-old stems (*see* **p.39**) and occasionally leaves in spring to early summer. The exterior of the gall is covered in a dense mass of mosslike growths that are reddish or yellowish green. In autumn, the mossy covering dries up.

CAUSE The mossyrose gall wasp (*Diplolepis rosae*), which lays eggs in buds in midsummer. Many white grubs live and feed inside the gall. Several related species make somewhat similar galls on roses.

CONTROL Apart from creating the galls, this insect has little adverse effect on the plant, so control measures are unnecessary. If the galls are unsightly, remove them.

MOTHS

Moths, like butterflies, have wings that are covered by many small, overlapping scales. Their arrangement on the wings gives the distinctive, sometimes colorful patterns by which different moth species can be recognized. Most moths fly at night. Moths vary considerably in size; some of the smallest, such as some of those with leafmining larvae, have a wingspan of about ⅛in (5mm), while the biggest hawk moths have a wingspan of up to 3in (8cm). It is the caterpillars that cause the damage to plants, rather than the adults, which take nectar from flowers or do not feed at all. Most moths are not pests, but those listed below can damage garden plants.

• see also ASH (LILAC) BORER *p.100;* BAGWORM *p.103;* CABBAGE BUTTERFLY *p.111;* CABBAGE LOOPER *p.112;* CANKERWORMS *p.113;* CASEBEARERS *p.113;* CLEARWING BORERS *p.115;* CODLING MOTH *p.116;* CORN EARWORM *p.117;* CUTWORMS *p.121;* EASTERN TENT CATERPILLAR *p.125;* EUROPEAN CORN BORER *p.127;* FALL WEBWORM *p.128;* FRUITTREE LEAFROLLER *p.131;* GYPSY MOTH *p.134;* HORNWORMS *p.137;* IRIS BORER *p.138;* JUNIPER WEBWORM *p.141;* LEAFROLLERS AND LEAFTIERS *p.143;* LILAC LEAFMINER *p.145;* NANTUCKET PINE TIP MOTH *p.149;* OAKWORMS *p.152;* ORIENTAL FRUIT MOTH *p.154;* PACHYSANDRA LEAFTIER *p.155;* PEA MOTH *p.156;* RHODODENDRON BORER *p.167;* RUSTY TUSSOCK MOTH *p.171;* SOD WEBWORM *p.175;* SOLITARY OAK LEAFMINER *p.175;* SPOTTED TENTIFORM LEAFMINER *p.177;* SQUASH VINE BORER *p.178;* WATERLILY LEAFCUTTER *p.188*.

MOWER INJURY

SYMPTOMS/CAUSE Tree and shrub trunks and stems are often battered and lacerated near the ground by the wheels and the deck of a mower (*see* **p.36**). Roots at the surface are scalped when run over. Any such bark injury opens the plant to boring insects and pathogens, many of which never attack intact bark. Repeated wounding alone can result in dieback. Death can eventually occur, particularly with young, thin-barked trees and certainly when the wounds strip the bark and girdle the trunk. Similar, although lighter, damage can come from string trimmers.

CONTROL Immediately trim any damaged bark and clean the wound. Prune off injured or dying twigs. Do not mow close to the trunk: trim there by hand or carefully with a string trimmer. Place a plastic guard, a screen, or another barrier around the base of the trunk. Do not grow grass right up to the trunk: surround it with a 1–2ft (30–60cm) ring of 3–4in (8–10cm) deep mulch or gravel, or a groundcover.

MULBERRY WHITEFLY

SYMPTOMS Leaves of mulberry, mountain laurel (*Kalmia*), *Itea*, flowering dogwood, holly, maples, sweetgum, and several other woody ornamentals are covered with honeydew and possibly sooty mold. The undersides may be infested by tiny black, scalelike insects with waxy white fringes, which are thickly peppered over the surface (*see* **p.15**). Clouds of small whitish flies may be present. Plants may appear to be generally unhealthy, with falling leaves.

CAUSE The very active mulberry whitefly (*Tetraleurodes mori*), which is less than ⅛in (3mm) long, but congregates in great numbers under leaves and flies up in a cloud when disturbed. They are present from late spring to September. The jet black, elliptical larva is only ⅛in (1mm) long and is circled with a white wavy fringe, which is lost in the second larval stage.

CONTROL Attract their natural enemies, which include parasitic wasps, lacewings, ladybugs, pirate bugs, and big-eyed bugs. Strongly spray infested plants with water, vacuum their tops, or simply handpick leaves covered with immobile larvae. Serious injury is relatively uncommon, and most plants tolerate an infestation. Adults can be controlled with horticultural oil, insecticidal soap, or another labeled insecticide. Sprays should be directed to leaf undersides.

MUSHROOM ROT
See HONEY FUNGUS *p.136.*

MYCOPLASMAS
SYMPTOMS Symptoms vary from host to host and with the precise identity of the organism. They may resemble those produced by viruses and may include greening of flowers and yellow markings on leaves, often combined with distortion and stunting.
CAUSE Various organisms that are similar in structure and activity to bacteria and viruses.
CONTROL Remove any affected plants promptly. Control leafhoppers, because they can spread some mycoplasmalike organisms.
•*see also* ASTER YELLOWS *p.102.*

MYROTHECIUM LEAF SPOTS AND ROTS
SYMPTOMS Any aboveground plant part on a wide range of hosts can develop water-soaked lesions that turn necrotic and dark brown to black (*see p.14*). A stem, for example, is frequently girdled at or near the soil line, and all growth beyond will die back. Covered with spore-producing lesions, a *Viola* petiole becomes dry and brittle. Other plants develop large, sunken cankers anywhere on the stem. Drying and cracking, the canker develops a thin, white layer, followed by black fruiting bodies, and the stem is broken easily.
CAUSE The fungus *Myrothecium roridum*. A few other *Myrothecium* species sometimes cause some of the same symptoms, especially in corn, but they are usually found on grasses and dead plant debris. *M. roridum* is a soil-dwelling saprophyte, living off dead vegetable matter, but it can also infect and flourish in living plants. It may be seedborne, or it may enter wounds of normally resistant varieties. Disease development is favored by temperatures of 70–80°F (21–27°C). When temperatures reach 90°F (32°C for 4 hours a day, development ceases.
CONTROL Plant resistant or less susceptible cultivars in sterilized soil. Avoid wounding plants during propagation and transplanting. Do not overfertilize, do not water from overhead, and provide for quick drainage of excess moisture. Dispose of any infected plant part. If the main stem, crown, or roots are diseased, destroy the entire plant. Fungicides give some protection.

NANTUCKET PINE TIP MOTH
SYMPTOMS In summer, the branch tips of a 2- or 3-needled pine, such as mugo, Scots, and Austrian pine, turn yellow then dry and brown, sharply standing out against the healthy evergreen foliage (*see p.38*). On close examination, the tips appear to have been mined with several chambers. Small, pinkish brown caterpillars may be inside. A young tree may be killed, and the affected pines may become abnormally bushy, crooked, or otherwise scrubby.
CAUSE The larva of the Nantucket pine tip moth (*Rhyacionia frustrana*), which bores into and feeds on branch ends as early as midspring. Several cream or reddish brown, ¾in (1.9cm) larvae pupate in the tips. There are 2 generations a year in northern areas and up to 5 in southern regions. Several related species cause similar damage to pines. European pine shoot moth is a common one, but is found singly in damaged tips. Diplodia (Sphaeropsis) tip blight causes similar injury, but the leaf tips are not hollowed out.
CONTROL Prune and destroy bored tips in winter and any other time before a brood matures locally. Pheromone traps are available for detecting flights and timing insecticide applications. Look for moths about ⅜in (10cm) long with reddish wings marked with 4 silvery bands. Several materials are available, and best results are usually with systemics. Apply Btk (*see p.110*) before larvae start boring.

NARCISSUS BASAL ROT
SYMPTOMS Infection occurs at the basal plate (the flattened area at the base of the bulb), causing it to discolor and rot. Discoloration and rotting spread upward through the inner scales, turning them chocolate brown. A pale pink fungal growth may develop on the basal plate and among the affected scales. Bulbs in storage turn uniformly brown, dry out, and become mummified. Those in the ground usually rot off completely, and by the end of the season there may be no trace of them. Leaf symptoms on growing bulbs include yellowing, stunting, and sparse foliage.
CAUSE The fungus *Fusarium oxysporum* f. sp. *narcissi*, which is soilborne. It persists in soil on infected bulbs that are not sufficiently affected for the symptoms to have been noticed. The disease is most damaging during or following hot summers.
CONTROL It may be beneficial to prevent infection by dipping the bulbs in a fungicide solution. This should be done before summer temperatures are at their highest, and within 48 hours of the bulbs being lifted. Dusting with sulfur, and early planting in autumn, may also reduce the risk of infection.

NARCISSUS BULB FLY
SYMPTOMS Bulbs fail to grow or produce only a few thin leaves in the spring. If the bulb is cut in half vertically, it can be seen that the center has been eaten away and filled with a fly larva's muddy excrement (*see p.54*). The plump maggot is a dirty cream color and is up to ⅜in (1.6cm) long. There is usually only a single maggot in each bulb.

CAUSE Narcissus bulb fly (*Merodon equestris*) resembles a small bumblebee and lays eggs on the necks of bulbs in early summer, when the foliage is dying down. It also attacks other bulbs, including amaryllis (*Hippeastrum*), hyacinth, lilies, tulips, and snowdrops. There is 1 generation a year.
CONTROL Cultivation techniques can reduce losses. Mound up soil around the stem bases when plants start to die down to make them less attractive as egg-laying sites. Valuable bulbs can be protected by growing them under rowcover, which needs to be in position from late spring to midsummer. When small bulb fly larvae are found, investigate whether the bulbs are suffering from other pests, such as nematodes or narcissus fly, or from fungal diseases. After lifting bulbs, sort them and discard any that appear soft or damaged. Soaking bulbs in hot (110°F/43°C) water for 2–3 hours (longer for large bulbs) provides control. Thoroughly dry or plant bulbs after treatment.

NARCISSUS LEAF SCORCH

SYMPTOMS As the leaves emerge, they become red-brown and scorched, and the symptoms then spread down the leaves (*see p.29*). Brown spots appear on the foliage, and numerous tiny, pinprick-size, raised fungal bodies may develop on damaged areas. Occasionally, flower stems and spathes may also be attacked. The bulbs do not show rotting or discoloration. In addition to *Narcissus*, amaryllis (*Hippeastrum*) and snowdrops (*Galanthus*) may be infected.

CAUSE The fungus *Stagonospora curtisii*, which may survive in the dry, papery outer bulb scales.
CONTROL Remove and dispose of infected leaf tips. Spray emerging foliage with copper or mancozeb. Dip bulbs for 30 minutes in the fungicide solution, according to the manufacturer's instructions, and dry off before storing.

NARCISSUS NEMATODE

SYMPTOMS Plants produce stunted and distorted foliage and flower stems. Some viruses cause similar symptoms, so the presence of nematodes has to be confirmed by cutting the bulb in half transversely. Nematode activity in the bulb causes concentric brown rings or arcs where the pest has damaged the tissues (*see p.54*). In large plantings of daffodils (*Narcissus*), the pest gradually spreads, so that each year the area of killed and damaged plants gets larger. New bulbs planted as replacements in infested soil quickly succumb to nematodes.
CAUSE Microscopic worms that live within the tissues of the bulb, foliage, and stems.
CONTROL Dig up and discard daffodils showing symptoms; others growing within a radius of 3ft (90cm) may be infested and should also be removed. Plant sound bulbs purchased from a reputable supplier.

NECTAR ROBBING

Many flowers produce nectar in order to attract bees and other pollinating insects. As these insects push their mouthparts into the nectaries at the base of a flower, their bodies become dusted with pollen from the anthers.

When they visit other flowers of the same type, some of this pollen rubs off onto the stamens, and pollination is achieved. Sometimes, however, bees cheat by biting a hole in the base of the flower (*see p.46*), enabling them to reach the nectar without touching the anthers and stamens. It is mostly short-tongued bees that do this when they cannot reach the nectaries from the front of the flower. For example, carpenter bees (*Xylocopa virginica*), which strongly resemble bumblebees, often damage blueberry flowers when searching for nectar. Flowers may die or may survive to set fruit. Sufficient competition from other pollinating bees can help discourage carpenter bee injury. Once a shortcut to the nectar exists, other insects will take advantage. Nectar robbing is most frequently encountered on beans and may contribute to poor fruit set. It is not possible to prevent nectar robbing, but fruit set is usually adequate if beans are kept well watered and do not suffer from high temperatures.

NECTRIA CANKER

SYMPTOMS Woody plants show roughened, flaky areas of bark on branches, twigs, and stems. The cankers enlarge and may girdle the stem, causing dieback. In summer, white fungal pustules may develop on cankered areas; in winter, they are replaced by many small, red fruiting bodies.
CAUSE Various species of the fungus *Nectria*.
CONTROL Prune out affected areas as soon as symptoms develop. Spray with a fungicide containing copper; on fruit trees, some sprays

used to control various mildews and scabs should also give incidental control of this disease.

NEEDLE BLIGHTS AND CASTS OF PINES

SYMPTOMS On young pines, the needles discolor, often showing diffuse brown or black lines. Infected needles may be shed prematurely. Damage to mature trees is insignificant, but young pines may be weakened. Another blight may cause distinct bands of discoloration to develop on the needles.
CAUSE *Dothiostroma pini* and *Lophodermium*.
CONTROL Rake up and dispose of infected needles as they fall.

NEEDLE RUSTS OF CONIFERS

SYMPTOMS On spruce (*Picea*), needles become discolored. If the fungus *Chrysomyxa abietis* has attacked them, they may develop orange fungal pustules but remain attached to the tree through winter. If attacked by *C. rhododendri*, they may become covered with orange pustules, followed by white spore tendrils, and then fall from the tree in autumn. The latter fungus is less common and spends part of its life cycle on rhododendrons. Norway and Sitka spruce are most frequently affected, but most spruces can be attacked. On pines, another fungus causes small yellowish spots on the needles, and resinlike exudations may occur. Later, off-white, columnlike growths develop on the needles and erupt to produce bright orange spores. This fungus may also attack herbaceous alternate hosts, including bellflowers (*Campanula*), and some weeds, particularly sow thistle and groundsel (*Senecio*).

CAUSE The fungi *Chrysomyxa abietis* and *C. rhododendri* on spruce; *Coleosporium tussilaginis* on pine and other plants.

CONTROL Dispose of infected needles and alternate hosts when possible.

NEMATODES

Nematodes are mostly microscopic wormlike animals, some of which are important plant pests. Chrysanthemum nematode *(see p.115)*, narcissus nematode *(see p.150)*, onion nematode *(see p.153)*, phlox nematode *(see p.159)*, potato cyst nematode (also called tomato cyst nematode, *see p.162)*, and root knot nematodes *(see p.169)* all feed within their host plants. Others, such as *Pratylenchus*, *Longidorus*, *Trichodorus*, and *Xiphinema*, live in the soil and attack the root hairs of plants. The last 3 are able to transmit some viral diseases of ornamentals and soft fruits.

CONTROL Areas of gardens from which virus-infected plants have been removed should not be replanted with the same types of plant; otherwise, they may quickly become infected by the nematodes. Not all nematodes are pests, however; the vast majority feed on bacteria, fungi, and other microorganisms, while some are predators *(see next entry)*.

• see also FOLIAR NEMATODES p.129.

NEMATODES (BENEFICIAL)

Certain species of nematodes are beneficial in the garden due to their parasitizing of pests. Also called predatory

or entomophathogenic nematodes, these microscopic worms move slowly through soil, water, or borer holes. Several *Steinernema* (syn. *Neoplectana*) species are commercially available, as is *Heterorhabditis bacterisopora* (syn. *H. heliothidis*), which ranges somewhat deeper in the ground. The various beneficial nematode species usually have the same applications, although some species are especially recommended for particular hosts. They are not harmful to humans, other vertebrates, or plants.

Fly larvae are highly sought after by nematodes. Among the pests controlled are fungus gnat and carrot rust fly larvae and cabbage root, onion, and seedcorn maggots. Nematodes destroy beetle grubs and other larvae in the soil, such as ones eating plant roots, and larvae boring into crowns and stems (and higher up, if the nematodes are so applied). Beetle groups and species attacked include billbugs, click beetle (wireworm), Colorado potato beetle, flea beetles, Japanese beetle, June bug, Oriental beetle, rose chafer, scarab grubs generally, spotted cucumber beetle (corn rootworm), and striped cucumber beetle. Related hosts include strawberry root weevil and black vine weevil. Many moth larvae, including codling moth, corn earworm, currant borer, cutworms, and sod webworms are also controlled. Among other pests attacked are various bugs, ants and wasps, carpenterworm, earwig, mole cricket, sowbug (pillbug), and slugs. Beneficial nematodes can be purchased in several formulations, such

as clay granules or sprays or in small spongelike packages. The release timing depends on the life cycle of the target pest, but you generally drench the soil or spray borer holes. Nematodes have a high survival rate in dark, moist places and are naturally abundant in compost piles. The third-instar juvenile, the infective "dauer" stage, is deadliest. It enters its much larger host through a body opening, such as mouth, anus, or breathing spiracles. The nematode releases a bacterium from its gut into the bloodstream of the host, which soon dies.

NITROGEN DEFICIENCY

SYMPTOMS Leaves are small and variably yellow (chlorotic), and general growth is reduced slightly to severely. On some plants, red or purple leaf discoloration may develop as the green pigment levels drop. The lower, older leaves are affected first, but if the deficiency progresses, all parts of the plant may be similarly affected. Flowering, fruiting, and tuber or root formation are also reduced.

CAUSE A deficiency of nitrogen, which can develop in any soil, particularly if it is light and has a low organic matter content or if it has been heavily farmed. The use of large quantities of fresh plant-derived mulches (especially grass clippings) may also result in nitrogen deficiency, since nitrogen is removed from the soil as soil bacteria break down mulch.

CONTROL Apply high-nitrogen fertilizers, composts, and mulches to the soil regularly. Grow legumes, which are capable of fixing nitrogen *(see **p.68**)* using bacteria in their root nodules.

NUT WEEVILS

SYMPTOMS In late summer, hazelnuts have a round hole, ⅒–¹⁄₁₂in (1–2mm) in diameter, in their shells (see ***p.52***) where beetle grubs have bored their way out before pupating in the soil. The kernel inside the nut shell is eaten by a white grub with a pale brown head.

CAUSE Small, brown or reddish black weevils: the hazelnut weevil (*Curculio obtusus*) in the East and the filbert weevil (*C. occidentis*) in the West. Almost half of their approximately ¼in (6.5–7mm) length is taken up by a slender snout. Hazelnut weevils are found in native beaked hazel, and filbert weevils also feed on acorns of certain oaks. In dry areas of southern California, infested acorns sometimes ferment and drip sap, creating a smelly andd messy nuisance. Hazelnut weevils lay eggs in early summer. Filbert weevils bore holes to lay eggs in late summer and mature when nuts drop. Filbertworm, the caterpillar of a small moth (*Cydia latiferreana*), causes damage similar to that done by filbert weevils and is an important pest of filbert, especially in the West.

LENGTH: APPROX. ¼IN (6.5–7MM)

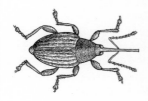

NUT WEEVIL

CONTROL Usually only a small proportion of the crop is attacked, so routine control measures are generally not required. Gather and destroy or discard infested nuts and acorns if feasible. Labeled insecticide can be applied when eggs are laid.

OAK GALL WASPS

SYMPTOMS Leaves, buds, twigs, and other plant parts develop small to large, massed or individual growths that may be round, irregular, feltlike, and other forms.
CAUSE Oaks (*Quercus*) are the host plants of more than 700 species of gall wasps in North America. Many of them have complex life cycles, involving alternating sexual and asexual (female only) generations that create different forms of gall (*see* **pp.17, 52**). The larval stage secretes chemicals that induce the plant to produce gall tissues. Gall wasps often encountered on oaks are the marble gall wasp (*Andricus kollari*), which makes woody spherical galls up to 1in (2.5cm) across on the stems, and the artichoke gall wasp (*Andricus fecundator*), which makes greatly enlarged buds at the shoot tips. The silk button gall wasp (*Neuroterus numismalis*) has galls shaped like tiny doughnuts, ⅛in (3mm) across, on the underside of leaves in late summer (*see* **p.17**). The cherry gall wasp (*Cynips quercusfolii*) produces reddish yellow spherical galls up to ⁷⁄₁₀in (1.8cm) across under leaves in late summer.
CONTROL Control measures usually are unnecessary, since gall wasps generally have little serious effect on the growth of oak trees, even when numerous. However, some occasionally can cause dieback and/or seriously detract from the oaks' appearance. If offensive and feasible, the galls can be pruned off and destroyed.

OAK LEAF BLISTER/CURL

SYMPTOMS Oak leaves have circular bulges, as seen from above; from underneath, the puckering appears as depressions. Each bulge, or blister, is ⅛–¾in (3–19mm) in diameter, starting yellow-green and then turning white or translucent. The blister finally turns brown. Several blisters may coalesce to engulf the whole leaf, which will strongly curl if narrow, as on willow oak. Usually, the damage is aesthetic, but severe premature defoliation can occur. Over 50 species of oaks, from both the red and the white oak groups, are vulnerable. The most frequent hosts include black, scarlet, live, water, laurel, and willow oaks. Sumac (*Rhus*) may also be affected.
CAUSE The *Taphrina caerulescens* fungus group. Infections spread during cool, moist conditions from early spring to midsummer. Leaves are vulnerable only when expanding.
CONTROL Spray a dormant fungicide at the time of bud swelling.

OAK LEAFMINERS

SYMPTOMS Leaves on a variety of oaks, especially white oak (*Quercus alba*), develop elongated, brownish white, discolored blotches on the upper surface. The corresponding areas on the lower surface look blistered. Leaves may be killed. Damage is particularly noticeable by late summer.
CAUSE Caterpillars of tiny moths (*Tischeria* and *Cameraria*), which are common pests of oaks. The gregarious oak leafminer (*C. cincinnatiella*) (mainly on white oaks) and the solitary oak leafminer

(*C. hamadryadella*) (on black, red, white, post, scrub, and blackjack oaks) are 2 common species.
CONTROL Oaks can support heavy infestations without adverse effects on their growth. Rake and compost or dispose of fallen leaves. Often, natural enemies provide control. Many trees may be too large for effective spraying and so the leafminers must be tolerated.

OAK WILT

SYMPTOMS From late spring to late summer, the leaves on any kind of oak, especially species in the red oak group (including red, scarlet, black, pin, shingle, and chestnut oaks), start wilting and discoloring, starting with the upper branches and the ends of lateral branches, quickly progressing down and in. Defoliation and branch death soon follow a similar progression, and most species die that same year. Young trees die very quickly, but mature trees that do not show wilting until late in the season may survive until the following spring, when they put out stunted leaves (which soon drop) and die, followed by death of the entire tree.
CAUSE Oak wilt (*Ceratocystis fagacearum*), which is the most destructive pathogen on oak. Nearly always lethal, the fungus invades and obstructs a tree's vascular system, causing leaves to droop and die and later killing twigs and finally branches and the trunk. Feeding and egg-laying sap and oak bark beetles as well as hatching larvae pick up spores and transmit them to nearby trees. Other vectors include other wood borers, such as the two-lined chestnut borer (*see p.185*)

and sometimes springtails and mites. The fungus also spreads to neighboring oaks by the roots, especially by natural root grafts but also by root insects.
CONTROL If your locality has a problem with oak wilt, it is probably best to avoid planting oaks altogether. Do not prune healthy oaks until very cold months, when the fungus and its carriers are dormant. A white oak can be helped at any time by pruning damaged areas immediately. To stop root transmission of the pathogen to healthy trees, isolate an infected tree by digging a 2–4ft (60–120cm) trench and cutting all roots, beyond the branch spread. Immediately backfill the trench.

OAKWORMS

SYMPTOMS From summer to early autumn, oaks are gradually defoliated (*see* **p.32**). Individual leaves are first skeletonized, eventually leaving only the midrib. The defoliation progresses from branch to branch. Droppings from the caterpillars may be present. White, live, and scrub oaks may be hard hit. Some other hardwood trees may be defoliated along with oaks, including beech, birch, elm, hickory, linden, hazelnut, and maple.
CAUSE Oakworms, which are caterpillars of several moth species. *Anisota* caterpillars have 2 distinctive black, flexible horns on the second segment behind the head. Among the *Anisota* species that feed on oaks is the orangestriped oakworm (*A. senatoria*), which is common and widely distributed. It is black with orange longitudinal stripes. Spiny oakworm (*A. stigma*) is brownish with a pinkish hue and lighter stripes and

whitish specks. Pinkstriped oakworm (*A. virginiensis*) is green-gray with pinkish stripes. California oakworm (*Phryganidia californica*) is a pest of landscape oaks in California. Older caterpillars are dark with yellow or olive stripes. Oakworm larvae range from about 1½–2⅓in (3.8–6.4cm).

CONTROL Oaks generally tolerate some defoliation, and oakworms have many natural enemies that usually keep them in check. If damage is intolerable, oakworms can be removed by hand from smaller trees or shaken off and destroyed. Handpick egg clusters, which are usually laid on lower branch foliage. Sticky bands around the trunk capture the larvae as they crawl down the tree to pupate. Cleaning up ground debris eradicates cocoons. Btk (*see p.110*) provides control, especially against younger caterpillars, but other labeled insecticides are also available

OLEANDER APHID

SYMPTOMS From early spring to early summer, the leaves of oleander (*Nerium oleander*) are distorted and discolored. Buds and young shoots also suffer damage. A large amount of sticky honeydew fouls the leaves and promotes the growth of sooty mold. Flowering may be reduced. Bright yellow and black, tiny aphids cover the shoots, buds, and undersides of leaves (*see* **p.35**). Milkweed (*Asclepias*) species are also attacked.

CAUSE The oleander aphid (*Aphis nerii*, also known as the milkweed aphid), which is a small, oval, soft-bodied insect that produces thick colonies. Also called the milkweed aphid, it is considered "pretty" by some,

the feeding colony making a striking color combination with, for example, the bright pink flowers of swamp milkweed (*Asclepias incarnata*).

Reproducing rapidly, the wingless early broods feed on the juices of the actively growing shoot terminals. Milkweeds are commonly infested in late summer. The colonies may stagnate in the natural dryness of midsummer or succumb to natural enemies late in the season, but a well-tended plant will continue to provide tender feeding material. In any case, with autumn rains there is some resurgence in aphid damage to oleander.

CONTROL Oleander aphids usually can be tolerated on oleander, but high numbers may cause milkweeds to decline. Avoid excessive fertilizing, pruning, and watering. Braconid wasps lay eggs inside aphids. The wasp larva matures inside its host, and then cuts a hole in its back to emerge an adult, leaving an aphid "mummy." A blast of water early in the day can knock aphids to the ground, from which they likely will not be able to return to their feeding site. Place sticky bands on trunks and stems to prevent aphid-herding and -milking ants from traveling to the "pastures"; similarly, prune back plants that are touching. An aphid-infested branch full of unhealthy foliage could be completely pruned off. Spray aphids with insecticidal soap or another labeled insecticide.

ONION MAGGOT

SYMPTOMS In early summer, young onion, leek, shallot, chives, and garlic plants may collapse as the roots are

eaten by white maggots up to ⅓in (8mm) long. Several plants in a row may be affected.

CAUSE Maggots of a fly, *Delia antiqua*, which resembles a housefly. There are several generations a year, with the first (in spring) the most damaging. Larvae of the second generation in late summer feed on roots and also bore into onion bulbs, especially those with other damage, allowing secondary rots to gain entry.

LENGTH: UP TO ¼IN (6-7MM)

ONION MAGGOT

CONTROL Onions grown from sets are less susceptible to first-generation maggots than seedlings. Infested plants should be lifted carefully and destroyed. Clean up old onion and plant debris in autumn, and rotate planting to a new area. Remove and replace infested soil. Rogue volunteer onions and related plants. Delay planting to minimize the window of infestation. Avoid damaging plants during cultivation, which attracts the flies. Labeled insecticides can be used only upon planting.

ONION NECK ROT

SYMPTOMS Scales of infected onions become soft, pale brown, and semitransparent (*see* **p.52**).

A dense, gray fungal growth develops over the affected areas and the tissues start to dry out, so that the onion becomes mummified. Sclerotia (black fungal resting bodies), which may be a few inches (several cm) in length, develop on the affected areas, particularly around the neck end of the

bulb. Symptoms are usually first noticed in storage.

CAUSE The fungus *Botrytis allii*, which can persist in the form of sclerotia on onion debris or, having fallen from the bulb, loose in the soil. Infections usually spread by spores or by sclerotia.

CONTROL Buy seed and sets only from reputable sources. Do not grow onions on the same site for more than 2 years in succession. Improve cultural conditions so that hard, well-ripened bulbs are produced. Do not apply fertilizers after midsummer, and avoid excessive use of high-nitrogen fertilizers. Keep crops evenly and adequately watered. Grow red or yellow bulbs instead of white, since they are generally less susceptible. Keep lifted onions dry.

ONION NEMATODE

SYMPTOMS Young onion plants are stunted and abnormally swollen. The tissues have a soft mealy texture and readily succumb to secondary rots (*see* **p.52**), so the plants usually die before reaching maturity. Onions attacked later in the summer do produce bulbs, but they rot in storage.

CAUSE Microscopic wormlike nematodes, *Ditylenchus dipsaci*, which infest the foliage, bulbs, and seeds of onion and related plants. They can also attack some other vegetables and common weeds, without necessarily causing obvious symptoms, but these alternate host plants allow onion nematodes to survive if onions are not present.

CONTROL Buy onion sets and seeds from reputable suppliers. Remove infested plants as soon as damage is spotted. Crop rotation can be effective in eliminating them.

ONION THRIPS

SYMPTOMS The foliage of onions and leeks develops a fine, white mottling during summer *(see p.23)*. Onions are more sensitive to damage as bulb formation begins, and red onions may be most prone to injury. Narrow-bodied, black or pale yellow insects up to ¹⁄₁₆in (2mm) long occur on and between the leaves. They are almost always more troublesome in hot, dry summers. Heavy infestations will severely check growth.
CAUSE The adults and nymphs of a sap-sucking insect, *Thrips tabaci*, which also feed on many ornamental plants.
CONTROL Light infestations can be tolerated. Some varieties of onions have greater tolerance to injury than others. Rain and/or overhead irrigation helps suppress infestations. While thrips have many natural enemies, if much of the green color is being lost before late summer, labeled insecticides can be used.

ONION WHITE ROT

SYMPTOMS Dense, white, slightly fluffy fungus grows around the base of the bulb and the roots *(see p.52)*. Numerous small, black sclerotia (fungal bodies) then develop among this growth. The sclerotia may fall off and into the soil, where they may remain viable for more than 7 years. The foliage on affected bulbs becomes chlorotic and wilts.
CAUSE The fungus *Sclerotium cepivorum*.
CONTROL Remove and discard infected plants as soon as they are noticed, and do not grow onions or related plants, such as leeks and garlic, on the same site for at least 8 years.

OPOSSUM

SYMPTOMS Tomatoes, corn, and other vegetables have chunks bitten out of them overnight. Berries, orchard fruits, and grain crops suffer significant losses. The compost pile and trash cans are raided.
CAUSE The opossum (*Didelphis virginiana*), more formally called the common or Virginian opossum. Although it may mutilate home-grown food crops, the opossum is primarily an insectivore and a carnivore, a usually nocturnal hunter of earthworms, insects, amphibians, reptiles, ground-nesting birds, shrews, mice, moles, and rabbits. Since much of its diet consists of major garden pests and it consumes road kill and other carrion, the opossum should be considered a mostly beneficial animal.
Larger than a housecat at 3ft (90cm) long, at least one-third of which is a nearly hairless white tail, the typical opossum weighs 5–6lb (2.3–2.7kg). In northern areas, its scraggly fur is a dirty gray; toward the subtropics, it is frequently much darker. The opossum is highly adaptable and finds residential sections of cities and suburbs quite desirable.
CONTROL Protect individual plants with wire cages, or surround the entire garden with wire mesh or an electrified fence. Keep garbage cans tightly covered. An opossum is easily caught by a large garbage can baited with sweets on an upside-down lid, which flips like a trap door under the animal's weight. Check local regulations regarding any trapping and releasing, and always wear heavy gloves: opossums will bite and may carry rabies.

ORIBATID MITES

Oribatid mites, such as *Humerobates*, also known as beetle mites, commonly occur on the bark of many trees and shrubs, under stones in soil, and sometimes on fences. They have shiny black or reddish brown bodies, about ¹⁄₂₅in (1mm) long, and during the day they tend to cluster together in crevices, where they can be mistaken for eggs. They are often noticed on dead or dying plants but are not the cause of the plant's decline. Oribatid mites are often scavengers, feeding on algae on the bark, and are mainly active after dark.
CONTROL No control measures are required, since these mites do no harm.

ORIENTAL BEETLE

SYMPTOMS Late in the growing season and the next spring, turf turns yellow, thins out, and dies. Nursery plants may wilt and die. In both cases, significant root damage is observed or roots are missing, and white grubs are present.
CAUSE The Oriental beetle (*Exomala orientalis*), which is most damaging as a larva, a brown-headed white grub that feeds on the roots of grass and, sometimes, other plants. This curved grub hatches from eggs laid in mid- to late summer and feeds until cold weather forces it to burrow nearly 1ft (30cm) deep. With spring warmth, it moves back toward the surface to resume feeding.
CONTROL Insect-pathogenic nematodes can be used to suppress infestations. Pheromone traps can be used to detect beetle activity but do not provide control. Pesticide and other control options are generally similar to those for the Asiatic garden beetle *(see p.101)* and the Japanese beetle *(see p.140)*.
• *see also* WHITE GRUBS *p.189*.

ORIENTAL FRUIT MOTH

SYMPTOMS From spring to early summer, the new terminals of fruit trees, especially peach, wilt and die. On close inspection, a small, white or pinkish caterpillar is seen inside the damaged terminal, or it is hollowed out. The new laterals that replace the killed ends give the branch an abnormally bushy look. Later, gum may ooze from damaged points on green fruit. When fruit is cut open, tunneling and perhaps a small caterpillar are seen inside. Fruit may rot and drop prematurely. Sometimes late peaches show tunneling or other interior damage, especially around the pit, with no exterior symptoms. Apples and other pome fruit can be attacked. Most stone fruits, such as nectarine, apricot, plum, cherry (including flowering cherry), and almond, are susceptible. Pear and particularly quince are also commonly attacked.
CAUSE The larvae of the Oriental fruit moth (*Grapholitha molesta*), which causes damage throughout the growing season. These caterpillars are pink-tinged white, maybe somewhat grayish, with brown heads. They are ½–⅝in (1.3–1.6cm). There are 3 or more generations, depending on location. The first-generation larvae bore into tender growth; later broods feed mainly on fruit but also on twigs. The third generation of this pest is a primary cause of wormy peaches. Feeding for 2–3 weeks, the

caterpillars are very active and swiftly move away when bothered. The early generation leaves twigs in early spring to pupate; later ones leaving the fruit make exit holes that fill with a gummy exudate.

CONTROL Early-ripening varieties of stone fruits may escape damage from the later generations of Oriental fruit moth. Destroy prematurely dropped fruit. Continually clean up weeds and rubbish, which may harbor cocoons. Attract parasitic wasps and flies with flowering plants around the fruit trees. Lacewings are another natural insect enemy, and mice eat cocoons that might be overwintering on trunks. Set up pheromone traps to monitor adult moth activity. For worm-free fruit, labeled insecticide applications are often necessary.

OVERWATERING
See WATERLOGGING *p.188.*

OYSTERSHELL SCALE
SYMPTOMS Pachysandra and the older stems of woody trees and shrubs, including apple (*Malus*), cotoneaster, boxwood (*Buxus*), dogwood (*Cornus*), willow (*Salix*), lilac (*Syringa*), and ceanothus, show grayish brown, ½–⅛in (2–3mm) long scales that resemble oyster shells. Heavy infestations can occur to the extent that the bark is entirely encrusted (*see p.36*), and scales may spread onto fruits and berries. Plants lack vigor, and shoots may die.
CAUSE Armored-scale, sap-feeding insects, *Lepidosaphes ulmi*.
CONTROL Horticultural oil applied before budbreak may provide some control. The use of horticultural oil

or another labeled insecticide can be timed for the newly hatched crawlers in mid-to late spring. Be sure that coverage is thorough. If the plant is in flower, spray at dusk to avoid harming bees.

PACHYSANDRA LEAFTIER
SYMPTOMS Leaves of pachysandra show feeding damage. Some are curled up and tied shut with webbing.
CAUSE The pachysandra leaftier (*Archips purpuranus*), the larva of a small moth. Pale bluish green, with 2 distinctive black spots near its rear end, this caterpillar grows to ⅜–1in (2–2.5cm). It hatches in midsummer and ties together 2 leaves for concealment and protection.
CONTROL Damage is generally only cosmetic and does not affect the health of the plant. If numerous or considered objectionable, handpick, or spray with Btk (*see p.110*) or another labeled insecticide.

PALM FRIZZLE TOP
SYMPTOMS A palm tree's leaflets are distorted and have interveinal chlorosis, the veins remaining dark green and looking netlike. Newly emerging fronds are stunted, not reaching normal length, giving the treetop a frizzy appearance. This new growth is often bronze-colored due to chlorosis. If the condition persists, the bud and then the tree will die. Royal (*Roystonea*), queen (*Arecastrum*), and date (*Phoenix*) palms are the species most commonly affected.
CAUSE Manganese deficiency. Technically a minor nutrient, manganese is essential in

chlorophyll synthesis and for enzyme activation. It may be lacking in soil depleted of nutrients by heavy leaching or by improper or absent fertilization. Even if present, manganese is not available for takeup if the soil pH is greater than 7.
CONTROL Analyze the soil pH; be sure it is no higher than 7 and preferably below 6. Apply either manganese sulfate or a palm fertilizer that contains it. The palm may take 6 or more months to recover after treatment. For an emergency situation where the frizzle top is about to overtake the bud, or a case where the soil is excessively alkaline, magnesium sulfate can be directly implanted into the trunk's sapwood. Warning: the addition of even a low concentration of manganese could be toxic to a particular tree, so a tissue analysis must verify a deficiency diagnosis before such implantation or injection.

PANSY LEAF SPOT
SYMPTOMS Brown, purple-brown, or very pale buff-colored spots develop on the foliage (*see p.13*). The older leaves are affected first and most severely. If the affected leaf tissue is killed, the entire area may fall away, producing shothole symptoms.
CAUSE Various fungi, including species of *Ramularia* and *Cercospora* as well as *Phyllosticta violae*.
CONTROL Remove affected leaves. If plants are growing very poorly, they should be removed and other bedding plants grown.

PAPERY BARK
SYMPTOMS Bark peels off as a thin, papery, brown sheet (*see p.40*). All woody parts

of a tree may be affected, but small- to medium-size shoots more frequently show these symptoms than do large branches or tree trunks. Shoots may also die back.
CAUSE Problems associated with inadequate functioning of the root system of the tree, most commonly waterlogging, which suffocates roots, excluding oxygen necessary for root function and eventually causing root death.
CONTROL Improve growing conditions, particularly soil drainage. Prune off all dead stems and those showing the symptoms. Prune back to a healthy bud growing from perfectly healthy-looking wood. The removal of the dead wood is necessary, not because the problem is infectious, but because once dead or injured, the wood is prone to invasion by opportunistic, secondary infection-causing organisms that may subsequently cause further dieback.

PEA APHID
SYMPTOMS On peas, beans, and other legumes, such as clover and alfalfa, at any time from spring through summer, leaves are distorted by thickening and curling. Some of this twisted or puckered foliage may wilt, yellow, and die. Leaves and food parts are covered with sticky spots of honeydew, which may lead to the growth of sooty mold. All parts – foliage, stems, blossoms, and pods – can be stunted. Blossoms may drop, and pods may be fewer in number and only partly filled with peas. Plants may eventually show signs of viral infection, such as bean yellow mosaic or alfalfa mosaic. The last results in tough, hard-to-shell pods.

CAUSE The pea aphid (*Acyrthosiphon pisum*), which is considered the worst pest on peas. It is also occasionally a pest of annual and perennial sweet peas. Hatching in early to midspring, the first generation is wingless and is composed entirely of females. This pest feeds by piercing soft plant parts and sucking out the sap, thereby often transmitting viruses. It is ⅛in (3mm) long and light to medium green with red eyes and black leg tips and cornicles ("tailpipes").
CONTROL Pea aphid has many natural enemies, which usually provide control. They include more than 70 parasites and predators, including braconid and other chalcid wasps; syrphid (hover) flies; big-eyed, soldier, and assassin bugs; aphid midges; spiders; and ladybugs and lacewings. Many of these beneficials are commercially available. Plant resistant varieties of peas and other hosts, such as vetch and clover. Avoid planting susceptible plants near alfalfa or clover fields. Clean up nearby weeds. Remove all crop residues, and till the soil after harvest to eliminate overwintering host plants. Keep plants vigorous, and do not overfertilize with nitrogen, which tends to favor aphids. Rowcover may help exclude aphids from young plants. Destroy plant parts completely infested with pea aphids. Rogue out plants showing virus symptoms. Aphids can be brushed or washed off plants by hard blasts of water. If necessary, they can be controlled with insecticidal soap or another labeled material or can be handpicked or knocked off the plant.

PEA LEAF AND POD SPOT

SYMPTOMS Brown or yellow, often sunken spots develop on the leaves (see **p.14**), stems, pods (see **p.51**), and flower stems. Numerous tiny, pinprick-size, raised fungal fruiting bodies may develop on the lesions.
CAUSE Various fungi, including *Ascochyta pisi* and *A. pinodes*, which most frequently attack fully grown peas. They may occasionally attack seedlings, which may be killed. The fungus carries over from year to year in infected plant debris, and, if seeds are gathered from infected pods, the resultant seedlings will succumb.
CONTROL Clear up all diseased plant material at the end of the season. Plant fresh seed on a new site. Do not save seed from infected plants.

PEA LEAF WEEVIL

SYMPTOMS Peas and broad beans have U-shaped notches eaten in their leaf margins (see **p.31**).
CAUSE Beetles, *Sitona lineatus*, which are grayish brown and ⅛–⅙in (3–4mm) long. The larvae live in the soil and feed on the nitrogen-fixing nodules on the roots of peas and beans. A related species, the clover root curculio (*S. hispidulus*), causes similar injury.

LENGTH: ⅛–⅙IN (3–4MM)

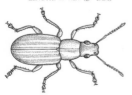

PEA LEAF WEEVIL

CONTROL Only a small proportion of the foliage is eaten, and plants can usually tolerate the damage. Control measures are required only when small plants are being heavily attacked. Rotate plantings to a new area. If intolerable, plants can be treated with labeled insecticide. Avoid spraying plants in bloom to protect bees.

PEA MOTH

SYMPTOMS Developing seeds in pea pods are eaten, and excrement pellets are evident.
CAUSE Caterpillars of a moth, *Cydia nigricana*, which live inside the pea pods. The caterpillars, up to ¼in (6mm) long, have black heads and small dark spots on creamy white bodies. Eggs are laid on peas that are in flower, so early- or late-sown peas that flower outside the moth's flight period from early to late summer will escape damage. Sweet peas also are susceptible.
CONTROL Till deeply in autumn to disrupt the overwintering stages in soil. Examine pods carefully, removing and destroying infested ones. Rotate plantings far from previously infested areas. If damage is intolerable, plants can be treated with labeled insecticide during the infestation period, starting about 1 week after flowering.

PEA WILT

SYMPTOMS Rapid wilting of the plant, usually in association with yellowing and dieback of the leaves (see **p.28**). Infection can occur on plants of any age but is most common toward the middle of the season. Dark brown discoloration of the vascular tissue (the conducting elements) in the stem develops but is visible only if the outer parts of the stem are stripped away.
CAUSE The fungus *Fusarium oxysporum* f. sp. *pisi*, which is soilborne and therefore particularly troublesome if peas or related plants are grown on the same site for several years in succession.
CONTROL Remove infected plants, and grow any replacements or future crops on a fresh site.

PEACH APHIDS

SYMPTOMS Peach, nectarine, plum, apricot, and almond foliage becomes crinkled, curled, and yellowish green during late spring to early summer. Green or black aphids suck sap from the underside of the leaves, although they may die out later in the summer, leaving only whitish cast skins.
CAUSE Several aphids occur on peach and related plants. The more important ones are the green peach aphid (*Myzus persicae*), which is yellowish green, and a black species, the black peach aphid (*Brachycaudus persicae*). The latter also may be found on bark or infesting roots.
CONTROL Look for aphids on the foliage or bark from midspring onward. Natural enemies may provide adequate control. In infestations are severe, insecticidal soap or another labeled insecticide can be used.

PEACH LEAF CURL

SYMPTOMS Leaves may become infected before or as soon as they unfurl in spring. They develop symptoms of puckering and blistering (see **p.26**), being pale green at first and soon turning bright red or purple. A white, powdery spore layer then develops over the leaf surface. Affected leaves drop prematurely. A second flush of foliage is usually produced later in the season, and this almost invariably remains healthy. The overall vigor and yield of the tree are likely to be affected only if the infection occurs for several years in succession. The skin of nectarines may develop slightly raised, rough patches. A very similar disease may affect poplars.

CAUSE The fungus *Taphrina deformans*, which produces spores that are carried by wind and rain and that lodge in cracks and crevices in the bark and in bud scales.

CONTROL Remove infected leaves promptly, preferably before the spore layer develops. Keep the tree well watered and fed to encourage the development of plenty of new replacement growth. Spray with a copper fungicide between mid- and late winter to protect the developing foliage from attack. The spraying must be completed before the flower buds start to open. Repeat the spray in the autumn, just before leaf fall to reduce spore survival over the winter.

PEACH SCAB

SYMPTOMS The leaves of a peach or another stone fruit tree have small, yellow-green spots. At first scattered on leaf undersides, the spots darken to brown or black, and then drop out, leaving circular holes. Twigs or branches may also have yellow to brown spots, which may be blue or gray on their almost circular margins, and eventually die. A few other trees sometimes show similar signs.

Half-grown fruit, about 6 weeks after the petals have fallen, also develops round spots. Only ½–⅛in (2–3mm) in diameter, these freckles are clustered around the fruit's stem end. On a peach, they turn black and velvety; on an apricot, brown. The fruit matures but is dwarfed, deformed, and, sometimes, cracked. It is edible if the mostly superficial damage is peeled away.

CAUSE The fungus *Cladosporium carpophilum* (syn. *Fusicladium carpophilum*, teleomorph *Venturia carpophila*), which is at its worst in warm climates. (A disease very similar to peach scab, or fruit freckle, on cherry and European plum is ascribed to the barely distinct *C. cerasae* [teleomorph *V. cerasae*].) Spores overwinter in twig lesions and then, in spring, are blown or splashed to young leaves and fruit. The fruit does not show signs of infection for a month. Meanwhile, continual spore development on the twigs, and then leaves and fruit, leads to the infection of healthy fruit to the end of the season.

CONTROL Peach scab is worst on late-fruiting cultivars. Plant resistant varieties. Destroy diseased parts, and clean up all fallen leaves, fruit, and twigs. After petals fall, spray or dust with sulfur, lime-sulfur, or a similar fungicide.

PEAR AND APPLE CANKER

SYMPTOMS Areas of bark sink inward and become pale. As the canker enlarges, it becomes elliptical, and the bark flakes in concentric rings. The branch may swell around the cankered area.

The growth above the canker is poor, and the foliage may be sparse and discolored. Cankers often enlarge sufficiently to girdle the stem or branch, and the growth above this point then dies completely. The canker usually starts near a bud or in a wound, such as a leaf scar or an insect injury. In summer, numerous small, raised, white, fungal spots develop on the cankered area, and in winter, they are replaced by similar but red fruiting bodies.

CAUSE The fungus *Nectria galligena*, which produces most of its windborne spores in spring. Poor growing conditions, such as a very heavy soil or inadequate fertility, may increase the likelihood of canker being troublesome.

CONTROL Remove cankered stems, and dispose of them well away from nearby apple, beech, ash, willow, mountain ash, and pear trees. On large branches or trunks, carefully cut out the cankered area using a sharp knife, so that diseased bark and wood are removed.

PEARLEAF BLISTER MITE

SYMPTOMS In mid- to late spring, the foliage of pears and ornamental flowering pear develop yellowish green or pink blisters or raised blotches. On expanded leaves, they form broad bands on either side of the midrib (see **p.16**). By midsummer, the blisters have darkened and become black. Less than ⅛in (3mm) in diameter, they should not be confused with the larger black lesions caused by pear scab disease. Pear fruit can be affected, resulting in russetted spots and possibly

deformed areas, especially on Bartlett. In rare cases, buds can be killed. Although rarely, it has been reported on apple and, possibly, mountain ash.

CAUSE Microscopic gall mites, *Eriophyes* (*Phytoptus*) *pyri*, which live within the leaves. The blistered appearance of the foliage is induced by chemicals secreted by the mites as they feed. Mites migrate to buds in late summer and autumn to overwinter.

CONTROL Although blister mite gives a tree an unhealthy appearance, it has little impact on the tree's ability to produce fruit. On small trees, affected leaves can be picked off if the infestation is light. Cultivars with russetted fruit do not suffer fruit damage. Horticultural oil may help control this pest, applied before green tissue shows in spring.

PEAR MIDGE

SYMPTOMS Pear fruitlets make rapid initial growth but, a few weeks after petal fall, start to turn black at the blossom end of the fruits (see **p.48**). In the center of the fruitlets are whitish orange maggots up to ½in (2mm) long. Affected fruitlets become extensively blackened and fall from the tree in late spring and early summer. Sometimes nearly all fruit is lost.

CAUSE Larvae of a small fly or gall midge, *Contarinia pyrivora*, which go into the soil when the fruitlets drop. They pupate inside silk cocoons and emerge as adults the next spring.

CONTROL On small trees, pick off and destroy infested fruitlets before the maggots complete their feeding.

PEAR PSYLLA

SYMPTOMS Pear leaves become very sticky with honeydew excreted by blackish green insects. Sooty molds frequently develop where honeydew has accumulated on the upper surface of leaves. Trees that are heavily infested over a long period decline.

CAUSE A sap-feeding insect, *Cacopsylla pyricola*, which has several generations during summer and overwinters as an adult on bark. The immature nymphs have flattened bodies, while the reddish brown, ½in (2mm) long adults resemble cicadas.

ACTUAL SIZE ➟

PEAR PSYLLA

CONTROL Pear psylla is less frequent on pears in gardens than in commercial orchards and is not usually a problem. Routine control measures are not needed, but check for adults from late spring to late summer by tapping branches over trays or by setting up yellow sticky cards before bloom. Keep watersprouts pruned off, since they provide ideal feeding sites for nymphs in summer. Apply labeled insecticide to control young nymphal stages, which are more susceptible than adults.

PEAR SAWFLY

SYMPTOMS In spring and late summer, the upper surface of pear and cherry foliage is skeletonized by sluglike caterpillars, causing the remaining damaged tissues to dry up and turn brown *(see p.19)*. Later damage tends to be more severe and can defoliate trees. Other plants attacked include hawthorn, quince, mountain ash, and plums.

CAUSE Larvae of a sawfly, *Caliroa cerasi*, which usually has 2 generations in summer. The olive green caterpillars secrete a black, slimy mucilage over their bodies, giving them a sluglike appearance. They are up to ⅜in (1cm) long and are swollen at the front end, making them club-shaped. Earlier stages are pale, darkening as they get older.

CONTROL Pear sawfly has many natural enemies that provide some control. For small trees, larvae and infested leaves can be removed. Several labeled insecticides are available.

PEAR SCAB

SYMPTOMS Blackish brown, scabby patches develop on the fruits *(see p.48)*, and similar but more greenish gray spots develop on the leaves. In severe cases, fruit may be almost entirely covered with scabby patches and is very small and misshapen. Infected fruits may crack or split and become infected with secondary organisms, such as brown rot or gray mold. Affected leaves yellow and fall early.

CAUSE The fungus *Venturia pirina*, which overwinters on scabby patches on the young stems and on fallen infected leaves. The disease is usually most prevalent on trees with crowded branches and in wet seasons.

CONTROL Rake up and dispose of affected leaves as they fall. Prune out cracked and scabby shoots to limit the overwintering of the fungus.

PEAR STONY PIT VIRUS

SYMPTOMS The fruits become knobby and pitted *(see p.48)*. Within the flesh are many dead sclerenchyma cells (stone cells), which make the fruits unpleasant to eat. The symptoms may be confused with those of boron deficiency *(see p.108)*. Affected fruits rarely appear all over the tree but are frequently borne on just one branch.

CAUSE Stony pit virus, which is most common on old trees. The virus particles are known to be transmitted only by grafting.

CONTROL Avoid planting cultivars known to be particularly susceptible. Trimming branches that bear damaged fruit may reduce the number of damaged fruits in subsequent crops.

PECAN WEEVIL

SYMPTOMS Starting in summer, the nuts of pecan and nearly all other hickory trees (*Carya*) drop prematurely, stained with dark patches. In contrast, ripe nuts cling to their branches and do not split from the hulls, each of which has a ⅛in (3mm) hole. The kernels inside are rendered worthless. Two-thirds of a local pecan crop can be destroyed.

CAUSE Larval and adult pecan weevils (*Curculio caryae*). In midsummer, the reddish brown to gray adult emerges from a 2- to 3-year pupation and starts feeding on unripe nuts, which fall. It has a slender snout that is longer than the oval body, which is elongated at ⁵⁄₁₆–½in (7.5–12mm). As nuts mature, the female drills a hole through the hull with mandibles at its beak tip and lays an egg. The curved, creamy white grub feeds within the nut for several weeks, growing to ½in (1.3cm). Infested nuts often drop. The larva drills a hole through the shell and husk and drops to the ground for its lengthy subsurface pupation. A closely related species (*C. sayi*) also infests pecan.

CONTROL Cultivate the soil under hickories (including pecan), if feasible, to expose the pupae. Gather fallen nuts daily before larvae emerge, and store them where the grubs cannot escape when they emerge. When adults start appearing, shake the tree limbs over sheets every couple of weeks, especially on cool mornings, and gather fallen weevils.

PEONY WILT

SYMPTOMS Shoots of herbaceous peonies wilt and turn brown at the stem base. In wet conditions, fuzzy gray fungal growth may develop at the base of the stem. The withered stem dies, shortly followed by other stems on the plant. Sclerotia (shiny black fungal resting bodies) form on and within the infected stem. Occasionally, the fungus attacks higher up the stem, causing similar symptoms *(see p.43)*. Wilt is most common on herbaceous peonies, but tree species may also be affected.

CAUSE The fungus *Botrytis paeoniae*, which produces numerous spores that are carried on air currents and by water splash. The sclerotia are usually responsible for wilt infections, which appear early in the season; subsequent infections may be due to spore spread.

CONTROL Cut out infected stems promptly, cutting back into healthy growth and below soil level if necessary. If the stems are not removed, the sclerotia fall into the soil, where they can persist for several years. Remove all debris at the end of the season, since it may harbor sclerotia. If a plant has been severely damaged by the infections, scrape off the uppermost few inches of soil in the autumn in case it contains sclerotia – this must be done with care.

PEPPER MAGGOT

SYMPTOMS The fruit of a pepper and, occasionally, an eggplant may become distorted as it matures, showing shallow dimples on the skin. Small, rotten spots may appear as it approaches ripening. Shallow, blotchy depressions may develop, and decay can cause fruit drop. The inner wall of peppers develops wartlike callus tissue in response to injury. The placenta (inner wall) can be infested with whitish maggots.
CAUSE The pepper maggot (*Zonosemata electa*), which is the ¼in (6mm) larva of a fruit fly. The flies, which emerge from a long pupation starting in early summer, are yellowish and about the size of a housefly, ¼–⅓in (6–8mm). The tip of the abdomen has a small, black dot, and each of the 2, mostly clear wings has 3 brown bands. The fly lays eggs in early to midsummer, depositing them in fruit walls, beneath skin, and in internal cavities.
The larva hatches and feeds inside the fruit or pod. It exits near the stem to pupate 2–4in (5–10cm) underground before emerging the next summer. Horsenettle, a weed related to both pepper and eggplant, is an alternate host. Tomatoes are rarely affected.

CONTROL Discourage egg laying by dusting fruit with diatomaceous earth, rock phosphate, or talc. Destroy damaged fruit promptly. Eliminate weed hosts, and rotate to uninfested ground or do not grow hosts plants for a year. Autumn tilling may help expose pupae to winter desiccation and predators.

PHLOX NEMATODE

SYMPTOMS In early to midsummer, phlox stems become abnormally swollen and are liable to split. Growth is stunted, and leaves at the shoot tips are greatly reduced in width, sometimes being little wider than the midrib (*see p.33*). Badly infested plants rot and often die.
CAUSE Microscopic nematodes, *Ditylenchus dipsaci*, which feed within the stems and foliage. They overwinter in dormant buds at the base of the plant.
CONTROL Phlox nematode does not attack the roots, so clean plants can be propagated by taking root cuttings. Affected plants should be removed before the pest spreads.

PHOMOPIS CANKER

SYMPTOMS Shoots die back, often accompanied by girdling of the stem by cankers. Girdled areas become constricted, leaving wider areas of stem above and below. On some species, the cankers are accompanied by resin production. Many conifers may be attacked, particularly Douglas fir and, occasionally, various species of cedar, larch, and other firs.
CAUSE The fungus *Phacidiopycnis pseudotsugae*, which enters stems and branches through wounds.

CONTROL Prune out and discard affected areas where feasible. Prune carefully, carrying out extensive pruning during the active growing season, and avoid leaving stumps.

PHOSPHORUS DEFICIENCY

SYMPTOMS Growth is weak and reduced, and leaves are small and may fall early. Leaves develop a blue-green or purplish discoloration or scorching around the edges. Plants may show delayed or poor flowering and fruiting.
CAUSE A deficiency of the major plant nutrient phosphorus, which is most likely to occur on acidic soils or after periods of heavy rain or watering.
CONTROL Apply high-phosphorus fertilizers or superphosphate at the rate and in the manner specified by the manufacturer.

PHYTOPHTHORA

SYMPTOMS Rotting at the roots and base (collar) of woody plants causes poor growth. Foliage is sparse and may become discolored. Stems show signs of dieback, and the whole plant may be killed. Inspection of the roots reveals that the finer ones are killed, and larger roots show a blackish brown discoloration. If the bark is removed at the base of the main stem or trunk, a reddish brown or blackish brown discoloration is plainly visible.
CAUSE Various species of the soil- or waterborne fungus *Phytophthora*, such as *P. cinnamomi*.
CONTROL Remove infected plants together with the soil in the immediate vicinity of the roots and crown.

Improve drainage, since a poorly drained soil may encourage the development and spread of the disease.
• *see also* WALNUT CROWN ROT *p.187*.

PHYTOTOXICITY

Phytotoxicity refers to the damage caused to plants by pesticides. Symptoms vary widely and can be confused with damage caused by insects, fungi, pollutants, deficiency disorders, and other stresses. Plants that have been damaged may suffer a significant check in growth but usually make a recovery, although their appearance may be spoiled. Serious phytotoxic reactions can result in the death of the plant. Seedlings are generally more susceptible than mature plants, and flower parts are more likely to be damaged than leaves. Annual and tender perennial bedding plants not yet acclimated to growing outside ("hardened off") are also more prone to damage. The risk of spray damage can be minimized by not treating plants that are already under stress as a result of exposure to bright sunlight, extremes of temperature, or dry soil. Where there is doubt and there are a number of plants to be sprayed, it is sensible to treat just a few and watch for adverse reactions over the next few days. When using any pesticide, always read the manufacturer's instructions and follow them carefully to ensure that the correct dilution is being applied. Plants known to be harmed by a pesticide will be listed by the manufacturer, but this information is not known for all potential plant/chemical interactions.

PIERCE'S DISEASE

SYMPTOMS In late spring and summer, the lower leaves on grape shoots show yellow mottling (see **p.24**). They scorch and dry on the edges, which roughly coincides with a general leaf yellowing or reddening. This is followed by the development of browning areas with diffuse yellow borders; the veins frequently stay green. The leaves are often quite distorted, and as they wither, the vine looks generally water stressed.

The xylem is brown, indicating vascular disruption and resulting in reduced vigor, with little or no new growth. Fruit production dwindles, and any grapes are dried and shriveled. Part or all of the vine wilts, succeeded by dieback.

In the second year of attack, both the roots and the growing tips of canes die back, the latter shriveling. Infected grape plants usually die within 5 years. These symptoms resemble those generally accompanying bacterial scorch diseases, which are caused by closely related organisms.

CAUSE The bacterium *Xylella fastidiosa* (syn. *Xylellum fastidiosum*). Pierce's disease is one of the most destructive problems of the vineyard. The pathogen reproduces and moves only in the xylem, the water-conducting, structural, and storage tissue of leaves, stems, and roots. Plugging up and degrading the xylem causes water stress, wilting, and dieback. The bacterium also releases phytotoxins that probably contribute to yellowing and scorching. Strains of *X. fastidiosa* have hosts in at least 28 plant families, most of which are externally symptomless when not infecting woody plants. Among the many ornamentals, grasses, and weeds that act as disease reservoirs are clover, ivy, fuchsia, rosemary, and zinnia. Common to areas with mild winters, the bacterium is linked to peach phony, periwinkle wilt, and leaf scorches of many trees, such as almond, elm, maple, mulberry, oak, and sycamore. Alfalfa is a prominently symptomatic herbaceous host whose stems and leaves are stunted by what is termed alfalfa dwarf.

The vector is nearly always a xylem-feeding sharpshooter leafhopper or spittlebug. Of course, with the huge amount of grafting occurring in viticulture, Pierce's disease can also be spread by means of infected cuttings.

CONTROL In an area where Pierce's disease is a frequent problem, do not grow susceptible grape cultivars. Be sure to propagate cuttings from only pathogen-free stock. Control insect vectors, and remove vines when they become unproductive.

PINE ADELGIDS

SYMPTOMS The new shoots or bark of pines develop a fluffy, white, waxy coating in mid- to late spring (see **p.39**). Black aphidlike insects can be found underneath the wax. The insects and wax persist through summer but gradually become less obvious.

CAUSE Several species of sap-feeding adelgids, most of which overwinter on the tree as immature nymphs and have several generations during the summer. Pine leaf adelgid (*Pineus pinifoliae*), Eurasian pine adelgid (*P. pini*), and pine bark adelgid (*P. strobi*) are three of the noteworthy species.

CONTROL Spraying is usually unnecessary; although the waxy secretions may be unsightly, the adelgids have little obvious effect on the tree's vigor once it has become established. Applying horticultural oil before budbreak in spring helps control some species. Other labeled insecticides can be used in summer if infestations are objectionable. The waxy coating acts as a protective barrier that can be overcome with wetting agents or low concentration of insecticidal soap added to the mix. Avoid fertilizing infested trees unless the infestations are controlled.

PINE NEEDLE SCALE

SYMPTOMS From midspring through autumn, most species of pines and spruces can develop distorted needles, which may whiten, brown, and eventually drop. Stems and needles have hardened, flat, white scales that can be picked or scraped off. The whole tree may appear whitened and become weak and susceptible to attack from borers and bark beetles. Even without these secondary invaders, when infestations are repeatedly severe, a young as well as an older tree can die. Douglas fir, hemlocks, and cedars are also sometimes attacked.

CAUSE White pine needle scales (*Chionaspis pinifoliae*), which often are seen covering needles of host plants. This armored scale inserts mouthparts into green needles and sucks out sap, also injecting toxic saliva. The obvious female scale grows to ⅛in (3mm). Eggs overwinter, and crawlers (nymphs) appear around midspring. There is often a second generation, with crawlers active in midsummer.

CONTROL Natural enemies commonly feed on this scale but do not always provide adequate control. Attract insect enemies, such as lacewings, chalcid wasps, and predatory mites, with pollen and nectar plants and standing water.

Prune heavily infested branches, if possible. Horticultural oil, applied just before budbreak, provides limited control. For best results, horticultural oil, insecticidal soap, or another labeled material should be applied when crawler stages are present.

PINES, NEEDLE BLIGHTS AND CASTS

See NEEDLE BLIGHTS AND CASTS OF PINES *p.150*.

PINE SAWFLIES

SYMPTOMS Pine needles are eaten at various times, often in spring (see **p.32**). Older foliage is generally preferred over younger. Sometimes needles are only partially eaten lengthwise, leaving strawlike wisps. At other times, entire needles are chewed to stubs or entirely consumed, sometimes causing serious defoliation. A smaller pine may be stripped bare, and any significant defoliation will weaken or kill a tree. Most pines are prone to damage.

CAUSE Dozens of species of sawflies. Most feed on foliage, while a few mine buds and shoots. Larvae, which often feed gregariously, are small caterpillars, usually reaching ¾–1in (1.9–2.5cm) long.

Redheaded pine sawfly (*Neodiprion leontei*) is one common species that feeds on a wide variety of pines and even other conifers. Caterpillars are white with black spots and a reddish head. They overwinter as cocoons in duff (decaying organic matter) beneath the host tree. European pine sawfly caterpillars are a grayish green and often feed on mugo, Scots, Japanese black, and other pines. Sawfly adults do not bother the trees, except for causing minor injury when inserting eggs in twigs or needles. There may be 1 or several generations a year, depending on species.

CONTROL Pine sawflies have many natural enemies, but they do not always provide adequate control. If plants or infestations are small, handpick larvae and destroy or prune off infested branches. For species that overwinter as cocoons, rake up ground debris and the cocoons in it under pines. Conifers do not tolerate extensive defoliation, and sawflies often seem to defoliate trees "overnight," so watch susceptible plants carefully for early signs of damage and/or infestation. Species such as European pine sawfly are cryptically colored, and the small larvae of all species are easily overlooked.

Insecticidal soap can control larvae when they are small; spot treat infested branches. Other labeled insecticides may be needed for extensive infestations.

PLANT (LYGUS) BUGS

SYMPTOMS Leaves at the shoot tips of many plants, such as fuchsias, roses, hydrangeas, currants, forsythias, mints, dahlias, and chrysanthemums, are misshapen, with many small holes *(see **p.29**)*. Foliage may be flaked with white spots. Flowers of dahlia and chrysanthemum open unevenly or are killed, and those of fuchsia *(see **p.46**)* abort at an early stage. Raspberry and strawberry fruits fail to develop normally and are distorted or "buttoned."

CAUSE Plant bugs, such as the fourlined plant bug (*Poecilocapsus lineatus*) and tarnished plant bug (*Lygus lineolaris*), both of which are about ⅕–¼in (5–6mm) long when adult. They feed on developing seeds or suck sap from the shoot tips, and some secrete a toxic saliva that kills some of the plant cells. Later, as leaves expand from the damaged shoots, these dead areas may tear into many small holes. At times, honey locust plant bug (*Diaphnocoris chlorionis*) and ash plant bug (*Tropidosteptes amoenus*), among others, are important pests of shade trees.

LENGTH: ⅕–¼IN (5–6MM)

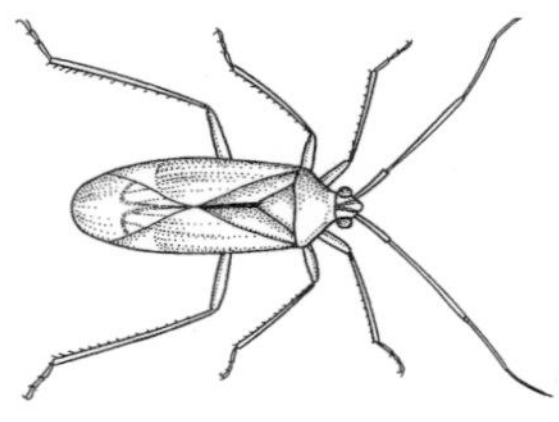

PLANT BUG

CONTROL Damage can occur at any time between late spring and autumn, depending on species. Check vulnerable plants during the summer, and knock insects off plants into soapy water. Control weeds, which serve as alternate hosts for some species. Insecticidal soap or another labeled material can be used.

• *see also* FOURLINED PLANT BUG *p.130;* TARNISHED PLANT BUG *p.180.*

PLUM CURCULIO

SYMPTOMS Starting when leaves and blossoms begin to open on plum, most other stone fruits, and apple and its relations, the buds, petals, and young fruit are nicked, slightly gouged, or eaten *(see **p.47**)*. The fruit will develop with scars that diminish its quality. Small, crescent-shaped holes ⅛in (3mm) deep are then cut into young fruit, resulting in depressions, followed by more scarring, worminess, and possibly distortion. The injury may open some fruit to attack by brown rot fungus. Some fruit drops early.

CAUSE Grub and adult plum curculios (*Conotrachelus nenuphar*), which are among the worst pests of tree fruit east of the Rockies. The adult curculio emerges from winter hibernation in soil or leaf litter around the time of apple bloom and soon causes the early, external bud and fruit damage by feeding and egg laying. A brown weevil that is sparsely covered with white hairs and is ¼–⅓in (6–8mm) long, it resembles a rounded beetle whose head tapers to a curved, cylindrical snout that is longer than the head and thorax.

The adult feeds for 6–17 days before laying round, white eggs singly in holes on young fruit. A crescent-shaped slit is often a distinctive feature of plum curculio activity. The legless larva grows to ⅓in (8mm) in its 2–3 weeks of summer tunneling inside the fruit. It cuts a clean hole to exit, drops to the ground, and burrows into the soil to pupate.

CONTROL Some types of fruit have resistant cultivars. For example, hard flesh in apples prevents larvae from maturing, and late-ripening blueberries do not accommodate the curculio's schedule.

Clean up and destroy fallen fruit every day, especially in warmer areas, where a second generation is possible. Remove damaged fruit from trees; check early for the telltale crescent slits. Clean up garden litter and brushpiles. Also, keep trees pruned open; since plum curculios do not like direct sun, they tend to avoid such trees.

Although plum curculio has many natural enemies, they do not provide sufficient control. Adult plum curculios drop when disturbed, so place a sheet under a branch and shake it or jar it with a padded pole during the period of spring activity. The weevils are most sluggish in the morning, but it is useful to collect and destroy them a second time every day, too. Some curculios will be on their backs playing possum, pulling their legs up and lying motionless as if they were already dead.

Plum curculio is difficult to control. Insecticides usually are needed for highest-quality fruit. Several applications are necessary, usually starting around petal fall in apple. Check local recommendations for timing and selection of controls.

POLLEN BEETLES

SYMPTOMS Shiny black or blue-green beetles cluster in flowers *(see **p.43**)* in spring and midsummer

CAUSE Pollen beetles (*Meligethes*), most of which feed on wildflowers. The beetles, 1/25–1/12in (1–2mm) long, feed on pollen but do not eat enough to interfere with pollination; they may even assist it. They can be a temporary nuisance when present in large numbers, especially when flowers are cut for the house, but generally cause little damage. **CONTROL** Before bringing cut flowers indoors, shake off pollen beetles. Alternatively, put cut flowers in a shed or garage for a few hours to allow the beetles to leave the flowers. Insecticides should not be used, since they also kill bees, butterflies, and other desirable flower visitors and may not ultimately be effective.

POOR POLLINATION
SYMPTOMS Fruits develop but are distorted, or they fail to develop entirely. On raspberry, for example, individual drupelets or small groups of them may be dry and brown, while adjacent drupelets are normal. The overall growth of the plant is not affected. **CAUSE** Poor pollination, which results in uneven swelling and development of the fruit. Tarnished plant bug (see p.180) can cause similar damage by feeding on developing seeds. **CONTROL** Grow problem plants in a sheltered area, and other flowering plants to attract bees and other pollinating insects.

POPLAR CANKER
SYMPTOMS In spring, a dense, off-white slime is exuded from cracks in young branches. The damaged areas may be girdled and die back. On older branches, the slime may also be apparent and roughened areas of bark may develop, measuring up to 1¼in (3cm) in diameter. Larger, more open cankered areas stand out clearly from the branch as they become surrounded by raised callus.

CAUSE The bacterium *Xanthomonas populi*, which is believed to enter the tree through wounds. The precise means of spread is not known, but rain splash and insects are probably the principal ones. **CONTROL** Prune out infected areas.

POTASSIUM DEFICIENCY
SYMPTOMS Most frequently, plants show poor flowering, undersize flowers, and/or poor fruit set. Leaf tips may appear scorched around the edges and have brownish purple spotting beneath (see **p.24**). **CAUSE** A deficiency of potassium in the soil, which is most common on light, sandy soils and those with a low clay content. On tomatoes, potassium deficiency is at least partially responsible for the disorder known as blotchy ripening. Potassium is also important in the maturation of wood and in the structure of the stem, and too little may increase the risk of cold damage. **CONTROL** Apply potassium sulfate in spring and autumn.

POTATO BLACK LEG
SYMPTOMS Foliage is chlorotic and stunted; the leaves are small and slightly incurled. These symptoms are easily confused with those of other problems, but with black leg the stem base is blackened and rotted at ground level. The vascular strands within the stem are similarly discolored, showing as distinct black spots when the stem is cut across. The parent tuber is completely rotted. The plant may be killed before a crop is produced. **CAUSE** The bacterium *Erwinia carotovora* var. *atroseptica*,

which is encouraged by wet soil conditions. It is often introduced on symptomless but mildly affected seed tubers. The bacteria may enter tubers through wounds while in the soil or at lifting. **CONTROL** Keep damage to a minimum when lifting potatoes. If possible, do not lift crops during wet weather, since infection is more likely then. Store only those tubers that appear quite healthy.

POTATO CYST NEMATODE
SYMPTOMS Potato plants die prematurely, during mid- to late summer, with leaves yellowing and drying from the bottom of the stems upward. First, small patches within the potato rows show symptoms. The patches gradually enlarge until it is impossible to grow a good crop of potatoes in that part of the garden. Tomato plants are also attacked. If infested plants are carefully dug up, spherical nematode cysts, up to ⅕in (1mm) in diameter, can be seen on the roots (see **p.55**). **CAUSE** Two species of cyst nematode: the golden cyst nematode (*Heterodera rostochiensis*), which has cysts that are white at first but pass through a yellow phase before becoming brown, and the white cyst nematode (*H. pallida*), which has cysts that change from white to brown without an intermediate stage. Both species develop inside the roots, where their feeding disrupts water and nutrient uptake; when mature, the females, which can contain up to 600 eggs, swell and burst through the root wall. **CONTROL** Potato cyst nematodes are particularly difficult to control because their eggs remain viable

inside the cysts for many years. The eggs are stimulated to hatch by chemicals that are secreted into the soil by the roots of host plants. Crop rotation can delay the buildup of damaging infestations, but once a serious nematode problem has arisen, the usual 3- or 4-year rotation is not long enough to eliminate the pest. Some cultivars have some resistance to the golden cyst nematode.

POTATO DRY ROT
SYMPTOMS The skin of tubers becomes wrinkled at one end, followed by rapid shrinking, the development of concentric rings of wrinkles, and discoloration (see **p.57**). The affected tissues turn black, gray, or brown. Pink, white, or blue-green pustules of fungal spores develop on the shriveled tissues. The symptoms are likely to be found only on stored tubers, although dry rot may also cause poor plant growth. **CAUSE** A species of the fungus *Fusarium*, which infects the tubers while they are in the ground or as they are being lifted. It enters through the pores, eyes, or wounds. **CONTROL** Handle potatoes very carefully at lifting and when storing. Minimize other problems, such as wireworm, slugs, and scab infections. Make sure that the potatoes are mature at harvest time and that they are stored in a frost-free but cool, dry place.

POTATO EARLY BLIGHT
SYMPTOMS Dark brownish black spots, often angular in outline and showing concentric rings, appear on the foliage of both potato and tomato. Sunken spots may develop on the stems,

and a dark rot and associated furry fungal growth may occur at the stem end of the fruits. Inadequately fed plants may be more susceptible. On tomato, this disease affects yield by causing fruit infections.

CAUSE The fungus *Alternaria solani*, which can carry over from year to year on infected plant debris.

CONTROL Rarely necessary, but some of the treatments for potato or tomato late blight (*Phytophthora infestans*, see later) should give incidental control.

• see also POTATO LATE BLIGHT *below*; TOMATO LATE BLIGHT *p.182*.

POTATO GANGRENE

SYMPTOMS Small areas of damage, slightly sunken with clearly defined edges, develop on tubers after lifting (see **p.57**). The skin may become slightly wrinkled. The affected tubers rot, turning wet and pale pink, and then darken. There is no visible fungal growth. If planted, a gangrene-infected potato produces a poor, gappy crop or no crop at all.

CAUSE The fungus *Phoma exigua* var. *foveata*.

CONTROL Avoid damaging tubers on lifting, and inspect all tubers carefully before planting and while storing. Dispose of any tubers with symptoms, and never use them as a source of eyes for future crops.

POTATO HOLLOW HEART

SYMPTOMS Tubers may look normal on the outside, as does the plant itself. When cut open, a tuber has an internal cavity: simple and surrounded by corky, somewhat darkened tissue; star-shaped; or 2 or more

interconnecting cavities. Large potatoes are particularly susceptible; small ones are rarely affected.

CAUSE Potatoes grow rapidly (perhaps from overwatering or -fertilizing) and then suddenly stop growing, usually due to lack of water. Conversely, plants in an overly dry soil are subjected to a sudden increase in the soil moisture from heavy rain or watering. In some instances, potato hollow heart appears to be induced by excessively high temperatures.

CONTROL Grow plants in uniform stands, and maintain regular and adequate but not excessive watering, particularly during dry weather.

POTATO LATE BLIGHT

SYMPTOMS Necrotic brown patches develop on the leaves, largely on the tips and around the edges (see **p.28**). As the spots enlarge, the leaves wither and die. In wet weather or humid conditions, slightly fluffy, white fungal growth may be visible around the spots, especially on lower leaf surfaces. The skin of infected tubers has slightly sunken, dark patches with reddish brown discoloration beneath. The discoloration may spread into the flesh (see **p.56**). Secondary organisms often invade, turning the dry, brown areas into unpleasant-smelling, slimy wet rot, which spreads through the tuber.

CAUSE The fungus *Phytophthora infestans*, which is also responsible for tomato late blight. Spores are carried by rain splash or irrigation or on air currents. Spores from the infected top growth are also washed down through the soil and may infect tubers.

CONTROL Hill deeply. Spray the foliage with a fungicide such as Bordeaux mixture, copper oxychloride, or mancozeb, before the symptoms appear.

• see also TOMATO LATE BLIGHT *p.182*.

POTATO LEAFHOPPER

SYMPTOMS The tips and edges of the foliage of almost 200 kinds of plants curl upward. These distorted areas become yellow or brown in bands or larger patches and turn brittle, often expanding toward the midrib (see **p.20**). The upper leaf surface is crinkled, looking scorched. Sometimes the symptoms are minor and tolerable, resembling drought stress. But half or more of each leaf may die, and the reduced photosynthesis results in dwarfed plants, short stalks, and no bloom or reduced, low-quality yield. Seedlings, especially, are sensitive to damage.

Foliar damage is often noticed first on potatoes, beans, and cowpeas. Among other plants affected are lupine, rhubarb, eggplant, dahlia, and hollyhock. Foliage and shoots on young trees, especially maple and birch, can be stunted, with marginal burn and yellowing of leaves.

CAUSE The potato leafhopper (*Empoasca fabae*), which is an important pest in eastern North America. The West has a similar species. The wedge-shaped leafhopper is ⅛–¼in (3–7mm) and pale or yellowish green, with white spots. It overwinters in the southeastern US, migrating north in spring and early summer. The leafhopper sucks sap and injects a toxin, causing the yellowing and scorching symptoms known as "hopperburn."

CONTROL Some potato and bean cultivars show resistance. Start plants early so that they will have attained good size and vigor before the leafhoppers' arrival. Since these pests prefer sunny, open areas, grow plants under some shelter. Inspect the underside of foliage carefully, or look for early symptoms of damage. Clear out weeds and plant residue. Nymphs and adults can be knocked off leaves by strong blasts of water. Insecticidal soap or other labeled materials can be used.

POTATO POWDERY SCAB

SYMPTOMS Small, nearly circular scabs with raised edges develop on tubers. They burst open and produce masses of brown spores that are released into the soil (see **p.56**). Occasionally, a canker form of this disease occurs when affected tubers are seriously deformed.

CAUSE The fungus *Spongospora subterranea*, which is particularly common in wet seasons and on heavy soils, especially those that have grown many crops of potatoes.

CONTROL Dispose of infected tubers; do not incorporate them into a compost pile. Do not grow potatoes on the infected site for at least 3 years, and improve soil aeration before planting.

POTATO SCAB

SYMPTOMS Raised scabs develop on the skin of tubers (see **p.56**). The skin ruptures, leaving the scabs with ragged edges. Damage may be superficial or result in cracking. The flesh is usually undamaged, although it may become discolored just beneath the scabs.

CAUSE The fungus *Streptomyces scabies*, which is particularly common on sandy, light soils with a low organic matter content. It is present naturally in most soils, and potatoes planted on former grassland are particularly prone to attack. Alkaline soil is likely to have more *Streptomyces* in it, whereas acidic soil has less.
CONTROL Improve the soil's organic matter content. Water regularly; there appears to be a link between scab and dry soil. Do not lime soil before planting potatoes. Use acidic materials, such as ammonium sulfate and superphosphate. Grow resistant cultivars.

POTATO SILVER SCURF

SYMPTOMS Inconspicuous silvery markings, usually lines, develop on the skin of tubers (see *p.56*). The flesh is not affected. The condition usually becomes apparent only when the tubers are stored, particularly if the storage conditions are too humid. The markings may turn black if the fungus produces spores.
CAUSE The fungus *Helminthosporium solani*.
CONTROL Control is not necessary.

POTATO SPRAING

SYMPTOMS The flesh of tubers is marked by tan-brown or red-brown rings or arcs (see *p.56*), and corky tissue may develop. Tubers may be distorted, and the stems and foliage may be mottled yellow. Sweet pepper, hyacinth, gladiolus, tulip, China aster, flowering tobacco, and many common weeds may also be affected.
CAUSE Tobacco rattle virus and, occasionally, potato mop top virus, which are spread by free-living nematodes in the soil.

Infection may be started if infected tubers are planted.
CONTROL Remove affected plants and control weeds, because tobacco rattle virus has a wide host range. Grow potatoes on a fresh site.

POTATO VIRUSES

SYMPTOMS Symptoms vary with the combination of viruses involved, the potato variety, and the growing conditions. Leaf symptoms include yellow flecking, streaking, or mosaicking; dark spotting and distortion; and upward rolling and stiffening of the leaflets. If home-saved seed potatoes are used for many years in succession, there may be a gradual but noticeable decline in the plant vigor and yield; this is often due to the buildup of viral diseases.
CAUSE Many viruses, including potato virus X, potato virus Y, and potato leaf roll virus.
CONTROL Buy tubers certified as virus-free. Grow potatoes on a fresh site, and do not save tubers for seed.

POWDERY MILDEWS

SYMPTOMS White, powdery fungal growth develops on the leaf surfaces (see *pp.24, 25*). The upper surface is usually affected before and more severely than the lower leaf. The mildew may also grow on the other aboveground parts of the plant, the location depending on the host plant and the mildew species. Affected plant parts may yellow and become puckered and otherwise distorted. Distortion is particularly common on young foliage. Fruits may crack and split because they are unable to expand normally (see *p.49*). Sometimes buff or pale brown fungal growth may be

seen, especially on rhododendron (where the mildew is often restricted to the lower leaf surface), gooseberry, and laurel. The mildew may kill small areas of leaf tissue, which then drop away, causing a shothole effect. Growth may be poor, and in extreme cases dieback or even death follows premature leaf fall.
CAUSE Various fungi, particularly many species of *Erysiphe*, *Microsphaera*, *Oidium*, *Phyllactinea*, *Podosphaera*, *Sphaerotheca*, and *Uncinula*. Each usually infects only 1 genus or a closely related group of plants, including oak, pea, phlox, and quince. These fungi are often encouraged by plants growing in dry soils and by humid air.
CONTROL Where available, grow resistant varieties. Remove infected leaves promptly. Keep plants adequately watered but avoid overhead irrigation. Apply a mulch to preserve soil moisture. Prune trees to improve air circulation within the crown. Spray with a suitable fungicide.
• *see also* APPLE POWDERY MILDEW *p.100*; BEGONIA POWDERY MILDEW *p.106*; CRAPE MYRTLE POWDERY MILDEW *p.118*; CUCUMBER POWDERY MILDEW *p.120*; RHODODENDRON POWDERY MILDEW *p.168*; ROSE POWDERY MILDEW *p.170*.

PRAYING MANTIDS

Large, arguably strange looking, and displaying fascinating mannerisms and behaviors, praying mantids (or mantises) are completely carnivorous insects that have an outsized reputation as beneficial predators of garden pests (see *p.61*). In fact, they are not heavy feeders, and their predations

are fairly indiscriminate. Preying on pest and nonpest insects, including caterpillars, moths, ants, true bugs, and one another, they are themselves occasionally pests around beehives, feeding on honeybees.
Of the 20 species in the US and Canada, 5 are fairly common in southern states. The Carolina mantid (*Stagmomantis carolina*), 2in (5cm) long, is the most frequently found. Mantids range from ⅜in (9mm) to nearly 6in (15cm) in length and are green or straw colored. The striking triangular head has large, bulging eyes. Unique for an insect, the neck allows the mantid to rotate its head and look back over its "shoulder." Its habit of waiting for prey with upraised front legs has led to the apt common name of "praying" mantid.
Stakes, shrubs, and other permanent plantings encourage females to deposit egg masses. The commercially available mantid eggs are generally of the Chinese (*Tenodera aridifolia sinensis*) or European mantid (*Mantis religiosa*).

PREMATURE AUTUMN COLOR

SYMPTOMS Too early in the growing season, the foliage of a deciduous woody plant takes on the colors normally associated with autumn and imminent leaf drop.
CAUSE Changes in the balance of foliage pigments. A reduction of chlorophyll, the green leaf pigment, unmasks the other differently colored pigments already present. When color change occurs early, the plant is often suffering stress from illness, damage, or

unfavorable environmental conditions, including drought and heavy rainfall. There are 2 notable exceptions: many immature leaves are reddish in spring, which possibly affords protection against ultraviolet light, and the sour gum (*Nyssa sylvatica*) normally has a few red leaves throughout summer.
CONTROL Keep plants healthy. Proper fertilization, watering, and drainage reduce stress. Avoid injuries by exercising proper pruning, and control pests and diseases.

PRIVET THRIPS

SYMPTOMS In summer, privet and lilac leaves turn dull green, becoming increasingly silvery brown or russetted on the upper surface *(see **p.22**).* Elongate, narrow-bodied insects appear on leaves.
CAUSE Sap-feeding insects, *Dendrothrips ornatus*, which are more troublesome in hot, dry summers. Up to 1⁄12in (2mm) long, adult privet thrips are black with 3 white wing bands The nymphs, which tend to be found under the leaves, are similar in shape but are creamy yellow and wingless.
CONTROL Clean up debris in which adults may overwinter. If damage is noticeable, thrips can be controlled with labeled insecticides.

PROLIFERATION

SYMPTOMS Additional buds appear in the center of existing buds *(see **p.44**).* They may never mature or may produce fully grown flowers that grow out from the center of the original flower.
CAUSE Most commonly, physical injury such as that caused by a late frost, which damages developing buds. Occasionally, viral infection

is responsible, especially if symptoms occur all over the plant and for several successive years.
CONTROL Rarely necessary, although affected shoots could be pruned out. If a virus is the cause, the plant should be removed. A few old-fashioned rose cultivars are valued for their ability to produce proliferations.

PSYLLIDS AND SUCKERS

Psyllids are small sap-feeding insects that cause damage on various garden plants in spring and/or summer. Some are also known as suckers. The immature nymphs are very distinctive, appearing squashed when viewed from the side. The adults, which are 1⁄12–1⁄8in (2–3mm) long, are rounded and resemble winged aphids or tiny cicadas. On its upper surface, an immature nymph has wing pads that become larger each time it sheds its skin, until the adult stage is reached with fully formed wings. Some psyllids cause gall formation on their host plants, while others live exposed on the leaf surface. Honeydew followed by sooty mold may be a more objectionable result of their feeding activity than any direct injury they cause.
• *see also* APPLE SUCKER *p.100;* BOXWOOD PSYLLID *p.109;* LAUREL PSYLLID *p.142;* PEAR PSYLLA *p.158.*

PYRACANTHA SCAB

SYMPTOMS Grayish black or dark khaki-colored scabs develop on the leaves and berries *(see **p.49**).* Infected leaves yellow and may fall prematurely. Infected berries may remain small, start to crack or split, and fall.
CAUSE The fungus *Spilocaea pyracanthae*, which is encouraged by wet weather.

It does not appear to overwinter on fallen leaves (unlike apple and pear scab), but on infected leaves that remain on the plant and as tiny pustules on the shoots.
CONTROL Prune out severely infected areas and twigs bearing the pustules. Some cultivars show some resistance.

PYTHIUM ROOT ROT

SYMPTOMS The entire plant wilts and dies back. Seedlings are particularly prone, but older plants may succumb, particularly if otherwise lacking in vigor. Roots are killed and may disintegrate, leaving the plant with only a few roots *(see **p.57**).* Sometimes the only symptom is stunting; at other times, the lower leaves are yellow. Plants with Pythium root rot are especially sensitive to water extremes. After being watered, an infected plant can decline rapidly.
CAUSE The fungus *Pythium*, which is soil- or waterborne.
CONTROL Remove infected plants, together with the soil or soil mix in the immediate vicinity of the roots. Use sterilized soil or soil mix for raising seedlings, and irrigate with only clean water. Wash containers with a 10 percent bleach solution if the previous crop is suspected to have had pythium root rot.

QUINCE RUST

SYMPTOMS Nearly 500 species of plants in the rose family, especially in the apple subfamily, can develop spots and growths that damage the fruit. They include apple, pear, quince, flowering quince, hawthorn,

serviceberry, chokeberry, cotoneaster, mountain ash, and photinia. Simultaneously, a slightly different set of abnormal growths strikes nearby species of *Juniperus*, including red cedar, and incense cedar (*Calocedrus decurrens*). Yellow specks on leaves, green twigs, petioles, and fruit grow into swollen, distorted spots. They may give rise to dirty white, columnar structures (aecia) that shred and "blossom" with bright orange spores, which are dispersed in the air. Disease signs are more numerous on twigs and petioles, where the swollen area can run about 2⅜in (6cm) along a twig; galls sometimes also form. *(see **p.39**).* After spore release, the stem or shoot dies. From an infected thorn or small shoot, the disease can spread as a canker into a small woody branch. If new leaf buds are infected internally through this twig, leaves come out early and grow dwarfed and deformed. If the rust girdles the woody twig, the twig dies back to a healthy bud or lateral, which is spurred into growth. The eventual branchful of antlerlike twigs is akin to a modified witches' broom. After the signs on twigs, some fruit, such as those of quince, hawthorn, and serviceberry, may be covered with aecia, and it usually dies. The fruit of other plants, notably apples and crabapples, may be spotted, scarred, distorted, and killed.
CAUSE Quince rust (*Gymnosporangium clavipes*), which requires 2 hosts, including a juniper or close relative, to complete its life cycle.
CONTROL Grow resistant cultivars. Never plant close to the alternate hosts.

Provide good air circulation, and do not wet the foliage. Clean up debris. Prune off infected parts. Fungicidal sprays and dusts, such as Bordeaux mixture or fungicidal soaps, may be helpful.

RABBITS
Rabbits (*Sylvilagus*) can feed on a very wide range of plants. Herbaceous plants may be grazed down to ground level, while the foliage and soft shoots of woody plants are eaten up to a height of about 1⅓ft (50cm). Rabbits also gnaw the bark from the base of trunks, especially on thin-barked woody plants and young fruit trees, and the tree may die. Bark feeding occurs at any time of year, but trees are particularly at risk when snow makes other food items unavailable. Damage around the snow line is one indication of rabbit feeding. Rabbits are inquisitive animals that often feed on newly planted plants, even if they have previously ignored similar established plants in the same garden.
CONTROL Keep rabbits away from plants by fencing or netting. Fences around the perimeter of a garden have to be at least 4–4½ft (1.2–1.4m) tall, with a further 1ft (30cm) sunk below soil level, and angled outward to discourage rabbits from burrowing underneath. The wire netting needs a maximum mesh size of 1in (2.5cm); otherwise, young rabbits may squeeze through. Individual plants or small flower beds can be enclosed with netting 3ft (90cm) high without the need to bury part of the netting. Gates also have to be rabbit-proof and kept closed. Tree bark can be protected by placing wire netting or spiral tree guards around the base of the trunks. Animal repellent products cannot be relied on to give long-term protection. Check with the Cooperative Extension Service for a list of less-favored plants, and look at nearby gardens for plants that local rabbits ignore.

RASPBERRY CANE BLIGHT
SYMPTOMS The shoots or the entire cane start to die back in summer. This is due to an infection at the base of the canes, which causes them to become brown and the bark to rupture. They also become very brittle and may snap off readily at or just above ground level. Tiny black fungal fruiting bodies develop on dead areas and exude spores.
CAUSE The fungus *Diapleella coniothyrium*, which is carried both by rain or water splash and on air currents. Infection usually takes place through wounds, such as those caused by cane midge attack, late-spring frosts, or pruning. The fungus can persist in the soil on infected plant debris.
CONTROL Prune and train the plant carefully to avoid infection. Control any pests that may cause wounds. If infection occurs, prune out affected canes and cut away any discolored wood from the crown. Then spray the crowns and any new growth with a copper-based fungicide.

RASPBERRY CANE BORER
SYMPTOMS Shoots or cane tips of raspberries, blackberries, and, occasionally, roses wilt in summer. About 6–8in (15–20cm) from the end of a cane, 2 rows of puncture wounds occur 1in (2.5cm) apart, typically girdling the tip and causing dieback (*see p.40*).
CAUSE The raspberry cane borer (*Oberea bimaculata*), which is the larva of a longhorned beetle. Beetles are active in June and lay eggs singly between the bands of perforations. The legless, white grub, about ¾in (1.9cm) long, bores into the cane and tunnels down several inches by winter. The next spring, it resumes its boring, and then spends a second winter in the plant crown, pupating during the second spring.
CONTROL As soon as the beetle is observed, prune off wilted terminals several inches below the lowest punctures. Destroy damaged canes or plants during late autumn or winter. Labeled insecticides are usually not needed but can be applied just before bloom to control the beetles.

RASPBERRY CANE SPOT
SYMPTOMS Purple spots with silvery white central areas develop on the stems of raspberries and other cane fruits. They may also appear on the leaves and flower stalks (*see p.34*). On loganberries and perhaps other brambles, the fruits may be infected. The bark may split as the spots enlarge, and entire canes may be killed.
CAUSE The fungus *Elsinoe veneta*, which usually appears on the canes in early summer and may spread to the foliage and the fruits.
CONTROL Prune out infected canes and discard them. Avoid growing susceptible cultivars.

RASPBERRY FRUITWORM
SYMPTOMS In spring, the foliage of cane fruits, especially red and purple raspberry, can be skeletonized and the flower buds damaged. The fruits may fall prematurely, and the stalk end of ripe berries has dried-up patches (*see p.50*). Grubs often are seen inside the berries after they have been picked.
CAUSE The larva of a small grayish brown beetle, *Byturus unicolor*, which lays eggs on the flowers from late spring to early summer. When fully grown, the larvae are up to ⅓in (8mm) long and are creamy white with pale brown markings on their upper surface. The grubs feed initially at the base of the berries and later in the inner core. The beetles, which are about ⅛–⅛in (3.5–4.5mm) long, damage the leaves and flower buds in spring.
CONTROL Autumn-fruiting varieties usually are not subject to damage. Cultivate between plants and rows to fill or expose pupae and larval stages. Labeled insecticides can be used, but timing of application is critical, with applications made as flower buds just appear and again just before flowers open.

RASPBERRY SAWFLY
SYMPTOMS In mid- to late spring, raspberry leaves start having small holes or are chewed from the edges. Soon the leaves are skeletonized and then consumed, except for large veins. Small pale green caterpillars may be feeding on leaf undersides. There may be damage to flower buds, fruit, or young bark on stems. Heavy defoliation in a patch can result in crop loss.

CAUSE The larvae of the raspberry sawfly (*Monophadnoides geniculatus*), which feed under bramble foliage or at leaf edges. The larva is a pale or bluish green, sometimes with dark brown striping down the back. By July at the latest, it is fully grown, at up to ⅜in (1.9cm), and it drops to the ground to pupate.

CONTROL Natural enemies, including several predators and parasites, usually are effective in regulating populations. Larvae can be handpicked. If defoliation is severe, labeled insecticides can be applied, directed to leaf undersides.

RATS

Rats damage stored fruits and vegetables and can also damage growing root crops. They also spoil foodstuffs by contaminating them with their droppings and urine. Rats often carry in their urine the bacterium that causes leptospirosis (Weil's disease), which can cause a serious illness in humans. The Norway, or brown, rat (*Rattus norvegicus*) and the roof rat (*R. rattus*) are of widespread occurrence in North America, the latter especially in coastal areas and the southern US. Besides feeding damage and gnaw marks, droppings and rub and greasy marks along paths and tracks are evidence of rats. Norway rats prefer high-protein and cereal foods, while roof rats favor vegetables, fruits, and cereals.

CONTROL Eliminate other food and water sources. Poisoned baits should be placed where rats are active but covered up so that children and pets do not have access to them.

Rats can be difficult to control, and the services of a professional exterminator may be required.

REDBERRY MITE

SYMPTOMS Blackberry fruits ripen unevenly, with some parts of the berries remaining red or green and hard *(see p.49)*. This problem is more frequently seen in hot summers. The first fruits to develop usually ripen normally, but later fruits show progressively more severe symptoms.

CAUSE Microscopic gall mites, *Acalitus essigi*, which feed by sucking sap from the flowers, foliage, and fruits. Only the fruits suffer damage, which is due to toxic saliva secreted by the mites as they feed.

CONTROL Some of the overwintering mites can be eliminated by pruning out to the ground and discarding the old fruiting canes. Destroy nearby wild blackberries. Applications of lime sulfur in spring and autumn may provide some control.

REDHEADED PINE SAWFLY

See PINE SAWFLIES *p.160*.

RED SPIDER MITE

See EUROPEAN RED MITE *p.127;* SPRUCE SPIDER MITE *p.178;* TWOSPOTTED SPIDER MITE *p.185.*

RED THREAD

See TURF RED THREAD *p.184.*

REPLANT PROBLEMS

See ROSE SICKNESS/REPLANT PROBLEMS *p.170.*

RHODODENDRON BORER

SYMPTOMS In autumn, rhododendron, and sometimes azalea or mountain laurel, begins to

wilt, the leaves turning pale and then yellow *(see p.33)*. A branch, ranging from a fairly small one to a main stem or even the trunk, has small holes in crotches, scars, or other irregular wood surfaces; it later develops longitudinal scars with loose bark and is substantially weakened. Broken branches reveal tunneling in wood. Fine sawdust is often seen around damaged areas and on the ground.

CAUSE The larva of a clearwing moth, the rhododendron borer (*Synanthedon rhododendri*), which chews long tunnels through the inner bark when young and into sapwood when larger. Hatching in early summer from eggs usually laid deep in crevices in rough bark or scars, it is whitish or pale yellow, with a dark head. The larva eats its way through outer bark and begins tunneling through the inner bark; by late autumn, it has bored either into the plant crown or deeper into sapwood. In early spring, the larva resumes feeding, producing greater quantities of sawdustlike frass as it grows to its full ½in (1.3cm). It then pupates for 1 month in an oblong cocoon just under the bark, at least several inches above the soil line if the larva was feeding inside the trunk.In midspring to early summer, the adult cuts an exit hole through the bark and emerges. The pupal shell can be seen protruding from the bark for a while.

CONTROL Carefully check potential rhododendron purchases for damage. Never injure the bark of the planted shrubs, and carefully observe landscape plants, particularly large specimens with rough

bark. Maintain plant vigor. Thread a wire down bore holes to destroy larvae. Prune off and destroy infested portions before the emergence of moths in spring. Beneficial nematodes have provided some control of other clearwing borers and could also be tried. Pheromone traps may be used to detect moth activity and to time controls. Bark sprays can be applied around 10 days after moths are first trapped.

• *see also* CLEARWING BORERS *p.115.*

RHODODENDRON BUD BLAST

SYMPTOMS Flower buds fail to open, turning brown and dry *(see p.41)*. They may remain on the plant for a few to several years. The surface of the bud is covered in tiny, black, bristlelike fungal outgrowths. Their presence differentiates rhododendron bud blast from dry bud *(see p.124)*, with which it is often confused. Quite often infected buds and healthy ones are seen growing side by side. Leaf, stem, and general growth are unaffected.

CAUSE The fungus *Pycnostysanus azaleae*, which is spread by rhododendron leafhoppers as they lay their eggs in the bud scales.

CONTROL The leafhoppers first appear in mid- to late summer, so pick off and dispose of infected buds before this time. Control of the leafhopper is possible but rarely fully effective in controlling the spread of bud blast because the pests simply reinvade from surrounding infested and untreated areas.

• *see also* BUD DROP *p.111;* DRY BUD *p.124.*

RHODODENDRON GALL MIDGE

SYMPTOMS In spring, new, young leaves on large-leaved species are distorted and may show yellow spotting and browned, inrolled edges (*see* ***p.27***). Tender growth later in the season is sometimes affected as well. In severe cases, individual leaves may be killed.
CAUSE The larva of the rhododendron gall midge (*Clinodiplosis rhododendri*), a tiny maggot whose feeding prompts abnormal growth of plant tissue that feeds and shelters the larva until it exits to pupate in the ground.
CONTROL Cultivars of *Rhododendron maximum* and *R. catawbiense* are particularly susceptible. Plant them in areas with good air circulation, or grow other cultivars. Prune off and destroy damaged leaves as soon as symptoms are observed. Damage is primarily of cosmetic concern and does not affect the health of the plant.

RHODODENDRON LACEBUG

SYMPTOMS In summer, the upper leaf surface of rhododendrons, especially those growing in sunny positions, develops a coarse, yellowish mottling. The underside of the leaves is covered in rusty-brown spots (*see* ***p.21***).
CAUSE Sap-feeding insects, *Stephanitis rhododendri*, whose excrement deposits are responsible for the brown spotting on the leaves. The lacebugs are present between late spring and early autumn. The wingless, immature nymphs are yellowish brown, while the adults are ⅙in (4mm) long and brownish black and have wings that are folded flat over their backs. The transparent wings have many veins, giving them a lacelike appearance.

LENGTH: ⅙in (4MM)

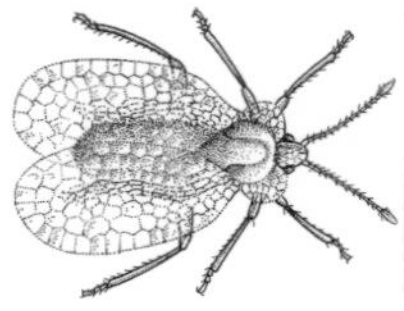

RHODODENDRON LACEBUG

CONTROL Avoid planting rhododendrons in warm, sunny spots. Although primarily a cosmetic concern and rarely a serious threat to plants, damaged leaves do not regain their green color; new growth develops normally once the pest has been controlled. Lacebugs can be dislodged with a blast of water. Labeled insecticides are available if damage becomes intolerable.

RHODODENDRON LEAF SPOT

SYMPTOMS Spots with clearly defined edges develop on the leaves of rhododendron. The older leaves are usually the worst affected, and, if severely damaged, some may fall prematurely. The spots are brownish purple, often with a distinct black or very dark purple ring around the edge (*see* ***p.14***). They often have concentric ringing, with numerous tiny, raised, black fungal fruiting bodies.
CAUSE The fungus *Gloeosporium rhododendri*, which, although causing unsightly damage to leaves, is likely to reach serious levels only on a plant that lacks vigor or is unhealthy.
CONTROL Remove severely affected leaves. Improve the general vigor of the plant. Avoid overhead irrigation and irrigating late in the day. Spray with a fungicide containing mancozeb or copper.

RHODODENDRON PETAL BLIGHT

SYMPTOMS Small spots – white on colored flowers and pale brown on white blooms – develop on the petals (*see* ***p.42***). The spots increase in size and appear water-soaked. The entire flower rapidly collapses and becomes slimy, and infected flowers often persist. This also attacks azaleas.
CAUSE The fungus *Ovulinia azaleae*, which is encouraged by mild, humid growing conditions. The spores develop on the petals and are spread by insects and on air currents.
CONTROL Remove and dispose of infected flowers promptly to minimize spread, since new infections start from flower debris that has accumulated under plants from the previous season.

RHODODENDRON POWDERY MILDEW

SYMPTOMS Yellow blotches develop on the upper leaf surface. Beneath each is a corresponding patch of felty, white to buff-colored fungal growth (*see* ***p.15***). Premature leaf fall can occur. Sometimes the fungal growth occurs on the upper surface and is then more off-white and powdery than buff and felty.
CAUSE The precise identity of the fungus or fungi is as yet undetermined, but the most important is probably a species of *Erysiphe*.
Dry soil and wet conditions around the foliage in late summer and autumn encourage its development and spread.
CONTROL Pick off severely affected leaves. Keep plants well watered and mulched, but avoid overhead watering. Spray with a suitable fungicide such copper or mancozeb.

ROOT APHIDS

SYMPTOMS Infested plants tend to have reduced vigor and are likely to wilt during sunny weather. A white, powdery or fluffy wax coats infested roots and soil.
CAUSE Several species of root aphids, some with alternate summer and winter hosts. They include *Pemphigus bursarius* on lettuce, which winters in poplar petiole galls; *Eriosoma lanigerum* on apple twigs and roots (*see* WOOLLY APPLE APHID *p.192*), which also causes rosetting of elm leaves; and elm leaf-galling aphid (*see* ELM LEAF GALL APHIDS *p.126*), which causes galls on elm leaves and overwinters on roots of some grasses. The aphids, up to 1/12–⅛in (2–3mm) long and usually a dirty cream color but sometimes bluish green, live among the roots or at the stem bases of host plants (*see* ***p.55***).

LENGTH: 1/12–⅛IN (2–3MM)

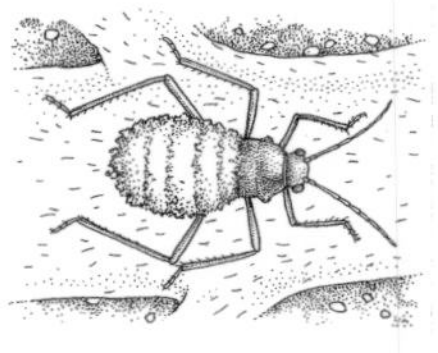

ROOT APHID

CONTROL Root aphids are more difficult to control than those that feed on the foliage. Crop rotation helps avoid infestation by aphids that have overwintered in the soil on the remains of the previous year's crops. Till soil and allow it to dry before replanting. To control aphids that depend on alternate summer and winter hosts, do not plant valuable crops near the alternate hosts, and keep alternate hosts (which include smartweed, foxtail, crabgrass and dock for corn root aphid) under control. Maintain infested plants in good condition.

ROOT KNOT NEMATODES

SYMPTOMS Knobby swellings (not to be confused with the nitrogen-fixing nodules normally found on the roots of legumes) appear on the roots of many plants, which lack vigor and have poor leaf color.

CAUSE Several species of *Meloidogyne*. These microscopic worms live within the roots, causing the swellings and disrupting the uptake of water and nutrients.

CONTROL Infested plants should be destroyed, together with the soil around the roots.

ROOT MEALYBUGS

SYMPTOMS Container plants, particularly cacti and other succulents, geraniums (*Pelargonium*), ferns, African violets, and fuchsias, lose vigor. Insects, roots, and soil particles are covered with a white, waxy powder (*see* **p.55**).

CAUSE Several species of *Rhizoecus*, especially *R. pritchardi, R. americanus,* and *R. dianthi*, which occur in greenhouses and on the roots of houseplants. They tend to be more troublesome on plants that are normally grown in a dryish soil mix. The mealybugs are up to ½in (2mm) long and have flatter, more elongate bodies than root aphids (*see p.168*), which have globular bodies.

CONTROL Root mealybugs are difficult to eliminate. Inspect roots regularly for the powdery white spots that indicate an infestation. The roots can be carefully washed to remove mealybugs, and the plant repotted in clean medium. Do not reuse potting media, or sterilize them first, and clean pots thoroughly before

using them again. Avoid growing infested plants or new introductions near uninfested plants. With many plants, it is better to discard the infested plants.

ROSE APHIDS

SYMPTOMS The younger leaves, shoot tips, and flower buds of roses are covered in dense colonies of green, yellowish green, or pink insects up to ½–⅛in (2–3mm) long (*see* **p.43**). Heavy infestations cause stunted growth and poor-quality blooms, while the foliage becomes sticky with sugary honeydew excreted by the aphids. Sooty mold may develop on the honeydew and trap the white skins shed by the aphids.

CAUSE Several species of aphid, the most troublesome of which is usually *Macrosiphum rosae*.

CONTROL Look for aphids from midspring onward. Aphids often can be washed off with a jet of water. They have many natural enemies, including ladybugs and lacewings, that help control infestations. Insecticidal soap, pyrethrin, or another labeled material can be used if numbers become too high.

ROSE BALLING

SYMPTOMS Rosebuds fail to open or start to do so but never open fully, generally in wet weather (*see* **p.44**). The outer petals become pale brown, dry, and papery. The inner petals are perfectly normal but are hidden beneath the outer casing of dead ones. If wet weather persists, the bud rots off, usually becoming covered in gray mold. The rose's general growth is not affected; healthy buds and flowers may appear among those showing balling.

CAUSE Most commonly, rain followed by hot sun.

CONTROL Little can be done to prevent rose balling. Water early in the day, especially when hot, and avoid wetting flowers, leaves, and stems. Prune out blooms showing the symptoms before they develop gray mold, because this secondary infection may then result in dieback.

ROSE BLACKSPOT

SYMPTOMS Diffuse purple-black spots or blotches develop on the leaves (*see* **p.13**), followed by yellowing and finally premature leaf drop. The spots enlarge and may sometimes join together. Much smaller purple-black spots may also develop on the stems, particularly on species roses. If blackspot occurs several years in succession, and particularly in early summer, the rose may be severely weakened.

CAUSE The fungus *Diplocarpon rosae*, which overwinters on stem lesions, bud scales, and fallen leaves.

CONTROL Plant resistant cultivars. Rake up and dispose of infected leaves promptly. In spring, prune out stems showing lesions. Spray with a suitable fungicide immediately after spring pruning or before the leaves start to break. Many applications are usually necessary to achieve control.

ROSE CANKER AND DIEBACK

SYMPTOMS Stems discolor and die back or fail to produce growth in spring. They may have a purple or blackish patch of discoloration (*see* **p.40**). During damp weather, fuzzy gray fungal growth may develop from areas damaged by gray mold; minute raised fungal bodies

may grow on the areas killed by the other fungi. In extreme cases, the plant is killed.

CAUSE Various fungi, particularly *Diapleella coniothyrium* and *Botrytis cinerea*. They gain entry to the stems, usually at the base, through wounds or other points of injury. These diseases are encouraged by poor growing conditions, such as overly wet soil, too deep planting, and excessive mulching. Poor pruning practices create wounds that are ideal entry points for dieback organisms.

CONTROL Prune out affected shoots completely, cutting back into healthy tissue. Clear mulch or excess soil away from the base of the plant. Provide good growing conditions.

ROSE CHAFER

SYMPTOMS Many ornamental and fruit plants, especially those with white petals, have partially or completely eaten flowers in late spring to early summer. Leaves are skeletonized, and developing fruit is chewed. Excrement dots the feeding site. Flower and fruit yields can be greatly reduced. Ornamentals frequently attacked include rose, peony, iris, hollyhock, and dahlia. Among the mostly small fruits damaged are grapes, brambles, strawberries, and cherries. Beans, beets, other vegetables, and small grains are occasionally affected. Grass roots may suffer from feeding injury from early summer to autumn and again in early and midspring.

CAUSE A sluggish scarab beetle, the rose chafer (*Macrodactylus subspinosus*), which is very damaging only in the occasional year when its population reaches a high level. The rose chafer appears suddenly in late spring, especially in an area with light, sandy soils. It is elongated at ⅓–⅜in (8–10mm), and its overall color appears grayish through yellowish tan or reddish brown. It swarms on plants and feeds for 3–4 weeks, then it disappears as suddenly as it appeared. The grub eats grass roots in summer and autumn.

CONTROL Cover plants or put up vertical fences of cheesecloth or mosquito netting: the low-flying beetle will not go up and over them. It is easy to handpick the slow-moving beetle, or on a cool morning shake an infested plant over a cloth and gather up the beetles. Cultivate deeply to expose overwintering larvae or pupae to the elements. Apply entomopathogenic nematodes to a lawn to kill grubs. To trap adults, set an open jar with decaying fruit in water under an infested plant. Labeled insecticides can be used if damage becomes intolerable.

ROSE GRAY MOLD

See GRAY MOLD (BOTRYTIS) *p.133*; ROSE CANKER AND DIEBACK *p.169*.

ROSE LEAFHOPPER

SYMPTOMS In summer, rose leaves develop a coarse, whitish mottling on the upper leaf surface (*see p.21*). Roses growing against a wall or in other sheltered positions may be heavily infested, and by late summer much of the green color will have gone from the leaves. Pale yellow insects live on the underside of the leaves and readily jump off when disturbed. Other possible hosts include apple, dogwood, elm, and maple.

CAUSE Sap-feeding insects, *Edwardsiana rosae*. They have narrow bodies, up to ⅛in (3mm) long, that are broadest at the head end and taper to the rear. The immature nymphs are creamy white and crawl on the lower leaf surface.

CONTROL Dislodge nymphs with a blast of water directed at the underside of leaves. Most insecticides for aphids, including insecticidal soap and pyrethrin, also control leafhoppers.

ROSE POWDERY MILDEW

SYMPTOMS Powdery white fungal growth develops on the upper leaf surface (*see p.20*). Leaves may be attacked when very young, and extensive distortion then results. On young foliage, the fungal growth frequently develops on both leaf surfaces. It is superficial and can be rubbed off, but the leaf tissue beneath is discolored. Powdery mildew may also develop on the stems, flower buds, and thorns. When flower buds are severely infected, they may fail to open fully. Affected leaves fall early.

CAUSE The fungus *Sphaerotheca pannosa*, which overwinters as stem infections and in dormant buds. The spores are airborne. Powdery mildew is encouraged by dry soil and by moist air.

CONTROL Plant resistant cultivars. Prune out badly infected stems. Keep roses adequately watered, particularly during dry weather, but avoid wetting the foliage. Apply an organic mulch to encourage moisture retention in the soil, and spray with a suitable fungicide according to label instructions.

ROSE RUST

SYMPTOMS Bright yellow or orange spots develop on the upper leaf surface, with corresponding bright orange spore masses beneath (*see p.16*). Severely infected leaves fall prematurely. The leaf infections develop in early summer and are the most common and most obvious. Later in summer, or in very early autumn, dark brown spore masses develop beneath the leaf as the winter spores are produced to replace the summer ones. Defoliation at this stage is almost inevitable. Spring infections may develop on the stems. The stem above may then wither, since the crack allows secondary organisms to invade.

CAUSE Species of the fungus *Phragmidium*. Moist, moving air is essential for spread and development. The spores can also overwinter on the soil surface and on fallen debris, stems, fences, and stakes.

CONTROL Prune out stems showing spring infections. This should be done promptly and thoroughly, so that no fungus is left within adjacent tissue. Improve air circulation by pruning and by avoiding planting too closely. Do not water from overhead. Spray with a suitable fungicide.

ROSE SICKNESS/ REPLANT PROBLEMS

SYMPTOMS Newly planted roses fail to thrive and may show signs of dieback. There is no obvious cultural problem, such as poor planting, very dry or very wet soil, or pest attack. The roots may appear poorly developed, compact, and dark in color, and the finer roots may rot. Roses are most often affected, but apple, cherry, peach, pear,

quince, and certain plums, may also be damaged. When planted on a site previously occupied by the same species, some plants fail to thrive. If they are removed promptly and replanted on a fresh site, however, they may recover.

CAUSE The precise cause is uncertain and may vary from plant to plant and location to location. The probable main causes are soil-living nematodes. Soilborne fungi, such as *Thielaviopsis basicola* and *Pythium*, may also play a part. Nutritional factors may also be involved.

CONTROL Replace the soil in the bed or area before planting. Soil must be changed to a depth of at least 1½ft (45cm), preferably deeper. Feeding with a high-nitrogen fertilizer and incorporating materials high in nitrogen into the planting hole may lessen damage.

ROSESLUGS

SYMPTOMS During summer, the upper leaf surface of roses is grazed, causing the remaining damaged tissues to dry up and become whitish brown (*see p.18*).

CAUSE Larvae of a sawfly (*Endelomyia aethiops*). The yellowish green, sluglike larvae, up to ½in (1.3cm) long, have pale brown heads. Bristly roseslug (*Cladius difformis*) has several generations a year and skeletonizes leaves from the underside, later chewing holes through the leaves.

CONTROL Natural enemies generally keep roseslugs in check. Dislodge them with a blast of water from a hose, or handpick and destroy them. If stronger measures are needed, insecticidal soap, pyrethrin, or another labeled material should provide control.

ROSE VIRUSES

SYMPTOMS Symptoms show up most clearly on leaves, usually as vein clearing, yellow flecking, or mottling (see **p.21**). The markings sometimes are quite indistinct and not as obvious as on most other virus-infected plants, but the plant may show some distortion and stunting. Symptoms may be confused with those caused by herbicide damage. **CAUSE** Numerous viruses, including strawberry latent ringspot, rose mosaic, and apple mosaic. Some viruses may be spread by soil-living nematodes; other methods may be involved as well. **CONTROL** Infected plants showing severe symptoms should be removed and destroyed.

ROSY APPLE APHID

SYMPTOMS Pinkish gray insects, up to ½in (2mm) long, cluster on the young foliage of apple trees in spring. Their feeding causes leaves at the shoot tips to become curled and yellowish and fruitlets to remain small, with a pinched appearance around the eye end (see **p.48**). The distribution of damaged fruits can be variable, with some branches producing normal fruits, and others having stunted ones at harvest time. Even low-level infestations can cause significant damage. **CAUSE** A sap-feeding insect, *Dysaphis plantaginea*, which overwinters on the tree as eggs. They hatch at bud burst, and the aphids are active on the tree until early or midsummer, when they migrate to buckhorn (narrow-leaved) plantain (*Plantago lanceolata*), a common weed. **CONTROL** Eliminate buckhorn plantain from the vicinity of apple trees. Horticultural oil applied before budbreak may provide some control of overwintering eggs. Inspect flower clusters carefully as they expand and through petal fall. If high-quality fruit is desired, the trees can be treated with labeled insecticide just before buds open and leaves are curled.

ROVE BEETLES

Rove beetles are very beneficial predators of garden pests, including cabbage maggots, bark beetle larvae, aphids, and slugs. Found in a wide variety of habitats, rove beetles are also important in the decomposition process, often feeding on decaying vegetation and carrion. They may also prey on or parasitize other insects, notably the eggs and maggots of flies. Most rove beetles are slender and parallel-sided. They range from ⅟₂₅–1in (1–25mm) long, but most are less than ⅟₂in (1.3cm). They are black or brown, shiny or covered with dense hair, and some have white or bright red markings. Some larger rove beetles can bite if disturbed while resting during the day on mushrooms, on flowers, or, most often, under objects on the ground. The beetles are generally most active at night, when many fly to lights (making yet another argument against light traps for moths and other pests). Rove beetles reside in and patrol a garden that offers daytime protection, such as permanent, undisturbed plantings and beds. Interplant cover crops between rows of vegetables. Mulch beds with materials that provide sheltering crannies, such as stones or large bark chips.

RUSTS

SYMPTOMS Many plants are hosts to rust diseases, including bean, fuchsia (see **p.18**), geranium (see **p.15**), hollyhock (see **p.17**), iris (see **p.15**), leek (see **p.17**), mahonia (see **pp.12, 24**), moraea (see **p.17**), periwinkle (see **p.15**), plum (see **p.22**), raspberry (see **p.40**), and snapdragon (see **p.15**). The symptoms may develop on the foliage, stems, and fruits, depending on both the host plant and the rust involved. Spores, as either spore masses or pustules, may be buff, yellow, orange, or any shade of brown, and their color may vary with the time of year. Rusts may produce several distinct spore stages, commonly known as spring, summer, and winter spores. Those produced early in the year are generally orange or bright yellow, and those later in the year are usually brown. Occasionally, the rust produces gelatinous masses, or "cluster cups," that contain the spores. Infected areas usually discolor and may become distorted and withered and die off, and the entire plant may be stunted or killed outright. Certain rusts have alternate hosts: both plants are needed for the fungus to complete its life cycle. On others, the life cycle requires only 1 host. **CAUSE** Various fungi, including species of *Chrysomyxa*, *Cumminsiella*, *Gymnosporangium*, *Melampsora*, *Phragmidium*, *Puccinia*, *Pucciniastrum*, *Tranzschelia*, and *Uromyces*. Many thrive in warm weather and on excessively soft growth. Most overwinter as spores on plant debris. The spores need a moist environment to germinate and infect, so rust infections are generally most severe in wet, but not very wet, conditions. The spores are ejected from the pustules, often by water splash, and spread on air currents. **CONTROL** Remove infected leaves, or discard entire plants. Improve air circulation, grow resistant cultivars, remove alternate hosts, and practice crop rotation. Avoid excessive nitrogen fertilization. Spray plants with a suitable fungicide, such as copper, triforine, or mancozeb. Fungicides cannot stop an established infection, but frequent spraying with Bordeaux mix or sulfur can prevent rust from taking hold. • see also APPLE RUSTS *p.100*; ASPARAGUS RUST *p.101*; NEEDLE RUSTS OF CONIFERS *p.150*; QUINCE RUST *p.165*; ROSE RUST *p.170*; WHITE PINE BLISTER RUST *p.190*.

RUSTY TUSSOCK MOTH

SYMPTOMS From late spring to late summer, holes are eaten around the edges of leaves of a wide range of trees and shrubs (see **p.31**). Hairy caterpillars, which are often evident on the plants, generally occur in small numbers but are sometimes abundant enough to cause significant damage. **CAUSE** Caterpillars of the rusty tussock moth (*Orgyia antiqua*), which emerges in mid- to late summer. The caterpillars, up to 1⅛in (3cm) long, are grayish black, with numerous orange-red spots on the body; there are 4 clumps of pale yellow hairs on the upper body surface. Tufts of black hairs point forward from the head end and backward from the rear. **CONTROL** Hand picking will deal with light infestations. Btk (see *p.110*) or another insecticide can be used.

S

SALT

SYMPTOMS Leaf browning and curling, often associated with the leaf veins. Leaves may be undersized and fall prematurely. Dieback may also occur. Most woody plant species could be affected, but symptoms are particularly common on maple, spruce, alder, linden, and sycamore, especially when grown as street trees.
CAUSE Sodium chloride (salt), usually as a result of a coastal location, excessive use of salt on roads in winter, or the presence of a salt pile too close to trees. Salt-laden coastal winds cause salt damage to trees growing by the ocean.
CONTROL Avoid contamination, and irrigate to leach excessive salt from the soil.

SAWFLIES

Sawfly larvae are mainly leaf-feeders, and many of the pest species are gregarious and capable of causing extensive defoliation. Unlike most butterfly and moth caterpillars, they are not susceptible to Btk sprays (*see p.110*). Other feeding habits include boring into developing fruits (*see* European Apple Sawfly *p.126*); causing galls or leaf distortion (*see* Willow Leafgall Sawflies *p.190*); or leafmining (*see* Birch Leafminer *p.106*).
• *see also* Imported Currantworm *p.138*; Pear Sawfly *p.158*; Pine Sawflies *p.160*; Raspberry Sawfly *p.166*; Roseslugs *p.170*; Willow Leafgall Sawflies *p.190*; Willow Sawflies *p.190*..

SCALE INSECTS

Scale insects are sap-feeding pests that attack the foliage and stems of many plants in greenhouses and gardens. The insects are hidden underneath waxy shells or scales. Newly hatched scales, called crawlers, move around looking for suitable places to feed, but they soon settle down and remain immobile for most of their lives. The color of the protective scale is usually brown or grayish white, and it may be flat or domed. The size of the scale varies according to the species, in the range of $\frac{1}{25}$–$\frac{1}{4}$in (1–6mm). Those in the "soft scale" group, such as European fruit lecanium, excrete a sugary liquid called honeydew, which makes the foliage sticky and permits the growth of sooty molds. Most scale insects lay their eggs under the protection of their own bodies, but the cushion and cottony scales deposit eggs among white, waxy fibers. With most outdoor species of scales, crawlers are present in midsummer, but on indoor plants breeding may occur all year. Horticultural oil sometimes is used to control over-wintering soft scales; it is not generally as effective against armored scales, such as oystershell and euonymus scales. The crawlers are most vulnerable to insecticides.

LENGTH: $\frac{1}{25}$–$\frac{1}{4}$IN (1–6MM)

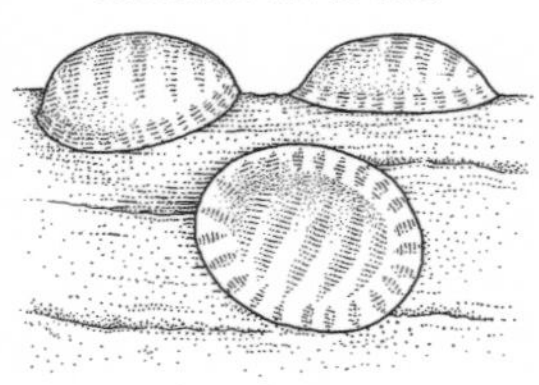

SCALE INSECTS

• *see also* Beech Scale *p.106*; Brown Soft Scale *p.110*; Cottony Camellia (or Taxus) Scale *p.118*; Cottony Grape Scale *p.118*; Cottony Hydrangea Scale *p.118*; Euonymus Scale *p.126*; European Fruit Lecanium *p.127*; Hemispherical Scale *p.135*; Horse Chestnut Scale *p.137*; Juniper Scale *p.141*; Oystershell Scale *p.155*; Pine Needle Scale *p.160*; White Peach and Prunicola Scales *p.190*.

SCLEROTINIA (WHITE MOLD)

SYMPTOMS After midspring, most soft aboveground parts of many plants, especially stem bases, flowers, and fruit, become discolored, brown, and wet as they rot. The rot quickly spreads, and flowers, leaves, and shoots wilt and die. The entire plant will die if the stem is girdled. The rot is followed by the development of fluffy, white mold scattered with large, black resting bodies (*see* ***pp.36, 45***). This may develop within the stems as well and on corms and tubers in storage. Creeping phlox, delphinium, and marigold, for example, are affected by crown rot. Underground rot includes rhizome rot (iris), root rot (peanut and delphinium), and bulb rot (tulip, narcissus, and hyacinth). Edible plant parts affected include tomato and pepper fruits, bean and pea pods, and lettuce and cabbage heads. Green fruit rot afflicts peach, apricot, almond, and strawberry; in addition, the flowers of camellia and rhododendron and the shoots and twigs of lilac and grape are affected. Some plants, such as euonymus and forsythia, develop basal cankers and dieback, but without the white mold.
CAUSE The fungus *Sclerotinia sclerotiorum*, which is encouraged by cool, wet conditions. It is called white mold, cottony rot, watery soft rot, Sclerotinia rot, wilt, or blight or by plant-specific names, such as dahlia stem rot. The sclerotia fall into the soil, where they remain dormant until spring, when spore-producing, cup-shaped fungal growths appear and discharge spores that are spread by insects or contact between plants. The sclerotia can remain dormant for up to 10 years.
CONTROL Remove and discard affected plants promptly, even if only a flower or a pod has symptoms. Eliminate nearby broadleaved weeds, and dispose of all debris at the end of the season. Do not grow susceptible plants on the site for at least 4 years following an outbreak of the disease. Before planting, sterilize the soil, and add sand to heavy soil. Keep soil moisture low.

SCORCH

SYMPTOMS Pale brown, scorched-looking patches develop on foliage. Damaged areas usually dry out, becoming crispy and brown. Leaves or petals are most commonly affected, but occasionally other aboveground plant parts may be damaged as well. Soft- or hairy-leaved plants are often most severely affected. Stems or trunks of trees and shrubs may show scorching only on the exposed side. Other growth remains normal.
CAUSE Most commonly, hot or bright sun. The problem may be worsened by droplets of moisture on the leaf surface. Similar damage may occur with chemical contamination or injury from an unsuitable pesticide or a contact herbicide. Less frequently, damage is due to the presence of moisture of any sort on the foliage, particularly if the leaves

remain wet overnight as temperatures drop. On bark, the injury is usually the result of the scorching effect of bright sun.

CONTROL Water carefully and in the early morning when leaves are not exposed to direct sunlight and have time to dry off before nightfall. In greenhouses and conservatories, provide adequate shading during the summer. Use pesticides properly.

• *see also* BACTERIAL LEAF SCORCH OF OAK *p.103*; BARK SCALDING *p.104*; FRUIT SCALD *p.130*; IRIS SCORCH *p.139*; LEAF SCORCH *p.143*; NARCISSUS LEAF SCORCH *p.150*.

SEEDCORN MAGGOT

SYMPTOMS Germinating seeds of peas, sweetpeas, beans, and corn are eaten. Seedlings sometimes are killed before the shoots emerge from the soil, but more usually ragged leaves and stems appear above soil level (*see p.51*). Such plants will usually survive, although they may grow slowly at first, especially if the growing points have been killed, causing sideshoots to develop.

CAUSE Maggots of a fly, *Delia platura*, which resembles a housefly. The white, legless larvae are soil-dwelling.

CONTROL Slowly germinating seeds are most at risk, so avoid sowing under adverse conditions, such as when the soil is cold or very wet. The female flies are attracted to soil that contains fresh organic matter, so apply it in autumn rather than spring. Germinate seeds in pots or seed trays and transplant after the first true leaves have expanded. Some insecticides are labeled for treating seed or furrows at planting.

SEIRIDIUM CANKER

SYMPTOMS Foliage of cypress (*Cupressus*), juniper (*Juniperus*), Leyland cypress (X *Cupressocyparis leylandii*), and arborvitae (*Thuja*) loses color, becoming slightly yellowed and losing its luster. It then turns brown and dies (*see p.35*). This deterioration is due to the development of a canker on the affected stem. The bark becomes slightly roughened, and resin is produced from around the cankers. Close inspection reveals black, raised, pinprick-size fungal bodies around the cankers. They may be rounded or may have burst, leaving minute craters. The infection is often first noticed as many small areas of dying foliage, but it may attack larger branches and cause dieback. The tree may be rendered unsightly and can be killed.

CAUSE The fungus *Seiridium cardinale* (syn. *Coryneum cardinale*), which enters branches through twig crotches or fine cracks in the bark and attacks most readily when the tree is growing slowly. The spores are produced from within the fungal bodies on the cankers and are carried on the wind. The fungus kills by girdling the affected stems as the canker enlarges.

CONTROL Prune out infected areas promptly.

SERPENTINE LEAFMINERS

SYMPTOMS Starting in midspring, long, narrow mines winding in all directions appear in the leaves of vegetables and flowers. More common on upper leaves, the mines are white or light colored. Leaves may become brown, and seedlings can die. The quality of leafy vegetables, such as spinach, chard,

lettuce, cabbage, and other brassicas, can be severely reduced. On ornamentals, such as chrysanthemum and nasturtium, the damage is mainly aesthetic.

CAUSE The small, white to yellow larvae of the serpentine leafminer (*Liriomyza brassicae*) and several related species, which are frequent leafminers on flowers, vegetables, and field crops. The vegetable leafminer (*L. sativae*) and the pea leafminer (*L. huidobrensis*) are common on many plants in the garden. *L. trifolii* is a notable greenhouse pest of chrysanthemums but also attacks other flower and vegetable plants. All feed on tissue between leaf surfaces, creating winding mines.

CONTROL Protect leafy vegetables with floating rowcover. Inspect plants carefully for early damage, including on the underside. Remove leaves with larvae, or they can also be pinched to death. Use screens to prevent leafminer flies from entering greenhouses. Yellow sticky cards can be used to detect the flies. Clean up plant residue immediately. Their great natural enemies, parasitic wasps, are commercially available. Several labeled insecticides are available.

SHOTHOLE

SYMPTOMS Holes develop on the leaves (*see p.30*), usually with an inconspicuous brown ring around the edge of each hole. Brown spots of dead tissue (*see p.18*) are present on the leaf.

CAUSE Various fungal and bacterial infections, including bacterial canker and, occasionally, powdery mildews. The pathogens kill off areas of leaf, producing

leaf spots. The damaged areas then fall away, leaving holes. A late frost can damage leaves, which then expand and leave circular holes. A few insects, such as some sawflies and leafminers, occasionally cause round shotholes.

CONTROL Determine the primary cause of the leaf damage, and then take the appropriate action. The host and history of environmental conditions often suggest a likely cause.

SHOTHOLE BORERS

SYMPTOMS Branches and sometimes the trunk of fruiting and ornamental forms of plums, cherry, almond, and (less frequently) apple and pear have many round holes, ⅟₂₅–⅛in (1–3mm) in diameter, in the bark. Underneath the bark is a maze of tunnels (*see p.33*), and boring may be seen in the heartwood. Frass ("sawdust") may be coming from the bark.

CAUSE Several species of beetles, collectively known as shothole borers on fruit trees. They include the shothole borer (*Scolytus rugulosus*), the lesser shothole borer (*S. mali*), and *Xyleborus dispar*, sometimes referred to as the pear blight beetle. The grubs, which are white and legless, feed under the bark, creating the tunnels. The dark brown, cylindrical adults, which are ⅟₂–⅛in (2–4mm) long, emerge from the shotholes in spring. The above are likely to attack branches or trees that are already in poor condition, and they are not a problem on vigorous trees. A few attack healthy trees.

CONTROL Prune out and discard infested branches, and improve the tree's vigor. Insecticides are available.

SKUNKS

SYMPTOMS In spring or late summer through autumn, small holes appear in the lawn overnight. Lower ears on a cornstalk may be eaten. A strong, musky smell may be noticed.

CAUSE Skunks, which may cause some lawn and garden damage, but are significant predators of beetle grubs, armyworms, grasshoppers, mice, gophers, rabbits, and moles. These and other small animals make up over half of their diet. The familiar striped skunk (*Mephitis mephitis*) is the size of a housecat. Its luxuriant, shiny black fur has 2 prominent, parallel white stripes running down the back from a white cap. For nearly certain defense it has 2 musk glands near the base of the tail, from which it can squirt a nauseating, temporarily blinding liquid. The curious, malicious, or otherwise imprudent gardener or pet will be warned, however, by forefoot stamping and tail curling before the pungent stream is emitted. Skunks are active primarily at night. They rest underground most of the day in burrows, which are often dug under structures, even houses, near woods and farmland. Skunks do not hibernate, but they do sleep through the severe parts of winter.

CONTROL Secure garbage can lids tightly, and do not leave pet food dishes out at night. Skunks may also be drawn to traps set for other mammals. Control grubs in turf so skunks do not come digging around. Discourage visits by surrounding the garden with a mesh or picket fence at least 2ft (60cm) high. Mothballs hung in mesh bags from trees are repellent. Check with your local animal control officer for regulations and special trap recommendations. Be extremely careful not to get sprayed or bitten, since skunks may carry rabies.

SLIME FLUX AND WETWOOD

SYMPTOMS Watery substances, sometimes slightly viscous and orange, pink, or white, ooze from the stems of affected plants. The slime flux usually first appears a few inches above soil level and may have an unpleasant odor. The bark beneath may be killed, and the upper parts of the stem wilt and die. Not all stems on the plant are affected at the same time.

CAUSE Injury to the stem early in the season, when the sap pressure is high, which causes sap to leak out. The high sugar content of the sap leads to its being colonized by various yeasts, fungi, and bacteria, which are responsible for the thickening and discoloration.

CONTROL Try to prevent stem injury. If they are injured, cut out affected stems, pruning back to perfectly sound wood.

SLIME MOLD

SYMPTOMS Gray, off-white, yellow, or orange growth develops, most commonly on stems. It is usually in the form of numerous tiny spheres that may appear to dissolve when wet, as the spores are released (*see p.53*). The plant's growth is not affected, and if the slime mold is washed or scraped off, the plant beneath is generally unharmed. Slime molds are particularly common on grass (*see p.58*).

CAUSE Various species of slime mold, nonparasitic funguslike organisms.

CONTROL Wash off slime molds with a strong jet of water from the garden hose.

SLUGS

Several species of slugs occur in gardens, including the gray garden slug (*Deroceras reticulatum*), marsh slug (*D. laeve*), banded slug (*Arion fasciatus*), and spotted garden slug (*Limax maximus*). They can damage a wide range of plants and are present throughout the year, continuing to feed in the winter if temperatures are above 40°F (5°C). Irregular holes are eaten in foliage (*see p.29*), flowers (*see p.43*), and stems (*see p.36*), but examination of plants by flashlight on a mild evening may be necessary to find slugs feeding. Slugs secrete slimy mucilage from their bodies that may leave a distinctive silvery deposit. Some slugs live mainly underground and damage potato tubers (*see p.57*) and tulip bulbs.

LENGTH: ⅛–7⅞IN (2–20CM)

SLUG

CONTROL Encourage natural enemies of slugs, such as toads, garter snakes, and predatory ground beetles. Remove slug hiding places under mulch, stones, and weeds, and eliminate leaves or mulch from around foundations. Boards or shingles placed over 6in (15cm) holes provide daytime resting places where slugs will gather and can be collected. Other nonchemical controls include hand removal after dark on mild evenings, and beer traps: sink jelly jars or similar containers half filled with beer in the ground almost to ground level. Slugs, attracted by the odor, fall in and drown. Sprinkle rings of diatomaceous earth, lime, or wood ashes around plants, repeating periodically or after heavy rain. Copper foil or screen encircling tree trunks or planters will provide an effective barrier for years. Slugs can never be eliminated, so control measures should be concentrated on protecting vulnerable plants, such as seedlings and soft new growth on herbaceous plants. Poisoned baits in the form of slug pellets can be scattered thinly among the plants. Results will be poor during cold or dry weather. The pellets can kill cats, dogs, and other pets and are toxic to humans.

SMUTS

SYMPTOMS Affected areas of the plant are discolored and may be distorted (*see p.35*). In a few cases, such as dahlia smut (*see p.122*), slight leaf spotting is all that is seen. In other plants, swellings develop and erupt to reveal large masses of soot-black spores (*see p.44*). Stems, leaves, flowers, and seeds may be affected. Most smut infections, are restricted to discrete areas of the plant.

CAUSE Various species of the fungi *Entyloma*, *Ustilago*, and *Urocystis*, which are spread by rain or water splash from nearby infected plant matter or from the soil surface.

CONTROL Remove affected areas from plants as soon as seen, preferably before the spores are released. Avoid splashing water around plants, and clear up all debris at the end of the season. Grow new plants on a fresh site.

• see also CORN SMUT *p.118*; DAHLIA SMUT *p.120*.

SNAILS

The most common snail pest is the garden snail (*Helix aspersa*), but banded snails (*Cepaea*) and others can also be troublesome. Many plants are eaten by snails between spring and autumn. Irregular holes are rasped in the foliage (*see* ***p.29***), stems, and flowers (*see* ***p.43***), particularly of annuals and other herbaceous plants. Snails are active primarily after dark or in wet weather. They secrete slimy mucilage from their bodies, and it often dries to leave a silvery deposit. Snails are less numerous in areas with acidic soils, which lack the calcium salts necessary to form a shell.

LENGTH: ¾–7⅞IN (2–20CM)

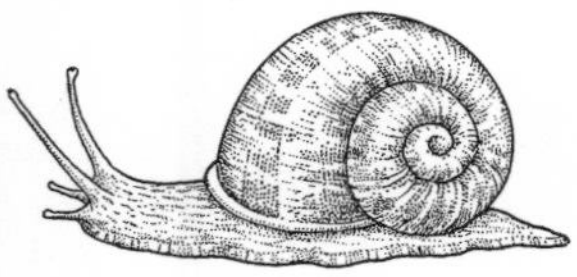

SNAIL

CONTROL Snails can be controlled by the methods used against slugs (*see p.174*). The predatory decollate snail (*Rumina decollata*) is sometimes sold as a biological control for brown garden snail. It is not recommended, however, and may even be illegal in some areas, since it also feeds on nonpest slugs and snails of ecological importance and may cause some limited plant damage.

SNAKES

Often found in country gardens and yards near woods or fields, snakes generally are beneficial predators that keep pest insect and rodent populations down. The bull snake (*Pituophis catenifer*), the pine snake (*P. melanoleucus*), and the king snakes (*Lampropeltis*) search the burrows of gophers and other rodents for prey. Other desirables are the rosy rat snake and the Great Plains rat snake (*Elaphe*). Even such small, harmless snakes as the familiar garter snake (*Thamnophis*) and green snakes (*Liopeltis vernalis* and *Ophiodrys aestivus*) contribute to pest control by eating innumerable grasshoppers, slugs, and other garden pests. If you see a beneficial snake or its molted skin, encourage it to take up residence by setting out shallow dishes of water. Provide a flat, dark surface, such as a large slab of slate, for it to sun on. A pile of boards, rocks, or other debris gives it shelter and possibly a winter hibernation site (some of these cold-blooded animals burrow underground in winter). Be careful when mowing, especially in tall grass, to avoid running over not only the snake but also its clutches of eggs, which may be laid in depressions in the ground. Discourage snake enemies, such as crows, raccoons, cats, and foxes.

SOD WEBWORMS

SYMPTOMS Especially in highly maintained turf and new lawns, irregular patches turn brown in late summer. The ragged spots may start out only saucer size, and then coalesce and expand to affect the entire lawn in only a few days. Brown areas are often permanently killed. Individual blades are cut right around the thatch line or soil line. Loose, white webbing may be seen in the grass, with short tunnels – silk lined and often incorporating grass and dirt particles – leading down into the thatch or ground. Bermudagrass, bentgrass, timothy, and, especially, bluegrass are most frequently attacked. Lifting up a patch of brown sod may reveal short, light-colored larvae. Small moths may be present.
CAUSE Sod webworms, also called sodworms, which are the larvae of several pyralid moths. The typical sod webworm has a thick body ¼–¾in (6–19mm) long. It is dirty white to yellowish or light brown and usually coarsely hairy. The larvae spin webbing as they actively move about near the soil surface, cut off grass parts, and drag this food into their silken tubes to eat. The sod of well-maintained lawns and golf courses is preferred, but meadows and former grassy areas tilled for planting may be infested, too. The larvae eat at night or during cloudy or rainy days.
CONTROL Rake up dead grass and all thatch. Mow the entire lawn, rake again, and green blades may reemerge. This is most likely with a watered and fertilized lawn. To detect an infestation, drench a section of lawn with a very dilute soap solution. The webworms can be seen coming to the surface. Several strains of beneficial nematodes are available to use against the larvae. *Beauveria bassiana* (*see p.105*) and Btk (*see p.110*) can also be used to suppress the pest. Several labeled insecticides are available.

SOFT ROT

See BACTERIAL SOFT ROT *p.103*.

SOLITARY OAK LEAFMINER

SYMPTOMS From late spring through autumn, many kinds of oak leaves, including those of white, red, scrub, post, blackjack, and black oaks, develop irregular, whitish blotches. At first, the damage may resemble spray or other injury, but the blotches may coalesce into larger areas. Inside each blotch between the leaf surfaces is a small larva.
CAUSE The solitary oak leafminer (*Cameraria hamadryadella*), which is the larva of a leaf blotch miner moth. It hatches in early summer from an egg laid on an oak leaf and spends the rest of the growing season eating out an area inside the leaf. Each blotch is caused by 1 larva.
CONTROL Damage is usually only cosmetic but may be objectionable, especially on lower-growing trees. Rake up leaves whenever they fall, whether in autumn or later, and destroy them to kill overwintering stages. In spring, cover oak seedlings. Remove blotched leaves, or pinch the miners in the leaves. Try attracting native parasitic wasps, which help keep populations under control. Insecticides are rarely needed.
• *see also* OAK LEAFMINERS *p.152*.

SOOTY MOLD

Sooty mold is a black or sometimes grayish green nonparasitic fungus that grows on foliage and other surfaces that have an accumulation of honeydew or other sugary substances, such as nectar, on them. Various sap-feeding insects, including aphids, whiteflies, mealybugs, and some scale insects and suckers, excrete honeydew, which falls down onto the upper surface of leaves below where the pests are feeding. Sooty mold can therefore be found on plants that are themselves free of pests, but are growing beneath trees that are infested with the insects, Heavy coatings of sooty mold spoil a plant's appearance and reduce the amount of light and air reaching the foliage. There is no direct control for sooty mold short of washing individual leaves, but dealing with the pest that is causing the problem will allow new growth to remain clean.

SOUTHERN BLIGHT

SYMPTOMS When temperatures exceed 70°F (21°C), over 500 tropical and temperate species of mostly herbaceous plants develop discolored, watersoaked stem lesions near the soil line. Lesions darken and die and sometimes girdle the stem base, resulting in the death of the plant. Similar symptoms can develop unnoticed on the roots or root collar just beneath the soil surface. Soon after, coarse, cottony webbing fans out over the stem base and surrounding soil. A conspic-uous white at first, it soon gives way to a sparser crust in which are many spherical, light reddish tan bodies $\frac{1}{25}$–$\frac{1}{12}$in (1–2mm) around. They soon become dark brown and hard and will persist on crop debris on or in the soil for up to 5 years. Diseased plants may be interspersed with healthy ones. Young, noncorky bark at the root collar can be girdled. Aboveground parts of bulbous flowers (amaryllis, narcissus, and other bulbs) and vegetables (onions) can be stunted and yellow and then die; the bulbs are soft and crumbly. The leaf bases and sometimes the rhizomes of bearded irises brown, dry, and rot, along with the

development of the cottony growth and round, black granules. Vegetables with fleshy roots, such as carrot and beet, are often attacked. Tomato, sweet potato, peanut, sweetpea, and melons are other major hosts. Pepper and bean leaves turn yellow and wilt and are shed, resulting in plant death.

CAUSE The fungus *Sclerotium rolfsii*. The complete set of symptoms of southern blight, also called southern wilt, southern stem rot, and southern stem blight, can be described as seedling damping-off, crown and root rot, stem canker, and leaf blight. A plant can die from infection in a month. The fungus can be saprophytic (living off dead plant material) but can also rest as dark brown sclerotia.
S. rolfsii is spread by flowing water, moved soil, transplants, and tools. Conditions of 86–95°F (30–35°C) for several days with intermittent rains are most conducive for fungal development, especially in acidic, well-aerated, sandy soil. The fungus germinates when certain host plant chemicals, up to 8in (20cm) away, stimulate it. Invading roots and crown, Southern blight soon spreads to stems.

CONTROL Some vegetables are relatively resistant. Rotate to corn and other non-susceptible grains. Clean up fallen plant parts and deeply plow under other debris after harvest. Keep the soil around plant bases disturbed by frequent cultivation, but be careful of roots. The soil in the bed should be well drained. Thin over-crowded plants. Carefully remove infected plants and the top 6in (15cm) of the surrounding soil.

SOUTHERN RED MITE

SYMPTOMS Broadleaved evergreens, particularly azaleas, rhododendrons, and hollies, show fine yellow stippling or russetting, especially on the lower surface; later, the upper surfaces can be affected (*see* **p.20**). The speckling may coalesce and give leaves a bronze or brown cast. Young, expanding foliage sometimes is distorted. Tiny reddish mites may be visible at the early stages of injury. Leaves bleach and dry, especially at the tips, and may drop. Plants are not usually killed, but the esthetic value is reduced.

CAUSE Immature and adult Southern red mites (*Oligonychus ilicis*), which feed by stabbing cells with mouthparts and sucking up the contents. This mite prefers cooler temperatures than most spider mites: its population is most dense in spring and autumn. (Indoors, these mites feed and reproduce all year.)

CONTROL While Southern red mites have several natural enemies (including other mites), plants sometimes may develop severe infestations. Watch susceptible plants, especially azaleas, hollies, and camellias, for early symptoms of injury or signs of infestation. Inspect evergreen foliage for eggs. Tap branches or foliage over a white board or piece of paper to dislodge and detect the mites. Horticultural oil can be used before budbreak in late winter or early spring to control eggs before they hatch. Other labeled pesticides are also available for severe infestations. Treat plants early in the infestation and when mites are active.

• *see also* MITES *p.147*.

SOWBUGS AND PILLBUGS

SYMPTOMS Dead plant matter is eaten and (sometimes) seedlings are damaged.

CAUSE Sometimes called woodlice, several species of sowbugs are common in gardens, including *Oniscus asellus*, *Porcellio scaber*, and *Cylisticus convexus*. The latter 2 roll up into a ball when disturbed and are commonly known as pillbugs. Sowbugs are gray or pinkish brown (*see* **p.53**), with a hard, segmented covering over their bodies and 7 pairs of legs. During the day, they are found in dark places and under pots, logs, and stones or in compost piles.

LENGTH: $\frac{1}{6}$–$\frac{3}{8}$in (4–15MM)

SOWBUG

CONTROL Sowbugs are such abundant animals in most gardens that there is little prospect of achieving any lasting reduction in their numbers. Where susceptible plants such as seedlings are being damaged, eliminate protected, damp locations and decaying plant material. Trap boards or stones can serve as shelters, from which they can be collected and destroyed during the day.

SPIDERS

There are about 2,500 species of spider in North America, and each is a predator that feeds mainly on insects. As such, they are beneficial in regulating insects and some pest populations. Although most do not bite if handled gently, very few spiders are dangerous. Widow spiders (*Latrodectus*) build webs in

dumps, trash, walls, buildings, and other similar sites and may (but rarely) bite when the strong web or the spider itself is disturbed. Serious illness and even death can result, so apply ice and get medical attention immediately. The female black widow (*L. mactans*), about the size of a quarter, is shiny and black except for a distinctive red hourglass under her abdomen.
The brown recluse (*Loxosceles reclusa*) is only ⅓–½in (8–12mm) and has a violin-shaped marking behind its head. Its irregular web may be located under rocks, brush piles, or debris or often in the shade of low-growing flowers and groundcovers, and sometimes in houses. Its bite sometimes causes no injury or it may lead to illness; it is almost never lethal. The slow-healing wound at the site of the bite can leave a pit or another large scar. Tarantulas may be 5in (13cm) across. Their very rare bite can feel like a bee sting, and their hairs may irritate bare skin. They are usually sluggish, though, and prefer to retreat to a dark cavity or burrow. To avoid trouble with these spiders, do not let wood and debris pile up. Wear gloves when cleaning up yard clutter, and wear long sleeves when turning over logs and pieces of debris.
Besides these, spiders should be welcomed to the garden for their beneficial roles and considered a normal part of the ecology. Many have fascinating habits and can be intriguing to observe as they spin webs and capture prey. Keep your garden's spider population healthy by minimizing applications of broad-spectrum insecticides.

SPINACH LEAFMINER
SYMPTOMS Leaves of beet, spinach, Swiss chard, and, sometimes, other leafy greens develop large brown areas (*see **p.17***). Early plantings are usually more affected than later ones.
CAUSE Larvae of the leaf-mining fly *Pegomya hyoscyami*, which has 3 or 4 generations in summer. The white maggots eat the leaves' internal tissues, which leads to the browning.
CONTROL Destroy weed hosts, especially lamb's-quarters, nightshade, plantain, and chickweed. Till soil deeply in spring to destroy pupae. With light infestations, remove affected leaves or crush the larvae inside the leaf mines. Parasitic wasps provide some control. Labeled insecticides can be applied.

SPITTLEBUG
SYMPTOMS Blobs of white frothy liquid appear on the stems of many plants in early summer (*see **pp.39, 43***). A sluggish, yellowish green insect lives in the froth, where it feeds by sucking the sap. Infested parts may be stunted.
CAUSE The immature nymph stage of froghoppers, such as the meadow spittlebug (*Philaenus spumarius*). Once they have reached the adult stage in early summer, they stop producing froth and become less noticeable. A few species, such as those on pine, may cause significant plant damage but are less commonly encountered.
CONTROL Dislodge nymphs with a blast of water. Picking off the pests by hand is usually sufficient to control most cases of infestation. Spraying is usually unwarranted.

SPLITTING
SYMPTOMS Fruits and occasionally stems may show cracking. This usually runs longitudinally, and initially the rest of the plant appears normal. The splitting allows other potential pathogens to enter, and so dieback or rot may occur later. The cracks may not necessarily become infected, and they may dry or heal over.
CAUSE Most commonly, an erratic supply of water or great fluctuations in temperature. Erratic availability of nutrients may be involved.
CONTROL Water and fertilize regularly, and use a mulch. Monitor damaged areas, and remove affected fruits so they are not infected by secondary organisms.

SPOTTED CUCUMBER BEETLE
See CUCUMBER BEETLES *p.120*.

SPOTTED TENTIFORM LEAFMINER
SYMPTOMS In midspring soon after apple petals fall, foliage of apple and several related trees, including crabapple, quince, and cherry. develop short, narrow, light-colored mines that are first visible under leaves and gradually widen (*see **p.13***). Within a few weeks, the mines become large, speckled, and blisterlike and are visible from the upper surface. If the leaf is held up to the light, a small worm is silhouetted within the blotch. White silk woven across the loosened, mined epidermis dries and shrinks, making a tentlike ridge lengthwise over the blister. The injury is mostly cosmetic, although a severe infestation can cause leaf and fruit drop.

CAUSE The spotted tentiform leafminer (*Phyllonorycter blancardella*), which is the larva of a small moth. There are several related species. The miner is a small, flattened, white to pale green caterpillar with a wedge-shaped, brownish head.
CONTROL Although spotted tentiform leafminer is rarely a serious pest in home gardens, it can be troublesome in orchards. Attract parasitic wasps, which are important in providing natural control. Inspect the undersides of middle-aged leaves from fruit clusters for the pale, tiny eggs. Rake up and destroy all fallen leaves from infested trees. Handpick foliage with egg clusters, larvae, or pupae, or pinch the larvae and pupae in their mines. Keep trees well watered. If large numbers are found, apply chemical controls before bloom.

SPRINGTAILS
SYMPTOMS Active white insects, up to ⅟₂₅in (2mm) long, live in the soil mix of container plants (*see **p.54***), especially those growing in peat-based types. They are most frequently seen when plants are being watered, since it washes them out of the bottom of the pot or onto the soil surface.
CAUSE Species of *Onychiurus*. The garden springtail (*Bourletiella hortensis*) sometimes chews small holes in leaves near the ground but rarely causes much damage. Springtails feed mainly on decaying plant material, algae, pollen, fungi, and, sometimes, young leaves or roots.
CONTROL No control measures are required, since most do not cause serious harm.

SPRUCE SPIDER MITE

SYMPTOMS Foliage becomes finely mottled and yellowish brown in early to midsummer, and it may fall prematurely. The damage may also appear again in autumn.

CAUSE Spruce spider mites (*Oligonychus ununguis*), which, when magnified through a hand lens, can be seen crawling among the foliage on fine silk webbing. These yellowish green mites with dark markings lay orange-red spherical eggs, which also can be found on the leaves and stems. Spruce is the most susceptible conifer, but this mite also attacks juniper, arborvitae, cedar, hemlock, Douglas fir, pine and other conifers, and cypress.

CONTROL Watch for early signs of infestation from late spring onward. Dwarf Alberta spruce is particularly sensitive and should be monitored carefully. Avoid planting mite-prone plants in areas of high sun and heat exposure. Tap branches over white paper to dislodge and detect mites. Horticultural oil applied just before budbreak helps control overwintering eggs (do not use on blue-colored conifers; the oil will spoil the color). Miticides are available.

SQUASH BEETLE

SYMPTOMS Squash leaves show feeding damage ranging from holes to skeletonization, often in circular areas (*see* **p.31**). Defoliation is rarely serious. Other cucurbits, such as pumpkin and gourd, are frequently attacked. Cucumber sometimes is damaged. Yellow, spiny larvae and black and yellow beetles may be seen under leaves.

CAUSE The squash beetle (*Epilachna borealis*). At ¼–⅜in (7–9mm) and looking like a pale orange-yellow ladybug, the squash beetle has 7 black spots on each wing cover. Both larval and adult squash beetles cause feeding damage.

CONTROL All methods of prevention and elimination of the squash beetle are the same as for the Mexican bean beetle (*see p.146*).

SQUASH BUG

SYMPTOMS At any point in the growing season, cucurbit leaves show pale green to yellow specks, which enlarge into brown patches. Leaves and shoots beyond the point of attack turn brown and die. Symptoms may be confused with those of wilt diseases, but gray or brown insects are present, typically in the interior of plants, under leaves, and on fruit (*see* **p.43**). Squash and pumpkins are most prone to attack. Cucumber, melons, and gourds are less so. Small plants can be killed early in the season. Older plants may lose one or more runners or leaves, and its yield is greatly diminished.

CAUSE Nymph and adult squash bugs (*Anasa tristis*), which feed by sucking sap from the leaves and stems of squash and related plants. The pest is active from midspring to midautumn. Because of the protracted egg-laying period, individuals of nearly every stage of the year's 1 generation can be found during the summer. When disturbed, the bugs give off an unpleasant odor.

CONTROL Plant more tolerant or resistant varieties. Timed planting may help. Grow susceptible plants far away from the previous season's site, or rotate out of vine crops altogether. Inspect plants in spring for adult bugs and later for the shiny eggs; remove and destroy them. Root disease, such as Fusarium (*see p.131*) and Verticillium (*see p.185*) wilts, spread by cucumber beetles (*see p.120*) and squash vine borers (*see below*), cause similar symptoms, so be sure the squash bugs are present before attempting control. Clean up the area to deprive adults of protected overwintering sites. After harvest, discard or plow under all plant debris. Use trap boards to attract overwintering adults, and destroy bugs that are found. Squash bug has several natural enemies, including the tachinid fly and the wolf spider, but they do not always keep numbers in check. Several labeled insecticides can be used to control squash bugs.

SQUASH VINE BORER

SYMPTOMS Starting in midspring in the warm areas to early summer in colder areas, the vines of squash, pumpkin, and, less often, other cucurbits wilt suddenly. This wilting should not be confused with physiological drooping due to hot weather or disease. Yellow to green or tan, crumbly sawdustlike material is evident at or under holes in the stems. Runners or stems tunneled near the base wilt and die. Winter and summer squash are especially susceptible. Cucumber and melons are less frequently attacked.

CAUSE The larva of a clearwing moth, the squash vine borer (*Melittia cucurbitae*), which is a common garden pest. Larvae hatch from eggs laid on stems in late spring to summer, tunneling inside and usually causing vines to wilt and die. The brown-headed white caterpillars, about 1in (2.5cm) long, often can be found inside affected stems. Later the squash vine borer will tunnel through other stems and the fruit.

CONTROL Squash and pumpkin cultivars exhibit widely varying degrees of susceptibility. Cucumbers and muskmelons may be less susceptible than squash and pumpkins. Early planting and encouraging vigor allows vines to grow large enough to tolerate infestation. Delayed planting may also help avoid some of the worst feeding damage. Check with the Cooperative Extension Service for local pest and planting timetables. Use floating rowcover to protect young plants during the early infestation period. To diminish the amount of lower stem surface available to egg-laying clearwings, mound moist soil or mulch right up to the flowers. This also promotes additional rooting at the leaf nodes. Clean up all vines and other residues immediately after harvest. Trichogramma wasps are natural egg parasites. Inject Btk (*see p.110*) or entomopathogenic nematodes directly into bore holes. Otherwise, insert a wire or slit a bored stem to kill the borer(s) – there may be several in each stem. Mound soil over damaged runners to encourage new roots. Pheromone traps are useful for detecting moth activity and timing control measures. Pyrethrin or another labeled insticide applied to vines and stem bases every week or 10 days can help control larvae.

• *see also* CLEARWING BORERS *p.115*.

SQUIRRELS

The gray squirrel (*Sciurus carolinensis*) and the red squirrel (*Tamiasciurus hudsonicus*) can be delightful to watch as they scamper around a garden, but squirrels can be very destructive. They dig up and eat crocus corms and tulip bulbs; eat flower buds and shoot tips; take nuts (*see* **p.52**), strawberries, and tree fruits; and strip the bark and eat buds from trees such as maple, beech, and ash. If bark is lost from all or most of the circumference of the trunk, the growth above that point may dry up and die. Squirrels can also cause annoyance by taking food put out for birds. Red squirrels sometimes make small, V-shaped cuts in bark for a source of sap in spring. Damage can lead to cankering.

CONTROL Squirrels are very mobile animals, and others will soon move in to occupy the territory of those that may have been removed by whatever means. Wrap barriers around individual trunks, and trim nearby limbs to prevent squirrels from gaining access to trees. Netting can give protection to fruits and flowering shrubs during periods when squirrels are showing an interest in them. Wire netting is better used for permanent structures, since squirrels can easily bite through plastic. Netting can also be placed over areas where bulbs and corms have been planted to deter squirrels from digging them up. Squirrelproof bird feeders are available from most garden centers.

STINKBUGS

SYMPTOMS Plants in the mustard family, legumes, fruit, and tomatoes have cloudy or white spots (*see* **p.50**). Fruit may be malformed. Bean pods can be bent or distorted. Cabbage can be wilted or sometimes killed.

CAUSE Stinkbugs, several species of which occur in gardens. The more common types include green stinkbug (*Acrosternum hilare*), harlequin bug (*Murgantia histrionica*), southern green stinkbug (*Nezara viridula*), and consperse stinkbug (*Euschistus conspersus*). They are up to ⅛in (1.3cm) long and are green or brown. Harlequin bugs are red and black. When viewed from above, stinkbugs have a shieldlike shape, with a large triangular plate in the middle of the back and a broad, flattened beetlelike appearance and sucking mouthparts. They emit a disagreeable odor when disturbed or handled. Some prey on other insects, but most feed on plant sap, although their impact on cultivated plants usually is negligible. They are most often a pest in late summer and early autumn, when numbers have increased.

CONTROL Clean up plant debris, and till overwintering sites. Handpick bugs and eggs. Keep areas free of weed hosts. Mustards have been used as a trap crop for harlequin bugs, destroying both trap and bugs to control overwintering insects. Labeled insecticide can be used to control heavy infestations.

STORAGE ROTS

SYMPTOMS Fruits, roots, and tubers in storage start to rot. In some cases, the infection may have begun without showing symptoms while the plant was growing, but the storage conditions encourage rot to develop visibly. In other instances, healthy plants or plant parts may become infected in storage, often from neighboring diseased material. Rot may be accompanied by the development of fungal growth on the surface or its spread within the plant.

CAUSE A very wide range of fungi and bacteria, some of which are described as secondary, enter only through injured areas; others, which are primary pathogens, cause damage to sound and uninjured tissue.

CONTROL Store only perfect fruits, roots, and tubers. Inspect stored items frequently, and remove any that show signs of deterioration, however slight. Provide storage conditions as close as possible to those advised.

STRAWBERRY BUD WEEVIL

SYMPTOMS Stems of strawberry, raspberry, and blackberry are partially cut ⅛–¼in (3–6mm) below the bud, which droops, falls over, dries out, and turns brown. Harvest may be reduced. Damage is usually more significant near weedy areas and in older plantings. Dewberry and potentilla flowers may also be affected.

CAUSE The tiny strawberry bud weevil (*Anthonomus signatus*), which is often a pest in home gardens. At only ½–⅛in (2–3mm), it is dark reddish brown with black wing patches. The female drills a hole in flower buds and inserts 1 egg. Aptly also called the bud clipper, she then cuts the stem nearly through to forestall further bud development. The small grub develops inside the hanging or fallen bud.

CONTROL Clean up all garden debris to eliminate overwintering adults. Use floating rowcover. Late-maturing strawberry cultivars may sustain less damage than early-maturing ones. Remove foliage during renovation to reduce attractiveness for overwintering adults. Watch for bud clipping as spring temperatures first reach 60–65°F (15–18°C). Labeled insecticides can be applied if clipping is significant, repeated after 10 days. An application after renovation may also help control any overwintering weevils.

STRAWBERRY LEAF SPOT

SYMPTOMS Reddish purple spots develop on the leaves (*see* **p.12**), each with a gray center. Off-white fungal growth and, occasionally, numerous tiny, raised, black fungal fruiting bodies may develop on the spots. The spots may join together and cover much of the leaf surface (*see* **p.17**) and may also spread to the flower and leaf stems. Although spoiling the appearance of the foliage, this infection may occur in spring but is usually fairly late in the season and so does little harm.

CAUSE The fungus *Mycosphaerella fragariae*, which forms sclerotia (black fungal resting bodies) that may overwinter in the soil and then cause the earlier infections in the spring.

CONTROL Remove badly infected leaves. Clear up all infected debris at the end of the season. Plant resistant cultivars.

SUCKERS

See PSYLLIDS AND SUCKERS **p.165**.

STRIPED CUCUMBER BEETLE

See CUCUMBER BEETLES *p.120.*

SYCAMORE ANTHRACNOSE (BLIGHT)

SYMPTOMS A brown patch develops at the base of leaf buds in winter. It may be hard to see, but in spring affected buds die without producing leaves. Adjacent areas of stem turn brown and die back, and a small cankered area may appear. Leaves that do open have very dark brown, necrotic areas and are rapidly killed. In summer, leaves that started off healthy may develop symptoms.
CAUSE The fungus *Apiognomonia veneta* (syn. *Gnomonia platani*), which is encouraged by cool weather in spring and may overwinter on fallen infected leaves.
CONTROL If the infection is mild and the tree is well sized, it may be possible to prune out all infected areas. Rake up and dispose of fallen leaves.

SYCAMORE MAPLE SOOTY BARK DISEASE

SYMPTOMS Leaves wilt and die back on infected branches but remain attached to the tree. If the bark is pared off, green or dark yellow staining may be visible (*see* **p.36**). Although these are the first symptoms, the problem may become apparent only at a later stage, when black spore masses or blisterlike outgrowths develop on the bark of affected stems and the tree fails to come into leaf in spring. The growths enlarge and may be associated with the extensive death and breaking up of the bark. The tree usually dies within a few years.

CAUSE The fungus *Cryptostroma corticale*, which appears to be encouraged by warm temperatures and, in particular, hot summers.
CONTROL Remove infected trees promptly.

SYRPHID FLIES

See HOVER FLIES *p.137.*

TACHINID FLIES

With about 1,300 species in North America, tachinid flies are parasites of many insects, helping to regulate pests. The adults, which resemble houseflies or wasps, are strong, relentlessly active fliers that feed on nectar and honeydew. Gray, brown, or black, often with colorful markings, the robust body has rows of bristles and is ⅛–⅝in (5–15mm) long. Tachinids usually lay eggs directly on hosts, such as caterpillars, but may deposit them on foliage; the eggs either are ingested by a host or hatch, with the larvae attaching themselves to a passing host. A few species inject larvae directly into a host. The white maggots gradually consume the internal organs of the host, which eventually dies. They remain in the body of the host or drop to the ground to pupate.
Tachinids have the greatest host range of any parasitic group, including caterpillars, beetles, grasshoppers, and many true bugs. They are the most important natural controls of many pest caterpillars, including armyworms, cabbage looper, Colorado potato beetle larvae, corn earworm

(tomato fruitworm), cutworms, gypsy moth, hornworms, many leafrollers, and tent caterpillars. One species is an important natural enemy of squash bugs, and another attacks both spotted and striped cucumber beetles.
Attract the nectar-loving tachinid flies with buckwheat, flowering herbs, and weeds such as dill, goldenrod, parsley, pigweed, sweet clover, wild carrot (Queen Anne's lace), and yarrow. Do not use broad-spectrum insecticides, and allow parasitized caterpillars or those carrying tachinid eggs to remain in the garden.

TARNISHED PLANT BUG

SYMPTOMS Strawberries are malformed or flattened and fail to develop normally, with seeds clustered in the tip. Bramble fruits may also be distorted. Peaches, peppers, and fruits of other plants are dimpled or distorted. Flower buds of asters and other plants, especially composites, are blasted or killed, or flowers are deformed on opening. Petioles, stems, or midribs of celery, lettuce, artichokes, chard, and other crops are pitted or distorted, as are bean pods.
CAUSE Nymph and adult tarnished plant bugs (*Lygus lineolaris*), also called lygus bug, which are significant pests of many garden plants. Several related species cause similar injury, including the western tarnished plant bug (*L. hesperus*) and the pale legume bug (*L. elisus*), both of which are important pests of alfalfa and seed crops in the western US.
CONTROL Natural enemies provide some control but are not always effective. Two parasitic wasps, *Peristenus*

digoneutis and *P. conradi*, have been released and appear to be regulating tarnished plant bugs. Grow nectar and pollen plants to attract the pest's natural enemies. Remove weeds and debris, which serve as overwintering sites. Do not plant near alfalfa or weedy areas, or disturb these sites around the time of bloom or fruiting of desirable crops. The bugs can be collected in sweep nets or monitored with white sticky panels. Tap strawberry or bramble flower clusters over a white plate to detect the nymphs. Labeled insecticides can be used after petal fall in small fruit or while flower buds form and expand for cut flowers.
• *see also* PLANT (LYGUS) BUGS *p.161.*

TARSONEMID MITES

SYMPTOMS Greenhouse plants and houseplants, including cyclamens, begonias, geraniums (*Pelargonium*), impatiens, delphinium, strawberry, and peppers, have distorted flowers with white or brown flecks on the petals. The new foliage fails to expand to its full size and becomes progressively more stunted and distorted (*see* **p.27**). In severe cases, growth comes to a complete halt, buds may be killed, and the stems have a brownish scarring.
CAUSE Microscopic sap-feeding mites, including broad mite (*Polyphagotarsonemus latus*) and cyclamen mite (*Phytonemus pallidus*, *see* p.121). These whitish brown mites infest developing leaves and flower buds, and their feeding causes flower distortion.
CONTROL Infested plants should be destroyed, although immersing plants in

water at 110°F (43°C) for 10 minutes (100°F/38°C for 20 minutes for strawberry) may provide control for important plants. This pest usually enters a greenhouse on an infested plant. Keep new plants away from older, healthy specimens until it is clear they are not infested.

TAR SPOT OF MAPLE

SYMPTOMS Large, slightly raised, shiny black blotches develop on the leaves of both wild and cultivated maples (see p.13). Each can measure up to ½–¾in (1.3–1.9cm) in diameter.
CAUSE Species of the fungus *Rhytisma*, particularly *R. acerinum*, which can overwinter on fallen infected leaves. In spring, it produces spores in a gelatinous coating that adheres to young leaves as they open. Leaves may fall prematurely, but the vigor of the tree is rarely significantly affected.
CONTROL Rake up and dispose of affected leaves as they fall.

TAXUS BUD MITE

SYMPTOMS The buds and growing tips of yew (*Taxus*) enlarge and become russeted (see **p.41**). If these parts are only lightly injured, the needles and shoots grow out distorted (see **p.27**). If the buds are heavily injured, they probably will die, so no new shoot growth occurs.
CAUSE The taxus bud mite (*Cecidophyopsis psilaspis*). The minuscule, slow-moving, orange or whitish adults crawl between bud scales to overwinter and frequently cause tiny bud galls. In late summer, they migrate to new buds and resume feeding. Although there may be 1,000 mites per bud, the decay and distortion of plant growth are caused by secondary micro-

organisms that infect the plant through feeding sites.
CONTROL Control usually is not needed, particularly for pruned plants or hedges from which distorted growth is removed. Dispose of prunings and other debris. Labeled insecticides applied in spring as mites emerge may help reduce injury.

TEXAS ROOT ROT

SYMPTOMS When midsummer temperatures reach 80°F (27°C), leaves may wilt, yellow or bronze, and dry. New growth is stunted and dies back, or the whole plant may die in a few days. By the time foliar damage is noted, most plants have advanced necrotic root lesions. The surface of moist soil and parts of the plant become covered with a cottony mat that changes from white to yellowish and then tawny brown. Dark brown strands spread along and beneath the surface for perhaps 30ft (9m) a season, killing every susceptible plant in their path. Small granules – at first light and roundish, later dark and warty – form along the strands, which can enlarge to a circle a few yards to over 1 acre (0.4 ha) in diameter. Over 2,000 species are vulnerable, including many summer annuals, perennials, and vegetables. Fruit trees and many other woody plants are slower to succumb, stunted new growth often being the only obvious symptom for several years, yet most eventually are killed.
CAUSE The fungus Texas root rot (*Phymatotrichopsis omnivora*, syn. *Phymatotrichum omnivorum*), which afflicts more plant species than any

other pathogen. Also called cotton root rot and Phymatotrichum root rot, it is the most damaging disease in Texas and is found from Arkansas and Louisiana west to southern California. The fungus develops most rapidly in warm conditions and heavy, calcareous, alkaline (pH 7.2–8.5) soils low in organic matter.
Spreading in the soil from roots, which it enters through wounds or other openings, Texas root rot can kill host cells by toxins in advance of direct contact. It winters as dormant mycelia in living roots or as resting bodies in the soil, where it can persist without a live host for several years.
CONTROL Plant resistant and winter-hardy vegetables – such as cucurbits, cabbage, and carrots – and ornamentals. Monocots, such as cereals and grasses, and many dicots native to the Southwest are resistant. Grow more susceptible plants from spring through early summer, and then follow them with a second crop of resistant plants from midsummer on. Acidify the soil and build up its organic content. Frequently, adding compost will favor soil saprophytes antagonistic to the fungus. Cover cropping and heavy manuring are also beneficial. Plant with the soil line somewhat higher than the surrounding ground, sloping away from the trunk. Cut irrigation moats 1ft (30cm) from stems and trunks. The soil should be well drained, water not pooling up at a tree base, and overwatering should be avoided. Do not cultivate near the roots, and mulch to keep down weeds. Sterilize tools and other equipment. Remove and destroy badly

infected plants. Some plants can be rescued by pruning the diseased roots and replanting in well-drained medium. Also prune the top of the plant to avoid moisture stress.

THRIPS

Thrips are narrow-bodied, elongate insects up to ⅟₁₂in (2mm) long. They usually feed by sucking sap and generally cause a fine silvery white mottled discoloration of the upper leaf surface or distorted growth of new foliage or flowers. Some are predatory or feed on fungus spores. Adult thrips are usually black or brown with 2 pairs of wings that are heavily fringed with hairs. The wings are folded back along the body when not in use and so are not readily visible. The immature nymphs are wingless and creamy yellow. Some species, such as western flower thrips, can spread plant viruses.
• *see also* DRACAENA THRIPS *p.123*; GLADIOLUS THRIPS *p.132*; ONION THRIPS *p.154*; PRIVET THRIPS *p.165*; WESTERN FLOWER THRIPS *p.189*.

TOADSTOOLS
See TURF FAIRY RINGS AND TOADSTOOLS *p.184*.

TOBACCO HORNWORM
See HORNWORMS *p.137*.

TOMATO BLOTCHY RIPENING

SYMPTOMS Patches of flesh remain unripened (see **p.51**). These hard, yellow or green areas may be anywhere on the fruit, and, unlike tomato greenback (see *p.182*), tomato blotchy ripening does not follow a regular pattern. The damage is visible only on mature fruits, and those on the lower clusters are generally the most frequently affected.

CAUSE Malnutrition, a deficiency of potassium probably being the most important factor. Dry soil or soil mix, or a poorly functioning root system, may also play a part. High temperatures in a greenhouse also increase the damage.

CONTROL Keep the plants well fertilized, particularly with potassium, the greenhouse well ventilated, and the plants well watered.

TOMATO CYST NEMATODE

See POTATO CYST NEMATODE *p.162.*

TOMATO FRUIT SPLITTING

SYMPTOMS Tomatoes develop normally but start to split, usually just before picking (*see **p.50***). The cracks may become infected by secondary organisms, such as *Alternaria* (*see p.98*) and *Botrytis* (*see p.109*), and then may rot. Occasionally, the split surface temporarily dries up and the fruit does not rot.

CAUSE Erratic growth and fruit swelling, which usually are caused by an irregular supply of water or unusual fluctuations in temperature.

CONTROL Make sure that plants are adequately watered at all times and are not subjected to temperature extremes. In greenhouses, provide shading and ventilation. Remove affected fruits before secondary organisms invade.

TOMATO GREENBACK

SYMPTOMS As tomatoes begin to ripen, a partial or complete ring of leathery tissue remains around the stalk end. It does not ripen, remaining green or yellow (*see **p.50***). The rest of the plant develops normally.

CAUSE Low levels of potassium and phosphorus may be involved, but hot, bright sunlight, which causes heat injury, is probably the most important factor.

CONTROL Provide appropriate shading for the plants, particularly once the fruits start to develop. Keep the plants well fed, especially with potassium and phosphorus.

TOMATO HORNWORM

See HORNWORMS *p.137.*

TOMATO LATE BLIGHT

SYMPTOMS Brown patches develop on the leaves, causing them to dry and curl. The stems may also show blackening. Infected fruits develop a brown discoloration and may appear to shrink inward. They may rot, either on the plant or a few days after being picked. Tomatoes grown outdoors are affected more frequently than those grown under glass. Potatoes may also be damaged (*see* POTATO EARLY BLIGHT *p.163*). Tomatoes usually succumb slightly later than potatoes.

CAUSE The fungus *Phytophthora infestans*, which is encouraged by moist or wet weather, particularly in late summer. The spores are carried on air currents or on water splash and need a minute film of moisture on the foliage if they are to cause damage.

CONTROL Preventive spraying with a copper- or mancozeb-based fungicide is worthwhile, particularly if tomatoes are growing in an area where blight is common and there are other potato or tomato crops in the vicinity.

In a wet season, spraying should be carried out as soon as the first tomatoes have set and then be repeated according to the manufacturer's instructions.

TOMATO VIRUSES

SYMPTOMS The symptoms that viruses produce vary, not only with the virus involved but also with the tomato cultivar and the growing conditions. Common leaf symptoms include yellow mottle or mosaic, distortion, and unusually small leaves. With tomato mosaic, in addition to these symptoms, the youngest leaves may curl downward. With fern leaf, the leaf blades are extensively narrowed and malformed, which may be mistaken for herbicide damage. Other symptoms of virus infection may include yellow streaking, stunting, and bronzing of the young fruits; yellow streaking of the fruits; or failure of the plant to set fruit.

CAUSE Most commonly, the viruses tomato spotted wilt, streak, tomato mosaic, potato virus X, and cucumber mosaic, either alone or in combination. They are readily spread by handling and/or by aphids and other sap-feeding pests. Many of these viruses have very wide host ranges, so they may be introduced from unrelated plants in the garden or may be spread to these plants from infected tomatoes.

CONTROL Remove and dispose of infected plants. Avoid handling plants unnecessarily, and always wash hands thoroughly after handling. Remove and discard all crop debris at the end of the season. Control aphids and other sap-feeding pests. Grow resistant cultivars.

TRICHOGRAMMA WASPS

Highly beneficial as natural parasites of the eggs of other insects, especially moths and butterflies, trichogramma wasps are widely distributed and often present, but rarely observed because of their small size. There are at least 40 species in the US and Canada, some of which are commercially reared and marketed for control of over 200 pests. Widely applied in releases within large crops, trichogramma wasps sometimes cost half as much as chemical controls. Trichogramma wasps range in length from $\frac{1}{100}$–$\frac{1}{25}$in (0.25–1mm). A female lays 80–100 eggs, each in a host egg, which stops developing and then blackens. The larva hatches, feeds, and pupates all within this egg. The adult wasp emerges to feed on nectar and is harmless to humans, pets, and everything else in the garden except butterfly and moth eggs. Some species of *Trichogramma* are general parasites, whereas others are highly specialized. The commercially available *T. minutum*, the minute egg parasite, does best in trees and other plants at least 5ft (1.5m) off the ground. *T. pretiosum* is widely marketed to fight garden and field pests occurring within 5ft of the ground, including armyworms, cabbage looper, casebearers, codling moth, corn earworm (tomato fruitworm), cutworms, European corn borer, hornworms, and imported cabbageworm.

Attract trichogramma wasps to the garden by growing small-flowered nectar plants. Well-fed wasps lay more eggs. When purchased, these beneficials arrive as thousands of parasitized eggs per square inch (6.5 sq cm), sandpapery card. Use the correct species for the pest or pests to be controlled, and plan releases when pest eggs are present. Set out pheromone traps to monitor adult pest moths and to time releases.

TULIP BULB ROT

SYMPTOMS Bulbs fail to emerge aboveground, leaving gaps in the bed. Shoots that do grow are extensively distorted and soon wither and die. Infected bulbs turn gray and dry as they start to rot. The roots and the basal plate may be all that remain. Soil tends to adhere to infected bulbs, especially at the noses. A dense, white or gray, felty fungal growth develops between the scales and on the outside of bulbs. Dark brown sclerotia (fungal resting bodies) appear amid the fungal growth and may reach up to ⅓in (7mm) in size, remaining viable in the soil for up to 5 years.
CAUSE The fungus *Rhizoctonia tuliparum*, which may attack many bulbs.
CONTROL Remove and discard affected plants, together with the soil around them. Do not grow susceptible bulbs on the same ground for at least 5 years.

TULIP FIRE

SYMPTOMS As the foliage emerges, it may be withered, distorted, and covered with numerous buff-colored flecks (*see* **p.22**) or scorched. It soon becomes covered in fuzzy, gray fungal growth. Elliptical gray-brown marks develop on the stalks. The plants may fail to mature, although some may flower, or flower buds may develop but fail to open. The petals

of those that open normally may have numerous small, bleached spots. The flower stems may topple over, and in wet weather the whole plant may become covered in the fungal growth and then rot rapidly. Bulbs may rot or may appear firm but bear black sclerotia (fungal resting bodies) clustered around the neck (*see* **p.55**).
CAUSE The fungus *Botrytis tulipae*, which overwinters as pinhead-size sclerotia in the soil or on infected bulbs. The spores produced on all the aboveground parts of the plant are readily spread on air currents and by water splash.
CONTROL Remove infected foliage promptly. Dispose of severely infected plants, together with the soil in the immediate vicinity of the roots. Check newly purchased bulbs carefully before planting, and plant only those that are apparently healthy and free from signs of sclerotia. Late planting may also decrease the chances of the disease developing. On sites where the disease has been identified, do not replant tulips for at least 3 years and for more than 2 years in succession. At the end of the season, lift tulip bulbs, examine them closely for infection, and discard those of poor quality.

TURF BROWN PATCH

SYMPTOMS In hot, humid conditions, turfgrass can develop purplish green patches in a few hours. As they expand in diameter, these circles quickly fade to brown or blackish. A dark purple ring 1–2in (2.5–5cm) wide sometimes remains as a border to the growing brown area. The grass in the patch may become matted, and the

blades covered with a moldy, filmy white tuft in the early morning. Several patches can coalesce and continue to expand. Even if the patch appears to have died out, recovery normally starts from the center after 2–3 weeks. Sometimes the patch does not recover, and algae invade the site. This is a more significant problem with short, high-maintenance grasses such as bentgrass than with bluegrass, but nearly every cultivated turfgrass is at least somewhat susceptible, particularly St. Augustine, zoysia, and rye.
CAUSE The fungus turf brown patch (*Thanatephorus cucumeris*), which is a very prevalent soilborne leaf and root rot in warm, moist climates. It progresses fastest in 75–80°F (24–27°C) weather and in grass with poor air circulation, such as lawns closed in by thick stands of trees, and treated with a high-nitrogen feeding program.
CONTROL Plant resistant grasses, such as several of the ryegrasses, tall fescues, and bluegrasses, particularly Canada bluegrass. Keep the grass as dry as possible, watering deeply at most once or twice a week. Fast lawn drying is crucial for the prevention and suppression of brown patch, so do not water late in the day. Good drainage is also necessary. Dethatch and aerate the lawn. Top-dress it with material that will build humus. Avoid excess nitrogen in fertilizer, but continue to provide adequate phosphorus and potassium. The soil should not have a low pH. Cut the grass neither as short nor as frequently as before brown patch attack, and never mow grass that

harbors spores. Rake out and replace completely dead patches.

TURF DOLLAR SPOT

SYMPTOMS Grass dies off in patches, becoming straw-yellow (*see* **p.58**). Patches usually measure between 3–4in (7.5–10cm) in diameter.
CAUSE The fungus *Sclerotinia homeocarpa*, which is most prevalent during warm, wet spells in early autumn and on lawns that have become compacted.
CONTROL Improve drainage by spiking the lawn in autumn. Avoid using grass seed mixtures containing a high proportion of fescues, since they are particularly prone to this infection. Treat infected areas with a suitable fungicide.

TURF DROUGHT

SYMPTOMS/CAUSE During a long dry spell, large areas of lawn yellow and brown. This occurs first in sunny spots, but can spread to more shaded areas. A wilting grass blade folds up and acquires a dark blue-green tinge. Its growth is stunted, and it turns slate gray, yellow, and then brown. A patch of such grass loses its springiness and starts to thin. It becomes strawlike and may die. If the grass goes into winter thus weakened, it will struggle to reestablish roots the following spring and will be yellowed due to iron-deficiency chlorosis. Damage from salts, which form a white or dark brown crust on the soil surface, is a serious problem in low areas of a lawn during a drought. The salts may come from fertilizer, evaporated irrigation water, or the soil. Dry lawns enhance the populations of pests, such as mites, chinch bugs, and sod webworms. Rust fungi are promoted by heavy dew on grass that is growing slowly due to dryness; the grass yellows, withers, and dies rapidly or is susceptible to winter kill. Species of *Fusarium* can blight drought-stressed turf during a 2- to 3-day period of high night temperatures (over 75°F/24°C) and high humidity. Dollar spot fungus also takes advantage of grass weakened by drought.

CONTROL Water a dry lawn immediately and deeply. Unless the roots are killed, some drought-induced wilting is normal during dormant periods. Even if the yellow blades take weeks to recover full greenness, the root systems can quickly start to come back. Every 5–7 days, water 6–8in (15–20cm) deep. Rains and cooler temperatures later in the season will complete the lawn rejuvenation.

Grow grasses appropriate for the climate and resistant to insect pests and pathogens. At least mix an equal amount of resistant varieties with more susceptible ones that are desired. Bluegrasses and fescues are generally hardy and tolerant of dry conditions. The Cooperative Extension Service or commercial landscaping specialists can recommend cultivars. To improve drainage, aerate compacted soil, and add organic material. Clear out thatch, clippings, and weeds. Conserve lawn moisture by not mowing grass too short. Do not overfertilize a drought-stressed lawn with nitrogen, which would result in excessive green growth that cannot be sustained by the inadequately functioning root systems.

TURF FAIRY RINGS AND TOADSTOOLS

SYMPTOMS Rings develop on the turf, increasing in size. Around the periphery grow 1 or more zones of very lush, green grass. There is also an inner zone of similarly luxuriant grass. The area between these green zones is dead and brown, or the soil may be completely bare. Occasionally, incomplete rings or other formations develop. Pale brown, slender toadstools, each 1½–4in (4–10cm) tall, may appear at the outer part of the middle zone in summer or autumn (*see* **p.59**). Toadstools may also appear as individuals or small groups independent of a fairy ring.

CAUSE Fungi that occur beneath the soil surface and around the bases of the grasses, forming a dense, off-white growth, or mycelium. The death of the middle zone of grass is caused by drought – the mycelium is so water-repellent that water cannot penetrate to the grass roots in this area.

CONTROL Rake up and dispose of all toadstools, preferably before their caps open to release spores. Mow the infected area, and discard the mowings. Dig out the affected grass and topsoil to a depth of at least 1ft (30cm).

TURF MELTING OUT

SYMPTOMS In early spring or late autumn, areas of lawn become yellow, dappled with remaining green. Patches eventually die, fading to reddish brown. Especially into summer, large, irregular areas can die quite suddenly. The lawn is substantially thinned out, and crabgrass and other weeds soon invade.

Scattered leaf blades start out with tiny brown lesions ringed with reddish brown to dark purplish or black. The center of the lesion turns gray, becomes straw-colored, and withers and drops. As the disease progresses, foot rot sets in and the grass dies.

CAUSE Several species of the fungus *Drechslera*, which causes turf leaf spots and melting out, sometimes known as fading out, going out, leaf blight, spot blotch, and zonate leaf spot blight. Spores of *Drechslera* overwinter in grass debris and in infected crowns and underground parts. During a cool, wet spring, the fungi become active; spores splash onto leaves, beginning the disease's early, or leaf spot, stage. The pathogen can also be introduced on contaminated seed. With continued moist or humid conditions in summer, especially in a shaded area of lawn, crowns and roots become diseased, marking the melting-out stage. Symptoms are worst on grass that is cut too low. In autumn, spores splash up and reinfect leaves.

CONTROL Kentucky bluegrass, bentgrasses, and fescues are the most susceptible, so grow resistant varieties. All grass seed must be certified clean. Keep grass vigorous. Reduce shade and fertilize properly, avoiding excessive soil nitrogen levels. Various mechanical techniques and soil amendments improve both aeration and drainage. Water deeply, but not late in the afternoon or in the evening so the grass can dry.

TURF RED THREAD

SYMPTOMS Patches of reddish or bleached grass develop, 3in (7.5–8cm) in diameter.

Among the grasses and attached to them, dark pink, hornlike, gelatinous, branching strands of fungus appear (*see* **p.59**). They then turn pale pink and slightly fluffy. Grass is rarely killed, but it is weakened and its appearance spoiled.

CAUSE The fungus *Laetisaria fuciformis* (syn. *Corticium fuciforme*), which is most common on lawns composed mainly of fine grasses, such as fescues. Low nitrogen levels and poor aeration encourage the disease. It is usually most prevalent in the year following a drought, because the dry weather in the previous year probably made carrying out the usual fertilizing routine difficult.

CONTROL Improve drainage by aeration, and make sure that the grass is adequately fertilized. Apply nitrogen in the form of ammonium sulfate. If a fungicide application becomes necessary, additional nitrogen must also be applied, or the problem will recur.

TURF SNOW MOLD

SYMPTOMS Primarily in autumn and mild spells in winter, small patches of grass die, gradually turn brown, increase in size, and may coalesce. In wet weather, the dying patches may become covered in a pale pink, fluffy fungal growth (*see* **p.59**).

CAUSE The fungus *Monographella nivalis* and occasionally other fungi. Snow mold is often encouraged by poor aeration and by wet conditions.

CONTROL Carry out regular aeration routine. Treat the lawn with a suitable fungicide according to the label directions.

TURF THATCH FUNGAL MYCELIUM

SYMPTOMS Bleached, yellowed, or, occasionally, reddish patches of grass develop on the lawn. A dense mat of fungus grows around the bases of the grasses, which are severely stressed or may be killed (see **p.58**).

CAUSE Various fungi, often described as thatch fungi, which are not directly pathogenic but live on organic debris, including thatch (mowings and other debris), at the base of the grasses. They form a strongly water-repellent layer that causes the grass to die from drought stress. Lawns that have not been properly maintained, and newly laid sod, are the most susceptible.

CONTROL Carry out lawn maintenance: scarification, spiking, and weed control. Do not allow mowings to be redistributed over the lawn. Buy sod from only a reliable, reputable supplier, and check it carefully upon delivery. The only solution may be the removal of badly affected areas followed by reseeding or resodding.

TWO-LINED CHESTNUT BORER

SYMPTOMS On oak, beech, chestnut, or ironwood, especially trees weakened by insect damage or disease, foliage may be thin, abnormally small, or off-colored. In severe cases, branches or entire trees can be killed. Lifting off the bark from dead wood reveals winding, zigzagging tunnels in the inner bark and outer sapwood (see **p.33**). D-shaped holes appear in the bark. These symptoms start at the treetop and gradually move down the trunk in succeeding years.

CAUSE Larvae of the two-lined chestnut borer (*Agrilus bilineatus*), which chew zigzag galleries mostly in the phloem, girdling branches or the trunk. The slender, flat-headed white larva is ½–1in (1.3–2.5cm) long, with constrictions between segments. There is 1 generation a year.

CONTROL Plant less susceptible or nonhost species. Maintain vigor. An infested branch should be pruned out and destroyed, and a severely infested tree may need to be completely removed. Labeled insecticides applied to bark before eggs are laid in late spring and early summer can also help control an infestation.

TWOSPOTTED SPIDER MITE

SYMPTOMS Leaves develop a fine pale mottling (see **p.22**), with the foliage dull green at first and later increasingly yellowish white. These symptoms can be confused with a mineral deficiency, but examination of the lower leaf surface reveals tiny spider mites and their spherical eggs. When plants are heavily infested, mites crawl over fine silk webbing spun between the leaves and the stems (see **p.43**). Leaves dry up (see **p.23**) and fall prematurely, so that only young leaves at the shoot tips remain.

CAUSE Sap-feeding mites, *Tetranychus urticae*, which attack a wide range of indoor and greenhouse plants. The mites are less than ⅟₂₅in (1mm) long and have 4 pairs of legs; they are yellowish green with 2 large dark markings toward the head. They become orange-red in the autumn and winter, when the adult

females are hibernating in sheltered places. They also cause problems outdoors, especially in warm dry summers, to beans, raspberries, strawberries, currants, roses, and many other ornamental plants.

ACTUAL SIZE ▪

TWOSPOTTED SPIDER MITE

CONTROL Biological control with the predatory mite *Phytoseiulus persimilis* can give good results if it is introduced before a heavy infestation has developed. It also requires warm daytime temperatures, moderate to high humidity, and an absence of pesticides if it is to become established. *Phytoseiulus* can also be used on outdoor plants in summer. Other predatory mites and a predatory ladybug (*Stethorus punctillum*) or flower bugs (*Orius*) can also be purchased and released against twospotted spider mites. Spider mites breed very rapidly under warm conditions, and some strains have become resistant to some pesticides. Insecticidal soap, horticultural oil, or another labeled miticide can be used to control an infestation.

VARIEGATION (SPONTANEOUS)

SYMPTOMS A plant with normally solid green foliage begins developing abnormal (often white or yellow) spotting, mottling, streaking, or banding. Flowers sometimes acquire abnormal colors without apparent viral infections or environmental stress. Sometimes only 1 branch or shoot is affected.

CAUSE Mutations cause leaf variegation when abnormal cells grow along with the genetically normal cells. This is different from temporary abnormal color due to injury, less than optimal growing conditions, or disease, where the pigment balance is disrupted by mechanical or chemical changes but the genetic identity of the cells remains unaltered. Variegation patterns result from mutations at various stages of cell division or in different cell components. Spontaneous variegation is often considered desirable by growers and consumers. Offspring with valued traits are usually propagated by buds and cuttings. Often, though, tissue that lacks chlorophyll prematurely dies, making variegated trees and shrubs easily subject to stress and long-term damage.

CONTROL If variegation is unwanted, prune the affected part. Propagate by cuttings from only the desirable parts of the plant.

VERTICILLIUM WILTS

SYMPTOMS Most or all of the leaves on a branch or stem show wilting (see **p.29**), but the entire plant is unlikely to be affected simultaneously. The leaves may show interveinal discoloration (usually as yellowing or browning between the veins) and then die. Stem death follows shortly, but it may be several years before a large shrub is killed. Smaller shrubs or herbaceous perennials and annuals may die within a single season. If the bark is removed from an affected stem, the vascular tissue (especially water-conducting tissue) is discolored, usually by brown or purple-brown streaks that run the length of the stem (see *p.33*) but are usually most apparent toward the base. Roots have a central core of discolored conducting tissue.

CAUSE The fungi *Verticillium dahliae* and *V. albo-atrum*, which are found in infested soil, on plant debris, and within the plant sap. The host ranges are wide, and many cultivated plants – including maples, Indian bean tree (*Catalpa bignonioides*), redbud (*Cercis*), smoke bush (*Cotinus*), golden rain tree (*Koelreuteria*), staghorn sumac (*Rhus typhina*), linden (*Tilia*), barberry (*Berberis*), daphnes, quince (*Cydonia*), apples, pears, and cherries – as well as several common garden weeds may harbor it.

CONTROL Remove affected plants promptly, together with the soil in the immediate vicinity of their roots. Because the infection can be spread on pruning tools, always thoroughly clean any tools with dilute bleach or alcohol after they have been used on an infected plant. Avoid replanting hosts on a site that had an infected plant.

VIBURNUM LEAF BEETLE

SYMPTOMS The foliage of viburnums – particularly laurustinus (*Viburnum tinus*), arrow-wood (*V. dentatum*), European cranberry bush viburnum (*V. opulus*), American cranberrybush viburnum (*V. trilobum*), and wayfaring tree (*V. lantana*) – is reduced to a lacework of eaten leaves during summer.

CAUSE Adults and larvae of a beetle, *Pyrrhalta viburni*. Most of the damage is caused by the creamy yellow, black-spotted larvae, which are up to ¼in (7mm) long, from late spring to early summer. The grayish brown beetles, ⅕–¼in (5–6mm) long, cause additional, but less extensive, damage.

CONTROL Plant resistant or less susceptible viburnums, such as Koreanspice viburnum (*V. carlesii*), burkwood viburnum (*V. burkwoodii*), and leatherleaf viburnum (*V. rhytidophyllum*). Look for signs of damage on the new foliage in late spring. Remove larvae and adults by hand. Labeled insecticides may be needed to avoid severe defoliation and should be applied when larvae are small.

VIRUSES

SYMPTOMS These vary widely, but the most common and widely spread symptoms of viral infection are stunting of the whole plant and distortion (see *pp.25, 27*), or the leaves and other aboveground parts of the plant become distorted and/or develop markings (see *pp.18, 21, 23*). They are usually yellow, although on some plants, such as orchids, they may be dark brown or black (see *p.12*). The markings are commonly seen as streaks, mosaic patterns, flecks, mottles, ring spots, or vein clearing, where yellow areas occur adjacent to the leaf veins. Flowers may show distortion or fail to develop, or they may form but show "flower breaking," where pale streaks of color develop on dark petals (see *p.42*) or colored streaks develop on pale petals. Other flowers may turn brown and dry up. Infected plants generally yield poorly or fail to bear at all, and death often is premature. Some viruses may infect certain plants without causing visible symptoms (latent infection). For example, cucumber mosaic virus (see *p.120*) can exist in a number of common weeds that, although appearing healthy, can act as a source of viral infection for other more desirable plants.

CAUSE A wide range of viruses, most of which may be found alone or in combination with other viruses. There are various methods of transmission, the most common being by sap-feeding insects, particularly aphids. Leafhoppers, whiteflies, plant hoppers, thrips, scale insects, mites, beetles, nematodes, and fungi are other vectors (carriers). Viruses may also be transmitted by handling, by grafting, by separating tubers, bulbs, and corms, and by performing routine horticultural operations, such as disbudding or removing sideshoots.

CONTROL Remove and dispose of affected plants promptly. Wash hands and tools thoroughly after handling infected plants. Do not put replacement plants of a similar type on the same site, and control potential vectors. Good weed and vector control is essential. Never propagate from visibly infected or even suspect plants. Where possible, choose virus-resistant cultivars (notably tomato) and buy plants (such as potatoes and strawberries) certified as virus-free.

• see also PEAR STONY PIT VIRUS *p.158*; POTATO VIRUSES *p.164*; ROSE VIRUSES *p.171*; TOMATO VIRUSES *p.182*.

VOLES

SYMPTOMS Bark from the trunks and branches of young trees and shrubs is gnawed (see *p.36*). This may occur around the entire stem (girdling), which prevents the uptake of water and nutrients, leading to the death of branches or the whole plant. Affected plants may also show yellowing foliage, low vigor or yield, or lodging (falling over).

CAUSE Voles, rodents with generally shorter tails and more rounded heads than the mice and rats that they resemble. They feed on a wide range of plant material, including seeds, flower buds, bulbs, corms, and plant roots. Several species can occur in gardens, including the meadow vole, also called the meadow mouse (*Microtus pennsylvanicus* and *M. californicus*), the pine vole, sometimes called the woodland mouse or pine mouse (*M. pinetorum*), and the montane vole (*M. montanus*).

CONTROL Keep vegetation mowed, and maintain a groundcover-free area underneath plants of approximately 4ft (1.2m) in diameter. Chicken wire, plastic mesh, or other guards can be placed around trunks, set about 4in (10cm) into the ground. Keep snow away from tree or shrub trunks. Remove fallen fruit and other debris promptly. For damaged plants, bridge grafting may help save important specimens. Set mouse or rat traps, as appropriate, in places where voles are active. Pieces of apple seem to be a particularly attractive bait. Traps must be placed under covers made of logs or bricks to keep birds away and to prevent harm to pets.

WALNUT CROWN AND ROOT ROTS

SYMPTOMS In a cool, wet, early spring, walnut leaflets become a dull green or yellow and are stunted. Foliage looks sparse and drought-stressed and, with the first warm weather, wilts and rapidly dies. These signs first develop on a single branch and then progress to the rest. In a wet late autumn, chlorotic symptoms resemble premature autumn coloring. Cankers are seen on the bark of the crown and of the upper roots. Soft and spongy, a lesion begins water-soaked then becomes reddish brown to dark brown or black, with an irregular but abrupt margin. Peeling off cankered bark reveals red-brown streaks. The sapwood may turn tan to black, with black fluid filling cavities. Saplings can be killed. A root attack takes some years to be fatal, although the tree is stunted. A peculiarly heavy crop may be followed by tree death the next year. Besides walnuts, almost all nut and fruit trees are susceptible to this disease. Cankers generally do not bleed sap on walnut, but they frequently do on fruit trees, exuding a dark reddish brown liquid.

CAUSE Species of *Phytophthora*, a fungus that infects first the base of the trunk and adjoining major roots. Wounds facilitate but are not essential for spore penetration. Spores are also transported by surface irrigation and runoff, splashing rain, movement of contaminated soil, and equipment.

CONTROL Choose only the most tolerant walnut varieties on Persian or 'Paradox' rootstock. Every tree must be certified clean. Plant in soil with very good drainage and aeration. If soil is shallow or tends to become waterlogged, build a raised mound, and do not place the crown any deeper relative to the soil line than it was at the nursery or another previous site.
Water only when necessary. Do not directly water the crown, lower branches, trunk, or ground right around it. Keep weeds and garden plants away from the crown. Excising the lesions may help. Fungicides may also be helpful but are difficult to use, since the entire root system must be treated.

WALNUT HUSK FLIES

SYMPTOMS Walnut husks, especially of black walnuts, become black and soft. When damage occurs early in the season, the kernels may become dark and shriveled.

CAUSE Maggots of walnut husk flies (*Rhagoletis completa* and *R. suavis*), which feed in nut husks and cause the shell to become stained. Kernels usually are undamaged. Black walnut is the favored host, but all kinds of walnuts can be attacked. Mid- and late-season cultivars are most affected. There is 1 generation a year.

CONTROL The infestation can be tolerated if stained nutshells are not a concern, since the nutmeats tend to be unaffected. Remove abandoned alternate host trees, clean up dropped nuts, and remove and destroy husks promptly. Grow early-maturing cultivars. Hang walnut-green sticky spheres, 3¼in (8.25cm) in diameter, and baited yellow sticky cards in the shaded canopy around susceptible trees from early summer to detect the adults and possibly suppress damage on individual, isolated trees. Labeled insecticides can be used but should be applied as soon as the first egg-laying damage is noticed.

WALNUT SOFT SHELL

SYMPTOMS Walnuts appear to develop normally, but the shell fails to form properly at an end. It may be thin or totally absent, so the nut within may become damaged or rotted by organisms that can gain entry through the faulty area.

CAUSE The precise cause is unclear, but soft shell is believed to be largely the result of nutrient deficiencies and an erratic supply of water.

CONTROL Keep trees fed, particularly if they have been bearing well. Mulch to promote soil moisture retention.

WASPS AND YELLOWJACKETS

Most wasps play a beneficial role in the garden as predators or parasites of other insects. Many species are quite small, rarely noticed and harmless to humans, such as the egg parasites *Trichogramma* (see *p.182*) and the aphid parasites *Aphidius* and *Diaeretiella rapae*. Some other species may appear large and menacing, but even they are generally nonaggressive and rarely sting humans. A few of the large predatory species, including paper wasps and yellowjackets, can be aggressive and likely to sting when nests are approached or disturbed. In addition to their helpful functions, some yellowjackets can be annoying as scavengers and occasional plant pests because of their interest in ripe fruits. On relatively soft-skinned fruits, such as grapes, plums, and peaches, they are capable of initiating damage (see *p.47*), but on apples and pears, they generally enlarge damage started by birds. Wasps eat the soft inner tissues and gradually hollow out large cavities (see *p.49*). Common wasp species include common yellowjacket (*Vespula vulgaris*), eastern yellowjacket (*V. maculifrons*), western yellowjacket (*V. pensylvanica*), and German yellowjacket (*V. germanica*). Some species make papery nests in the branches of trees and shrubs, which can make hedge-cutting hazardous. Others nest in the ground and become defensive when trampled or lawns are mowed. Problems with these species tend to be worse in summer, when populations are high.

CONTROL To deter scavenging yellowjackets, use tight lids on garbage cans and soft-drink or other containers. Traps for yellowjackets are commercially available and usually require baiting with cat food, jam, ground ham, or other foods, the choice of which depends on species. (The Cooperative Extension Service can help with identification, and suggestions are included with traps.) Wasps can be vacuumed – watch for secondary holes – and the vacuum bags sealed and placed in the freezer to kill the wasps. Nests can be dug up or treated with labeled

insecticides. Those with hypersensitivity to stings should consider the services of a professional exterminator.
• see also BRACONID WASPS *p.109*; GALL WASPS *p.132*; MOSSYROSE GALL WASP *p.148*; OAK GALL WASPS *p.152*; TRICHOGRAMMA WASPS *p.182*.

WATERLILY APHID

SYMPTOMS Olive-green or brownish insects, about ½in (2mm) long, cluster on the upper surface of leaves of waterlily, lotus, cattail, and other pond plants and on the flowers during summer. They often gather on leaf veins. Heavy attacks result in poor growth and flowering, with waterlily leaves appearing dirty due to the accumulation of aphids and their whitish cast skins.
CAUSE An aphid, *Rhopalosiphum nymphaeae*. It overwinters as an egg on wild and cultivated plums, apricot, almond, and cherries, feeding on the foliage of these plants in spring before migrating to waterlilies in early summer. On this host, they appear white and powdery.
CONTROL Avoid planting alternate hosts near desirable waterlilies and other pond plants. Forceful spraying with plain water reduces infestations. Fill the pond to overflowing, and allow aphids to wash onto the surrounding lawn or ground. Labeled insecticides can be used on woody hosts if there is no danger of contaminating water and endangering fish, frogs, and other pond wildlife.

WATERLILY LEAF BEETLE

SYMPTOMS Beginning in late spring and continuing through summer, irregularly

shaped slots are eaten in lily pads, starting on the top surface (see *p.30*). Infested leaves are unsightly and deteriorate rapidly as secondary rots develop on the damaged tissues. The flowers are also eaten.
CAUSE Adults and larvae of a beetle, *Galerucella nymphaeae*. The yellowish brown beetles, ¼in (7mm) long, begin the damage, which is continued in midsummer by the larvae, which have elongate bodies up to ⅓in (8mm) long and are black on the upper surface but pale yellow underneath. Only the adults feed on the flowers. The entire life cycle takes place on the upper surface of waterlily leaves, and there are usually 2 generations in summer.

LENGTH: ¼IN (7MM)

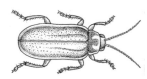

WATERLILY LEAF BEETLE

CONTROL Adults, larvae, and pupae can be removed by hand from small ponds. Forceful spraying with water will dislodge the larvae, some of which will fail to find their way back onto the leaves. Leaves can be submerged for a few days using netting or another material, which also deters the pest. Insecticides cannot be used, since they harm fish and other pond life.

WATERLILY LEAFCUTTER

SYMPTOMS In summer, the leaves of waterlily (*Nymphaea*) and other aquatic plants, including pondweed, duckweed, and arrowhead, become very ragged and rotted.

CAUSE The larva of a small moth, the waterlily leafcutter (*Synclita obliteralis*). The larva mines the host leaf for a short time and then emerges and makes a case by cutting lens-shaped leaf pieces and fastening them with silk it produces. The case is open on both ends, yet it surprisingly keeps water out. Creamy, with a small, light brown head and a dark line down its back, the larva feeds from its case. Although the case is elastic, the larva must build a series of larger ones as it grows to 1in (2.5cm).
CONTROL Wash off the cases by submerging the plant by hand or flooding the pond; fish will then feed on the dislodged larvae. Remove cases by hand if necessary. Avoid using insecticides around ponds, since they are harmful to fish and other aquatic life.

WATERLOGGING

SYMPTOMS The plant appears to be suffering from drought (in the absence of drought), with wilting foliage (see *p.34*) and flowers (see *p.71*); in severe cases even stems wilt, and the plant collapses. The leaves may be yellowed and may fall early. Inspection of the roots may reveal that they have disintegrated, often peeling readily, to leave just the dead vascular strands.
CAUSE Overwatering, excessive rain, or poor drainage in the soil or soil mix may be involved.
CONTROL Attempt to improve soil conditions, and avoid overwatering. Lighten heavy soil by incorporating plenty of coarse sand or grit or organic matter. The application of a foliar fertilizer to any remaining

green leaves may help counteract the effects of slight waterlogging.

WATER SPOTS

SYMPTOMS The upper leaf surfaces of African violet (*Saintpaulia*), gloxinia (*Sinningia*), Cape primrose (*Streptocarpus*), other members of the gesneriad family, and sometimes other fleshy-leaved plants in other families an have white, yellow, or brown rounded to nearly perfectly circular, slightly sunken spots (see *p.12*). From the spots, islands of thick, green tissue seem to arise. The spots do not disappear with time and may die, ruining the appearance, if not the overall health, of the leaves and the enitre plant.
CAUSE When leaf temperature is suddenly lowered (such as from cold water splashing onto foliage) the green chloroplasts in the cells break down, so the tissue loses its chlorophyll. Even seemingly warm water can cause damage if the foliage temperature is substantially higher, the important factor being the difference in temperatures. *Saintpaulia* is particularly susceptible to noticeable water spots, also called ring spots, because all of its chloroplasts are in a cell layer near the upper leaf surface. Other plants generally have chloroplasts distributed in multiple layers in the leaf, so green color prevails despite superficial chloroplast destruction.
CONTROL Avoid wetting the foliage by watering plants from below. Use water that is the same temperature as the air, and be sure that the foliage is not hot at watering from sitting in direct sunlight. If spots are too unsightly, cut off affected leaves.

WEEVILS

Weevils, sometimes called snout beetles, are insects characterized by having clubbed antennae that are bent at right angles about halfway along their length. The front of the head projects forward to form a snout or rostrum, which may be long, as in nut weevils (*see p.151*), or short, as in the black vine weevil (*see p.107*).

• see also BEAN AND PEA WEEVILS *p.105*; LEAF WEEVILS *p.144*; PEA LEAF WEEVIL *p.156*; PECAN WEEVIL *p.158*; PLUM CURCULIO *p.161*; STRAWBERRY BUD WEEVIL *p.179*.

WESTERN FLOWER THRIPS

SYMPTOMS Foliage and flowers of primarily houseplants and greenhouse plants, but also outdoor plants, are damaged. On some plants, such as tomato and cucumber, the upper leaf surface shows a silvery mottling. On ornamentals, such as African violets, roses, streptocarpus, gloxinias, chrysanthemums, verbenas, geraniums (*Pelargonium*), fuchsia, cyclamen, and impatiens, flower petals show a pale flecking (*see pp.42, 45*), blooms can deteriorate rapidly, and buds can fail to open.
CAUSE A sap-feeding insect, *Frankliniella occidentalis*. Adult western flower thrips are ¹⁄₁₂in (2mm) long and have narrow, elongate, brown bodies. The immature nymphs have a similar shape and are pale yellow. This pest can transmit tomato spotted wilt and other viruses. It breeds continually in heated greenhouses and has many generations a year.
CONTROL Biological control is available with a predatory mite, *Amblyseius cucumeris*,

but it must be introduced before heavy infestations arise. When buying houseplants, check flowers carefully and reject any with thrips or signs of feeding damage on petals. Remove infested flowers regularly and promptly. Yellow or blue sticky cards can be used to monitor thrips in greenhouses. Discard plants that show virus symptoms. Most insecticides have little effect on this species, since it is difficult to treat thrips hidden in flower buds or in folded leaves. Check with the Cooperative Extension Service for current labeled controls.

WHITE BLISTER

SYMPTOMS Raised, shiny white fungal pustules develop, primarily on the lower leaf surface of brassicas (*see p.14*). Occasionally, they may develop on other aboveground plant parts. The pustules are arranged either singly or in concentric rings. Affected leaves may become puckered and distorted, and the upper leaf surface develops yellow, slightly sunken pits.
CAUSE The fungus *Albugo candida*, which is encouraged by humid or moist air. The spores are spread on air currents or by water splash, or occasionally by insects. A resistant resting spore stage may also be formed, and it may persist in the soil.
CONTROL Remove infected leaves, and dispose of severely infected plants. Where feasible, grow resistant varieties.

WHITEFLIES

Whiteflies are sap-feeding insects about ¹⁄₁₂in (2mm) long and, when adult, have

white wings, sometimes with gray or darker bands. They live on the underside of leaves and readily fly up when the plant is disturbed. They lay eggs that hatch into flat, oval, scalelike nymphs. Like the adults, they excrete sugary honeydew. It falls onto the upper surfaces of leaves, which become sticky and covered with black sooty molds. The final nymphal stage is thicker, often with hairs or white, waxy secretions on the upper surface. Some plants, such as azalea, rhododendron, and holly, are occasionally attacked by whiteflies specific to these or a narrow range of plants. Indoor plants may require special treatment. Parasites and predators are commercially available, and some have been effective in controlling infestations of greenhouse whitefly.

• *see also* AZALEA WHITEFLY *p.103*; GREENHOUSE WHITEFLY *p.134*; MULBERRY WHITEFLY *p.148*.

WHITE GRUBS

SYMPTOMS Plants may suddenly wilt. Those species of white grubs that eat grass roots cause yellow patches in lawns (*see p.58*). Heavy infestations attract raccoons, skunks, crows, and other birds, which make holes in the grass to feed on the grubs during late summer to spring.
CAUSE Plump, white-bodied grubs with brown heads and 3 pairs of legs that live in the soil and feed on roots (*see p.53*). Their bodies are curved like the letter C. They can kill small plants and gnaw cavities in root vegetables. Several species of occur in gardens. Japanese beetle grubs (*Popillia japonica*) are a common

lawn pest, and the adults often seriously defoliate many garden plants. Oriental beetle grubs (*Exomala orientalis*) feed on turfgrass roots and many other plants. European chafer (*Rhizotrogus* [*Amphimallon*] *majalis*), masked chafer (*Cyclocephala*), Asiatic garden beetle (*Maladera castanea*), and green June beetle (*Cotinus nitida*) are among the species common as pests in lawns. Most grubs pupate in the soil and emerge as adult beetles in late spring to early summer.

LENGTH: UP TO 1½IN (4CM)

WHITE GRUB

CONTROL Infestations in flower borders and vegetable gardens are generally light, and it is feasible to search for the grubs in the soil near plants that have suddenly wilted. Problems in lawns are sporadic but can be devastating when they do occur. Well-maintained lawns may attract a heavier infestation but may tolerate greater damage. Turf that is allowed to dry and go dormant in midsummer may be less attractive to egg-laying females. Milky disease (*see p.147*), a natural pathogen, can be used where Japanese beetle is the dominant pest. Insect-pathogenic nematodes can be watered into moist soil in late summer and in the temperature range 57–68°F (14–20°C). The nematodes enter the bodies of the grubs and kill them by releasing bacteria that cause a fatal infection. White grubs are hard to kill with insecticides once they have grown large enough to cause damage.

WHITE MOLD
See SCLEROTINIA *p.172*.

WHITE PEACH AND PRUNICOLA SCALES
SYMPTOMS The trunk or large limbs of peach, cherry, privet, lilac, and other woody plants is covered with small, white and grayish white scales. In a severe infestation, the entire surface is encrusted or powdery. Limbs or an entire tree may die.
CAUSE The white peach scale (*Pseudaulacaspis pentagona*), also called the West Indian peach scale, a southern species similar to the white prunicola scale (*P. prunicola*), which is found in temperate regions. These armored scales are protected by waxy coverings of molted skins and excretions, bright white (male) to grayish (female). The scales usually feed directly on bark, often at the base of branches or in cracks and crevices if bark is thick, but sometimes are found on leaves or fruit. Damage can be significant. Both kinds have more than one generation during the growing season.
CONTROL Both species are treated similarly. They have many natural enemies, including the twice-stabbed ladybug (*Chilocorus stigma*) and other predators and parasites. However, control may not be adequate to prevent plant damage. Scales can be scrubbed off trunks with a brush, with or without a mild soap solution. Bark sprays with horticultural oil (during the dormant season or summer), insecticidal soap (spring, early autumn), or another labeled insecticide can be used. Applications timed for crawlers or young stages are probably most effective.

WHITE PINE BLISTER RUST
SYMPTOMS A series of abnormalities from needle spotting to wood cankers and branch girdling takes years on 5-needled pine trees, including bristlecone, limber, sugar, and white pines. Currants and gooseberries host complementary symptoms, mostly as leaf blisters, that are not nearly as damaging. The most noticeable sign is flagging, an entire dead branch standing out in the midst of normal branches. This begins as a small yellow to reddish brown spot on an individual needle spreads into the twig and becomes a yellow, blisterlike lesion on wood with an orange margin. This area swells and exudes a sweet, sticky, yellowish or clear resin for several days. The lesion site can leave a superficial, rough, brown scar, and the drying resin crystallizes on bark. The lesion enlarges, cuts off circulation, and the branch dies. The infection eventually spreads to the larger branches and finally the trunk. A small pine dies in only a few years, whereas a large tree might live for another 20 or more years. Not all attacks are lethal, however, as the infection itself is often stopped by the death of the twig or branch.
CAUSE White pine blister rust (*Cronartium ribicola*), a fungus that is considered to be the most destructive pine pathogen. It requires 2 different hosts to complete every stage of its lengthy, complex life cycle. Also called currant rust, there are many races with varying severity on both hosts.
CONTROL Select pines for resistance. European and Asiatic white pines are less susceptible, and *Pinus peuce* is generally resistant. Even within a susceptible species, there are many resistant individuals. Cultivated red- and whitecurrants are basically little affected, so they will produce few spores to inoculate pines. Do not work on a rust-afflicted plant when the needles are wet. Sterilize tools between cuts. Compost all debris, or dispose of it properly. Improve air circulation. State quarantine and eradication regulations govern the growing of wild currants and gooseberries in many areas. Fungicides such as Bordeaux mixture, sulfur sprays or dusts, and soaps may have some effect when used preventatively.

WHITE PRUNICOLA SCALE
See WHITE PEACH AND PRUNICOLA SCALES *above*.

WHITE RUST
See WHITE BLISTER *p.189*.

WILLOW LEAFGALL SAWFLIES
SYMPTOMS Hard swellings form in the leaf blades of willows during summer (*see p.17*). They are yellowish green or red, and their rounded oval shape resembles that of certain bean seeds.
CAUSE Several species of sawfly (*Pontania*), including willow redgall sawfly (*P. proxima*), *P. californica*, and willow leafgall sawfly (*P. pacifica*). There are often 2 generations between late spring and early autumn. The galls are initiated when the female lays eggs in the leaf. She secretes chemicals that induce the leaf to produce a gall around each egg. The egg later hatches into a caterpillarlike larva that gradually hollows out the gall.

WILLOW LEAFGALLS

CONTROL Natural enemies help keep infestations in check. Apart from causing galls on the foliage, these sawflies have no harmful effect on willows. Affected leaves can be removed from small trees if they are considered unsightly, but spraying would not be justified.

WILLOW LEAF SPOT
SYMPTOMS In early spring, irregular spots develop on the young foliage, spreading and causing it to turn black and die. Olive-brown pustules appear on the lower leaf surface and on affected stems. Black lesions develop on the stems and may cause girdling (*see p.41*).
CAUSE The fungus *Pollaccia saliciperda* (syn. *Fusicladium saliciperdum*), which overwinters as pustules on the stems.
CONTROL Prune out affected stems.

WILLOW SAWFLIES
SYMPTOMS Willow leaves are devoured, leaving larger veins and ribs, sometimes suddenly, by gregarious small larvae. Coloration varies, but they are often black with orange or yellow spots along the side, greenish yellow with dark spots or lines and black heads, or shades of gray. Some have a distinctive defensive posture, arching the abdomen when disturbed.
CAUSE Willow sawflies, some species of which also feed

on poplar or a few other hosts. The larvae have more than 5 pairs of prolegs (false hindlegs), distinguishing them from caterpillars of butterflies and moths, which have 5 or fewer.

CONTROL Despite occasionally dramatic defoliation, infestations usually are not life-threatening to plants. The larvae can be removed by hand or dislodged into a container of soapy water. Branches with heavy infestations can be pruned off and destroyed. Sawflies have many natural enemies, but labeled insecticides can be applied to control outbreaks. Btk is not effective. Insecticidal soap and horticultural oil can be used when larvae are small.
• *see also* WILLOW LEAFGALL SAWFLIES *p.190*.

WILLOW WATERMARK DISEASE

SYMPTOMS In mid- to late spring, young leaves turn red and wither. Ooze that contains the bacteria is produced from the stems. Leaves deteriorate further, and affected branches die back. The tree loses much of its growth but is rarely killed. The wood develops a watermark-like stain internally, and infected cut surfaces show complete or partial red or black rings. *Salix alba* var. *coerulea* and other white willows may be affected.
CAUSE The bacterium *Erwinia salicis*, which persists in the wood and produces toxins that cause the leaf discoloration and dieback. The bacteria enter the tree through wounds and are probably spread by birds and insects and on air currents.
CONTROL Remove and discard affected trees.

WILTS

SYMPTOMS Wilting of the foliage is followed by dieback. The whole plant is rarely affected simultaneously and may take several seasons to die, or it may progress quite rapidly: smaller woody plants or herbaceous or annual plants may be killed in a season. Staining may develop, associated with the vascular or conducting tissues in stems and roots.
CAUSE Various fungi, including species of *Verticillium*, *Fusarium*, and *Ceratocystis*. Much damage is caused by the blocking of vascular elements and the subsequent deterioration of stems and leaves. The fungi may be spread by pruning, root contact, grafting, or sap from a contaminated plant coming into contact with that of a healthy plant.
CONTROL Where feasible, grow resistant plants. Remove and dispose of affected plants with the soil in the vicinity of the roots.
• *see also* ASTER WILT *p.102*; BLOSSOM WILT *p.108*; CLEMATIS WILT *p.116*; DROUGHT *p.124*; DUTCH ELM DISEASE *p.124*; FUSARIUM WILT *p.131*; OAK WILT *p.152*; PEA WILT *p.156*; PEONY WILT *p.158*; VERTICILLIUM WILTS *p.185*; WATERLOGGING *p.188*.

WIND

SYMPTOMS Leaves appear scorched. One side or face of the plant is usually more severely affected than the others. The most damage occurs on the side facing the prevailing wind. Flowers may be similarly affected (*see p.45*). If winds are salt-laden, the effect is usually much more severe and the whole plant may suffer extreme dieback or even be killed. Trees on exposed sites may develop a lopsided growth habit, leaning away from the prevailing wind.
CAUSE Wind, often worsened if wind tunnels are created or if a windbreak is removed.
CONTROL Where possible, plant or erect windbreaks to prevent wind damage. If stems are killed, prune them out to prevent invasion by secondary organisms.

WINTER MOTH

SYMPTOMS Between bud burst and early spring, small holes are eaten in newly expanded leaves of many fruit trees and other deciduous trees and shrubs (*see p.31*), and the leaves are bound loosely with silk threads. Fruit blossoms are eaten, and holes appear in swelling blueberry buds and apple fruitlets, causing them to develop as badly misshapen fruits. Affected plants include apple, red oak, American elm, basswood, red maple, hop hornbeam, willow, alder, and poplar.
CAUSE Caterpillars of a moth, *Operophtera brumata*. The yellowish green caterpillars, up to 1in (2.5cm) long, have paler lines along their bodies. They walk with a looping action. The moths emerge between late autumn and midwinter. Several other species with similar habits are collectively referred to as winter moths, including the closely related Bruce spanworm (*O. bruceata*), which often attacks beech, sugar maple, quaking aspen, willow, and other hardwoods.
CONTROL Place sticky grease bands on tape around tree trunks, especially those of fruit trees, in midautumn to stop female moths from reaching the branches. Look for early signs of damage, such as feeding on or in buds. Check first in warmer locations, where caterpillars may be more frequently found. Labeled insecticide can be applied.

WIREWORMS

SYMPTOMS Larger seeds are eaten or the stems of seedlings are bitten just below soil level, killing the seedlings. In late summer, sweet potato roots, potato tubers (*see p.56*), and other root crops can be extensively tunneled. Fruits lying on the soil surface can be damaged.
CAUSE The larval stage of click beetles, including the eastern field wireworm (*Limonius agonus*), Columbia Basin wireworm (*L. subauretus*), Gulf wireworm (*Conoderus amplicollis*), and southern potato wireworm (*C. falli*). Wireworms are slender and orange-brown and have 3 pairs of short legs near the head end (*see p.54*). They are up to 1in (2.5cm) long and have a small protuberance on the underside of the rear end of the abdomen. They live in the soil and are found in the greatest numbers in newly dug grassland; their numbers decline over 3–4 years if the ground is kept in cultivation.

LENGTH: UP TO 1IN (2.5CM)

WIREWORM

CONTROL Where wireworms are troublesome, dig up potato tubers as soon as they have matured in order to limit damage. Damage may be most severe on unrotated or minimum-tillage fields; rotate to other crops or maintain fallow periods. Good drainage and shallow summer cultivation may help deter or control infestations. Insecticide-treated seed can be sown.

WITCHES' BROOMS
SYMPTOMS Abnormal, extensively branched twigs grow in the crowns of trees or other plants (see **p.41**). Large numbers of them spoil the appearance of deciduous trees in winter, but they usually are unobtrusive when the trees are leafed out. Conifers may develop large witches' brooms, and many dwarf conifer cultivars were originally propagated from them.
CAUSE Various fungi, particularly species of *Taphrina*, which are spread by water splash and on air currents. Occasionally, other factors, especially mite infestations and perhaps viruses, may be responsible.
CONTROL Prune out the growths, if desired. Spread seems to be very slow, but removal will help limit the problem.

WOODCHUCK
SYMPTOMS In early spring before foliage sprouts, the bark, twigs, and buds of low-growing shrubs or trees are torn or gnawed off. During the growing season, a wide range of garden, orchard, and crop plants can be eaten in a short period. In woods or a field, a burrow's entrance hole is fronted by a mound of soil. Grass and other vegetation are cut short near this entrance, and trails radiate from it.
CAUSE The woodchuck (*Marmota monax*), also known as the groundhog or whistle pig (for its loud alarm), which is a large, stocky rodent. Active during the day, it feeds close to its forest or farmland den. It is almost entirely herbivorous, with a very small percentage of its diet consisting of insects. Before hibernating in late October, the woodchuck

puts on fat by eating extensively. The male, slightly larger than the female, can be 2⅛ft (66cm) long, counting a 5–6in (13–15cm) tail. The fur is brown, shaded reddish to blackish, with a grizzled appearance. The woodchuck's barrel-shaped body has short but mighty legs, the front feet outfitted for digging with lengthy, curved claws.
CONTROL Woodchucks avoid tomatoes, eggplant, and peppers. Remove their protective foraging cover by getting rid of debris and brush piles and by mowing a wide strip around the garden. Although woodchucks are good tree climbers in an emergency, a low (6–12in/15–30cm) fence is usually a sufficient barrier. For greater security, set up a flexible 3ft (90cm) fence whose unreinforced top will flop back with the weight of a climbing animal. Sink the fence 1ft (30cm) deep, although the typical woodchuck will not try to dig under a fence. High-tensile electric deer fence can be modified to include wires at 5–6in (13–15cm) intervals to 1½ft (45cm) high. The urine of predators, sprayed on bases of trees, has been effective in reducing bark damage and works well in combination with electric fencing. Young woodchucks are preyed on by hawks, and even adults fall victim to eagles, red foxes, and dogs. Live traps baited with apple are useful for capturing woodchucks for removal. Flushing burrows with water or gassing burrows can be done, but persistent efforts may be needed: woodchucks recolonize old burrows from surrounding areas. Check

with the local animal control officer regarding humane traps and release.

WOOLLY APPLE APHID
SYMPTOMS A fluffy, white, waxy substance develops on the bark of apple and crabapple trees, hawthorn, mountain ash, pyracantha, and cotoneaster in summer (see **p.35**). The wax is secreted from the bodies of pinkish brown aphids. During mid- to late spring, they are seen mainly around old pruning cuts and in splits in older bark. Later in summer, the aphids spread to young branches, where their feeding causes soft, knobby swellings to develop. These galls often split during cold weather, creating wounds that apple and pear canker (see p.99) can infect.
CAUSE A sap-feeding insect, *Eriosoma lanigerum*. This species overwinters on roots of its hosts, causing knobby galls to form. Eggs are also laid on American elm, on which infestations, in spring, appear as distorted foliage or rosettes.
CONTROL Natural enemies help regulate populations. 'Northern Spy' apple and Merton Malling rootstocks are resistant. Avoid planting susceptible hosts near elm, and inspect plants for infestations before purchase. Watch for signs of woolly apple aphid during spring, especially on twigs, callus areas, and watersprouts of apple and related plants. Heavy infestations in late summer are difficult to control. There are no satisfactory controls for root infestations, but insecticidal soap or another labeled material can be used for aboveground populations.
• see also BEECH APHIDS p.106.

WORMS
See CANKERWORMS *p.113*; CORN EARWORM *p.117*; CORN ROOTWORM see CUCUMBER BEETLES *p.120*; CUTWORMS *p.121*; EARTHWORMS *p.124*; FALL WEBWORM *p.128*; HORNWORMS *p.137*; IMPORTED CURRANTWORM *p.138*; JUNIPER WEBWORM *p.141*; NEMATODES *p.151*; OAKWORMS *p.152*; RASPBERRY FRUITWORM *p.166*; SOD WEBWORM *p.175*; WIREWORMS *p.191*.

YELLOWJACKETS
See WASPS AND YELLOWJACKETS *p.187*.

YUCCA LEAF SPOT
SYMPTOMS Circular brown spots develop on affected leaves. On variegated yuccas, the spots may be most prevalent on pale portions of the leaf (see **p.18**). The spots show concentric ringing, and numerous, pinprick-size, raised, black fruiting bodies develop on them. The spots enlarge and may merge.
CAUSE The fungi *Cercospora concentrica* and *Coniothyrium concentricum*, which produce similar symptoms. The spores are spread by water splash.
CONTROL Remove severely affected leaves. Spray badly affected plants with a fungicide such as mancozeb.

INDIVIDUAL PLANT PROBLEMS

COMMON PROBLEMS TO which different garden plants are subject are listed here grouped by plant type, then under the name of the plant within its type. For each individual plant problem, cross-references are given to the illustration(s) of the problem's effects in the *Gallery of Symptoms* (*pp. 12 – 63*) and to its detailed entry in the *A–Z Directory* (*pp. 98 – 192*).

GARDEN TREES

ONCE ESTABLISHED, trees are usually sufficiently vigorous for many problems to seem insignificant. However, if seriously attacked by a pest or a disease, an established tree's size can make it difficult – sometimes impossible – to treat. Many problems can be avoided by careful maintenance. With deciduous trees, autumn leaf-fall also helps, removing many pathogens on foliage.

A number of common problems may affect a wide range of unrelated trees (*see right*). Some, however, are more host-specific; trees that are particularly prone to certain problems are listed below. Resistant species or cultivars may be suggested in the entry for the problem in question in the *A–Z Directory*.

COMMON PROBLEMS

The most common tree ailments are:

APHIDS 99
BAGWORM, 103
BARK BEETLES, 104
BRACKET FUNGI 109
CATERPILLARS 114
CORAL SPOT 117
DROUGHT 124
FROST 130
HERBICIDES 135
HONEY FUNGUS 136
LEAFROLLERS AND LEAFTIERS, 143
LEAF SPOTS (FUNGAL) 143
LIGHTNING 144
MAGNESIUM DEFICIENCY 146

MOWER INJURY, 148
PHYTOPHTHORA 159
POOR PRUNING, 94
POWDERY MILDEWS 164
SCORCH 172
VERTICILLIUM WILTS 185
VIRUSES 186
WATERLOGGING 188
WIND 191

A

Alder (*Alnus*)
COTTONY GRAPE SCALE, 118
FALL WEBWORM, 128
FELT GALL MITES, 128
GYPSY MOTH, 134
SALT, 172
WINTER MOTH, 191

Apple *see* FRUITS AND NUTS

Arborvitae (*Thuja plicata*)
JUNIPER SCALE, **37**
KEITHIA THUJINA NEEDLE BLIGHT, **28**, 141
LEAF WEEVILS, 144
SEIRIDIUM CANKER, 173
SPRUCE SPIDER MITE, 178

Ash (*Fraxinus*)
ASH (LILAC) BORER, 100
ASH SPANGLE GALL MITE, 101
ASIAN LONGHORNED BEETLE, 101
EASTERN TENT CATERPILLAR, 125
EUTYPA DIEBACK, 128
FALL WEBWORM, 128
LILAC LEAFMINER, **19**
PEAR AND APPLE CANKER, 157
SQUIRRELS, 178

Aspen
WINTER MOTH, 191

B

Bay (*Laurus nobilis*)
BROWN SOFT SCALE, 110

HORSE CHESTNUT SCALE, 137
LAUREL PSYLLID, **26**

Beech (*Fagus*)
APPLE AND PEAR CANKER, 99, 157
BEECH APHIDS, **32**, 99
BEECH SCALE, **35**, 106
CANKERWORMS, 113
ENDOTHIA CANKER, **35**, 126
HONEY FUNGUS, 136
LEAFHOPPERS, 142
OAKWORM, 152
SQUIRRELS, 178
TWO-LINED CHESTNUT BORER, 185
WINTER MOTH, 191
WOOLLY BEECH APHID, 99

Birch (*Betula*)
BAGWORM, 104
BIRCH LEAFMINER, **19**, 106
BLEEDING CANKER, 107
BRONZE BIRCH BORER, 110
CASEBEARERS, 113
COTTONY GRAPE SCALE, 118
EASTERN TENT CATERPILLAR, 125
FELT GALL MITES, 128
HONEY FUNGUS, 136
JAPANESE BEETLE, 140
LEAFHOPPERS, 143
OAKWORM, 152
POTATO LEAFHOPPER, 163

Boxelder
BAGWORM, 104
MAPLE ERINEUM GALL MITE, 146
MULBERRY WHITEFLY, 148

C

Cedar (*Cedrus*)
HONEY FUNGUS, 136
PHOMOPSIS CANKER, 159
PINE NEEDLE SCALE, 160
QUINCE RUST, 165
SPRUCE SPIDER MITE, 178

Cherry (ornamental)
LEAF WEEVILS, 144

Chestnut
TWO-LINED CHESTNUT BORER, 185

Crabapple
APPLE MAGGOT, 99
APPLE POWDERY MILDEW, **25**
APPLE RUST, 100
CEDAR-APPLE RUST, **18**, **37**
EASTERN TENT CATERPILLAR, 125
ENTOMOSPORIUM LEAF SPOT, 126
FELT GALL MITES, 128
LEAF WEEVILS, 144
QUINCE RUST, 165
SPOTTED TENTIFORM LEAFMINER, **13**, 177
WOOLLY APPLE APHID, 192

Cypress, Leyland Cypress (*Cupressus*, X *Cupressocyparis leylandii*)
JUNIPER SCALE, **37**, 141
SEIRIDIUM CANKER, **35**, 173
SPRUCE SPIDER MITE, 178

D

Dogwood (*Cornus*)
CLEARWING BORER, 115
DOGWOOD ANTHRACNOSE, **18**, 98, 123
EUTYPA DIEBACK, 128
FOURLINED PLANT BUG, 130
HORSE CHESTNUT SCALE, 137
MULBERRY WHITEFLY, 148
OYSTERSHELL SCALE, 155
ROSE LEAFHOPPER, 170

E

Elm (*Ulmus*)
BAGWORM, 104
BARK BEETLES, 104
CANKERWORMS, 113
CASEBEARERS, 113
DUTCH ELM DISEASE, 124
ELM LEAF GALL APHID, 126
ELM SACKGALL APHID, **16**
ENDOTHIA CANKER, 126
EUROPEAN ELM BARK BEETLE, 127
FALL WEBWORM, 128
HORSE CHESTNUT SCALE, 137
JAPANESE BEETLE, 140
LEAF WEEVILS, 144
OAKWORM, 152
PIERCE'S DISEASE, 160
ROOT APHIDS, 168
ROSE LEAFHOPPER, 170
WILT, 191
WINTER MOTH, 191

F

Filbert *see* FRUITS AND NUTS

Fir
BALSAM TWIG APHID, 104
BALSAM WOOLLY ADELGID, 104
PHOMOPSIS CANKER, 159

Fir, Douglas (*Pseudotsuga menziesii*)
ADELGID, 98
COOLEY SPRUCE GALL ADELGID, **38**, 117
PHOMOPSIS CANKER, 159
PINE NEEDLE SCALE, 160
PINE SAWFLY, **32**
SPRUCE SPIDER MITE, 178

Fringetree (*Chionanthus*)
ASH (LILAC) BORER, 100

G

Golden Rain Tree (*Koelreuteria paniculata*)
VERTICILLIUM WILT, 186

H

Hawthorn (*Crataegus*)
APPLE AND PEAR CANKER, 99
APPLE MAGGOT, 99
ENTOMOSPORIUM LEAF SPOT, 126
FIREBLIGHT, 129
GYPSY MOTH, 134
LEAF WEEVILS, 144
PEAR SAWFLY, 158
QUINCE RUST, 165
WOOLLY APPLE APHID, 192

INDIVIDUAL PLANT PROBLEMS

SHRUBS AND CLIMBERS

CORRECT PRUNING is one of the keys to maintaining healthy shrubs and climbers, thinning overcrowded and old growth to prevent a stagnant environment. Prompt recognition of problems is also vital; the removal of much badly affected growth can spoil an attractively shaped shrub or carefully trained climber.

Some common problems may affect many unrelated plants (*see right*). Others are more host-specific; plants particularly prone to certain problems are listed below. Resistant species may be suggested in the entry for the problem in question in the *A–Z Directory*.

COMMON PROBLEMS

The most common ailments affecting shrubs and climbing plants are:

APHIDS 99
BAGWORM 103
BLIND SHOOTS 107
CANKERWORMS 113
DEER 122
FOURLINED PLANT BUG 130
FROST 130
HERBICIDES 135
IRON DEFICIENCY AND LIME-

INDUCED CHLOROSIS 139
LEAF SCORCH 143
LEAF SPOTS (FUNGAL) 143
MAGNESIUM DEFICIENCY 146
PHYTOPHTHORA 159
POWDERY MILDEWS 164
RABBITS 166
VERTICILLIUM WILTS 185
VIRUSES 186

A

Azalea
AZALEA GALL, 102
AZALEA LACEBUG, **20**, 102
AZALEA WHITEFLY, 103
COTTONY CAMELLIA (OR TAXUS) SCALE, 118
CYCLAMEN MITE, 121
FOURLINED PLANT BUG, 130
IRON DEFICIENCY AND LIME-INDUCED CHLOROSIS, 139
RHODODENDRON BORER, **33**, 167
RHODODENDRON LEAF SPOT, 14
RHODODENDRON PETAL BLIGHT, **42**
SOUTHERN RED MITE, 176

B

Barberry
VERTICILLIUM WILT, 186

Bittersweet
EUONYMUS SCALE, 126

Boxwood (*Buxus*)
BOXWOOD PSYLLID, **26**, 109
HONEY FUNGUS, 136
OYSTERSHELL SCALE, 155

Butterfly Bush (*Buddleja*)
JAPANESE BEETLE, 140

C

Camellia
BUD DROP, 111
CAMELLIA GALL, **26**, 112
CAMELLIA YELLOW MOTTLE, **22**, 113
COTTONY CAMELLIA (OR TAXUS) SCALE, **15**, 118
FROST ON BUDS AND FLOWERS, **44**
HEMISPHERICAL SCALE, 135
SCLEROTINIA (WHITE MOLD), 172
SOUTHERN RED MITE, 176
WIND, **45**

Ceanothus
OYSTERSHELL SCALE, 155

Chamaecyparis
LEAF WEEVILS, 144

Chokeberry
QUINCE RUST, 165

Clematis
BLISTER BEETLE, 108
CLEMATIS WILT, 116
EARWIGS, **46**, 125
HONEY FUNGUS, 136

Cotinus
HONEY FUNGUS, 136

Cotoneaster
ENTOMOSPORIUM LEAF SPOT, 126
FIREBLIGHT, 129
HONEY FUNGUS, 136
OYSTERSHELL SCALE, 155
QUINCE RUST, 165
WOOLLY APPLE APHID, 192

Crape Myrtle
CRAPE MYRTLE POWDERY MILDEW, 118

D

Daphne
FOOT AND ROOT ROTS, **55**
VERTICILLIUM WILT, 186

Deutzia
LILAC LEAFMINER, 145

Dogwood *see* GARDEN TREES

E

Elaeagnus
CORAL SPOT, 117
HONEY FUNGUS, 136

Elder (*Sambucus*)
JAPANESE BEETLE, 140

Euonymus
COTTONY CAMELLIA (OR TAXUS) SCALE, 118
EUONYMUS SCALE, **21**, 126
JAPANESE BEETLE, 140
LILAC LEAFMINER, 145
SCLEROTINIA (WHITE MOLD), 172
SOUTHERN RED MITE, 176

F

Forsythia
FORSYTHIA GALL, **40**
FOURLINED PLANT BUG, 130
HONEY FUNGUS, 136
PLANT (LYGUS) BUGS, 161
SCLEROTINIA (WHITE MOLD), 172

G

Grape *see* FRUITS AND NUTS

H

Hackberry
MULBERRY WHITEFLY, 148

Heathers (*Erica* and *Calluna*)
JAPANESE BEETLE, 140

Hibiscus
JAPANESE BEETLE, 140

Honeysuckle (*Lonicera*)
APHIDS, 99
EUTYPA DIEBACK, 128
HONEYSUCKLE APHID, 137
FOURLINED PLANT BUG, 130

Hydrangea
COTTONY HYDRANGEA SCALE, 15, 118
FOURLINED PLANT BUG, 130
HONEY FUNGUS, 136
LEAFROLLERS AND LEAFTIERS, 143
PLANT (LYGUS) BUGS, 161

I

Ivy, English (*Hedera helix*)
BEAN APHID, 105
BROWN SOFT SCALE, 110
IVY ANTHRACNOSE, **12**, 139
PIERCE'S DISEASE, 160

J

Juneberry
APPLE MAGGOT, 99

Juniper (*Juniperus*)
BAGWORM, 104
CEDAR-APPLE RUST, **18**, 37
JUNIPER SCALE, **37**, 141
KABATINA SHOOT BLIGHT, 141
LEAF WEEVILS, 144
QUINCE RUST, 165
SEIRIDIUM CANKER, 173
SPRUCE SPIDER MITE, 178
WEBWORM, **32**

L

Lavender *see* VEGETABLES AND HERBS

Lilac (*Syringa*)
ASH (LILAC) BORER, 100
BLIGHT, **33**
HONEY FUNGUS, 136
LILAC LEAFMINER, **19**, 145
OYSTERSHELL SCALE, 155
PRIVET THRIPS, **22**, 165
SCLEROTINIA (WHITE MOLD), 172
WHITE PEACH AND PRUNICOLA SCALES, 190

M

Magnolia *see* GARDEN TREES

Mahonias
RUST, **12**, **24**, 171

INDIVIDUAL PLANT PROBLEMS

HERBACEOUS PERENNIALS

PERENNIALS DO NOT suffer from many serious problems. The annual dying back of foliage and stems gives an opportunity for the removal and disposal of plant tissue harboring many diseases and pests. Regular division of established clumps also helps keep plants healthy. A number of common problems may affect a wide range of unrelated plants (*see right*). Some, however, are more host-specific (*see below*). Resistant species may be suggested in the entry for the problem in question in the *A–Z Directory*.

COMMON PROBLEMS

The most common ailments affecting herbaceous perennials are:

APHIDS 99	GRAY MOLD 133
ASTER YELLOWS 102	LEAF SPOTS (FUNGAL) 143
CATERPILLARS 114	POWDERY MILDEWS 164
CROWN ROT 119	RABBITS 166
DEER 122	SLUGS, SNAILS 174, 175
DOWNY MILDEW 123	VIRUSES 186
DROUGHT 124	WATERLOGGING 188
FROST 130	WESTERN FLOWER THRIPS 189

A

Alyssum see ANNUALS AND BIENNIALS

Anemone, Japanese
CHRYSANTHEMUM NEMATODE, 115

Aster
ASTER WILT, 102
BLISTER BEETLE, 108
CYCLAMEN MITE, 121
EUROPEAN CORN BORER, 127
TARNISHED PLANT BUG, 180

Astilbe
BLACK VINE WEEVIL, 107

Aubrieta
FLEA BEETLES, 129

B

Bellflower (Campanula)
NEEDLE RUSTS OF CONIFERS, 151

Buttercup
BLISTER BEETLE, 108

C

Canna
JAPANESE BEETLE, 140
LEAFROLLERS AND LEAFTIERS, 143

Carnation (Dianthus)
BEAN APHID, 105
CABBAGE LOOPER, 112
FUSARIUM WILT, 131

Cattail
WATERLILY APHID, 188

Chickweed
SPINACH LEAFMINER, 177

Chrysanthemum (Dendranthema)
BLISTER BEETLE, 108
CABBAGE LOOPER, 112
CHRYSANTHEMUM LEAFMINER, **25**, 115
CHRYSANTHEMUM NEMATODE, 115, 151
CORN EARWORM, 117
CYCLAMEN MITE, 121
EARWIG, 125
EUROPEAN CORN BORER, 127
FOURLINED PLANT BUG, 130
JAPANESE BEETLE, 140
LEAF-CURLING PLUM APHID, 142
MELON (COTTON) APHIDS, **43**, 146
PLANT (LYGUS) BUGS, 161
SERPENTINE LEAFMINER, 173
WESTERN FLOWER THRIPS, 189

Columbine (Aquilegia)
COLUMBINE LEAFMINER, **19**, 117

Coreopsis
FOURLINED PLANT BUG, 130

D

Daylily (Hemerocallis)
EARWIGS, 125

Delphinium
CYCLAMEN MITE, 121
DELPHINIUM BLACK BLOTCH, **12**, 122
LARKSPUR LEAFMINER, **18**, 142

SCLEROTINIA (WHITE MOLD), 172
TARSONEMID MITES, 180

E

English Daisy (Bellis perennis)
CUCUMBER POWDERY MILDEW, **15**

Epimedium
LEAF-CUTTING BEES, 142

Evening Primrose
JAPANESE BEETLE, 140

G

Geranium
POWDERY MILDEW, **25**, 164

Globe Thistle (Echinops)
FOURLINED PLANT BUG, 130

H

Hellebore (Helleborus)
HELLEBORE LEAF BLOTCH, **20**

Hollyhock see ANNUALS AND BIENNIALS

I

Indian Mallow
JAPANESE BEETLE, 140

L

Lavender see VEGETABLES AND HERBS

Lotus (Nelumbo)
WATERLILY APHID, 188

Lupine (Lupinus)
FOURLINED PLANT BUG, 130
LUPINE APHID, **41**, 99, 145
POTATO LEAFHOPPER, 163

M

Mallow
RUST, **17**

Milkweed (Asclepias)
OLEANDER APHID, **35**, 153

Monkshood see Delphinium

P

Penstemon
CHRYSANTHEMUM NEMATODE, 115

Peony (Paeonia)
HONEY FUNGUS, 136
PEONY WILT, **46**, 158
ROSE CHAFER, 169

Periwinkle (Vinca)
PIERCE'S DISEASE, 160
RUST, **15**, 171

Phlox
JAPANESE BEETLE, 140
PHLOX NEMATODE, **33**, 151, 159

POWDERY MILDEW, 164
SCLEROTINIA (WHITE MOLD), 172

Pinks see **Carnation**

Primrose
BIRDS, 46, 106

Q

Queen Anne's Lace
CARROT RUST FLY, 113
MEXICAN BEAN BEETLE, 147
TACHINID FLIES, 180

S

Shasta Daisy
FOURLINED PLANT BUG, 130

Succulents
CACTUS CORKY SCAB, **22**, 112
MEALYBUGS, 146
ROOT MEALYBUGS, 169

V

Violet (Viola)
DOWNY MILDEW, 123

W

Waterlily (Nymphaea)
WATERLILY APHID, 188
WATERLILY LEAF BEETLE, **30**, 188
WATERLILY LEAFCUTTER, 188

LAWNS

MANY GARDENERS happily tolerate a certain quantity of weeds in the lawn, and indeed some would say that a crop of clover adds to a lawn's appeal. A possible exception is moss, which can be pernicious, particularly on damp ground. Eradication of severe moss infestation may also have to be combined with re-seeding.

Pests and diseases, however, are always disfiguring, and controls are necessary. In many cases of disease, chemical control must be combined with cultural improvements if the lawn's health is to be improved in the long term.

COMMON PROBLEMS

The most common ailments affecting lawns are:

ANTS **59**, 98	TURF DROUGHT, 183
BLUEGRASS BILLBUG, 108	TURF FAIRY RINGS AND
BURROWING BEES **58**, 111	TOADSTOOLS **59**, 184
CHINCH BUG, 114	TURF MELTING OUT, 184
EARTHWORMS **58**, 124	TURF RED THREAD **59**, 184
MOLES **59**, 148	TURF SNOW MOLD **59**, 184
ORIENTAL BEETLE, 154	TURF THATCH FUNGAL MYCELIUM
ROSE CHAFER, 169	**58**, 185
SLIME MOLD **58**, 174	WHITE GRUBS **58**, 189
SOD WEBWORMS, 175	
TURF BROWN PATCH 183	
TURF DOLLAR SPOT **58**, 183	

GREENHOUSE AND HOUSE PLANTS

A SHELTERED environment not only protects plants but also pests and diseases. They may therefore build up very rapidly, and exotic species may flourish that would have little chance to cause serious problems out of doors. However, an enclosed environment also lends itself to effective and thorough treatment, and to the use of biological controls (*see pp.84–85*) to eradicate pests.

Some common problems may affect a wide range of unrelated plants (*see right*). Others are more host-specific (*see below*). Resistant species may be suggested in the entry for the problem in question in the *A–Z Directory*.

COMMON PROBLEMS

The most common ailments affecting plants grown in the greenhouse or conservatory, or as house plants, are:

APHIDS 99	SPRINGTAILS 177
FOOT AND ROOT ROTS 130	TWOSPOTTED SPIDER MITE 185
FUNGUS GNATS 131	VIRUSES 186
LEAF SCORCH 143	WATERLOGGING 188
MEALYBUGS 146	WESTERN FLOWER THRIPS 189
POWDERY MILDEWS 164	WHITEFLIES 189
ROOT MEALYBUGS 169	
SCALE INSECTS 172	
SLUGS 174	

A

African Violet (*Saintpaulia*)
CYCLAMEN MITE, 121
EDEMA, 125
ROOT MEALYBUGS, 169
WATER SPOT, **12**, 188
WESTERN FLOWER THRIPS, 189

Asparagus Fern
ASPARAGUS RUST, 101

B

Begonia
BEGONIA POWDERY MILDEW, **23**, 106
BLACK VINE WEEVIL, 107
CYCLAMEN MITE, 121
MELON (COTTON) APHIDS, 146
TARSONEMID MITES, 180

C

Cacti
CACTUS CORKY SCAB, **22**, 112
MEALYBUGS, 146
ROOT MEALYBUGS, 169

Carnation *see* HERBACEOUS PERENNIALS

Chrysanthemum *see* HERBACEOUS PERENNIALS

Cineraria (*Senecio* x *hybridus*)
CHRYSANTHEMUM LEAFMINER, 115
LEAF-CURLING PLUM APHID, 142

Citrus *see* FRUITS AND NUTS

Cyclamen
BLACK VINE WEEVIL, 107
CYCLAMEN MITE, **26**, 121
TARSONEMID MITES, 180
WESTERN FLOWER THRIPS, 189

F

Ferns
BROWN SOFT SCALE, 110
ROOT MEAYLBUGS, 169

Ficus
DRACAENA THRIPS, 123

Fuchsia
PIERCE'S DISEASE, 160
PLANT (LYGUS) BUGS, 161
ROOT MEALYBUGS, 169
RUST, **18**, 171
WESTERN FLOWER THRIPS, 189

G

Gardenia
HEMISPHERICAL SCALE, 135
IRON DEFICIENCY AND LIME-INDUCED CHLOROSIS, 139

Gerbera
CHRYSANTHEMUM LEAFMINER, 115
CYCLAMEN MITE, 121

Gloxinia (*Sinningia*)
WATER SPOT, **12**, 188
WESTERN FLOWER THRIPS, **42**, 189

O

Oleander (*Nerium*)
HEMISPHERICAL SCALE, 135
OLEANDER APHID, **35**, 99, 153

P

Palms
DRACAENA THRIPS, 123
HEMISPHERICAL SCALE, 135
PALM FRIZZLE TOP, 155

S

Streptocarpus
WATER SPOT, 188
WESTERN FLOWER THRIPS, 189

BULBOUS PLANTS

THE PLANTING OF bulbs, corms, and tubers in a suitable site is crucial to their health. Many will not tolerate soils that become heavy or wet in winter, soon succumbing to disease. In most cases, too, it is essential for the foliage to be left in place for several weeks after flowering in order to allow the bulbs to build and store up energy reserves for the following year.

Division of established clumps allows for the removal of less vigorous or unhealthy looking portions before problems can spread. Many bulbs are prone to virus infections, and regular inspection and removal of those showing symptoms is advised. Other problems are more host-specific; the particular problems affecting various plants are listed below. Resistant species may be suggested in the entry for the problem in question in the *A–Z Directory*.

COMMON PROBLEMS

The most common ailments affecting bulbs are:

SLUGS 174   VIRUSES 186

A

Amaryllis (*Hippeastrum*)
BLISTER BEETLE, 108
NARCISSUS BULB FLY, **54**, 150
NARCISSUS LEAF SCORCH, **29**, 150
SOUTHERN BLIGHT, 176

C

Crinum
NARCISSUS LEAF SCORCH, 29

Crocosmia *see* MONTBRETIA

Crocus
BIRDS, **46**, 106
DRY ROT OF BULBS AND CORMS, 124
GLADIOLUS CORM ROT, **55**, 132
SQUIRRELS, 178

D

Daffodil (*Narcissus*)
BLINDNESS OF BULBS, **41**, 107
NARCISSUS BASAL ROT, 149
NARCISSUS BULB FLY, **54**, 137, 149
NARCISSUS LEAF SCORCH, **29**, 150
NARCISSUS NEMATODE, **54**, 150, 151
SCLEROTINIA (WHITE MOLD), 172
SLUGS AND SNAILS, **43**
SOUTHERN BLIGHT, 176

Dahlia
BLISTER BEETLE, 108
CORN EARWORM, 117
CYCLAMEN MITE, 121
DAHLIA SMUT, 122
EARWIGS, **46**, 125
EUROPEAN CORN BORER, 127
FOURLINED PLANT BUG, 130
JAPANESE BEETLE, 140
LEAF-CURLING PLUM APHID, 142
MELON (COTTON) APHIDS, 146
PLANT (LYGUS) BUGS, 161
POTATO LEAFHOPPER, 163
ROSE CHAFER, 169

F

Freesia
DRY ROT OF BULBS AND CORMS, 124

G

Gladiolus
CORN EARWORM, 117
DRY ROT OF BULBS AND CORMS, 124
EUROPEAN CORN BORER, 127
GLADIOLUS CORM ROT, 132
GLADIOLUS THRIPS, **45**, 132, 181
POTATO SPRAING, 164

H

Hyacinth (*Hyacinthus*)
NARCISSUS BULB FLY, 150
POTATO SPRAING, 164
SCLEROTINIA (WHITE MOLD), 172

I

Iris (bulbous)
BULB BLUE MOLD, 111
GLADIOLUS CORM ROT, **55**, 132

Iris (rhizomatous)
IRIS BORER, 138
IRIS LEAF SPOT, 139
IRIS RUST, **15**, 171
IRIS SCORCH, 139
IRIS SOFT ROT, **55**, 139
ROSE CHAFER, 169
SCLEROTINIA (WHITE MOLD), 172
SOUTHERN BLIGHT, 176

L

Lily (*Lilium*)
LILY LEAF BEETLE, 145
NARCISSUS BULB FLY, 150

M

Montbretia (*Crocosmia*)
DRY ROT OF BULBS AND CORMS, 12

N

Narcissus *see* **Daffodil**

S

Snowdrops
NARCISSUS BULB FLY, 150
NARCISSUS LEAF SCORCH, 150

T

Tulip
BEAN APHID, 105
BULB ROT, 183
NARCISSUS BULB FLY, 150
POTATO SPRAING, 164
SCLEROTINIA (WHITE MOLD), 172
SLUGS, 174
SQUIRRELS, 178
TULIP FIRE, **22**, **55**, 183
VIRUS, **42**
SMUTS **35**, 176

ANNUALS AND BIENNIALS

MANY PROBLEMS affecting annuals and biennials can be avoided by careful initial choice of plants, good planting, and regular feeding and watering. To avoid the foot and root rots to which many are prone, do not grow the same (or closely related) plants on any site for more than one year. Some problems affect a wide range of unrelated plants (*see right*); others are more host-specific (*below*). Resistant species may be suggested in the entry for the problem in question in the *A–Z Directory*.

COMMON PROBLEMS

The most common ailments affecting annual and biennial plants are:

APHIDS 99	POTASSIUM DEFICIENCY 162
ASTER YELLOWS 102	POWDERY MILDEWS 164
BLISTER BEETLES 108	RABBITS 166
CUTWORMS 121	SLUGS 174
FOOT AND ROOT ROTS 130	SNAILS 175
FROST 130	VIRUSES 186
LEAF SPOTS (FUNGAL) 143	WESTERN FLOWER THRIPS 189

A

Alyssum
CABBAGE MAGGOT, 112
FLEA BEETLES, 129

B

Bellflower (Campanula)
see HERBACEOUS PERENNIALS

C

Calendula
BLISTER BEETLE, 108
CABBAGE LOOPER, 112
CORN EARWORM, 117
CYCLAMEN MITE, 121
SCLEROTINIA (WHITE MOLD), 172

Canna *see* HERBACEOUS PERENNIALS

China Aster (Callistephus)
ASTER YELLOWS, 102
JAPANESE BEETLE, 140
POTATO SPRAING, 164

Cosmos
EARWIGS, **46**
EUROPEAN CORN BORER, 127
JAPANESE BEETLE, 140

G

Geranium (Pelargonium)
BACTERIAL FASCIATION, **39**
CABBAGE LOOPER, 112
CYCLAMEN MITE, 121
DOWNY MILDEW, 123
EDEMA, 125
FOURLINED PLANT BUG, 130
GRAY MOLD, **45**
JAPANESE BEETLE, 140
LEAFROLLERS AND LEAFTIERS, 143
ROOT MEALYBUGS, 169
RUST, **15**, 171
TARSONEMID MITES, 180
WESTERN FLOWER THRIPS, 189

H

Hollyhock (Alcea)
EUROPEAN CORN BORER, 127
JAPANESE BEETLE, 140
POTATO LEAFHOPPER, 163
ROSE CHAFER, 169
RUST, **17**, 171

I

Impatiens
TARSONEMID MITES, 180
WESTERN FLOWER THRIPS, 189

N

Nasturtium (Tropaeolum)
BEAN APHID, 105
CABBAGE BUTTERFLY, 111
FLEA BEETLES, 129
SERPENTINE LEAFMINER, 173

P

Pansy (Viola)
DOWNY MILDEW, 123
MYROTHECIUM LEAF SPOTS AND ROTS, 149
PANSY LEAF SPOT, **13**, 155

Petunia
COLORADO POTATO BEETLE, 116
HORNWORMS, 137
POTATO LATE BLIGHT, **28**

S

Salvia
LEAFHOPPERS, 142

Snapdragon
CYCLAMEN MITE, 121
RUST, **15**, 171

Stocks (Matthiola)
CABBAGE MAGGOT, 112
CLUBROOT, 116
FLEA BEETLES, 129

Sunflower
LEAF-CURLING PLUM APHID, 142

Sweet Peas (Lathyrus)
PEA APHID, 155
PEA MOTH, 156
PEA WILT, **28**
SEEDCORN MAGGOT, 173
SOUTHERN BLIGHT, 176
VIRUS, **23**

T

Tobacco, flowering (Nicotiana)
COLORADO POTATO BEETLE, 116
POTATO SPRAING, 164

V

Verbena
WESTERN FLOWER THRIPS, 189

Viola *see* **Pansy**

W

Wallflower (Cheiranthus)
CABBAGE MAGGOT, 112
CLUBROOT, 116
FLEA BEETLES, **29**, 129

Z

Zinnia
BLISTER BEETLE, 108
EUROPEAN CORN BORER, 127
FOURLINED PLANT BUG, 130
JAPANESE BEETLE, 140
PIERCE'S DISEASE, 160

VEGETABLES AND HERBS

SOME PROBLEMS affect a wide range of vegetables (*right*); others are more host-specific (*below*). Even more so than with fruit, the choice of locally disease-resistant cultivars can help ensure healthy crops and minimize the need for pesticides.

FRUITS AND NUTS

MANY GARDENERS might use pesticides on ornamentals, but when it comes to edible plants, most prefer to avoid them wherever possible. Good cultivation, preventive measures taken at the correct time, and the use of resistant cultivars will all help. Some problems affect many fruits (*see right*). Others are more host-specific; plants so affected are listed below. More resistant species may be suggested in the entry for the problem in question in the *A–Z Directory*.

COMMON PROBLEMS

The most common problems affecting plants and trees bearing edible fruits and nuts are:

APHIDS 99
BACTERIAL SOFT ROT, 103
BIRDS 106
CORAL SPOT 117
FRUIT SPLIT, 131
GRAY MOLD 133
MAGNESIUM DEFICIENCY 146

PLUM CURCULIO, 161
POWDERY MILDEWS 164
RABBITS 166
SQUIRRELS 179
VIRUSES 186
WASPS AND YELLOWJACKETS 187

A

Almond (*Prunus dulcis*)
ORIENTAL FRUIT MOTH, 154
PEACH APHID, 156
PIERCE'S DISEASE, 160
SCLEROTINIA (WHITE MOLD), 172
SHOTHOLE BORERS, **33**, 173
WATERLILY APHID, 188

Apple
APPLE AND PEAR CANKER, **36**, 99, 157
APPLE BITTER PIT, **48**, 99
APPLE MAGGOT, 99
APPLE POWDERY MILDEW, **25**, 100
APPLE RUSTS, 100
APPLE SCAB, **16**, 100
APPLE SUCKER, **43,** 100
BIRDS, **47**, 106
BLEEDING CANKER, 107
BLOSSOM WILT/SPUR BLIGHT, **41**, 108
BRACKET FUNGUS, **39**
BROWN ROT, **47**, **49**, 110
CANKERWORMS, 113
CASEBEARERS, 113
CEDAR-APPLE RUST, **18**, **37**
CODLING MOTH, **47**
EASTERN TENT CATERPILLAR, 125
ENTOMOSPORIUM LEAF SPOT, 126
EUROPEAN APPLE SAWFLY, **47**, **48**, 126
EUROPEAN RED MITE, **40**, 127
FALL WEBWORM, 128
FIREBLIGHT, **35**, 129
FRUIT SPLIT, **48**
FRUITTREE LEAFROLLER, 131
GYPSY MOTH, 134
JAPANESE BEETLE, 140
LEAFHOPPERS, 143
LEAFROLLERS AND LEAFTIERS, 143
MEALY PLUM APHID, 142

ORIENTAL FRUIT MOTH, 154
OYSTERSHELL SCALE, 155
PAPERY BARK, **40**
PEARLEAF BLISTER MITE, 157
PLUM CURCULIO, 161
PROLIFERATION, **44**
QUINCE RUST, 165
REPLANT DISORDERS, 96
ROOT APHIDS, 168
ROSE LEAFHOPPER, 170
ROSY APPLE APHID, **48**, 99, 170
SHOTHOLE BORERS, 173
SPOTTED TENTIFORM LEAFMINER, **13**, 177
VERTICILLIUM WILT, 186
WASPS AND YELLOWJACKETS, 187
WINTER MOTH, 191
WOOLLY APPLE APHID, **35**, 99, 192

Apricot
APPLE MAGGOT, 99
BACTERIAL CANKER, 103
BLOSSOM WILT, 108
EUTYPA DIEBACK, 128
MEALY PLUM APHID, 142
ORIENTAL FRUIT MOTH, 154
PEACH APHID, 156
PEACH SCAB, 157
SCLEROTINIA (WHITE MOLD), 172
WATERLILY APHID, 188

B

Blackberry
DRYBERRY MITE, 124
LEAFHOPPERS, 142
PYRACANTHA SCAB, 165
REDBERRY MITE, **49**, 167
RUST, **40**
STRAWBERRY BUD WEEVIL, 179

Blueberry
NECTAR ROBBING, 150

WASPS AND YELLOWJACKETS, **47**, **49**, 187
WINTER MOTH, **31**, 191

C

Cherry
BACTERIAL CANKER, 103
BIRDS, 106
BLACK CHERRY APHID, **24**, 99, 107
BLOSSOM WILT/SPUR BLIGHT, **41**, 108
BROWN ROT, **47**, **49**
CYTOSPORA CANKER AND BRANCH DIEBACK, 122
EASTERN TENT CATERPILLAR, 125
ORIENTAL FRUIT MOTH, 154
PEACH SCAB, 157
PEAR SAWFLY, 158
ROSE CHAFER, 169
ROSE SICKNESS/REPLANT PROBLEMS, 170
SHOTHOLE BORERS, **33**, 173
SPOTTED TENTIFORM LEAFMINER, 177
SUCKERS, 94
VERTICILLIUM WILT, 186
WATERLILY APHID, 188
WHITE PEACH AND PRUNICOLA SCALES, 190

Citrus (*Citrus, Fortunella*)
BROWN SOFT SCALE, 110
FRUITTREE LEAFROLLER, 131
HEMISPHERICAL SCALE, 135
SPRINGTAILS, **54**
TWOSPOTTED SPIDER MITE, **22**, **23**, 185
WESTERN FLOWER THRIPS, 42

Currants (*Ribes*)
CURRANT APHID, **17**, **27**, 121
BIRDS, 106
CLEARWING (CURRANT) BORER, 116

CORAL SPOT, 117
COTTONY GRAPE SCALE, **39**, 118
FOURLINED PLANT BUG, 130
GOOSEBERRY MILDEW, **25**, **49**, 132
HONEY FUNGUS, 136
IMPORTED CURRANTWORM, **31**, 138
PLANT (LYGUS) BUGS, 161
WHITE PINE BLISTER RUST, 190

D

Dewberry
STRAWBERRY BUD WEEVIL, 179

F

Filbert
LEAFROLLERS AND LEAFTIERS, 143
NUT WEEVIL, 151

G

Gooseberry
CLEARWING (CURRANT) BORER, 116
COTTONY GRAPE SCALE, 118
FOURLINED PLANT BUG, 130
GOOSEBERRY MILDEW, **25**, **49**, 132
IMPORTED CURRANTWORM, **31**, 138
POWDERY MILDEW, 164
WHITE PINE BLISTER RUST, 190

Grape
COTTONY GRAPE SCALE, **39**, 118

DOWNY MILDEW, 123
EUTYPA DIEBACK, 128
FELT GALL MITES, 128
GRAPE BUNCH ROTS, 133
GRAPE ERINEUM MITE, **15**, 133
GRAPE GALL MIDGES, **16**, 133
JAPANESE BEETLE, 140
LEAFROLLERS AND LEAFTIERS, 143
PIERCE'S DISEASE, **24**, 160
POWDERY MILDEW, **49**
ROSE CHAFER, 169
SCLEROTINIA (WHITE MOLD), 172
WASPS AND YELLOWJACKETS, **47**, **49**, 187

Guava
HEMISPHERICAL SCALE, 135

H

Hazelnut
NUT WEEVIL, **52**, 151
OAKWORM, 152
SQUIRRELS, **52**

Hickory *see* GARDEN TREES

M

Melon
CHIPMUNKS, 114
CUCUMBER BEETLES, 120
CUCUMBER SCAB, 120
CUCURBIT DOWNY MILDEW, 121
FOOT AND ROOT ROTS, 130
MELON (COTTON) APHID , 99, 146
SOUTHERN BLIGHT, 176
SQUASH BEETLE, 178
SQUASH VINE BORER, 178

REFERENCE
SECTION

THIS SECTIONS CONTAINS a glossary of terms
and the comprehensive index.

GLOSSARY

ABDOMEN The hind part of an insect's body.

ACARICIDE A pesticide effective against mites.

ACIDIC (of soil) With a pH value of less than 7; see also *Alkaline* and *Neutral*.

ADVENTITIOUS (of roots) Arising above ground from a stem or leaf.

AERATE (of soil) 1. Loosen by mechanical means in order to allow air to enter. 2. Alter soil texture and structure by creating more air spaces.

ALKALINE (of soil) With a pH value of more than 7; see also *Acidic* and *Neutral*.

ALTERNATE HOST One of two host plants needed for some pathogens or pests to complete their life cycles. The alternate host is often unrelated to the other host: most pathogens and pests are able to complete their life cycles using a single host plant.

ANNUAL A plant or fungus that completes its life cycle, from germination through to death, in one year.

ANTENNA (*pl.* antennae) A jointed sensory organ on the head of insects and mites.

ANTHER The part of a stamen that produces pollen; it is usually borne on a filament.

ANTHRACNOSE A term used to describe several unrelated fungal diseases which are seen as dark spots or lesions on foliage, stems, pods, or fruits.

ARTHROPODS Invertebrate animals which have jointed legs, such as. insects, mites, sowbugs, centipedes, and millipedes.

ASEXUAL REPRODUCTION A form of reproduction not involving fertilization.

AXIL The upper angle between a leaf and stem, between a main stem and a lateral branch, or between a stem and a bract; where an axillary bud develops.

BACTERIUM (*pl.* bacteria) A microscopic single-celled organism. Some are beneficial to plants; others may be pathogenic or cause secondary rotting.

BACTERICIDE A chemical capable of controlling bacteria.

BARK The surface layer of the trunk and branches of woody plants, protecting the tissue within; usually composed of dead corky cells.

BARK-RINGING The controlled removal of a partial ring of bark from the trunk or branches of certain fruit trees, to reduce vigorous growth and encourage fruit cropping. Complete removal or girdling of a trunk, as in damage by rabbits, squirrels, voles, and black vine weevil grubs, can lead to the death of woody plants. See also *Girdling*.

BASAL PLATE The flattened base of a bulb, from which the roots grow.

BIENNIAL A plant that produces leafy growth in the first year and then flowers, sets seed, and dies in the next year.

BIOLOGICAL CONTROL The control of pests, diseases, and weeds by the use of natural enemies such as predators, parasites, and pathogens.

BLEEDING The oozing of sap through a cut or wound.

BLIGHT A term loosely used to describe a fungal, or occasionally an insect, attack.

BLIND SHOOT A shoot that does not form a terminal flower bud, or one where the growing point has been destroyed.

BOLT To produce flowers and seed prematurely.

BORDEAUX MIXTURE A fungicide mixture containing copper sulfate and lime.

BRACT A modified leaf at the base of a flower or flower cluster, sometimes resembling a flower petal or leaves. Bracts may also be reduced to scalelike structures.

BROADLEAVED Of trees or shrubs that bear broad, flat leaves, rather than needlelike foliage as in conifers.

BROAD-SPECTRUM Used to describe a chemical that has an effect on a wide range of often unrelated organisms.

BUD A condensed shoot containing an embryonic leaf, leaf cluster, or flower.

BULB A storage organ consisting mainly of fleshy scales and swollen, modified leaf-bases on a much reduced stem. Bulbs usually, but not always, grow from underground.

CALLUS The corky wound tissue formed by a plant in response to wounding. Callus frequently grows in from the edges of a wound created when a tree limb is removed, or at the base of a cutting.

CATERPILLAR The larval stage of moths and butterflies.

CERTIFIED STOCK Plants sold guaranteed to be of good quality and free from pests and diseases, especially virus infection, at the time of sale.

CHEMICAL In a garden situation, a fungicide, pesticide, weedkiller, repellent or fertilizer used to control pathogens, pests or weeds, or to increase the soil fertility.

CHLOROPHYLL The green pigment in plants that absorbs light, providing the energy for photosynthesis.

CHLOROSIS Yellowing of plant tissue due to a deficiency or loss of chlorophyll (the green pigment). It may be brought about by a range of physiological disorders, nutrient deficiencies, pests, and diseases.

CHLOROTIC Showing the symptoms of chlorosis.

CHRYSALIS The stage between the fully fed caterpillar and the adult moth or butterfly. See also *Pupa*.

COCOON A protective outer covering, usually of silk, produced by caterpillars and some other larvae before they pupate.

COLOR-BREAKING A term used to describe a patterned change in flower color, where the original color is "broken" into elaborate feathered patterns. It is usually caused by virus infections.

COMPANION PLANTING Positioning plants together that are reputed to have a beneficial effect on neighboring plants by discouraging pests and diseases or improving growth.

COMPLETE METAMORPHOSIS See *Metamorphosis*.

COMPOST An organic material formed by decomposed plant remains and other organic matter, including material from the kitchen and garden, used as a soil improver or mulch.

COMPOUND Made up of several or many parts, for example a leaf that is divided into two or more leaflets.

CONTACT Used to describe a chemical that remains on the outside of a plant and is absorbed by a pest or pathogen when it is sprayed or comes into contact with a treated surface.

CORM A bulblike underground storage organ, consisting mainly of a swollen stem base and often surrounded by a papery tunic.

COTYLEDON A seed leaf; the first leaf or leaves to emerge from some seeds after germination, often markedly different from mature leaves. Flowering plants (angiosperms) are classified into monocotyledons (one) and dicotyledons (two) depending on how many cotyledons are contained in the mature seed. In gymnosperms (conifers) they are often produced in whorls.

CRUCIFEROUS Of the family Cruciferae, to which brassicas belong.

CULTIVAR A plant that has developed from the original species in cultivation (and rarely selected from the wild), either by accident or by deliberate breeding; a contraction of "cultivated variety." See also *Variety*.

DECIDUOUS Plants that shed their leaves at the end of the growing season (in autumn and winter) and renew them at the beginning of the next season.

DEFOLIATION Loss of leaves.

DIEBACK The death of shoots, often spreading down from the tip of the stem, caused by damage or disease.

DORMANCY 1. The state of temporary cessation of growth in plants, and slowing down of other activities, usually during winter. 2. Seed dormancy: non-germination of seed when placed in conditions suitable for germination, due to physical, chemical, or other factors inherent in the seed.

DRUPES, DRUPELETS See *Stone fruits.*

DRENCH Pest or disease control applied as a liquid to the roots of a plant to control soil-borne pests or pathogens.

DUST Pest or disease control applied as a fine dust, usually to the plant, but occasionally to the soil round it.

ELYTRON (*pl.* elytra) A beetle's wing case; when not in flight these are folded back and form a covering for the top of the abdomen.

EYE On a stem or, more commonly, on a tuber such as a potato, a dormant or latent growth bud that is visible.

f. [Lat.] *forma*; a variant within a species.

FAMILY A category in plant classification, grouping together related genera. All these genera have characteristics which are all constant or which are clearly different from those of other families.

FERTILIZATION The fusion of a pollen grain nucleus (male) with an ovule (female) to form a fertile seed.

FERTILIZER A plant "food" (usually in concentrated form), naturally or synthetically produced, applied to the soil or to plant foliage. A balanced fertilizer contains a balance of nitrogen, phosphorus, and potassium. A complete fertilizer contains both these and other nutrients.

FOLIAR FEED Liquid fertilizer formulated for application direct to healthy plant foliage. Nutrients applied in this manner are very rapidly taken up by the plant.

FRASS Insect excrement pellets, especially of caterpillars.

FREE-LIVING An organism such as a nematode which is associated with but not attached to its host.

FRUITING BODIES (of fungi) Spore-bearing structures of larger fungi, commonly known as toadstools, mushrooms, or bracket fungi. May be annual or perennial.

FUNGICIDE A pesticide capable of controlling a fungus.

FUNGUS (*pl.* fungi) A very variable group of organisms, which obtain their food materials from living or dead organic matter (see also *Parasite* and *Saprophyte*). They vary greatly in size, from microscopic to clearly visible with the naked eye.

GALL An abnormal growth produced by a plant in response to chemicals secreted by an animal, fungus, or bacterium that lives within the galled tissue.

GENUS (*pl.* genera) A category in plant classification, grouping related species. Denoted by the first part of the scientific name. See also *Species.*

GERMINATION The physical and chemical changes that take place as a seed starts to grow and develop into a plant.

GIRDLING The removal of bark around a trunk, stem, or branch by animals or physical injury. See also *Bark-ringing.*

HABIT Characteristic, natural form of growth of a plant – for example upright, prostrate, or weeping.

HEAVY (of soil) Having a high proportion of clay, and often poorly drained.

HERBACEOUS 1. A nonwoody plant in which the aboveground part dies down to the rootstock at the end of the growing season. 2. Dying down at the end of the growing season.

HERBICIDE A chemical used to control or kill weeds.

HERBIVORE A plant-feeding animal.

HERMAPHRODITE Animals with both female and male sexual organs, e.g. slugs, snails, and earthworms.

HONEYDEW A sugary liquid excreted by sap-feeding insects including many, but not all, aphids, whiteflies, psyllids, mealybugs, and scale insects.

HOST The plant on which a pest or pathogen develops or feeds; also the insect or other animal in which parasitic animals develop.

HOST RANGE The range of host plants that a given pest or pathogen will attack. The host range is often restricted to closely related plants.

HYPHA (*pl.* hyphae) The minute thread-like growths formed by fungi.

IMMUNE A plant with characteristics that prevent a given pest or pathogen from attacking or colonizing it. A plant immune to one disease or pest may, however, be susceptible to others.

INCOMPLETE METAMORPHOSIS See *Metamorphosis.*

INORGANIC 1. Used generally, not of plant or animal origin, i.e. a mineral or synthetically produced material. 2. Of a chemical compound, one that does not contain carbon. Many manmade pesticides contain carbon-based chemicals and so are organic compounds as defined by a chemist, but not in the sense in which gardeners use the word organic. Inorganic fertilizers are refined from naturally occurring minerals or produced artificially. See also *Organic.*

INSECT Invertebrate animal whose body is divided into a head, thorax, and abdomen. Adult insects have three pairs of jointed legs on the thorax and usually two pairs of wings, e.g. moths, butterflies, beetles, ants, bees, wasps, sawflies, some aphids, whiteflies, and earwigs.

INSECTICIDAL SOAP A pesticide containing fatty acids, used against some pests, diseases, and weeds.

INSECTICIDE A pesticide capable of controlling insects.

INSTAR The stage(s) in the development of larvae and nymphs of insects and mites.

INTEGRATED CONTROL A combination of chemical and biological controls with good cultivation techniques, aimed at keeping pests and diseases below the level at which damage occurs.

INVERTEBRATE Animals without backbones, such as insects, mites, sowbugs, mollusks, nematodes, earthworms, and millipedes.

LARVA (*pl.* larvae) The immature feeding stage in the life cycle of an insect undergoing complete metamorphosis, e.g. moth caterpillars, beetle grubs, and fly maggots. See also *Nymph.*

LEACHING The loss of nutrients when they are washed down through the soil to areas out of reach of plant roots, often caused by excessive watering or rain.

LEGUME A plant of the family Fabaceae (formerly Leguminosae), to which peas and beans belong.

LENTICEL A breathing pore found in the stems of woody plants. Often enlarged and clearly visible to the naked eye.

LESION Point or area of damage caused by pests, pathogens, or physical injury.

LIME Compounds of calcium. The amount of lime in soil determines whether it is alkaline, neutral, or acidic.

MANDIBLES The biting mouthparts of insects, especially leaf-eating types.

METAMORPHOSIS The changes undergone during an insect or mite's development. Incomplete metamorphosis, as shown by aphids, plant bugs, earwigs, and mites, involves little more than an increase in size and the gradual development of sexual organs and sometimes wings. Complete metamorphosis involves a dramatic change of form with the larva bearing no resemblance to the adult, as in moths, flies, beetles, and sawflies.

MOLLUSCICIDE A pesticide capable of controlling slugs and snails.

MULCH 1. A material applied in a layer to the soil surface to suppress weeds, conserve moisture, and maintain a cool, even root temperature. In addition to organic materials such as manure, bark, and compost, which also enrich the soil, plastic, foil, and gravel may also be used.

MULTISTEMMED Tree or shrub with several main stems arising either directly from the ground or from a short main stem.

MYCELIUM A compacted mass of fungal hyphae, often developed into a distinct sheet of fungal growth.

MYCOPLASMA Microscopic organism closely related and with similar characteristics to a virus.

MYCORRHIZA (*pl.* mycorrhizae) Soil fungi that live in mutually beneficial association with plant roots, helping them absorb nutrients from the soil.

NECROSIS The deterioration and death of plant tissues.

NECROTIC Dead, frequently brown or black, areas of plant tissue.

NECTAR A sweet, sugary liquid secreted by nectary glandular tissue, usually found in the flower, but sometimes on the leaves or stem.

NEMATICIDE A pesticide capable of controlling nematodes.

NEMATODES Microscopic, unsegmented, wormlike animals. Some are used as pest predators of slugs and other pests.

NEUTRAL (of soil) With a pH value of 7, the point at which soil is neither acidic nor alkaline. See also *Acidic* and *Alkaline*.

NITRATE Salts of nitric acid having a high nitrogen content that is available to plants. They are produced by bacterial activity in the soil or manufactured.

NITRITE A salt of nitric acid in which the nitrogen is not readily available to plants.

NODE The point on a stem where one or more buds, leaves, shoots, or flowers are attached.

NODULE A small swelling.

NOSE (of a bulb or corm) The pointed upper end.

NUTRIENTS Minerals (mineral ions) used to develop proteins and other compounds required for plant growth.

NYMPH The immature stage of an insect or mite that undergoes incomplete metamorphosis. See also *Larva*.

ORGANIC 1. Of garden chemicals, referring to compounds containing carbon derived from plant or animal organisms. 2. Loosely, mulches, composts, or similar materials derived from plant or animal-derived materials. 3. A system of crop production and gardening without using synthetic or nonorganic materials.

OVICIDE A pesticide capable of controlling the egg stage of pests.

OVIPOSITOR The egg-laying organ of an insect.

PARASITE An organism that gets all or part of its food from another plant or animal over a period of time, often without killing its host. Parasitic insects that eventually kill the insect in which they have developed are more correctly termed parasitoids.

PARTHENOGENESIS The ability of some female pests to reproduce without fertilization. Many aphids have this ability, as do black vine weevils, some sawflies, scale insects, and mealybugs. Males are rare or nonexistent in these species.

PATHOGEN A parasitic, disease-causing organism. Pathogens include certain bacteria, fungi, viruses, and mycoplasmas.

PATHOVAR A distinct strain or type of a named pathogen.

PEDICEL The stalk of an individual flower.

PERENNIAL Living for at least three seasons. In this book the term when used as a noun, and unless qualified, denotes a herbaceous perennial. A woody-based perennial dies down only partially, leaving a woody stem at the base.

PERSISTENCE (of chemicals) The length of time a chemical persists in an active form either on the plant or in the soil or soil mix after it has been applied.

PESTICIDE A chemical substance; a term usually applied to chemicals that control pests, but in its broader definition also includes fungicides, herbicides, animal repellents, and wood preservatives.

PETIOLE The stalk of a leaf.

pH The scale by which the acidity or alkalinity of soil is measured. See also *Acidic*, *Alkaline*, and *Neutral*.

PHEROMONE Volatile chemicals produced by insects as a means of communicating with others of the same species. Males often locate virgin females by tracking down the source of the pheromone or scent released by the female.

PHLOEM Conducting elements within plant tissue, largely associated with the transport of food materials in solution, produced in the leaves and distributed to the rest of the plant.

PHOTOSYNTHESIS The synthesis of carbohydrates in green plants from carbon dioxide and water, using light energy from sunshine or artificial light absorbed by the green pigment chlorophyll.

PHYTOTOXIC Harmful to plants. Usually used to describe a chemical (usually an insecticide or fungicide) that can damage a plant onto which it has been sprayed.

POLLEN The male cells of a plant, formed in the anthers.

POLLINATION The transfer of pollen from the anthers to the stigma of the same or different flowers, often carried out by insects, especially bees, or by air movement, resulting in fertilization of the embryonic seeds in the ovary.

POME FRUIT A firm, fleshy fruit, with seeds enclosed in a central core, as in apples and pears.

PROBOSCIS Insect mouthparts used for sucking up liquids, especially nectar.

PROLEGS The clasping legs on the abdomen of a caterpillar or sawfly larva.

PUPA (*pl.* pupae) The non-feeding stage in the life cycle of an insect undergoing complete metamorphosis.

PUPATION The period of time during which larval tissues are dissolved and reconstructed into the form of the adult insect.

PYCNIDIUM (*pl.* pycnidia) Minute raised, rounded fungal fruiting body, produced on the surface of infected plant tissue.

RACE (of fungi) A specific strain of a named fungus which may vary in its physical or pathogenic characteristics from other races of that fungus.

REPELLENTS Substances that deter pests without causing them harm.

RESISTANT A plant is described as resistant to a pest or disease when it is attacked by it but shows no ill effects. A fungus may also develop resistance to a fungicide or to a closely related group of fungicides. Fungicide resistance occurs most commonly when a particular fungicide or closely related ones have been used repeatedly for many years. Similar resistance problems also occur with some pests and weeds that are no longer controllable by insecticides and herbicides that were formerly effective.

RHIZOME A specialized, usually horizontally creeping, swollen or slender underground stem that acts as a storage organ and produces aerial shoots at its apex and along its length.

RHIZOMORPH A cordlike fungal structure that is very resilient and withstands extremes of temperature and moisture. Honey fungus rhizomorphs are dark and tough and grow from host to host.

ROOT The part of a plant, normally underground, that anchors it and through which water and nutrients are absorbed.

ROTATION Growing different types of plants on a given piece of land from season to season. By rotating plants, some pest and disease outbreaks can be avoided. Rotation is a particularly effective method of avoiding problems with soil-borne pests and pathogens.

ROWCOVER Synthetic material composed of very fine fibers woven or compressed together into a fabric that can be draped over plants to protect them from weather extremes and certain pests.

RUSSETING A discoloration, generally brown and roughened, of a plant surface (usually the skin of fruits).

SAPROPHYTE An organism (most commonly a fungus) which that on dead or decaying organic material but does not attack living material.

SCLEROTIUM (*pl.* sclerotia) The resilient fungal resting bodies formed by some fungi to allow them to overwinter successfully and withstand extremes of weather.

SHOOT The aerial part of a plant which bears leaves. A sideshoot arises from a bud along the length of a main shoot.

SOIL MIX A potting medium consisting of a mixture of soil, sand, peat, leaf mold, coir, bark, or other ingredients. There are many formulations for a variety of uses.

SPECIES A category in plant and animal classification, consisting of individuals in the same genus that are alike and naturally breed with each other. Denoted by the second part of the scientific name. See also *Genus*.

SPORE Microscopic reproductive structure of fungi and bacteria. Certain non-flowering plants such as ferns also produce spores.

SPUR A short fruiting branch on fruit bushes and trees, particularly apples and pears.

SSP. Subspecies; a higher category in plant classification than *forma* or variety.

STAMEN The male reproductive organ in a plant, consisting of the pollen-producing anther and usually its supporting filament (stalk).

STEM The main axis of a plant, usually above ground and supporting leaves, flowers, and fruits.

STOLON A horizontally spreading or arching stem, usually above ground, that roots at its tip to produce a new plant, such as in strawberry.

STONE FRUITS Fruits, also known as "drupes," with one or more seeds ("stones") surrounded by fleshy, usually edible, tissue. They are common in the genus *Prunus* (e.g. apricots, plums, cherries).

STOOL A group of shoots emerging from the base of a single plant. In propagation the term refers to the roots of a plant such as a chrysanthemum after it has finished flowering.

STRAIN (of bacteria, etc.) A distinct form of a named pathogen.

STYLETS The mouthparts of sap-feeding insects and mites, used for piercing plant tissues.

SYMBIOSIS A relationship between two organisms where neither harms the other and both derive benefit from the relationship, for example the nitrogen-fixing bacteria in root nodules.

SYSTEMIC 1. Insecticides and fungicides that are absorbed into a plant's sap and translocated within the plant. Systemic fungicides are, however, rarely able to move great distances but may move from one leaf surface through the leaf to the lower surface. 2. Of diseases, some pathogens, in particular the viruses, that are systemic within the host plant, moving with the plant sap and being found in all or a large part of the host.

THORAX The mid-part of an insect's body, between the head and abdomen.

TOLERANT Having the ability to tolerate an attack by a pest or a pathogen. A pest or pathogen may be described as tolerant if able to withstand the effects of a pesticide.

TRACE ELEMENTS Chemical elements needed by plants, but only in very small amounts, such as boron, copper, manganese, iron, molybdenum, and zinc.

TRANSPIRATION Loss of water by evaporation from leaves and stems.

TUBER A swollen, usually underground, organ derived from a stem or root, used for food storage.

VARIEGATED Irregularly marked with various colors, particularly of leaves patterned with markings in white, yellow, or other colors.

VARIETY A plant that has developed with a slight difference from a wild plant species. Plant varieties are often brought into cultivation once developed.

VECTOR See *Virus vector.*

VIRUS A submicroscopic particle often responsible for causing plant virus diseases.

VIRUS VECTOR An insect, mite, or nematode that transmits plant viruses, usually on its mouthparts or in its saliva. Some fungal and bacterial diseases can also be spread by plant pests.

WETTING AGENT A material used to lower the surface tension of liquids on a plant surface, so allowing a spray to form a film over the surface rather than forming into droplets. Many garden pesticide formulations contain wetting agents (also known as wetters or spreaders).

WIND SNAP Wind causing a tree to be broken off at ground level; this can be made more likely by decay round the base of the trunk.

WIND THROW Wind causing a tree to be uprooted. Decay in the tree roots can make the tree unstable and therefore susceptible to wind damage.

WORM Various animals with elongate, cylindrical bodies. Nematodes have simple, unsegmented bodies; earthworms are more advanced animals with bodies divided into many segments.

XYLEM Vascular tissue under bark taking water and nutrients up a stem.

REFERENCE SECTION

INDEX

References to illustrations
and tables are in **bold**.
Subheadings are arranged
with symptoms first.

A

Acer see maple
acidity of soil, 68–9
adelgids, 98
  leaf damage by, **32**
  mechanism of plant
    damage, 74, 75
  stem damage by, **39**
aecia, 165
aerosol pesticides, 89
Aesculus see horse chestnut
air pollution, 98
alfalfa mosaic, 155
algae, 98, 183
alkalinity of soil, 68–9
almond (*Prunus dulcis*)
  stem symptoms, **33**
alternaria leaf spot, **13**, 98
amaryllis (*Hippeastrum*)
  symptoms, **29**
Amblyseius spp., 85
amphibians, beneficial, **63**
andromeda lacebug, 98
animals
  barriers to, 82–3, 122
  beneficial see beneficial
    creatures
  contamination by
    droppings of, 166
  flower damage by, 74
  lawn damage by, **59**, 140
  nut damage by, **52**
  pesticide injury, 89, 90
  repellents, 83, 106, 114,
    122
  stem/bark damage by,
    36, 40, 41, 70
  vegetable/fruit damage
    by, **51, 70**, 75, 154
anthracnose, 98
  symptoms, **12, 18**
Antirrhinum see
  snapdragon
ants, 98–9, **99**
  biological control, 151
  lawn problems from, **59**
  traps for, 81
Aphidius spp., **85**
aphidlions see lacewing
Aphidoletes aphidomyza,
  85
aphids, 74, 99
  biological control, **60–1**,
    63, 84, 85, 105, 109
  flower damage by, **43**
  fruit damage by, **48**
  honeydew from, 136
  leaf damage by, **16, 17,
    24, 27, 32, 35**
  lifespan, 77
  mechanism of plant
    damage, 74, 75
  "mummies," 153
  reproduction, 77, **77**
  resistance to pesticides,
    87
  root damage by, **55**
  stem and bud damage,
    35, 36, 41, 43
apple
  flower symptoms, **43, 44**

fruit symptoms, **47, 48,
  49**
  leaf symptoms, **16**
  fruit protection, 82
  replanting, 96
apple bitter pit, **48**, 99, 112
apple canker, **36**, 99, 157,
  192
apple maggot, 99
apple mosaic virus, 171
apple powdery mildew, **25**,
  100
apple rusts, **37**, 100
  see also rusts
apple scab, **16**, 87, 100
apple sucker, **43**, 100, **101**
application see chemical
  controls, application of;
  fertilizers, application of;
  safety issues
Aquilegia see columbine
arborvitae
  symptoms, **37**
  see also seiridium canker
arborvitae weevil, 144
armyworm, 109, 180
artichoke, Jerusalem, **36**
artichoke gall wasp, 152
ash borer, 100
  see also clearwing borer
ash spangle gall mite, 101
Asian ladybug, 141
Asian longhorned beetle,
  101
Asiatic garden beetle, 101,
  188
asparagus
  symptoms, **40**
asparagus beetle, **40, 101,
  101
asparagus rust, 101
aster wilt, 102
aster yellows, **44**, 102
Australian ladybug, 141
autumn color, premature,
  164–5
azalea see rhododendron
azalea gall, 102
azalea lacebug, **20**, 102
azalea leaftier, 131
azalea whitefly, 103

B

Bacillus popillae, 140, 147
Bacillus thuringiensis, **81**,
  85, 88, 110–11, 115, 125
bacteria
  infections, 72, **73**
  nitrogen fixation by, 69
  see also secondary
    infections
bacterial canker, **35**, 103
bacterial fasciation, **39**, 103
bacterial leaf scorch see
  scorch
bacterial leaf spot see leaf
  spot
bacterial soft rot see soft rot
bactericides, 88
bagworm, 103–4
bait, **88**, 89, **89**, 115, 147
baking soda spray, 118
balsam twig aphid, 104
balsam woolly adelgid, 104
banded slug, 174
banded snail, 175

bark
  girdling, 186, 190
  herbicide damage, 172
  lightning damage, **70**,
    144–5
  papery see papery bark
  scalding, 104
  splitting, 104–5, 177
bark beetles, **33**, 75, 104,
  104, 109
barriers, **78**, 80, 81, **82**,
  82–3, **83**
  to beetles, 170
  to birds, 106
  to deer, 122
  to rabbits, 166
  to squirrels, 179
  to voles, 186
  to woodchucks, 192
basal rot see foot rot; root
  rot
bats, 84
bay see laurel
bean anthracnose, 105
bean aphid, 105
bean halo blight, 105
bean weevil, **51, 105**, 105
beans
  leaf symptoms, **29, 31**
  root symptoms, **55**
  seed symptoms, **51**
  vegetable symptoms, **51**
Beauveria bassiana, 105,
  108, 114
beech (*Fagus*)
  leaf symptoms, **32**
  stem symptoms, **35**
beech aphids, **32**, 105
beech blight aphid, 106
beech scale, **35**, 106
bees
  beneficial, **62**
  burrowing, 111
  flower damage by, **46**
  lawn/ground nests of, **58,
    62**
  leaf damage by, **30, 31**,
    75
  leaf-cutting, **30**, 142
  nectar robbing by, **46**,
    150
beetle mites, 154
beetles, 106
  beneficial, **63**
  biological control, 109,
    110, 147, 151
  flower damage by, **43, 46**
  lady see ladybug
  leaf damage by, **29**, 75,
    101
  stem damage by, **33, 40**,
    101
  vegetable damage by, 155
beet
  vegetable symptoms, **51**
begonia powdery mildew,
  23, 106
beneficial creatures, **60–3,
  67, 79**, 82, 83, **83**, 154
  flies see tachinid fly
  ladybugs, **60, 77, 85**, 126,
    135, 147, 185, 190
  mites, **85**, 131, 185, 188
  nematodes, **85**, 107, 121,
    151, 188
  snakes, 175
  spiders, 177

wasps see trichogramma
  wasp; wasps, parasitic
  see also *Bacillus* spp.
berries see specific berries
Betula see birch
billbug, 151
biological controls, **84**,
  84–5, **85**
  see also *Bacillus
    thuringiensis*; nematodes,
    beneficial; wasps,
    parasitic
birch (*Betula*)
  leaf symptoms, **19**
birch borer see bronze
  birch borer
birch leafminer, **19**, 106,
  172
birds, 75, 106
  beneficial, **63, 84, 84**
  control, 83, 106
  flower damage by, **46**
  fruit damage by, **47**
  lawn damage by, 58
  leaf damage by, **30**
bitter pit see apple bitter pit
black cherry aphid, **24**, 107
black currant, **49**
black leg of cuttings, 108
black vine weevil (adult),
  29, 75, **107**, 107, 144
  barriers to, 81
  biological control, 85, 151
black vine weevil (larvae),
  53, 75, 107
black widow spider, 177
blackberry
  symptoms, **40, 49**
blackspot see rose
  blackspot
blasting see blindness of
  bulbs
bleeding canker, 107
blight, **73**
  flower damage by, 42
  leaf damage by, **28**, 105
  stem damage by, **33, 41**
  vegetable/root damage
    by, **51, 56**
blind shoots, **40**, 107
blindness of bulbs, **41**, 107
blister beetle, **30, 43**, 108
blossom end rot, **50**, 108,
  112
blossom wilt, **41**, 108
blueberries
  fruit symptoms, **47**
  leaf symptoms, **31**
bluegrass billbug, 108
bolting, **44**, 108
borax, 108
Bordeaux mixture, 79, 103,
  118
borers
  stem damage by, **33, 40**
  vegetable damage by, **48**
boron deficiency, 108, 158
Botrytis see gray mold
bottom rot, 109
boxwood (*Buxus*)
  leaf symptoms, **26**
boxwood leafminer, 109
boxwood psyllid, **26**, 109
bracket fungi, **37, 38, 39**,
  109
braconid wasp, **62**, 109–10,
  153
branching, abnormal see
  witches' brooms

brassica wire stem, 110
brassicas
  leaf symptoms, **14, 29,
    30, 32**
  root symptoms, **55**, 75
  stem symptoms, **39**
  pest control, 83, **83**
  resistant cultivars, **92**
bristly roseslug, 170
broad mite, 180
  see also tarsonemid mite
broccoli see brassicas
bronze birch borer, 110
brown rot, **47, 49**, 110
  see also sclerotinia
brown soft scale, 110
Bruce spanworm, 191
Bt see *Bacillus thuringiensis*
bud clipper see strawberry
  bud weevil
bud drop, 111, 124
buds
  problems, **40, 41**, 165
  pruning considerations,
    95
bulb blue mold, 111
bulb rot, 124, 172
bulbs
  symptoms, **54–5**
  blindness see blindness
    of bulbs
  hot water treatment, 83,
    132, 150
  how to buy, **92**
bumblebees, **62**
bunch rot, 132
burn see fertilizers, damage
  by
burrowing bee, 111
butterflies see caterpillars

C

cabbage see brassicas
cabbage aphid, **32**, 111
cabbage butterfly (imported
  cabbageworm), **76**, 83,
  111
cabbage looper, **30**, 112,
  180
cabbage maggot, 83, **83**,
  112, 151
cacti, adaptations of, **71**
cactus corky scab, **22**, 112
calcium deficiency, **69**, 99,
  108, 112
California oakworm, 153
camellia
  leaf symptoms, **15, 22,
    26**
camellia gall, **26**, 112
camellia yellow mottle, **22**,
  113
cane tip blight, 133
cankers, 113
  symptoms, 14, **35, 36,
    38, 40**, 73, **73**
  excision of, 126
  see also crown rot; root
    rot
cankerworm, 113
  leaf damage by, **30**
  traps for, 81
Capsicum see pepper
carabid beetles see ground
  beetles
Carolina mantid, 164
carpenter bee, 150

ACKNOWLEDGMENTS

AUTHORS' ACKNOWLEDGMENTS

Pippa Greenwood would like to thank all the colleagues past and present, and friends and family, who helped her to retrieve obscure but useful information and continued to put up with her while she was writing this book. In particular, Dr John Fletcher, her plant pathology "guru," who taught her so much and who really does share her fascination with diseased plants! She would also like to thank Justine for her word-processing help and the numerous people at Dorling Kindersley who have been involved in this project and who have all been so tirelessly enthusiastic and such fun to work with.

Andrew Halstead is indebted to Dorothy Gibson for her speedy and accurate conversion of hand-written pages to a word-processed script. He would also like to thank the companies and colleagues who have given assistance and encouragement in writing this book.

Daniel Gilrein would like to thank Lucille Siracusano and Sandi Mulvaney for their assistance with the work.

PUBLISHER'S ACKNOWLEDGMENTS

SPECIAL THANKS GO TO PETER ALAN NELSON FOR RESEARCH, WRITING, AND GENERAL CONTRIBUTIONS TO THIS BOOK.

PICTURE RESEARCH
Melanie Simmonds, Louise Thomas, and Victoria Walker

DESIGN ASSISTANCE
Fay Singer and Heather Dunleavy

EDITORIAL ASSISTANCE
James Nugent

ADDITIONAL ILLUSTRATIONS
Karen Cochrane

CREEPY CRAWLY FONT
Mark Bracey

INDEXERS
Nanette Cardon and Beverley Nightenhelser

Dorling Kindersley would also like to thank Susanne Mitchell, Karen Wilson, and Barbara Haynes at the Royal Horticultural Society and Ian Hodgson at *The Garden* magazine.

PHOTOGRAPHY CREDITS

The publisher would like to thank the following for their kind permission to reproduce photographs.

t=top, b=bottom, c=center, l=left, r=right.

A–Z Botanical Front Jacket bc, 39br. DW Bevan: 47c, 60tr. Martin Stankewitz: 67tr.

Biofotos/Heather Angel Front Jacket tr. 10 title page, 37bl, 38tl, 39cl, 43bc, 44cr, 59br, 61tl, 63tc, 63tr, 63cl, 72bl, 75tl, 96tl.

A. R. Chase 12cl,12bc, 14tr, 14bl, 15bc, 17tl, 21bl, 22c, 24bl, 25cr, 28br, 40bl, 44tr, 45tc, 57bl.

Bruce Coleman Jane Burton: 62bl. Kim Taylor: 63tl, 90tr.

Margery Daughtrey 13tc, 17c, 18tl, 30tl.

Forestry Commission 36cr, 38br, 39tl, 40cr, 41tc, 70cr.

The Garden magazine Tim Sandall: Front Jacket bcr, bcl, cbl, tl, tcr. Back Jacket bl, tl. 5bl, 12tc, 12cr, 12br, 13tl, 13cr, 13tr, 14bc, 15tc, 15cr, 15bl, 16tl, 16bl, 16bc, 17tc, 17cl, 17cr, 17br, 18br, 18tc, 19bc, 19tl, 20cr, 20tl, 21tl, 21tc, 22tr, 22cl, 22cr, 22bl, 22bc, 22tl, 23bl, 23bc, 23tr, 23cr, 24tc, 24tr, 24br, 25tr, 25cl, 25c, 26cr, 26tl, 27tl, 27bc, 27c, 27cr, 27bl, 28tr, 29c, 29cr, 29br, 30tc, 30cr, 31tl, 31br, 32tl, 33tr, 34tl, 34cr, 35c, 35tl, 35bc, 36cl, 37tr, 38bl, 39tr, 43tr, 44bl, 45tl, 45bl, 46bl, 47tc, 47c, 48tc, 48bl, 49tl, 50tr, 51tc, 51tr, 52cl, 53tr, 53tc, 53c, 53bl, 54tl, 54cr, 54br, 55cl, 55cr, 56bc, 57br, 58bl, 58br, 75cr, 75cb. Derek St Romaine: 15tr, 27br, 42bl, 55tl.

Garden/Wildlife Matters 48cr, 48bc.

The Garden Picture Library John Glover: 20tr, 74bl.

Daniel Gilrein 13bl, 15tl, 16tr, 16br, 17tr, 18cr, 19cr, 19bl, 20bl, 20bc, 20br, 23br, 26bl, 27tr, 27cl, 29tr, 29bc, 30tr, 30c, 30bl, 30br, 31tr, 31cr, 32tc, 32tr, 32cl, 32bl, 33tl, 33bl, 35tc, 35cr, 36tc, 36bc, 37tl, 38cr, 38bc, 39c, 40tr, 41bc, 43bc, 43br, 45cl, 47cr, 48c, 48br, 50br, 53br, 61bl, 62br, 63bl, 67br.

Jerry Harpur 83bl.

Michael Hoffmann 29cl, 43bl, 46cl.

Holt Studios John Adams: 28bl, 44tr. Gordon Roberts: 45tr. Inga Spence: 51bl. Nigel Cattlin: Front Jacket cr, br, bl, cl, tl, tcl, tc. Back Jacket cr, br, clb, cl, tcl, tc. Inside Jacket flap bl. p6, 12tr, 12bl, 14tl, 14cr, 17bc, 21br, 23tl, 24tl, 25tc, 25br, 25bl, 28tl, 28cr, 28bl, 28bc, 29tl, 29tc, 33bc, 35bl, 37br, 38tr, 40tc, 41cr, 42bc, 42tr, 43c, 43cl, 44tl, 46tr, 47tr, 47br, 48tr, 49bc, 50tl, 50bl, 51cr, 52tl, 52br, 55tc, 55tr, 56br, 56tl, 56cr, 57cl, 58bc, 59tc, 59cl, 60bl, 60bc, 61cl, 62tl, 72bl, 80cl, 91tr, 96br.

Oxford Scientific Films 68cl. Marshall Black: 75trb. Scott Camazine: 72br. Harry Fox: Back Jacket cal, 61tc. Harold Taylor: 60br, 77bc, 77br. Terry Heathcote: 70bl. John McCammon: 81tr. Colin Milkins: 77tl. James Robinson: 75tr. Tony Tilford: 83tr. Thorsten Klapp/Okapia: 81bl, 81bc.

Photos Horticultural 15c, 18tr, 41cl, 43cr, 44bc, 44br, 62cr, 64, 71br, 75crb, 75br, 90bl. BT: 34br, 40c, 40cl. RB: 49tr.

RHS Wisley Front Jacket cra, cbr. Spine tc. 14br, 15br, 18bl, 19tr, 21cl, 22tc, 26bc, 27bl, 30bc, 31bl, 31bc, 32br, 32cr, 32bc, 33br, 33c, 33cr, 36tl, 36tr, 39cr, 45tl, 46tc, 46tr, 46tl, 47bl, 48tl, 49cl, 51c, 51cl, 51bc, 52tc, 52bl, 53bc, 53cr, 54bc, 55br, 55bc, 58cr, 58c, 58tc.

Harry Smith Collection 50cr.

Unwins Seeds Ltd Calabrese 'Trixie', 92c.

Jerry Young 74tr.

Additional photography by Peter Anderson.

Every effort has been made to trace the copyright holders. Dorling Kindersley apologizes for any unintentional omissions and would be pleased, in such cases, to add an acknowledgment in future editions.